FREE SPEECH AND THE SUPPRESSION OF

DISSENT DURING WORLD WAR I

Free Speech and the Suppression of Dissent during World War I

Eric T. Chester

MONTHLY REVIEW PRESS

New York

Library of Congress Cataloging-in-Publication Data
available from the publisher.

ISBN paper: 978-1-58367-868-8
ISBN cloth: 978-1-58367-869-5

Typeset in Minion Pro

MONTHLY REVIEW PRESS, NEW YORK
monthlyreview.org

5 4 3 2 1

Contents

Acknowledgments

Most of the research upon which this book is based was done at the National Archives in College Park, Maryland. The National Archives holds a vast amount of archival documents and I would like to thank the archivists in College Park for their help in locating relevant documents. I went to other archives in both the United States and England. The archivists at these libraries were of great assistance.

I would also like to thank Susan Dorazio, my partner, for her support and encouragement during the long period between the initial conception of this project and its fruition in a published book.

Freedom is always for those who think differently.

—Rosa Luxemburg

1

Introduction

The era since the terrorist attack on the Twin Towers on September 11, 2001, has been marked by the continuing erosion of fundamental rights. Successive administrations have defended this unceasing attack on the Bill of Rights with the claim that civil liberties need to be balanced against security concerns and thus, in a time when further terrorist attacks are a genuine threat, individuals have to give up some of their basic rights for the good of the entire society.

This concept that fundamental freedoms are not absolute rights but must be balanced against security concerns has become dogma. It is often taken to be self-evident, but the reality is that it is one of several theories concerning free speech that have been advocated over the years. Furthermore, it first arose out of the specific circumstances of the First World War and the draconian measures that the federal government imposed on those who dared to oppose the war effort.

The First World War was a catastrophic event that had a tremendous impact throughout the world. In the United States, President Woodrow Wilson's decision to lead the country into the war was intensely unpopular. As opposition to the war increased, the government responded by initiating a coordinated effort to silence any expression of a dissenting viewpoint. This effort could only be

implemented through a drastic erosion of fundamental civil liberties. The legal battles that ensued continue to resonate even now, a
century later.

Although Wilson adamantly insisted that his policies had the support of the vast majority of the American people, and that those who
dissented from the administration constituted a small and insignifi-
cant minority, most observers understood that opposition to the war
was widely held and deeply felt. Dissidents were convinced that their
views represented the majority opinion. In private, supporters of the
administration assessed public opinion in similar terms.

It was in this context that the Wilson administration was spurred
to propose repressive legislation intended to suppress any organized
opposition to the war effort or to the draft. In crafting its program of
repression, the Wilson administration relied heavily on the wartime
experience of Britain. The government of the United Kingdom (UK)
adopted an intricate web of rules and regulations that stifled dissent
and curbed walkouts at the workplace.

As the war continued, and became even more unpopular, the
U.S. government widened the range of those subject to repression.
Increasingly, progressives who dared to question official war policies
found themselves marginalized and reviled as traitors.

Many of these progressives were influential figures who had played
a prominent role in mainstream politics. The government's decision
to target them inspired a broad movement to defend civil liberties.
As a result, the defense of free speech became a major focus for many
of those on the Left. Even some of those who endorsed the administration's decision to enter the war found themselves opposing the
draconian measures taken to repress dissent.

This clash, between a government intent on suppressing all dissent
and an anti-war opposition with strong roots in popular opinion, lies
at the heart of this book. The question of the extent to which the First
Amendment of the Bill of Rights protected those who dissented from
the government's policies was widely debated. Different and conflicting theories were formulated and contrasted. The federal government
defended its decision to crush the opposition as a necessary price to

pay during wartime. Indeed, the president was convinced that the decision to enter the war had created a crisis situation in which fundamental rights could be disregarded. He therefore gave government agencies a wide scope for action, even though the result was a trampling of basic rights and the creation of a society where anyone who even thought of presenting a dissenting view lived in fear.

During the First World War, the federal government launched a sustained attack on its opponents that remains without equal to this day. Woodrow Wilson was prepared to use virtually every possible method to disrupt the opposition. The post office refused to mail antiwar journals or leaflets. Soldiers were used to suppress strikes and indefinitely detain activists. Military intelligence conducted intensive surveillance of civilian antiwar activities. Of course, the Justice Department was the primary agency used in this campaign of repression. Prosecutors took advantage of the nebulous wording found in the Espionage Act of June 1917 to bring charges against those who argued that the United States should open peace talks with Germany. Those convicted often served lengthy sentences in the harsh conditions of a high-security prison.

At the same time as it openly implemented a coordinated series of repressive actions, the federal government engaged in a series of covert operations to demoralize and divide the opposition. This book discusses two of these operations, the effort to pressure Eugene Victor Debs into supporting the war and the illegal surveillance and harassment of the National Civil Liberties Bureau, the predecessor of the American Civil Liberties Union.

The government's flagrant campaign of repression could only occur with the approval of the judicial system. Most judges, at every level from district courts to the U.S. Supreme Court, wholeheartedly supported the war effort and were willing to leave the decision as to the limits of dissent to the discretion of the president and the Justice Department. Even the "clear and present danger" doctrine, which Justice Oliver Wendell Holmes Jr. first formulated in a case arising from wartime dissent, granted the Justice Department a wide scope in determining who to prosecute.

Both the clear and present danger doctrine and the doctrine of the balancing of conflicting interests developed out of the historical context set by the First World War. Those who propounded these theories, Oliver Wendell Holmes Jr., Justice Louis Brandeis, and Zechariah Chafee, viewed themselves as centrists, seeking to find a reasonable alternative to extremists on both sides. They were uneasy with the administration's eagerness to harshly suppress all dissent, even that coming from mainstream progressives, but they also disagreed with radicals such as Eugene Debs who argued that the right to free speech held without restriction even during wartime. Instead, the Holmes-Chafee school argued that, although free speech was an important right, it could be significantly circumscribed in certain circumstances such as wartime.

After analyzing this argument in its historical context, an alternative theory is formulated, one that holds that the right to debate matters of public policy is absolute and that this principle holds even in wartime.

This book has four distinct sections. The first examines the methods used by the UK to quash dissent, looking as well at how elements of this campaign of repression became a model for legislation in the United States. During the war, the UK issued an extensive series of regulations intended to implement the Defence of the Realm Act. These DORA regulations gave the government enormous power to suppress dissent and punish those who opposed the government's policies.

In the second section, two important cases that arose in the United States during the First World War are thoroughly examined. The first case study looks closely at the experience of the National Civil Liberties Bureau. Although the NCLB insisted that it was only defending the civil liberties of the antiwar opposition, the federal government viewed it as an integral component of the opposition and targeted it for surveillance and repression. As a result, the NCLB engaged in secret negotiations that led to a dubious agreement with the Department of Justice.

The second case looks at the prosecution of Eugene Victor Debs. The first chapter on Debs looks at the efforts made by the government, both covertly and openly, to silence him. Debs had enormous popular support. He used his standing to speak out forcefully against the war. When the Wilson administration found it could not coerce Debs into silence, it initiated a prosecution under the Espionage Act that resulted in a ten-year prison sentence.

The second chapter concerning Debs examines the amnesty campaign that followed his imprisonment. Debs was old and frail when he was jailed. This and the respect he commanded as a person of integrity gave a strong push to the amnesty campaign. The chapter looks at the different approaches taken by Woodrow Wilson and Warren Harding in their effort to stymie the effort to free Debs. It also describes the sharp differences that arose within the campaign between socialists who were convinced that only a mass movement could free Debs and Samuel Gompers and the leadership of the American Federation of Labor that were insistent on relying exclusively on quiet lobbying.

The third section examines issues related to the role of the military in suppressing dissent. The first chapter of this section examines a proposal to extend the jurisdiction of military courts to include civilian dissidents. Under this proposal, those who opposed the war could have been tried for treason or espionage and sentenced to death by a military court. Although legislation along these lines garnered considerable support in Congress, President Woodrow Wilson intervened to block it.

The second chapter in this section focuses on a strike of timber workers organized by the Lumber Workers' Industrial Union, an affiliate of the Industrial Workers of the World. The strike spread rapidly throughout the Pacific Northwest in the spring and summer of 1917. From the start, Wilson was determined to crush the strike. Soldiers were dispatched to patrol picket lines and began detaining Wobbly activists. Hundreds of strikers were held for weeks in deplorable conditions and without being charged with any specific offense. These detentions constituted a flagrant violation of fundamental constitutional rights.

The fourth and final section of the book looks at the evolution of free speech theory during the First World War era. The first chapter analyzes the overall context in which the new theories developed, with a focus on *The New Republic* and its influence on a tendency within progressive thought that supported the war effort. The next chapter looks at Zechariah Chafee Jr. and his legal theory of free speech that premised a balance of conflicting interests. This proposition continues to underpin much of the discussion concerning civil liberties. The third chapter concentrates on Oliver Wendell Holmes Jr. and the development of the "clear and present danger" doctrine, an argument that complements Chafee's more general theory. It examines closely Holmes's decision in the *Schenck* case, where his doctrine was first formulated, as well as his views on the *Debs* case. A fourth chapter in this section presents a legal theory that is intended as an alternative to the Chafee-Holmes doctrines. Instead of viewing free speech as a right whose limit varies with the specific circumstances, the alternative theory holds that statements intended to influence the debate on matters of public policy have an absolute right to be expressed and to be protected from repression of any sort.

The final chapter of conclusions brings together the various strands of the book. It seeks to place the defense of free speech as an essential component of a popular movement for fundamental social change. Those on the Left should be in the forefront in the defense of free speech, even when this means defending the rights of those whose beliefs they find to be reprehensible. Free speech has to be for everyone, not just for those whose views you find congenial.

2

The British Experience in Suppressing Dissent

From the time the United States entered the war, the Wilson administration looked to the British experience as a model of how to suppress dissent. This was hardly surprising. Initially, the campaign to defeat Germany had won the support of most of the British populace. Nevertheless, as casualties increased, and it became clear that the war would not be quickly won, opposition increased. This was particularly true after conscription was instituted in January 1916. Still, even then, the British government proved to be extremely effective in devising repressive mechanisms that divided and demoralized the antiwar opposition.

U.S. officials were anxious to benefit from the British experience. Furthermore, the U.S. legal system had been constructed on the foundations of British common law. Indeed, sections of the U.S. Constitution directly copied phrases from key British legal documents. Thus the debate on the issue of civil liberties during wartime that flared in the United States can only be understood in the context set by the previous evolution of British policy.

THE OFFICIAL SECRETS ACT

Relations between Great Britain and Germany had been deteriorating well before the outbreak of the First World War in August 1914. Popular tabloids had been fanning a hysterical and paranoid fear of German spies since 1909. In the midst of a tense confrontation over Morocco, which nearly led to war, the Liberal government of Herbert Asquith introduced the Official Secrets Act of 1911.[1] It provided for heavy penalties for those conveying sensitive secret information to unauthorized sources. The terms of this legislation were broadly drawn, so that a civil servant leaking embarrassing information to a newspaper could be charged with a violation of the act.[2]

An even more ominous aspect of the 1911 statute specified that the government's prosecutors did not have to prove that a defendant who retained or transmitted secret information had deliberately intended to undermine national security, or to aid an enemy state, in order to gain a conviction. Instead, the "circumstances of the [alleged] act" or the "known character" of the defendant could provide sufficient grounds to establish intent. The burden of proof would then shift from the presumption of innocence to the defendant's need to demonstrate his innocent intentions.[3]

This provision constituted a critical erosion of the legal foundation protecting essential civil liberties. By suffocating dissent, governments often sought to imprison those who were engaged in activities that were permissible during normal peacetime conditions. For instance, radicals who called for the repeal of conscription were accused of deliberately seeking to disrupt the draft. The question of intent was crucial. With the Official Secrets Act of 1911, the UK began laying the groundwork for a comprehensive assault on civil liberties.

This groundbreaking legislation was pushed through the House of Commons in one hour during a quiet Friday afternoon, when attendance was predictably low. Attorney General Rufus Isaacs, who was later named Chief Justice and awarded the title of Lord Reading, reassured Parliament that "there would be no danger to anyone engaged in something perfectly innocent."[4] Even today, government apologists still voice versions of the same specious rationale.

The Defence of the Realm Act

On August 4, 1914, Great Britain declared war on Germany, and began mobilizing for the first global, total war. The Liberal Party government led by Prime Minister Herbert Asquith moved rapidly to erect an elaborate legal apparatus to crush any opposition. On August 7, only three days after the onset of war, the government introduced the Defence of the Realm act. During the next six months, the government would return to Parliament three more times, revising and consolidating the Act, while refining its enforcement procedures.

In its initial version, the Defence of the Realm Act banned any action hampering the war effort at docks and railways and authorized the government to issue regulations to ensure that this goal was met. Those accused of violating the statute or the regulations would be tried by courts-martial, that is, military tribunals. The home secretary, Reginald McKenna, presented the legislation as an "emergency bill" that would authorize the government to issue regulations prohibiting actions that could "jeopardise the success" of military operations, or could otherwise "assist the enemy." He insisted that this drastic legislation was needed to ensure an immediate response "in case of tapping wires or attempts to block bridges." In reality, the Defence of the Realm Act would be used to suppress perfectly peaceful protest.[5]

Having played to wartime paranoia, the government was able to ram through the statute in one day. The following day, August 8, 1914, the bill sailed through the House of Lords without debate, and was given royal assent the same day.[6] In neither of the houses of Parliament was a formal vote recorded, with not one voice being raised in dissent.

Three weeks later, the government returned with an expanded version of the act. The revised statute extended the zones in which UK citizens could be tried before a military tribunal to include any area used for the "training or concentration" of troops. The British

Army and Navy high command then declared that the coastal areas of southern and western England, as well as the entire coast of Scotland and Ireland, were covered by the revised statute.[7]

In addition, the second version provided that the government could issue regulations designed "to prevent the spread of reports likely to cause disaffection or alarm." This marked a substantial widening in the scope of government suppression of dissent. Similar wording would find its way into the U.S. Espionage Act, which was approved by Congress in June 1917.[8]

When the amended bill came up in the House of Commons, the issue of military tribunals was not addressed. Nevertheless, Charles Trevelyan, a Liberal MP who had opposed the decision to declare war on Germany, questioned the section restricting the right of dissent. He was concerned that the provision could be "interpreted by military authorities to prevent the expression in speech or in writing of any political opinion on the action of the Government."[9]

As usual, those defending the bill evaded the fundamental issue involved by spuriously focusing on a narrowly defined problem. McKenna argued that the bill was only intended to prevent the spread of reports that exaggerated casualties suffered by British troops. In reality, the government sought to minimize the enormous loss of life suffered by British troops along the Western Front. Furthermore, this provision in the Defence of the Realm Act would be used to prosecute those who criticized the war as the outcome of imperialist rivalries.[10]

In the House of Lords, the Liberal Party politician Wentworth Beaumont, Lord Allendale, explained that because the initial version of the Defence of the Realm Act had been "hurriedly drawn" the revised version had been formulated to fill in "certain omissions." The clause restricting dissenting opinions was intended to prevent "the spreading of false reports." Furthermore, he noted, extending the zone where military tribunals could try civilians would only make it possible to punish those who violated the curfew set at military training camps.[11] With this deliberately misleading explanation, the amended version was approved without further discussion, and without a vote.

The first two versions of the Defence of the Realm Act sailed through Parliament with minimal discussion and little opposition. In November 1914, the Asquith government returned to Parliament with a new, consolidated version of the Defence of the Realm Act that retained previous clauses while expanding the scope of the statute. This time UK citizens could be tried by a military tribunal for allegedly violating the statute, or the regulations issued to enforce it, anywhere within the United Kingdom, not only in narrowly defined war zones. Furthermore, the death penalty could be levied against those who were found to be acting "with the intent of assisting the enemy."[12]

In the House of Commons, the debate focused on the provision prohibiting "the spread of reports likely to cause disaffection or alarm." Conservative leaders were concerned that the wording permitted the government to move beyond the suppression of those opposed to the war to a censorship that curtailed mainstream newspapers, even those that avidly supported the war and yet were critical of the official war policy. Robert Cecil objected that the clause would "enable the Government to suppress any report of any kind of which they disapprove."[13] A few months after this debate, in May 1915, the Conservatives would join a coalition government and Cecil would hold a high post in the Foreign Office.[14] During this period, the Foreign Office pressed the government to zealously enforce the DORA regulations aimed at censoring the press.

Debate in the House of Lords on the provision authorizing military tribunals to try civilians was extensive and heated. Extending the zone in which civilians could be tried by military tribunals to the entire country represented a major step in the suspension of fundamental civil liberties. Peers were dismayed with the willingness of the Liberal government to nullify a key mainstay of British liberty going back to the Magna Carta of the thirteenth century. Richard Haldane, as Lord Chancellor and government spokesperson, admitted that "the principle of trial before a jury is a principle which is very deep" in British jurisprudence, "and one which we should all respect."[15]

As a result of this debate, the Liberal government agreed to come back to Parliament with a revised version of the statute. For a period of several months, from November 1914 to March 1915, the issue remained unresolved. In the course of a debate on this issue in the House of Commons in February 1915, Attorney General John Simon conceded that "courts-martial are for the purpose of the discipline of those who serve in the Army and Navy."[16] The question of military tribunals having jurisdiction over civilians accused of a crime would be a controversial issue in the United States as well.

The government finally returned with the fourth and final version of the Defence of the Realm act, which was approved by Parliament in March 1915. The revised Act permitted UK citizens charged with violating the statute or the regulations to choose which court system would be utilized to try them. Needless to say, civilians opted to be tried in a civilian court. One clause of the 1915 legislation gave the government an escape valve. An official proclamation could mandate military tribunals for UK citizens violating the regulations "in the event of invasion or for special military emergencies arising out of the present war." This section was never invoked in Britain (England, Scotland and Wales), but such a proclamation was issued for all of Ireland in the immediate aftermath of the Easter Uprising of April 1916.[17]

DEFENCE OF THE REALM REGULATIONS

The regulations issued by fiat to enforce the Defence of the Realm Act proved to be as dangerous a threat to civil liberties as the act itself. Taken as a whole, the DORA regulations provided the authorities with the legal basis to bar virtually every form of opposition to the war or the draft. In the beginning, the government issued sweeping regulations that were nebulously phrased, thus granting the judicial system and the military enormous leeway in their interpretation. As the war progressed, the government issued detailed regulations so that everyone was fully aware of the tremendous power delegated to the government under the Defence of the Realm Act, while also making it easier to prosecute dissidents in civil court.

Regulation 9 was one of the many regulations that were initially issued in November 1914. It enabled the "competent military commander" to "require" all unauthorized individuals to leave a certain area. The army used this regulation to force dissidents to leave their homes and move elsewhere within the UK. Regulation 52 was also issued in November 1914. It gave any soldier the right to stop and search any vehicle anywhere in the UK and to seize any contents deemed to be in violation of the regulations.[18] Thus, from the start of the war, the military, in particular the British Army, was given tremendous power to deny individuals their basic rights and to do so without any review by the judiciary, or without providing those affected with any forum in which to appeal these decisions.

Regulation 14, also initially issued in November 1914, authorized a local military commander, with the approval of his superiors in the Army Council, to order individuals "suspected" of "being about to act" in "a manner prejudiced to the public safety" to move from one area of Britain to another. In other words, it introduced internal deportation. Further additions to this regulation gave the military the power to monitor the movements of those forced to move, and to require them to regularly report to the authorities.[19]

This regulation not only granted the military enormous power to suppress dissent, it did so in a way that blatantly disregarded fundamental human rights. There was no way to defend against a charge that you might do something suspect in the future. Regulation 14 was enforced in Glasgow, Scotland, in March 1916 when eight strike leaders were deported from Scotland for a year.[20] This highly visible case acted to intimidate union activists throughout Britain.

The power given to the military by the DORA regulations led to a drastic elimination of fundamental liberties. Indeed, the DORA regulations underscored the influence and authority of the armed forces in determining every aspect of public policy, domestic and foreign, throughout the First World War. In fact, many of the DORA regulations were formulated in the War Office by army officers charged with suppressing domestic dissent.

Major General Frederick Maurice was director of military operations, a key post reporting directly to the chief of the imperial general staff, William Robertson, who was also Maurice's close friend. In the summer of 1917, Maurice wrote to Herbert Samuel, the former home secretary, to explain that the DORA regulations "were modelled" on rules that he had written while "administering Martial Law for two years in the Cape Colony."[21]

Maurice had served from 1899 to 1901 as an intelligence officer in South Africa during the Boer War.[22] The drive to integrate Dutch colonial areas into the British Empire had been met with bitter resistance. British troops burned Dutch farms and forced thousands of civilians into concentration camps. Initially, the UK only controlled the Cape Colony. Even here, guerrilla units harassed military units. In January 1901, under pressure from Alfred Milner, the High Commissioner for South Africa, the Cape Colony government imposed martial law.[23] Any form of dissent, no matter how peaceful was suppressed. Maurice helped to draft the rules that implemented martial law. Using this experience, he then oversaw the drafting of the DORA regulations that suppressed dissent in Britain, a country where peaceful conditions prevailed. The lessons of colonial rule in the British Empire would then be passed on to the United States in the form of the Espionage Act.

The power granted to the British military to suppress those who opposed the war through the use of the Defence of the Realm Acts and the regulations that followed was vast. Once the United States entered the war in April 1917, President Woodrow Wilson was intent on retaining civilian control. He was therefore more circumspect in ceding to the U.S. military the authority to quash dissent.

Still, even in Britain the prime responsibility for curbing the opposition remained with civilian legal authorities, most importantly the home secretary, the attorney general, and the director of public prosecutions. The DORA regulations created the basis for the prosecution of dissidents in civilian courts for a wide array of alleged acts.

In general, the first regulations set forth sweeping measures while later ones were more specific. Regulation 42 was initially issued in November 1914, prohibiting any acts that were "likely to cause mutiny, sedition, or disaffection within the military." In early 1916, the government amended this regulation to specifically ban "attempts" to "restrict the production, repair or transport of war materièl." The amended regulation authorized the prosecution of union activists who led strikes or slowdowns in any of the war industries.[24]

The government was also eager to suppress any organized opposition to its war policies, whether this took the form of public meetings or printed matter. Regulation 27, issued in November 1916, banned the distribution of any newspaper or other printed document that "spread false reports," or contained reports "likely to cause disaffection" with either the UK or any of its allies. The regulation also prohibited any statements, oral or written, that were "likely to prejudice the recruiting of persons" to the armed forces.[25] This sweeping regulation provided the model for key sections of the U.S. Espionage Act of June 1917.

Regulation 27 totally undercut the freedom of the press, but additional regulations went even further to suppress any dissident opinions. Regulation 51, also initially issued in November 1914, authorized the local military commander to search any premises in which it was suspected that printed material in violation of DORA or the regulations issued to enforce it was being produced, and to seize anything found there. Furthermore, the local military, with the approval of the Army Council, could order the destruction of the seized property, including printing presses. This meant that a printer could be ruined if a suspect document was produced on its premises.[26] Few commercial presses would risk these harsh penalties, so those who opposed the war were forced to print their own newspapers and leaflets.

The enormous power given to the military to suppress domestic dissent left even some of those in the government uneasy. Charles Matthews, the director of public prosecutions, wrote a confidential memorandum in which he concluded that Regulation 51 was "so drastic" that its implementation would "closely approach the application of martial law." Matthews therefore drafted a supplementary amendment, which became Regulation 51A as issued in July 1915. This authorized a local magistrate to issue a warrant permitting the police to raid a premises suspected of being the source of newspapers or flyers in violation of the DORA regulations. A court hearing would ensue during which the magistrate would determine whether printed material or printing equipment seized during the raid actually violated the Defence of the Realm Act.[27]

Regulation 51A provided the basis for most of the raids on newspapers that questioned the government's war policies. Nevertheless, Regulation 51 remained in effect and was used to shut down newspapers without a court hearing. John Maclean's newspaper, the *Vanguard*, was seized by the military authorities in Glasgow in January 1916, without a hearing during which this order could be challenged.[28] Indeed, in a real sense Glasgow was under martial law during much of the period from 1916 to 1919.

The DORA regulations also set out the legal basis for suppressing public meetings. This was a crucial aspect of the effort to quash any organized opposition to the government's policies. Regulation 9A, issued in October 1916, allowed the home secretary to ban any meeting or procession that might "give rise to grave disorder" or "promote disaffection." He could delegate to a local magistrate or police chief the authority to issue the order banning a specific meeting or procession.[29]

DORA and the regulations issued to implement it established a dense set of rules curbing every form of opposition to the war and the draft. Although the military targeted a few dissidents for internal deportation and detention, the great majority of dissidents who were deemed to have violated the rules were prosecuted in civilian courts.

Regulation 56A, issued in March 1915, specified that those convicted for violating one of the DORA regulations in a civilian court could be sentenced to a term in prison up to a life sentence. Indeed, the death penalty could be imposed by a jury if it determined that the defendant had deliberately violated a regulation with the intent of aiding the enemy.[30] In spite of the threat of executions, no British civilian received a death sentence for violating one of the DORA regulations.

In general, the authorities were eager to avoid public trials before a jury. The final version of the Defence of the Realm Act had specified that those violating its provisions were guilty of a felony and could be tried by a jury in a secret trial, if this was deemed to be "in the public interest." Regulation 58, issued in November 1914, provided for summary court hearings on lesser charges before a magistrate. Acting without a jury, the magistrate could impose sentences of up to six months. A further amendment, dated March 1915, allowed the magistrate to close summary trials to the public "in the interests of national safety."[31]

The government chose to interpret this section in the broadest terms, so it frequently requested that court hearings involving the Defence of the Realm Act be closed and magistrates usually acceded to this request. Furthermore, a person released from jail after serving a six-month sentence could be rearrested and given another six-month sentence. All of this without a trial by jury or any public notice.

The DORA regulations were vigorously enforced. These were not hollow paper threats. On the contrary, MI5, the counter-intelligence agency that operated autonomously under the nominal authority of the army's director of intelligence, directed considerable resources to their enforcement. Overall, during the four years of the war, roughly five thousand individuals and organizations were investigated by MI5. In about one-third of these cases some repressive action was actually taken. Six hundred and sixty individuals received orders under Regulation 14 forcing them to leave their homes and relocate to another region of the country. More than four hundred individuals were convicted in civilian courts for allegedly violating one of the DORA regulations and received a jail sentence as a result.[32]

REGULATION 14B AND INTERNMENT

In order to have the Defence of the Realm Act approved by Parliament with a minimum of resistance, Asquith's Liberal Party government had agreed that anyone charged with violating the act or the regulations issued to enforce it would have the right to be tried in a civilian court. This concession was codified in the last version of the Defence of the Realm Act enacted in March 1915. Nevertheless, in June 1915, the government issued Regulation 14B, which enabled the government to indefinitely detain those it believed were acting in violation of the DORA regulations because of their "hostile origins or associations."[33]

By issuing Regulation 14B, the government was violating the pledge that it had given to Parliament only three months previously. Regulation 14B gave the ultimate authority as to who would be detained into the hands of the home secretary. There was no provision to challenge the internment order in court. An advisory committee appointed by the home secretary was given very limited powers. It provided those who had been detained with their sole opportunity to contest their continued internment in a hearing where they had few rights. Witnesses for the government were heard in secret, without the person detained being present. Furthermore, many of those detained were not provided with a specific set of charges. Needless to say, the advisory committee failed as a check on executive powers, approving almost every detention order.[34]

When the validity of Regulation 14B was challenged in court, judges ruled that Parliament had granted the government the right to suspend the writ of habeas corpus when it enacted the Defence of the Realm Act. The writ of habeas corpus guaranteed that those charged with a crime would receive a trial in a civilian court. In fact, Parliament had only approved the statute when the government explicitly agreed that those charged with violating the act would have the option of a trial in a civilian court in which defendants retained significantly more rights than those interned were being granted.

THOSE DETAINED

Most of those detained were held because of reports coming from MI5. The great majority of those detained from anywhere in Britain were held in a former workhouse located in Islington, then a working-class neighborhood in north London. The names of those detained were not made public, so it could be a considerable time before their families became aware of their detention, as well as where they were being held. Many were held for a year after the war had ended. The Islington detention center was only closed in November 1919.[35]

The number of those interned under Regulation 14B was fairly small. During the entire wartime period, 225 individuals were held indefinitely for their alleged "hostile origins or associations." A majority of them had emigrated from Germany and were being held for their possible ties to the German government, although quite a few of these individuals had lived long enough in Britain to become naturalized citizens. Still, among those interned were individuals born in Britain who were citizens by birth.[36]

In general, internment targeted those who were suspected of having ties to the German government, rather than being used to silence those who dissented from the government's war policies. One exception to this rule involved radicals coming from tsarist Russia who had received asylum as political refugees. Peter Petroff was a Russian left-wing socialist who became a close confidant of John Maclean, a key figure in the socialist movement of Glasgow. Indeed, he sought to convince the Clyde Workers' Committee, a network of shop stewards who organized strikes in key war industries, to openly oppose the government's war policies. Petroff was interned in March 1917 on the basis of Regulation 14B and then deported to the Soviet Union in January 1918.[37]

The intelligence community sought to extend internment to include not just foreign radicals, but also British citizens working within the organizations of the radical Left. Alphonso Samms, an active member of the British Socialist Party in Sheffield, was given a two-month jail sentence for violating the DORA regulations by vocally protesting the war at a military hospital. In September 1915, MI5 tried to have Samms indefinitely detained under Regulation 14B. The home secretary, Herbert Samuel, rejected this request in the absence of any evidence "of hostile origins or associations."[38]

The issue of internment was highly controversial in Britain. In the United States, a similar issue would arise as soldiers indefinitely detained those engaged in a peaceful strike. In Britain, unlike the United States, the lack of a written constitution guaranteeing basic rights made it easier for the government to circumvent the most minimal guarantees of individual rights. Furthermore, in Britain the judicial system approved the government's actions without any meaningful review.

The DORA regulations gave the government enormous power to suppress those who opposed the war. Generally, the government relied on those provisions of the DORA regulations that allowed for the prosecution of dissidents in civilian courts, rather than resorting to internment. Yet for political reasons the government was wary of targeting leading members of the moderate opposition. This led to the tricky issue of delineating the permissible limits for any resistance to the official policy.

The issue was discussed in broad terms in a speech in 1930 made by Vernon Kell, the chief of MI5. Kell had been directly responsible for implementing the government's policy of repression during the First World War. His confidential speech, given at a school that trained MI5 officers, was aptly titled "Control of Civil Populations in War." Although Kell framed his speech as a set of guidelines for a future conflict, his talk was based on experiences gained during the first years of the war.

Kell started by outlining those statements that would not be permitted during wartime. Condemnations of the war would not be tolerated and any discussion of conscription would be bound to hit upon sensitive issues. Thus "propaganda against volunteering" or "attempts to induce men liable to compulsory service to disobey the law" would leave one open to prosecution. Furthermore, "attempts to foment strikes or disaffection amongst the workmen in munitions factories or shipyards" would be expressly prohibited. (Many workers in the munitions factories were women, but Kell's traditional, patriarchal bias led him to ignore these newcomers.) Under these guidelines, strike leaders would be jailed or deported to other places in Britain, even though the strikes they led might not have involved workplace issues and would not have been directly related to the war.[39]

Having delineated those forms of opposition that would not be tolerated, Kell then detailed the expressions of dissent that could be allowed. Dissidents could state that a "war could have been avoided by better statesmanship," or that it "should be ended straightaway by negotiation." As long as the draft was under consideration, one could argue that "conscription ought not to be adopted." Once it was in force, dissidents could suggest that it "ought to be repealed," presumably once the war was ended.

Kell's guidelines are instructive, but in reality the limits for dissent were not fixed, but varied with the readiness of people to listen to those who opposed the war. As the war progressed and popular disillusionment deepened, the War Cabinet that took power in December 1916 began to target even those who limited their opposition to calls for a negotiated peace.

The Moderate Opposition

The authority delegated by Parliament to the government made it possible to ban every form of dissent, no matter how moderate. Instead, the Liberal Party government that ruled during the first months of the war, and then the coalition government that took power in May 1915, set in motion a calibrated series of repressive measures that varied with the militancy of the opposition.

The government was quick to quash any activity undertaken by the radical Left. Open, radical criticism of the war as an imperialist conflict, as well as any effort to encourage resistance to the draft, were met with harsh measures designed to crush those who ventured along this path. The case of John Maclean is the most important example of this, as he was repeatedly jailed for condemning the war as an imperialist adventure.[40] Those who organized strikes in the munitions and armament industries risked jail and internal deportation. Trade union activists in the Glasgow area who joined the Clyde Workers' Committee were the most significant cases of this type of opposition. In both of these cases, the authorities had no hesitation in using every means at their disposal to quash dissent.

The issue became more complex in responding to the moderate

opposition. This involved a network of closely linked organizations, with overlapping memberships. Influential figures in this network were prominent members of the Labour Party or the Liberal Party, and several were members of Parliament. It was thus difficult for a Liberal government to initiate a policy of harsh repression against this segment of the antiwar opposition. Furthermore, those who held power were eager to maintain the enthusiastic support of union officials. They understood that harsh measures aimed at the moderate opposition could lead to a break with the official union structure and the Labour Party.

In responding to the threat posed by those who questioned the UK's war policy, the authorities had to take into account the different components of the interlinked network that constituted the moderate opposition. The three main organizations within this informal network, the Independent Labour Party, the Union of Democratic Control, and the No Conscription Fellowship, shared a common perspective. They sought to put pressure on the government to enter into meaningful negotiations with the German government in order to conclude a peace treaty that would be based on the principle of no annexations of territory and no punitive reparations. At first, the UK was evasive in setting its terms for peace, but as the war proceeded it became increasingly clear that the Allies were intent on forcing the German government to accept an unconditional surrender. Furthermore, the peace resulting from such a total victory would bring a peace treaty that imposed harsh terms on the defeated Central Powers.

Many of those active in the peace movement were in more than one of these three organizations and yet each organization had a distinctive purpose and base of supporters. The government had to take these distinctions into account as it developed a program that could stifle the informal network of organizations calling for a negotiated peace.

THE INDEPENDENT LABOUR PARTY

The Independent Labour Party (ILP) provided the mass base for the moderate opposition to the war, gaining most of its support from within the working class. With thirty thousand members, the ILP was an organization with a solid base of support in northern England and Scotland. Wherever there was support for a militant resistance to the war, the ILP grew in strength, despite becoming the target of government sanctions. This was particularly true in Glasgow. Some of the most prominent leaders of the Clyde Workers' Committee were ILP members, although a small organization of radical socialists, the Socialist Labour Party, was even more influential.[41]

In addition to a significant base of support within working-class communities, the ILP played a critical role within the Labour Party. Indeed it had been instrumental in the formation of the Labour Party at the turn of the twentieth century.[42]

Although the Labour Party had been formed on the basis of a working agreement between the ILP and union leaders, this coalition became frayed during the war. Most union officials enthusiastically endorsed the war effort, while the Independent Labour Party called for a rapid end to the war through a negotiated settlement.[43]

During the war, the Independent Labour Party and the Union for Democratic Control developed very close relations. The ILP's newspaper, the *Labour Leader*, frequently printed articles by UDC leaders. ILP branches distributed UDC pamphlets and organized public meetings for UDC speakers. In general, the ILP hewed closely to the position advocated by the UDC as the war progressed.

THE UNION OF DEMOCRATIC CONTROL

Although the ILP provided the mass base of support for the moderate opposition, the Union of Democratic Control (UDC) formulated its strategic vision and produced much of its printed material as well. The organization was formed in early August 1914, days after the UK entered the war. It was created by Liberal Party politicians who had sought to block Britain's entry into the war. From the start, the UDC sought to forge an alliance with the ILP.

Charles Trevelyan was a Liberal Party MP from northern England. who opposed the drift toward war with Germany. On August 5, 1914, the day after Britain declared war on Germany, Trevelyan wrote to Edmund Morel to ask him if he would be willing to act as the secretary of a new organization. Morel was living in France at the time, but he rushed back to London to join the effort.[44]

Morel was primarily a journalist. He had led an effective public campaign to expose the brutalities of Belgian rule in the Congo. As Europe drifted toward a total war, Morel wrote a series of articles calling for a peaceful resolution of imperial rivalries. He was therefore a logical choice to direct the new organization.[45]

An intense and dedicated activist who worked himself to exhaustion, Morel was also a prolific writer. Many of those who joined the peace movement found him to be an inspiring role model, although some viewed him as "vain [and] obsessive."[46] In any case, the UDC came to depend on Morel to coordinate its activities and to provide it with a strategic direction.

In addition to Morel, the UDC leadership included several well-known figures. In addition to Trevelyan, Arthur Ponsonby, another Liberal Party member of Parliament, was an active participant in the organization. Ramsay MacDonald, a leading figure in the Independent Labour Party, was also brought into the planning process at an early stage. MacDonald acted as a crucial liaison with the leadership of the Labour Party. Although Morel wrote many of the UDC's pamphlets, MacDonald acted as a primary spokesperson for the group.

During the second week of August 1914, Morel, Trevelyan, and MacDonald sent out a letter to a list of progressives informing them of the formation of the UDC. The letter outlined a program that included an end to secret diplomacy and called for an end to the war that would not lead to "the humiliation of the defeated nation." Such an imposed peace could well be "the starting point" for "future wars." This was a prediction that proved to be all too correct. The letter was published by the *Morning Post*, a right-wing Tory newspaper that castigated the UDC for its tepid enthusiasm for the war.[47]

At first, the UDC refrained from proposing an immediate start to peace negotiations. The core group of the organization was concerned that the German Army would gain a rapid victory and they therefore gave tacit support to the British war effort. A year later, near the end of 1915, Morel started calling for immediate negotiations leading to a negotiated treaty based on the formula of no annexations and no punitive reparations.

The Union of Democratic Control was eager to avoid direct conflicts with the authorities. For the first six months after it was formed, it opted to not organize any public meetings. When the UDC did begin holding events in the spring of 1915, it quickly became a target of the tabloid press. When Parliament enacted legislation enforcing conscription in January 1916, Morel convinced the UDC's executive committee that the issue should be avoided.

The UDC presented a very moderate opposition to the war and yet, as the war dragged on and popular discontent grew, the government became increasingly vexed by its activities. Still, an open assault on an organization with such influential leaders carried significant risks. Furthermore, the UDC was funded by wealthy benefactors, most of them devout Quakers. The Cadbury and Rowantree families provided the money to pay for Morel and the UDC's staff.

The methods to be used to restrict the activities of the UDC and the ILP became a point of controversy within the coalition government that ruled Britain from May 1915 to December 1916. The War Cabinet that held power from that point to the end of the war took a more aggressive stance toward the moderate opposition. As the government ratcheted up its repressive actions, the UDC accepted the narrowing range of activities that were permitted in order to avoid an open clash with the government.

No Conscription Fellowship

The most militant of the three organizations was the No Conscription Fellowship (NCF). Since the primary purpose of this organization was providing assistance to those who resisted conscription, it was bound to become a target of repression under the DORA regulations. The leadership of the NCF came from the middle-class intellectuals who identified with the Independent Labour Party. Many of them resisted conscription and served time in prison as conscientious objectors who refused to undertake alternative service. Yet a more radical strand functioned within the NCF as well. In Glasgow, members of the Socialist Labour Party joined the NCF and were instrumental in creating underground networks to hide young men who refused to report for conscription into the military. This caused tension within the organization, but the two tendencies were able to continue to work together throughout the war within the organizational framework of the No Conscription Fellowship.[48]

The NCF realized that it would not be allowed to operate as a legal organization, so it prepared for the worst. Even in 1915, prior to the advent of conscription, the organization developed a shadow system of officers. Every officer at the local and national level had an alternate who was ready to step in should the original officer be jailed. The NCF also decided that it would make several copies of every vital document and that these would be hidden in several sites scattered around the country. During the last years of the war, the organization decided that it would print its flyers on small, mobile presses without the prior permission of the authorities, thus flaunting Regulation 27C of the DORA regulations. The presses were inexpensive, so if one were seized by the authorities it could be easily replaced.[49]

THE LABOUR LEADER

The *Labour Leader* was the national newspaper of the Independent Labour Party (ILP). Since the ILP had been instrumental in the formation of the British Labour Party, the *Leader* provided unstinting support for Labour Party candidates.

With the advent of the First World War came a very different set of circumstances. The *Labour Leader* furnished a forum for E. D. Morel and the Union of Democratic Control. Of course, the *Leader* also printed many articles from Ramsay MacDonald, the most prominent member of the ILP. The editor of the *Leader* for most of the war was Fenner Brockway, a pacifist and a founder of the No Conscription Fellowship.

The Asquith coalition government viewed the *Labour Leader* as nuisance and a potential threat. Nevertheless, the newspaper had influential supporters and the editors carefully set limits to its criticisms of the war. By February 1915, Morel was writing that "the time" had come for the UK to declare "the terms of an eventual settlement."[50] This would become a recurring theme in the critique of official policy presented by the UDC and its allies. The Liberal government was urging millions of men to volunteer for military service and yet it would not provide a detailed list of its war aims. Policymakers continued to insist that it was too early to do this and that a formulation of war aims would require the agreement of all of the Entente Allies. In fact, the UK entered into a series of secret treaties that set out in detail the division of enemy territory once the war had been fought to a successful conclusion.

In late May 1915, the Liberal Party and the Conservative Party entered into a coalition government. This maneuver led to a shift in the attitude of the government toward the moderate opposition and, in particular, the *Labour Leader*. Edward Carson was the leader of the Protestant loyalists in the north of Ireland and a prominent member of the Conservative Party. A zealous supporter of the war effort, he had little regard for civil liberties. His appointment as attorney general signaled a greater readiness to use the DORA regulations against those who voiced any disagreement with the government's policies. Intelligence agencies intensified their surveillance of the ILP and the *Leader* as government prosecutors looked for a good opportunity to bring a case to court.

In its issues of August 5 and August 12, 1915, the *Labour Leader* printed small, classified advertisements from the No Conscription Fellowship. The ads announced that NCF members would not "take part in military service," or the production of war materièl, but that some members were willing to be conscripted into alternative service, such as driving ambulances on the Western Front.

These ads were brought to the attention of Charles Matthews, the director of public prosecutions, who reported to Carson. Matthews and Carson agreed that the ads urged readers to resist the draft and thus were printed in violation of Regulation 27 of the Defence of the Realm Act, which prohibited any statements, oral or written, that were "likely to prejudice the recruiting of persons" to the armed forces. Acting under Regulation 51A, Special Branch officers accompanied by officers from the local police force raided the offices of the National Labour Press in Salford, England, a suburb of Manchester on August 18, 1915. The National Labour Press was a large print works that had been founded in 1909 by the Independent Labour Party. It printed the *Labour Leader* as well as pamphlets produced by the Union of Democratic Control.[51]

Soon after this raid, Brockway met with the Special Branch and "offered to delete anything to which the authorities took exception." The next issue, dated August 19, 1915, had blank spaces where a letter and an ad deemed to be in violation of the DORA regulations had been removed.[52]

Nevertheless, Brockway, as editor of the *Labour Leader*, had to appear before a magistrate in Salford on the charge that the earlier issues had violated the DORA regulations. Brockway promised the magistrate that the ads placed by the No Conscription Fellowship "would not appear again." This despite his being a founding member of the NCF and one of its most influential members. With this promise in hand, the magistrate ordered the government to return the copies of the *Leader* that had been seized and declared that the newspaper was not in violation of Regulation 27.

The precedent set by the *Labour Leader* in the fall of 1915 would hold for all of the moderate opposition throughout the war. As the war dragged on and casualties mounted into the millions, opposition to official policies gained support. In response, the government narrowed the scope of permissible dissent. The moderate opposition was unwilling to confront the government and thus agreed to further limit its criticism of government policy. Thus, in effect, the opposition began policing itself.

By January 1916, the coalition government had come to the conclusion that it had no choice but to institute conscription. Asquith had been very reluctant to introduce the draft realizing that it would further accentuate the divisions within the Liberal Party that had arisen during the course of the war. Home secretary John Simon resigned his post in the cabinet in protest.[53] He was replaced by another Liberal Party politician, Herbert Samuel, who gave his reluctant support to conscription.

The decision to introduce conscription represented a turning point in the war, catalyzing a broad and spirited movement of resistance. Articles in the *Labour Leader* reported that "mass meetings" were held around the country denouncing conscription. Workers in a key munitions factory threatened to go on strike if legislation enacting a draft was approved by Parliament.[54]

This was a critical moment for the antiwar movement. There was a genuine possibility of organizing a mass movement to oppose conscription, one that might soon lead to demands that the UK immediately enter into peace negotiations for an equitable peace that did not require the unconditional surrender of Germany. In an editorial on January 20, 1916, the *Labour Leader* declared its "apprehension of the results of a revolt upon the part of organized Labour at this moment." In other words, the *Leader*, and thus the leadership of the Independent Labour Party, acted as a brake on a grassroots, militant opposition to the draft.

Indeed, in the two years from the spring of 1916 to the spring of 1918 the *Labour Leader* generally avoided any discussion of the war. Brockway was jailed as a conscientious objector in November 1916 and his successor as editor, Katherine Glasier, was even more cautious in her approach than he had been.[55]

In spite of its efforts to avoid prosecution, key elements within the government continued to view the *Labour Leader* as a threat. Victor Ferguson, the MI5 officer assigned the responsibility for keeping track of the *Leader*, estimated its circulation in late 1916 at thirty to forty thousand copies, with its strongest base in Scotland and Wales. He remained convinced that the newspaper gave "every encouragement" to "the movement demanding that peace negotiations should be undertaken now." By the end of 1916, Ferguson and MI5 were insisting that further restrictions on the moderate opposition were essential.[56] (In his speech in 1930, Vernon Kell had explicitly included calls for immediate negotiations as one form of dissent that would remain legal.)

Ferguson had met earlier with Matthews in June 1916. At that time, Matthews had insisted that he was "as anxious as anyone to prosecute the *Labour Leader.*" Nevertheless, as director of public prosecutions Matthews had to concede that "not one single item" in the paper had "overstepped the mark." It would therefore not be possible to initiate a successful prosecution even under the expansive guidelines established by Regulation 27 and the rest of the DORA regulations.

In a memorandum written in December 1916, Ferguson again reported that Matthews still believed that a prosecution of the *Labour Leader* was "not likely to succeed." Instead, there was an agreement "to go after the National Labour Press" as one "method of hindering its production." As a result, the London office of the Labour Press was raided on August 14, 1916, and thousands of copies of a pamphlet concerning conscientious objectors were seized. This pamphlet, produced by the No Conscription Fellowship, was included in the Home Office's Black List of banned pamphlets and flyers, so Samuel and the Home Office approved the raid.[57]

The pressure from within and outside the government to prosecute the *Labour Leader* was intensifying during the winter of 1916. Still, key Liberals were unwilling to proceed further. The Foreign Office was among those calling for harsher measures. While serving as home secretary, Herbert Samuel had informed Charles Hardinge, the permanent under secretary at the Foreign Office, that he had "given very careful consideration" to those calling for prosecution of the *Leader* for printing articles by Morel and others active in the UDC. He had come to the conclusion that "the points at issue" were "less for courts of law to determine than for Parliament and public opinion." Banning the *Labour Leader* and prosecuting its editors and contributors "would cause more harm than good."[58]

The debate within the coalition government had reached a stalemate and a further decision on prosecuting the *Labour Leader* was postponed until January 1917, when a newly installed regime began considering the entire range of issues raised by the increasing popular discontent with the war.[59] This was the situation as the Asquith coalition cabinet, in which the Liberal Party had the most influence, was unseated and replaced by a small and secretive executive body, the War Cabinet. Led by a Liberal, Lloyd George, it was, nevertheless, dominated by the Conservative Party. The War Cabinet would prove to be significantly more vindictive than the Asquith coalition in its refusal to tolerate even the mildest criticisms of its policies.

D-NOTICES AND THE PRESS BUREAU

The government not only attempted to prevent left-wing newspapers from criticizing the war, it also sought to ensure that the mainstream press hewed to the official line. This remains one of the least known aspects of the curtailment of civil liberties in Britain during the First World War. The Official Secrets Act was enacted in 1911, three years before the First World War began. This legislation provided stiff criminal sanctions for those who passed military secrets to an enemy, primarily Germany, but it was also designed to punish those leaking embarrassing information to the popular press. Insiders who furnished the press with secret documents could be prosecuted under the Official Secrets Act, but the ban went further. Reporters and editors of newspapers that published official secrets could also be arrested and jailed.[60]

The passage of the Official Secrets Act was a major blow to press freedom, but the government went even further. In 1912, a secret committee was established, initially named the Admiralty War Office and Press Committee. This committee had the authority to issue notices to newspaper editors warning them that there were certain topics that were not to be covered. These warnings were the infamous D (for defense) notices that continue to be dispatched to this day. The committee included representatives from the War Office (the British Army), the Admiralty (the British Navy), the Foreign Office and the Cabinet, representing the prime minister. These four representatives determined the agenda for the D-notice committee, which also included representatives from the mainstream press.[61]

The D-notice committee operated entirely in secret. Indeed, the existence of the committee did not become publicly known until 1952.[62] To protect it from public notice, D-notices were sent to newspapers by another government agency, the Press Bureau. The two committees worked closely together, but the D-notice committee retained the ultimate authority to determine policy.

In theory, the D-notice committee operated as a voluntary advisory board, providing editors with helpful advice. As patriotic defenders of the British Empire, editors and publishers would happily heed the messages contained in the D-notices. Yet everyone understood that this was not a truly voluntary system. Edward Cook, the director of the Press Bureau, was clear that the "instructions" in many of the D-notices were "mandatory."[63] During the First World War, newspapers believed to be flouting a D-notice were subject to harsh sanctions levied under the DORA regulations, as well as possible prosecution under the Official Secrets Act. The D-notice system acted as an effective method of pre-publication censorship, thus preventing articles from appearing in the press that could embarrass the government.

Those who defended the D-notice system argued that it kept information that might be of use to the German military out of the mainstream press. In fact, D-notices encompassed a wide range of topics, going well beyond strategic plans, the movement of troops and individuals and the development of new weapons. Seven hundred notices were sent during the First World War on a wide array of topics, including one that instructed newspapers as to how they should cover the progress of the war.[64] The existence of the committee was kept a secret, as was the content of specific D-notices, which were "strictly private and confidential."[65] A newspaper that published a D-notice, thus informing its readers of a topic that could not be discussed in its columns, could be prosecuted under the Official Secrets Act, or punished under the DORA regulations, for making public a secret document aimed at keeping other documents and topics secret.

THE PRESS BUREAU

Nevertheless, specific D-notices were mentioned during debates in the House of Commons. Occasionally, a government spokesperson would refer in general terms to a D-notice, without mentioning the actual source. More frequently, one of the few members of Parliament willing to challenge the government would mention the contents of a specific D-notice. At no time did anyone actually point to the D-notice committee, or, if they did, this reference was deleted from the official record of parliamentary proceedings. Instead, members of Parliament would ascribe the source of a notice as the Press Bureau, although, in reality, the Press Bureau sent the D-notices at the behest of the Admiralty, War Office and Press Committee. The Press Bureau also distributed official statements from the War Office and the Admiralty on recent events in the war.[66]

The Press Bureau and the D-notice committee worked closely together during the First World War and yet the two were distinct bodies. Although the Press Bureau had been created under the aegis of the War Office in August 1914, in June 1915 it was transferred to the Home Office.[67] This made sense since the home secretary and his advisors decided whether to pursue a prosecution for violating a DORA regulation. Although the existence of the Press Bureau was openly acknowledged, the D-notice system was a tightly held secret. Furthermore, the Press Bureau had a large staff of censors and publicists, while the D-notice committee remained small and shadowy.

The Press Bureau had several areas of authority that extended beyond its links to the mainstream press. Under the War Cabinet, it was given the power to review all flyers prior to publication. The Press Bureau also censored all printed material, from books to flyers, that were sent abroad or received from a foreign country. Yet its role as an overseer of the popular press was most crucial. All cables and photos sent by journalists from the Western Front were carefully vetted and censored. Articles concerning military affairs were sent by the mainstream newspapers to the Press Bureau on a voluntary basis. Needless to say, the advice provided editors as to publication was almost always followed.[68]

The Press Bureau's most sensitive task was producing an official version of controversial incidents. The Bureau sent out bulletins to every major newspaper in the United Kingdom. Some of these bulletins were either false or deliberately misleading. A D-notice was often sent in tandem, in effect warning the editor that this was the only version of the incident that should appear in print. Newspapers that violated this notice could be targeted under Regulation 51 or 51A, allowing the government to seize the issue and the printing press that had produced it. Thus, the Press Bureau and the D-notice committee could act together to stifle the press and insist that editors publish items they knew to be false or misleading.

Disrupting UDC Public Events

As the government asserted its control over the information that could be published in newspapers, it also tried to limit the ability of antiwar groups to reach the public through open meetings. From its formation, the UDC understood that it had to spread its message through public meetings and open-air rallies. The organization had its strongest base in London, but its close ties to the Independent Labour Party meant that it could send speakers to northern England, Wales, and Scotland as well. At first Morel was worried that holding public meetings would energize the organization's opponents and make it more difficult for the UDC to organize itself.[69]

In the spring of 1915, the UDC began holding public events and, as expected, its meetings were frequently disrupted by mobs of pro-war zealots. That July, the UDC held a rally in Kingston upon Thames, a small town on the outskirts of London. In response, the *Daily Express,* one of the popular tabloids, printed an anonymous letter that denounced it as a "loathsome body of pro-Germans." An editorial in the *Express* urged its readers to prevent the meeting from occurring, with the result that a hostile crowd overwhelmed the meeting and Arthur Ponsonby was physically attacked.[70]

This was an early indication of a continuing pattern. The tabloid press, especially the *Daily Express*, would print articles denouncing the Union of Democratic Control, while calling for "patriots" to disrupt the meeting. A mob would then assemble, many of them in military uniform. These may have been soldiers who had been discharged or perhaps they had been given leave so that they could disrupt the meeting. In any case, the mob would storm the platform, assault speakers and forcibly disperse the audience. The police would stand by as observers, although no one would be charged with rioting or assault.

The first disruptions of UDC public events were small-scale incidents, but the confrontations soon escalated. In November 1915, the UDC booked a public event for the Memorial Hall on Farringdon Street in central London. The large auditorium in Memorial Hall held fifteen hundred and was one of London's largest venues. It had been the site for the founding conference of what would become the British Labour Party.

The *Daily Express* countered with a series of letters and articles denouncing the UDC and calling for a disruptive counter-protest. An editorial in the *Express* urged its readers to protest the UDC event, holding that those who disrupted the UDC were "as surely fighting for their country" as the soldiers in the trenches.[71]

On the day of the meeting, November 29, 1915, organizers of the counter-protest handed out forged tickets. This was by no means a spontaneous protest of enraged pro-war zealots. Many of those crashing the meeting were soldiers from New Zealand, Canada, and Australia visiting London while on leave. Before the gathering could convene, the mob charged the platform and attacked members of the audience. Once those who had hoped to attend the meeting had fled, the members of the mob passed a resolution supporting the government's war policies. The few police on hand did nothing to hinder those disrupting the meeting.[72]

On the following day, the *Express* gave its approval to the actions of the counter-protest. The mob had engaged in a "great patriotic demonstration" that had "put the pro-Germans to flight." After this incident, the UDC found it impossible to rent halls in the London area because landlords feared halls could be destroyed by angry mobs. The Metropolitan Police then made it official by sending out a list of organizations that were prohibited from holding public meetings in the London area. Several peace organizations, including the UDC, were among those on the list.[73]

When the UDC complained to the government, it found the government to be totally unsympathetic. Prior to the clash at Memorial Hall, Charles Trevelyan wrote to John Simon, the home secretary, complaining that the articles being printed in the *Express* were "almost as direct an incitement to violence as possible." Simon ignored the letter.[74]

A few months later, Simon had been replaced by Herbert Samuel in the Home Office. In May 1916, Phillip Snowden wrote to Samuel to protest the unwillingness of the Home Office to protect meetings held by the UDC and the ILP from mob violence. Snowden was one of the most prominent figures in the ILP and a Labour Party member of Parliament. He was convinced that "a certain sector of the press" was "inciting the hooligan elements to break up public meetings." Furthermore, the Home Office was giving its tacit approval to the violent suppression of dissent "by its inaction."[75]

Samuel responded that the Home Office could not "guarantee the safety of everyone who attends public meetings, especially during wartime." Although the police would make some effort to maintain order outside a hall, the responsibility for controlling protestors inside rested with "those who summoned the meeting." This for a large number of violent demonstrators intent on disrupting a peaceful meeting.[76]

THE CONSERVATIVE PARTY AND THE *DAILY EXPRESS*

The Asquith coalition was unwilling to confront the mobs breaking up UDC meetings because they had the covert backing of powerful forces that had allies within the government. This can be seen by looking more closely at the funding behind the *Daily Express*. In 1911, the owner of the paper, Arthur Pearson, on the verge of going blind, decided to dispose of his shares. He approached the Conservative Party to see if the rich donors funding it would be interested in purchasing the newspaper.

As a result, the Conservative Party established a *Daily Express* fund. In the period from 1912 through 1914, the Tories purchased £50,000 in shares, thus gaining a controlling interest in the paper. In current terms, more than a million pounds was invested in a failing newspaper. The wealthy individuals contributing to the fund did not wish to be identified, so the Conservative Party named dummy directors to the *Daily Express* board. One of those was James Lowther, a Conservative Party member of Parliament who also served as the speaker of the House of Commons.

The editorial policy of the *Express* was determined by Arthur Steel-Maitland, who controlled the fund as chair of the Conservative Party. He consulted closely with Andrew Bonar Law, the leader of the Tory contingent in the House of Commons. Thus as the Tories participated in a coalition government with the Liberals, the party engaged in clandestine efforts to undercut the government policy on the moderate opposition. Disagreements about how to cope with the moderate opposition added to the tensions within the coalition government and ultimately led to its collapse in December 1916.

THE CONFRONTATION AT CORY HALL

The mobilization of mobs to disrupt meetings called by the Union of Democratic Control and the Independent Labour Party succeeded in significantly stifling open opposition to the war. Nevertheless, the media tied to the Conservative Party, and their allies within the intelligence community, were not satisfied. Public meetings continued to be held in which the antiwar opposition was strongest, in Glasgow and South Wales. The coalition government harassed the moderate opposition, but it did not entirely suppress its public meetings.

The flashpoint was the convening of a mass meeting called by the National Council for Civil Liberties (NCCL) in a large hall in Cardiff,

Wales. The NCCL arose out of the struggle to prevent the introduction of conscription. Alongside the No Conscription Fellowship, organized in support of conscientious objectors, a broad coalition of those who opposed conscription was formed in the summer of 1915 to mobilize popular opinion. The National Council Against Conscription was transformed into the National Council for Civil Liberties after Parliament instituted the draft in January 1916. Most of those active in the NCCL were members of one of the groups within the moderate antiwar opposition, in particular the Independent Labour Party. Nevertheless, the NCCL was able to recruit from a wider base, including some who supported the war effort.

J. H. Thomas was the general secretary of the National Union of Railwaymen (NUR) and an active supporter of the Labour Party. Although Thomas promoted the war effort, he opposed the government's decision to ban strikes, as well as its efforts to inhibit the ability of workers in the key war industries to switch from one employer to another. Lloyd George, the minister of munitions, had pushed through regulations that penalized workers who left their jobs without first gaining permission of their employers. Thomas viewed the NCCL as a way of mobilizing popular opposition to further encroachments on the rights of workers during the wartime emergency.

In October 1917, James Winstone, the president of the South Wales Miners Federation and an ILP member, announced that the NCCL would hold a conference at Cory Hall in the following month. His announcement triggered a storm of controversy. The conference would draw hundreds of delegates from around Britain. Most of the affiliated organizations were branches of the ILP and the NUR. Cory Hall was one of the largest venues in Cardiff, originally built to host temperance meetings.

Although the NCCL primarily concentrated its activities on criticisms of the government's autocratic actions in suppressing dissent, its scope went beyond this narrow focus. A leaflet distributed prior to the conference listed a series of resolutions that would be considered by the delegates. In addition to a defense of civil liberties during wartime and a condemnation of "industrial conscription," the list included a resolution urging a repeal of conscription once the war came to an end. Another resolution came close to endorsing the stance of the Union of Democratic Control. It called on the government "to seek the earliest opportunity of promoting negotiations," with the aim of achieving "a just and lasting peace."[77]

These demands had considerable support among rank-and-file Welsh miners, but they also placed the NCCL firmly within the orbit of the moderate antiwar opposition. The pro-war element within the South Wales Miners' Federation was incensed. An ad hoc coalition was hastily formed to pressure the government into cancelling the conference and, if that failed, to prevent the conference from happening. A closed meeting was held during the latter part of October to plan a coordinated assault on the conference.

Among the twenty-five attending the initial planning meeting were the owners of some of the largest coal companies in the area. One of them, David Davies, was also a member of Parliament representing the Liberal Party. Several of those active in the pro-war faction of the Miners' Federation were also present. Most prominent of these was Charles Butt Stanton who would act as the public spokesperson for the group. Stanton had been a militant in the miners' union until he opted to become a fervent supporter of the war. Stanton was elected to Parliament as an independent Nationalist, defeating Winstone, who stood as the Labour Party candidate, in a 1914 by-election. Edward Tupper, the national organizer of the National Sailor's and Firemen's Union, also attended the closed planning meeting. Merchant ships carrying vital supplies were often attacked by German submarines, so some sailors were among the most fervent supporters of the war effort.[78]

This was already an odd cross-class alliance of union officials and industrialists, but the coalition was even odder than that. Representatives of military intelligence and the intelligence unit of the ministry of munitions, PMS2, also participated in planning the disruption of the NCCL conference. Thus, a government agency was sending representatives to a meeting to organize a mob to forcibly prevent the holding of a peaceful meeting that was perfectly legal.

The Asquith coalition government was working at cross-purposes. Furthermore, Lloyd George, then the minister of munitions, sent greetings to the meeting. Even though he was a member of the Cabinet, Lloyd George was acting to undermine the authority of one of its most important members, Herbert Samuel, the home secretary.[79]

Although the planning meeting was held in secret, the informal group was quite open as to its intentions. Captain Atherly Jones, a former army officer, attended the meeting as the Welsh organizer of the British Empire Union, a far-right group that demanded the suppression of even the mildest form of dissent. In a letter to the *Western Mail*, the local newspaper, Jones demanded that the rally be cancelled and warned that patriotic elements would act if the government did not.[80] (The *Western Mail* had close links to the coal-mining corporations.)

Behind the scenes, the government came under intense pressure to ban the conference. Vernon Kell, as the head of MI5, wrote to the Home Office urging Samuel to invoke the powers provided by the DORA regulations to prohibit the meeting from taking place. This regulation, issued in early October 1916, authorized the home secretary to ban any meeting or march that might "give rise to grave disorder" or might "promote disaffection." The regulation also permitted a local magistrate or police chief to issue such an order, but only with the express permission of the home secretary. Edward Troup, the permanent secretary and chief civil servant in the Home Office, responded that there were no legitimate grounds to cancel the meeting. If the local police chief applied for an order to "stop the meeting" on the basis that it would cause a disturbance of the peace, the request would "have to be considered." Troup was clear that the Home Office would not consider a request to ban the meeting that came from the MI5, the Security Service.[81]

Once it became known that the government would not block the NCCL conference from opening, the pro-war coalition began mobilizing its forces for a direct confrontation. Although the tabloids liked to claim that Welsh miners had acted out of patriotic fervor to prevent a dangerous meeting from taking place, the reality was that the disruption was carefully organized and that trains brought many of the protesters from outside of Wales to Cardiff.[82]

On the morning of Saturday, November 11, 1916, prior to the opening of the NCCL conference, the pro-war faction held an open-air rally some distance away. Stanton was the main speaker, but he was joined by the owner of one of the largest Welsh coal companies, D. A. Thomas (Lord Rhondda). The speakers at the rally made it clear that they were intent on preventing the conference from occurring. Once the speeches ended, the crowd marched to Cory Hall where a large number of protesters were already besieging the hall.

By the time the march from the rally reached Cory Hall, the angry mob numbered fifteen hundred. The chief constable of Cardiff had only 150 constables available to police this volatile situation, an entirely inadequate number.

Inside the hall the audience consisted of about 450 delegates and an equal number of observers. They awaited the keynote speech to be delivered by James Henry Thomas, the general secretary of the National Union of Railwaymen. Although Thomas would be vilified by the tabloid press for participating in a conference of antiwar dissidents, he was a moderate union official who supported the war effort. Still, Thomas objected to a law that made it more difficult for workers in war industries to quit and move to a new job. Ramsay MacDonald, the most prominent ILP leader, was to follow Thomas to the podium.[83]

Before the conference could begin, the mob brushed aside the police cordon and broke up the meeting. Stanton directed the mob by shouting, "Clear the Germans out!" MacDonald left quickly by a back exit, but Thomas and Winstone were caught up among the hostile crowd. They were pelted with mud and tomatoes before being escorted by police from the hall. Once those attending the conference had been forced to flee, the leaders of the counter-demonstration addressed the mob and a resolution was passed without dissent calling on the government to continue the war until Germany was totally defeated.[84]

The police stood by while a peaceful, legal meeting was violently dispersed and a member of Parliament fled the hall in fear of being physically assaulted. In this case, there was no doubt who had led the mob. Indeed, Stanton defended his actions in a speech to Parliament. The coalition government had done nothing to prevent the meeting from being held and it had done nothing to stop a mob from disrupting it.

The miners of South Wales and the railroad workers were furious that their leaders had been subject, to a humiliating assault. A follow-up meeting of two hundred was held in Merthyr Tydfil shortly after the Cory Hall fiasco. The participants in the second meeting came primarily from ILP branches in Wales. There was no effort to mob the meeting, which took place without incident. Railroad workers informed the government that they would not operate any trains carrying those intent on disrupting the follow-up meeting. Furthermore, Welsh miners threatened to strike if the Merthyr gathering was disrupted. Herbert Samuel then insisted to Stanton that any plans for a further confrontation would be resisted and peace prevailed.[85]

Clearly the situation as it stood in the latter part of 1916 was untenable. The coalition government found itself unable to formulate a coherent policy in dealing with the moderate antiwar opposition. Divisions within the government deepened as the war became increasingly unpopular. For the Conservatives and a segment of the Liberals, the necessity of a harsher policy was becoming even more crucial. On the other hand, most of the Liberals continued to believe that a more nuanced approach would prove to be more effective. This division was one factor catalyzing the crisis of December 1916.

The War Cabinet and Civil Liberties

The confrontation at Cory Hall underlined the deep divisions within the coalition government led by Asquith. As the stalemate continued along the Western Front, the British casualty toll rose rapidly and popular support for the war effort plummeted. By the fall of 1916, radical critics who viewed the war as an imperialist conflict were beginning to gain a mass audience, although this was still a minority position within the working class. Still, beyond the radical core of activists were a large and growing number in the broader populace who had been through enough and who wanted the UK to immediately negotiate a peace treaty with Germany on the basis of no annexations and no reparations. The network of organizations calling for an immediate peace was gaining in strength and becoming a significant threat to the government.

It was within this context that the confrontation at Cory Hall exacerbated the underlying tensions within the government. Although the Asquith Liberals were prepared to continue the war until the Germans unconditionally surrendered, they were not willing to ruthlessly suppress those calling for an immediate peace. Several of the most prominent members of the Union of Democratic Control had been elected to Parliament as Liberals. Thus, quashing the moderate opposition would inevitably trigger a bitter split within the Liberal Party.

The Conservative Party was divided as well. The more pragmatic leaders such as Arthur Balfour, a former prime minister, and Andrew Bonar Law, the leader of the Tory contingent in Parliament, were wary of precipitating the downfall of the Asquith coalition, fearing that this might further isolate the United Kingdom from potential allies such as the United States. Since President Woodrow Wilson viewed himself as a progressive, Bonar Law and his group were concerned that a government dominated by the Conservative Party would have a more difficult time gaining Wilson's support. They were therefore unwilling to demand that the coalition government further restrict the permissible limits of debate.

Hardliners within the Conservative Party were convinced that the moderate opposition had to be suppressed so that the war could be continued until a final and total victory. This position was expressed by Edward Carson in a speech he gave to the House of Commons in November 1917, after the coalition government had collapsed. Carson warned Parliament that there was "an organised system of misrepresentation by the pacifists of this country," often "in the interests of the enemy." This peace propaganda came from those who were "doing their best to thwart those" who were "trying to carry on the war to a victorious conclusion."[86] These views were shared by the small segment of the Liberal Party that supported Lloyd George.

In December 1916, divisions within the coalition government led to its fall and its replacement by the War Cabinet. Although David Lloyd George, a prominent member of the Liberal Party, served as prime minister, the War Cabinet was dominated by those tied to the Conservative Party. A small, secretive body, the War Cabinet met virtually every day and set the overall policy for the government in every area of responsibility.[87] Minutes of the meetings were kept and circulated to a small group of top-level officials. Unfortunately, some minutes were deemed to be especially sensitive and have still not been released to the public.

The idea of an all-powerful but small executive had been widely discussed well before December 1916. In November 1915, Newton Wallop, the Earl of Portsmouth, had complained in a speech to the House of Lords that certain controversial issues were still being determined in the cabinet, a broader body of twenty-two members of Parliament. This, he claimed, was inefficient. It was time to recognize that war was "a business" and that "success" was "the sole criterion." After all, Wallop argued, Britain was "fighting" for its "existence as an Empire."[88]

The spokesperson for the coalition government in the House of Lords, Robert Milnes, the Earl of Crewe, responded that such a concentration of power in a small body would soon become "something like a genuine dictatorship and it is one of the postulates of a dictatorship that it should be immune from criticism." The result would be "the silencing of the Press" and a government that did not feel itself responsible to Parliament.[89] These predictions proved to be entirely correct, but unfortunately neither Asquith nor the majority of the Liberal Party that aligned with him challenged the autocratic measures that were adopted by the War Cabinet.

Once in power, the War Cabinet took as a priority the disruption and silencing of the network of peace organizations led by the Union of Democratic Control. Yet the War Cabinet did not stop there. As it consolidated power, it increasingly came to see any opposition, no matter how limited and cautiously worded, as a threat and this aggressive hostility was soon extended to critics from within the mainstream media. In the view of those in the War Cabinet, the United Kingdom could only succeed in achieving its wartime goal, total victory over the imperial German government, if the people of the United Kingdom remained unified. Any criticism had to be immediately and ruthlessly suppressed.

THE WAR CABINET CONFRONTS THE PEACE MOVEMENT

The War Cabinet, intent on suppressing the activities of even moderate opposition, tightened controls over a range of activities. On the issue of public meetings, there seems to have been a tacit understanding that the network of organizations within the moderate opposition would not convene any more large-scale public conferences and rallies, so there were no more major confrontations such as the one at Cory Hall. In addition, George Cave, the attorney general who replaced Herbert Samuel, had no hesitation in invoking the DORA regulations to prohibit smaller public meetings sponsored by the UDC and the ILP.

Nevertheless, local conflicts occurred. In May 1918, the Leicester Labour Party organized an outdoor rally featuring Ramsay MacDonald, the member of Parliament representing that constituency. The National War Aims Committee held a counter-rally and a large group from it mobbed the platform of the Labour Party rally and prevented MacDonald from speaking. Although there had been similar incidents under the coalition government, this was a somewhat different affair. Previously, the tabloid press urged off-duty soldiers and veterans to disrupt antiwar meetings. This time it was the National War Aims Committee, an organization created to promote popular support for the war, that spearheaded the disruption. Since the Committee was funded by the government, the War Cabinet was directly responsible for the physical disruption of public meetings that were legal even under the restrictive provisions of the DORA regulations.[90]

The *Labour Leader* had been viewed as an important problem for the coalition government, but it was less so under the War Cabinet. With Fenner Brockway in jail as a conscientious objector, the newspaper became even more cautious in printing articles critical of the government's war policies. Government threats had succeeded in stifling the *Labour Leader* as a forum for the antiwar opposition.

Still, opposition to the war continued to increase as the war dragged on and casualties continued to mount. Demands for immediate negotiations and a just peace treaty were gaining the support of a wide segment of popular opinion. In this context, the War Cabinet came to view the Union of Democratic Control as a significant threat that had to be suppressed. The government developed a concerted plan of action that began with a heightened censorship of UDC literature and led to the prosecution and jailing of E. D. Morel, the driving force within the Union of Democratic Control.

THE WAR CABINET AND NEWSPAPERS

The War Cabinet began by targeting the brochures coming from the Union of Democratic Control. George Cave, an attorney and a Conservative Party member of Parliament, was eager to tighten government control over printed material. In a memorandum dated November 1917, Cave insisted that "further powers" under DORA were "required." He warned the War Cabinet that "a very large number of pacifist pamphlets and leaflets" were being circulated with the "funds supplied either by the enemy or by anarchists or peace cranks."[91] In fact, MI5 and the Special Branch initiated repeated efforts to uncover any financial links between organizations such as the Union of Democratic Control and the German government, but they were unable to discover the slightest evidence to bolster this spurious charge. Instead, intelligence reports discovered that the funds needed by peace groups came from wealthy Quakers such as the Cadbury family, presumably the "peace cranks" referred to by Cave.

To counter the threat posed by printed material calling for a negotiated peace, Cave argued that a more rigorous form of censorship was essential. Furthermore, this "would not be an interference with freedom of opinion and speech" since leaflets promoting an immediate peace were "not expressions of opinion, but propaganda intended to influence others." This was an absurd argument. Any comment on public affairs that is distributed to the public represents an effort to persuade the reader of that point of view. The fact that an experienced attorney acting as home secretary could advance such an argument, and not have it immediately dismissed, is indicative of the total disregard for fundamental civil liberties that characterized the War Cabinet.

In spite of the faulty logic of Cave's rationale, much of his proposal was adopted by the War Cabinet. A further regulation, 27C, to implement the Defence of the Realm Act was approved and implemented. One section of the new regulation was particularly aimed at controlling the content of newspapers. The government's concern extended from the *Labour Leader* on the Left to conservative newspapers such as the *Morning Post*, which strongly supported the war, but disagreed with the War Cabinet on how to conduct it. Cave believed these newspapers were "mischievous," and needed to be more tightly controlled. He was concerned that regulations already in force, Regulations 51 and 51A, which permitted the authorities to raid the premises of the printers and seize their presses, and had been used successfully to silence smaller newspaper published by the radical Left, could not be readily employed against the larger newspapers. Cave was concerned that seizing the printing presses of the larger print shops, such as the National Labour Press, was not a viable option since this "would interfere with the publication of other matter and might attract the sympathy of more reputable newspapers."[92]

Instead, Cave proposed that the new regulation authorize the home secretary, that is, himself, to order the suspension for a specified period of time of any newspaper found to be in violation of the DORA regulations. He was convinced that "the mere existence of such a power would be a strong deterrent" to any newspaper with a sizable circulation from engaging in a sharp criticism of the government's war policies.

Within the War Cabinet, this proposal was rejected both as to its "efficacy and desirability." There was concern that an order suspending publication of a major newspaper would be bound to trigger "an almost unanimous outcry" by all the mainstream papers and, furthermore, the ensuing "storm of controversy" would provide "a great advertisement to the suppressed newspaper."[93]

Still, the War Cabinet recognized that it had a problem. Carson suggested that a censor be stationed at every "offending newspaper," with the power to reject any article considered to be in violation of the DORA regulations. This would have significantly tightened press censorship, but it would have also risked a direct confrontation with the mainstream newspapers, which were prepared to submit articles to the Press Bureau for review prior to publication but were strongly opposed to any measure that would make the publication of a rejected article in itself a crime.

Another proposal, which seems to have been carried out quietly, was a strict control over the supply of paper. Newspapers seen as unfriendly would see their supply substantially reduced, thus creating a major financial loss. Although the War Cabinet had its doubts as to whether such a plan could be implemented, even the threat could act as a significant deterrent.

THE WAR CABINET AND PEACE LITERATURE

Home Secretary Cave was also intent on targeting suspect leaflets and flyers, in particular those coming from the Union of Democratic Control. Flyers being distributed by small, radical organizations could already be suppressed under Regulations 51 and 51A. Those responsible for the flyers could also be prosecuted under Regulation 42, causing disaffection within the military, or deported to another area under Regulation 14.

There were, therefore, no lack of repressive measures aimed at those producing flyers criticizing the war. Nevertheless, Cave was aware that the government was not prepared to prosecute the leaders of the UDC for advocating immediate peace negotiations and it was not willing to summarily seize the printing presses of the National Labour Press, its printers. Furthermore, by the time the government could go to court to order the seizure of flyers it disliked, they would have been already been distributed.

Cave therefore proposed that the War Cabinet issue a new regulation requiring that every leaflet "dealing with the continuance of the war or the conclusion of peace" be "passed by the Press Bureau before publication." He presented a draft of a new regulation mandating that every leaflet, flyer, or brochure must "have been submitted and approved" by the Press Bureau prior to publication. In addition, each copy of every leaflet had to carry the name and address of the author and the printer.[94] There can be little doubt that this new regulation was specifically aimed at the Union of Democratic Control and its ally the Independent Labour Party.

This new DORA regulation, numbered as 27C, was approved by the War Cabinet at its meeting held on November 15, 1917, with no objections and few alterations. Cave then defended it before the House of Commons, insisting that the new regulation was needed "to deal effectively with propaganda in the interest of the enemy," but that it would not be used in any way to suppress criticism of the Government.[95] Of course, Cave had written the regulation specifically to quash those who criticized the government's policy of continuing the war until Germany unconditionally surrendered.

Shortly afterward, Herbert Samuel wrote to Cave that he and the group around Asquith had a significant problem with the new regulation and would raise the issue on the floor of the House of Commons. Samuel had no objection to the War Cabinet's efforts to subject the flyers coming from the Union of Democratic Control to some form of prior censorship, but he did object to the flyers having to be "approved by the Press Bureau" before they could be printed. This clause gave the government, through the Press Bureau, the final authority to determine the legality of a written document without any judicial review. To Samuel, and the others in his group in Parliament, this was going too far.[96]

Samuel pointed out that the clause was not required since the provisions requiring prior notice in the new regulation would be sufficient to handle the problem posed by flyers calling for an immediate peace. Furthermore, the new regulation represented a further step away from due process. Although the military was already authorized to seize newspapers and printing presses and deport citizens to other localities in the United Kingdom without prior approval from any court, citizens could not be imprisoned on the basis of an administrative ruling.

Samuel warned Cave that the Liberal group led by Asquith would raise this issue on the floor of the House of Commons unless this issue was resolved. In response, the War Cabinet agreed to delete the clause requiring the prior approval of the Press Bureau, while adding an additional section requiring every leaflet to be presented to the Press Bureau seventy-two hours prior to publication.[97] This gave the government time to go to a magistrate's court to obtain a court order prohibiting distribution of any flyer found to be in violation of the DORA regulations.

Confronted by this new and more stringent set of DORA regulations, the UDC muffled its critique of government policy. The organization undertook self-censorship, publishing a sharply limited number of pamphlets during the last months of the war. Those that were issued were presented to the Press Bureau for a pre-publication review and were printed only after they received official approval.

This policy of compliance raised concerns within the ranks of the UDC's membership. In February 1918, the General Council approved a resolution that challenged the DORA regulations by insisting that the UDC should publish its pamphlets whether or not the government gave its permission. The resolution was introduced by Lt. Col. Maitland Hardyman, an infantry officer then posted to the Western Front. Even as he fought in the trenches, Hardyman remained a critic of the government's war policies. He would be killed in action in August 1917.[98]

The General Council was a large body with representatives from UDC branches from around Britain. It met three times a year in order to determine general policy guidelines. In spite of this, the executive committee, a smaller body of ten that met weekly, ignored Hardyman's resolution and the UDC continued to submit all of its literature for prior review by the Press Bureau.[99] The Union of Democratic Control understood the limits that were being set and censored itself rather than confront the government. Thus, the War Cabinet succeeded in its determination to stifle those calling for a negotiated peace.

TARGETING MOREL

Tightening government control over the pamphlets being distributed by the Union of Democratic Control was only part of the War Cabinet's campaign to suppress its activities. E. D. Morel was the "chief inspiration" of the UDC and, as such, a prime target of the government.[100] In spite of the campaign of repression directed at it, the UDC continued to gain a hearing for its call for a negotiated peace that would not be based on the total defeat of either alliance.

On August 22, 1917, Morel's house was ransacked by the police. Morel had been completely open in his opposition to the government's war policies, but the authorities were looking for a pretext to bring charges without directly prosecuting him for his point of view. He was arrested and charged with violating the DORA regulations on August 31, 1917. Arraigned the following day, Morel was held in Brixton Jail with the presiding magistrate refusing to grant bail. On September 4, Morel was given a summary trial without a jury, convicted of the charges and sentenced to the maximum six months in jail.[101]

Although the government claimed that this was a simple police matter, the extremely rapid judicial process and the refusal to set bail provide obvious indications that the War Cabinet considered this to be a matter of urgent importance. George Cave, the home secretary, informed Parliament that Morel's prosecution was "undertaken in the ordinary way." Cave insisted that he "knew nothing" of the matter until he saw "the reports in the papers." Still, Cave believed that Morel's "offense" had been "a very serious one in war-time."[102]

In reality, the government had pounced on a technical violation of one of the many DORA regulations as an excuse to imprison an influential figure among those who called for peace. Regulation 24 had prohibited anyone residing in Britain from sending a letter or printed material to a person living outside of the country "otherwise than through the post." This regulation was issued in July 1917. It was followed by a supplementary regulation, 24B, that specified that those who sent documents or letters "by an indirect route" with the intent "to evade examination" by postal censors was guilty of violating the Defence of the Realm Act.[103] This was very detailed, but it was issued in April 1918, after Morel's prosecution and imprisonment.

Nevertheless, the intent of Regulation 24 was clear. The DORA regulations gave the Army Council the authority to ban certain material from the overseas post. Literature criticizing the government's war policies was not permitted in posted mail being sent to Germany and its allies. On the other end, mail to countries allied with Britain was less severely censored. Mail sent to neutral countries was placed in a third and more ambiguous category. In November 1915, the Union of Democratic Control had been granted the right to send pamphlets and literature to readers residing in neutral countries. This privilege was withdrawn in November 1916 as the government placed greater constraints on the activities of the UDC.[104]

Thus by August 1917 Morel had been warned that any effort to send UDC literature to a person living in a neutral country would be blocked. Nevertheless, he attempted to evade this restriction that month. Morel heard through friends that Ethel Sidgwick knew French union leaders who opposed the war and that she was about to tour Europe. Although he did not personally know Sidgwick, Morel wrote to her about the possibility of bringing some of UDC's literature to France. Sidgwick answered that she was in contact with Romain Rolland, a famous author who was outspoken in his opposition to the First World War. Sidgwick offered to bring a copy of one of Morel's pamphlets, *The African Problem and the Peace Settlement*, to Rolland in Switzerland. Although Rolland was French, he had moved to Switzerland, a neutral country, so that he could freely express his opposition to the war. Morel agreed with Sidgwick's proposal and added that he hoped she could deliver another of his pamphlets to Rolland, *Tsardom's Part in the War*.[105]

UK intelligence agencies had placed Morel under close surveillance so the correspondence between Morel and Sedgwick was intercepted, opened, copied, and resealed.[106] Intelligence agents observed Sidgwick reading Morel's letter on August 21, 1917, and the searches and arrest followed quickly. Although Morel claimed that he did not know Rolland had moved to a neutral country, the evidence strongly indicates that he was aware that he was attempting to evade a DORA regulation when he responded to Sidgwick's letter. It was a mistake that would have disastrous consequences.

Morel served his sentence in Pentonville jail, a high-security prison holding men convicted of serious violent crimes. Located in northern London, Pentonville was built in 1842 and was thus already old and outmoded in 1917. Several prisoners had been executed by hanging and buried in the prison's grounds. Pentonville consisted of five wings radiating from a central ward. Morel was the only political prisoner on his wing, although another wing held a few conscientious objectors.

Prison conditions were harsh. Morel was confined to his solitary cell from 4 p.m. to 8 a.m. every day of the week. Coal was scarce, so even during the height of winter there was no heat in the cells. Morel was put to work sewing bags for postal carriers, but part of this job involved carrying 100-pound bags of jute. The food was nutritionally deficient with porridge and bread making up the bulk of the meals. (The diet of prisoners had always been unhealthy but it became worse in 1917 as the food available from small harvests was directed to the soldiers at the front.)[107]

Silence between prisoners was strictly enforced throughout the day. Morel was allowed outside exercise one hour a day, walking silently around a courtyard. He was almost totally cut off from the outside world. He was granted a fifteen-minute visit with his wife every month, a provision that was altered in the middle of his sentence to one brief visit every two weeks. Morel could also send one short letter to his wife every month and she could write to him once a month as well.[108] The harsh conditions and the imposed isolation left Morel in a fragile mental state, suffering severe depression.

English prisons were designed to break the health and morale of those incarcerated. Most of the prisoners were young, used to hard physical work and in good health. Morel was none of these. He was forty-four, in poor health, and accustomed to working in an office.

Morel suffered from a severe heart problem, later diagnosed as angina. In October 1916, he had fainted and was ordered to rest and stop working. Six months earlier, he had collapsed during a train ride.[109] Morel was a sick man and his stay in Pentonville Prison greatly exacerbated his condition. Since he had been under intense surveillance by the intelligence agencies for some time prior to his arrest, the government fully understood that treating Morel as a youthful, violent criminal was certain to have severe consequences to his health.

When Morel's wife realized that his health was rapidly deteriorating, she convinced Arthur Ponsonby to write a series of letters urging the home secretary, Cave, to grant Morel an early release. Morel served five months of his sentence, with a month off for good behavior. Cave finally agreed to release Morel three days early, so Morel left prison in January 1918.

Morel left prison "in a state of nervous exhaustion" leading to a "short period of near-collapse." Although he began attending UDC events within weeks of his release, Morel could only return to work on a full-time basis after several months of rest. The impact of prison on Morel's health was permanent. Indeed, according to a sympathetic biographer, "Ill health continued to plague him for the rest of his life." Morel died in 1924 at the age of fifty-one, only seven years after serving his sentence at Pentonville.[110]

The members of the War Cabinet despised the Union of Democratic Control. They viewed it as a serious threat to popular support for the government's war policies. By greatly restricting the right of the UDC to issue pamphlets and by imprisoning its leading figure, the War Cabinet succeeded in effectively undercutting the ability of the UDC to function as a focal point for the antiwar opposition.

THE X COMMITTEE

The X Committee was an interesting twist in executive decision-making. The December 1916 parliamentary coup had brought to power a small, secretive War Cabinet with total power to make decisions of enormous import without being accountable to Parliament or the wider Cabinet. The X Committee took this one step further. Important decisions concerning the conduct of the war were unofficially delegated to a small committee consisting of Lloyd George, Alfred Milner, and General Henry Wilson.[111] (Alfred Milner was an influential figure in the Conservative Party and a member of the House of Lords, while Henry Wilson was the army's chief of the Imperial General Staff.)

The three men met almost daily after Milner left the War Cabinet in April 1918 to become the Secretary of State for War, usually for an hour immediately prior to a meeting of the War Cabinet. Meetings were kept small and informal, unlike meetings of the War Cabinet, with Maurice Hankey acting as an aide to Lloyd George and Leo Amery acting as an aide to Milner. (Hankey was a naval officer who became a key policy advisor. He served as the secretary of the War Cabinet. Amery was a Conservative Party member of Parliament. Earlier, as a journalist covering the Boer War, he worked closely with Milner who was then British High Commissioner to South Africa.) In spite of the informality, action minutes were kept and decisions were made and implemented.[112]

The UK frequently attacked Germany as an undemocratic autocracy, since major decisions were made by the Kaiser and his personal advisors rather than an elected government. In addition, the German military high command held enormous power, especially as it related to decisions that determined the military strategy to be followed. Yet here was a small executive committee that not only made decisions that were kept secret, but whose very existence was a tightly held secret. Furthermore, only one of its three voting members had ever been elected to public office, while the other two were directly related to the military, Milner as minister of war and Wilson as a career army officer.

Although the X Committee had been created to give Milner an opportunity to discuss the evolving military situation with Lloyd George, with Wilson and Hankey contributing their expertise to the discussion, the scope of concern often went beyond issues of military tactics and strategy. Topics that were viewed as particularly sensitive could also be placed on the agenda. These topics might concern the repression of dissent, making sure that the government led by Lloyd George remained in power, and even the possible outcome of the war.

This raises the issue of why sensitive topics were discussed in the secretive and small confines of the X Committee rather than being brought before the War Cabinet. Milner frequently attended War Cabinet meetings as minister of war, so his direct participation in the making of key decisions could not have provided the sole compelling reason for initiating a parallel structure.

There were two additional plausible reasons for the creation of the X Committee. First, the spring and early summer of 1918 were especially difficult times for Allied forces along the Western Front. War Cabinet meetings were often large, so total secrecy was difficult to maintain. Though the War Cabinet was small, various other officials might be asked to attend to contribute their expertise on a particular issue. Although the deliberations of the War Cabinet were treated as sensitive secrets, word of its decisions sometimes filtered to the members of Parliament. X Committee meetings were far smaller and thus its deliberations could be more carefully guarded.

Second, the War Cabinet included a representative of the Labour Party. By 1918, Arthur Henderson, the most influential Labour figure, had been replaced by George Barnes, a Labour Party member of Parliament. In the December 1918 election, Barnes would break with Labour and win election as the government's candidate from a Glasgow district. Still, during the last months of the war, when the X Committee met frequently, Barnes remained in close contact with Henderson and the Labour Party executive committee. Lloyd George and Milner may well have believed that certain sensitive topics were better discussed within a smaller setting that excluded Barnes.

THE X COMMITTEE AND PARLIAMENT

One case that involved the X Committee in issues that went well beyond questions of military strategy occurred in June 1918. The war was not going well along the Western Front as Germany launched an aggressive attack hoping to capture Paris and perhaps the coastal ports along the English Channel. In this context, the X Committee discussed the possibility of a forced evacuation of troops from France.

News of this discussion leaked to dissident members of Parliament who raised the issue of a forced evacuation during an extended debate on the war. Although most members of Parliament provided the government with uncritical support, a few became increasingly skeptical. William Pringle, a Liberal, was the most outspoken dissident. Pringle had initially supported the war, but he opposed the imposition of conscription and he sharply disagreed with the coalition government's efforts to silence the antiwar opposition. Pringle despised Lloyd George and bitterly criticized the War Cabinet.[113] He was dismayed by the War Cabinet, which seemed to combine an autocratic arrogance with incompetence. Pringle had good sources within the government who provided him with information that he then introduced into the official record of parliamentary debates.

During a debate on the course of the war held on June 18, 1918, Pringle informed Parliament that the situation in France was "so serious" that ports in England along the British Channel were "in great peril" should France collapse. Another member of Parliament, and an informal ally of Pringle, Richard Holt, confirmed that there was a genuine danger that France would be "overwhelmed by the Germans." He then queried the government spokesperson as to whether any arrangement had "been made with the French authorities" concerning the rapid evacuation of UK troops should the German assault succeed.[114]

Obviously, Pringle and Holt knew of the earlier discussion within the X Committee covering this topic. The following day this interchange in Parliament was a subject of concern within the X Committee. Lloyd George reported that Geoffrey Dawson, the editor of the *Times*, had drawn his attention to the "indiscreet and mischievous speeches" that had been given in Parliament. Dawson had been quickly informed of these speeches and had then ordered that no mention be made of them in the *Times*. He had then gone further to ensure that none of the other major London newspapers took any notice of this important debate.[115]

The speeches made by Pringle and Holt caused quite a stir. Amery reported to the X Committee on the following day that he had discussed the question with the director of military intelligence, Lt. General George Macdonogh, and that they had agreed that the relevant pages of the official record of Parliament would not be permitted to be sent abroad. Yet this was not enough. Amery had also spoken with the speaker of the House of Commons, James Lowther, to look into the possibility of an "alteration in Hansard," that is, the deletion of the pages providing a report of the speeches by Pringle and Holt. This was a truly Orwellian effort, an attempt to rewrite history. Fortunately, Amery failed and the actual record remains intact.

Amery also met with Andrew Bonar Law, the leader of the Conservative Party's contingent in Parliament and a member of the War Cabinet. Bonar Law agreed to speak with Lowther to urge him to warn the "offending members." The Speaker of the House held enormous power within Parliament, so he could prevent Pringle and his group of disaffected Liberals from gaining a chance to speak. In fact, Pringle was not able to raise any difficult and controversial issues for three months after the June debate. Only in October 1918, as the war came to an end, was he permitted to raise a question concerning the coming peace talks.

THE X COMMITTEE AND THE *MORNING POST*

As the War Cabinet tightened the pressure on those calling for a negotiated peace, it also acted to further widen the range of opinion subject to repression. The members of the War Cabinet became increasingly convinced that anyone who criticized the government's policies was obstructing the war effort and thus must be silenced. As a result, even the most conservative newspapers became a target of repression. These initiatives were too sensitive for the War Cabinet and, instead, the X Committee took the lead. Ironically, the elaborate web of DORA regulations came to be used against those who had most stridently called for a total war to the finish and who had enthusiastically applauded the government's concerted efforts to suppress those calling for a negotiated peace.

The *Morning Post* was an influential daily newspaper, second only to the *Times* among conservative newspapers. The *Post*, and its editor Howell Gwynne, had close ties to the military command. Gwynne despised Henry Asquith for being too soft on dissidents and eagerly supported the parliamentary coup that deposed the coalition government headed by Asquith and replaced it with the War Cabinet.

It would seem that Gwynne would have been enthusiastic as the War Cabinet acted to suppress all of those who opposed a continuation of the war until Germany unconditionally surrendered. Nevertheless, his support for the War Cabinet was short-lived. The coalition government had left issues related to the overall strategy followed by British forces to the military high command, frequently with disastrous results. Lloyd George was adamant that the War Cabinet gain tighter control over the military. Needless to say, Gwynne's contacts in the Army Council vehemently rejected these efforts. Gwynne also opposed Lloyd George's military strategy, which involved shifting some troops from the Western Front to the Middle East.

As the *Post* became increasingly disenchanted with the government's war policies, the War Cabinet began to consider how to quash it. At its meeting on November 15, 1917, the War Cabinet had discussed possible measures of repression that could target newspapers it viewed as unfriendly, although no action was taken.[116]

The problem was magnified after January 1918 when Charles Repington left the *Times* to become the chief military correspondent of the *Post*. Repington had undertaken a successful career in the army until he became involved with a married woman. The resulting scandal resulted in his being forced to resign. Repington left the military to become a freelance journalist. He was soon hired by the *Times*, where he became a notable member of its staff.[117]

The ill will between the *Post* and the War Cabinet became a matter of public record in February 1918 when the *Post* printed an article by Repington detailing decisions made at a high-level conference of the commanding officers of the Allied military forces. Repington had been given a confidential briefing by France's premier, Georges Clemenceau. Both the French government and Repington opposed the War Cabinet's effort to transfer troops from the Western Front to Italy and the Middle East.

The censor assigned to the *Morning Post* warned Gwynne that the article contained military secrets and thus its publication would violate the DORA regulations. Gwynne and Repington insisted that the German government was already well informed of the decisions made at the conference in Versailles. They contended that the government was using the DORA regulations to stifle debate on a crucial policy issue rather than protecting national security. Of course, the *Post* had enthusiastically supported the government when it suppressed those calling for a debate on British war aims. In any case, the *Morning Post* was prosecuted for printing the article and both Repington and Gwynne were fined £100 for violating the DORA regulations.[118]

Another issue in dispute concerned the creation of a reserve of Allied forces that would be held back from the front lines and be available to stop any German advance. The reserve forces would be placed under the command of a French general. William Robertson, the army's chief of staff, tried to block this transfer of forces, insisting on direct control over all UK troops along the Western Front. At Lloyd George's insistence, General Robertson was dismissed in February 1918 and replaced by General Henry Wilson. Robertson and Gwynne were allies. Gwynne was furious and the *Morning Post* printed a series of articles and editorials that were critical of Wilson and of the War Cabinet.[119]

Milner was very conscious of the importance of the media in influencing popular opinion, so he secretly moved to counter Repington and the *Post*. Waldorf Astor was one of Milner's closest allies. A wealthy American living in England, Astor owned the *Observer*, a London newspaper that zealously defended the government's war policies. At Milner's behest, Astor told J. L. Garvin, the editor of the *Observer*, to write a hatchet piece excoriating Repington. The lengthy article appeared on May 12, 1918. It denounced Repington as a "devious troublemaker" whose articles "encouraged and delighted the enemy."[120]

At this point, the entire X Committee stepped into the controversy. Needless to say, Wilson was not pleased with the *Morning Post*'s persistent criticism of his leadership. As a result, he raised the issue at a meeting of the X Committee a few days after the *Observer* article had been published. Wilson warned the others that the *Post* was "much read by the younger staff." Its criticism of the War Cabinet and the military command "did a great deal of harm" by "engendering hatred of the Prime Minister and the government."[121]

Milner agreed and held that further "steps would have to be taken" to prevent the publication of further articles challenging the policies of the government. If a warning proved to be insufficient, "it might be necessary to stop the paper." Lloyd George agreed that Repington's articles "could hardly assist the enemy more." Repington was "making trouble" between the army's top command and officers stationed in the trenches.

The members of the X Committee were not engaging in idle threats. A range of measures could be taken against the *Post*. There could be more leaks to friendly newspapers of information that could be used to attack the staff of the *Post*. Gwynne could have been prosecuted again under the DORA regulations. The *Post*'s supply of newsprint could have been disrupted. It was not necessary to actually implement such measures. The mere threat could well be sufficient.

In any case, the warning from the War Cabinet seems to have been effective. Repington's reputation had been significantly tarnished. Although the *Morning Post* continued to publish, it was more cautious in its criticisms of the government's war policies. Still, the fact that a powerful and secretive executive committee could even consider closing a conservative newspaper such as the *Post* is indicative of how wide the scope of repression had become and how perilously close the UK came to exercising an autocratic suppression of every form of dissent.

SECTION I

———

CIVIL LIBERTIES AND THE FIRST WORLD WAR

3

Stifling the National Civil Liberties Bureau

The American Civil Liberties Union (ACLU) has established itself as the foremost organization defending fundamental civil liberties. This requires upholding the free speech rights of every citizen and resident, no matter what their political viewpoint might be. The ACLU has taken the lead in defending the rights of Islamic fundamentalists since the attack on the Twin Towers in September 2001. This has meant defending the constitutional rights of those who hold views that are antithetical to the secular progressive perspective held by most ACLU members.

Yet the ACLU evolved out of a very different set of circumstances. Its immediate predecessor, the National Civil Liberties Bureau (NCLB), was formed during the First World War by a group of progressives who had opposed the entry of the United States into the war, but who, when confronted by repressive legislation targeting dissidents, retreated to a position of countering the worst excesses of wartime hysteria. Although the NCLB was eager to avoid a direct conflict with the federal government, it was soon under intensive surveillance from intelligence agencies. Indeed, the National Civil Liberties Bureau came under severe pressure to curb its activities. Covert efforts were made to disrupt its program and defame its executive secretary, Roger Baldwin.

The NCLB managed to get through the war without its leaders being incarcerated, but the threat of prosecution led the organization to enter into questionable arrangements with the authorities.

PROGRESSIVES CONTEST THE DRIFT TO WAR

When the First World War erupted in August 1914, popular sentiment strongly supported President Wilson's decision to remain neutral. The United States had a long history of avoiding all entanglements in European wars. Furthermore, the United States had steadfastly avoided the creation of a large standing army or a powerful naval fleet. Nevertheless, there were indications from the beginning that the United States could be drawn into the war as a combatant nation allied with Great Britain.

In September 1914, a few weeks after the start of the First World War, Lillian Wald issued a call for an informal conference of prominent progressives. Wald was a venerated and celebrated figure, having founded one of the first settlement houses, the Henry Street House, a social work agency situated in the heart of the Lower East Side, the Jewish ghetto of Manhattan.

Wald was a close friend of Jane Addams, the founder of Hull House, which was the first settlement house in the United States. Hull House was located on the west side of Chicago. Addams endorsed Wald's invitations for an initial meeting of prominent progressives who were opposed to the drift toward war. The meeting was held in New York City at Henry Street House. Although the first meeting of the group was viewed as a success, no formal structure emerged.[1]

A second conference was held at Henry Street House in January 1915. This time there was a general agreement on the need to create an organizational framework. An "informal committee" was established, the American Committee to Limit Armaments, with Wald acting as chair.[2]

The Committee remained a paper organization. Although the Henry Street group convened a third conference in July 1915, organizational efforts remained stalled. Still, the third meeting did include several figures who would be instrumental in the formative years of the ACLU. Wald began reaching out beyond the initial core group, adding several prominent leaders from liberal Protestant churches, such as Levi Hollingsworth Wood, an outspoken figure in the peace activities of the Friends Society, the Quakers. Wood attended the third Henry Street conference and joined the executive committee of the American Committee to Limit Armaments.[3]

The core group of activists was also expanded to include influential secular progressive activists. These new members understood how political organizations functioned, so they quickly took central roles in the anti-militarist group. Crystal Eastman, an attorney who attended the third conference, was the secular progressive who had the greatest impact on the new organization.[4]

Eastman, who had worked to strengthen consumer protection laws, was also an active suffragist. In November 1916, Eastman supported Woodrow Wilson's bid for a second term as president, although she moved into the orbit of the Socialist Party after the United States entered the First World War in April 1917. Eastman served as the unpaid secretary of the committee until its dissolution.[5]

The American Union Against Militarism

During the first years of the First World War, the Henry Street group's efforts to organize an opposition to militarism were stalled. Only the president's decision to prepare for war would catalyze their efforts. In the fall of 1915, Woodrow Wilson reversed his previous policy and began calling for a sharp increase in military spending. Preparedness marches were organized in large cities around the country and in early 1916, Wilson began touring the country promoting his program for a larger military. The United States began drifting toward a declaration of war on Germany.[6]

In response, the American Committee to Limit Armaments created an Anti-Preparedness Committee in January 1916, with the goal of organizing a viable opposition to Wilson's military program. The committee sought to accomplish this goal by distributing literature and lobbying key members of Congress. No thought was given to mobilizing popular opinion through marches and demonstrations.

Unlike the Henry Street group or the American Committee to Limit Armaments, the Anti-Preparedness Committee became a viable organization, with a public presence and a paid staff. Crystal Eastman was hired as its executive secretary. By April 1916, the Committee had come to the realization that a wider campaign to oppose militarism was needed. A more broadly focused program was developed, one that included opposition to conscription and to the introduction of military training into the public schools. An additional plank called for the "creation of institutions for judicial settlement of international disputes," pointing toward the establishment of the League of Nations, and, ultimately, the United Nations.[7] To reflect its revised and more broadly based program, the organization also adopted a new name, the American Union Against Militarism (AUAM).

Coping with the Onset of War

By the spring of 1917, a year after its formation, the American Union Against Militarism had become an influential component of the progressive antiwar movement that had come together to make a last ditch effort to block U.S. entry into the war. At this critical moment, the organization confronted an urgent problem. Crystal Eastman was experiencing serious health problems after steadily working sixteen-hour days. She had high blood pressure, heart problems, and nephritis, a painful kidney ailment. In addition, she was pregnant. Once her child was delivered, she was forced to take an extended leave of absence.[8]

As a result, in March 1917, the AUAM asked Roger Baldwin to join its staff.[9] Initially, Baldwin was hired as a temporary replacement for Eastman and then to "assist" her once she had returned to work on a full-time basis. As it turned out, Eastman was unable to return to her grueling schedule, although she was well enough to resume her role as the AUAM's primary policymaker through the summer and early fall of 1917.[10]

Born in 1884, Roger Baldwin came from an old-line family of Boston merchant aristocrats. His ancestors had arrived in the United States on the *Mayflower* and had prospered since then. Baldwin grew up in Wellesley, Massachusetts, an affluent suburb of Boston. After receiving his undergraduate degree from Harvard, Baldwin was offered a job teaching sociology at Washington University in St. Louis. Soon afterward, he became chief probation officer at the municipal juvenile court there. In 1910, Baldwin was hired as secretary of the St. Louis Civic League, an organization backed by leading business executives, which sought to end corruption and introduce progressive municipal reforms.[11]

A pacifist who would later become a conscientious objector, Baldwin eagerly accepted the AUAM's offer of a job. At first, he divided his time between New York and Washington, lobbying government officials. Crystal Eastman continued to formulate the organization's strategic perspective during the first months after the U.S. entry into the war. The congressional vote on April 6, 1917, declaring war on Germany, placed the American Union Against Militarism in a quandary. Eastman and the executive board scrambled to devise a new strategy that would permit the AUAM to oppose the rush to a militarized society and yet would not bring the organization into direct conflict with the federal government.

On May 1, 1917, the AUAM executive board adopted a wartime program, almost certainly drafted by Crystal Eastman. The plan established the general guidelines that the organization would follow for the next eighteen months, that is, until the armistice finally brought the war to an end. From the start, executive board members understood that a continuation of open opposition to the war effort would, almost certainly, lead to indictments and lengthy jail sentences. Instead, the wartime program shifted the focus of the organization to one of seeking a clarification of U.S. objectives. Specifically, the AUAM called for the publication of secret treaties and a "clear and definite statement of the terms on which the United States" would "seek peace."[12] These were the standard demands of the moderate wing of the peace movement.

Congress was debating the Selective Service Act while the AUAM developed its new program. It was clear that the legislation would narrowly define those eligible for conscientious objector status to those who belonged "to a well-recognized [religious] sect whose creed opposes participation in war." Although the AUAM lobbied Congress to broaden this definition to include anyone who morally opposed war, whether or not they subscribed to any religious belief, the bill as enacted retained a narrow definition of those eligible for conscientious objector status.[13]

Eastman understood that conscription as legislated was bound to lead to difficult questions. The AUAM's wartime program therefore included a promise of legal advice for those seeking to be exempted from military service. It also pledged to facilitate a legal test challenging the constitutional basis of the draft. Finally, the AUAM agreed that it would publicly oppose efforts to extend the draft even after the war had ended.

Although one section of the AUAM's wartime program focused on issues related to the draft and conscientious objectors, there was also the recognition that the AUAM should be committed to a defense of a broad range of civil liberties. The administration was preparing legislation that would greatly restrict any opposition to the war.

The wartime program provided the bare outline of a strategy, but Crystal Eastman was more forthright in an internal memorandum written a few months later. Eastman began by noting that once war was declared the AUAM "ceased all opposition to it. This was a policy dictated not only by loyalty, but by common sense." Specifically, the AUAM "*never* in the slightest degree counseled resistance to the selective service law nor any other policy of obstruction."[14] In other words, the committee did not participate in any organized effort to stop the war or end the draft, and it did so, in large part, to avoid its members going to jail.

Eastman posed the problem clearly. The American Union Against Militarism, as an organization "dedicated to fighting militarism in all its phases," had formulated a policy that would allow it to remain "law abiding" while the United States mobilized for war. It sought to establish a middle ground, implementing a course of action that would spur "extreme patriots" to call for the AUAM "to go out of business." Nevertheless, the organization would also reject "extremists of another sort" who insisted that it hold to its principles "until, individually and collectively," all of its leaders arrived at "a final resting place in the federal penitentiary."

Eastman concluded that an appropriate strategy neither required "continual opposition to the war" nor "organization for the repeal of conscription during the war," nor "any other action which must inevitably be interpreted as obstructing" the war effort. Instead it was the AUAM's "duty to prevent and oppose all those extreme manifestations of militarism, such as brutal treatment of COs, [and] the denial of free speech" that were "not essential to the prosecution of the war."

Eastman, as executive secretary of the American Union Against Militarism, played a crucial role in developing the policy of the forerunners of the American Civil Liberties Union. Her perspective was explicitly opportunistic. The civil liberties committee created by the AUAM defended activists who had the courage to persist in organizing against the war and the draft even after the United States entered the war, that is, to continue to do what the AUAM had opted to abandon in an effort to avoid becoming a target of repression.

CONSCIENTIOUS OBJECTORS' BUREAU

In early May 1917, shortly after adopting its wartime program, the American Union Against Militarism created a Conscientious Objectors' Bureau. The Selective Service Act of 1917 mandated that every male between twenty-one and thirty-nine had to register for the draft on June 5. This gave the newly created bureau several weeks to publicize its existence prior to registration day and to lobby government officials to interpret the statute in a way that did not arbitrarily limit those eligible for conscientious objector status.

Seven members of the AUAM executive board were chosen as the Directing Committee of the newly created Conscientious Objectors' Bureau. The members of this committee would become influential figures in the early years of the American Civil Liberties Union. Levi Hollingsworth Wood, a committed pacifist, was chosen to serve as chair of the Bureau, while Roger Baldwin was named as the bureau's director.[15]

Within days of the passage of the Selective Service Act, the AUAM issued a public statement on the draft signed by an array of prominent progressives, among them the members of the Conscientious Objectors' Bureau. The statement declared: "Obedience to the law" was "the basis for good citizenship." Accordingly, the statement specified that "all conscientious objectors should register" for the draft and should then proceed through the system established by the new law in order to be exempted from military service.[16]

This was not good advice. Those who registered for the draft and then sought conscientious objector status but who were not religious pacifists were almost certain to have their request for exemption denied. With the consent of a federal district court judge, government prosecutors could have draft resisters transferred to the authority of a military tribunal, which was likely to sentence them to serve lengthy terms in military jails, where conditions were often brutally harsh. On the other hand, those who refused to register could only be tried in civilian court. They were then sentenced to civilian jails, where conditions, in general, were less oppressive.

The public statement advocating draft registration was an unfortunate first step for the Conscientious Objectors' Bureau, but it reflected the underlying beliefs held by those who would form the American Civil Liberties Union. The members of the AUAM executive board were convinced that once Congress declared war in Germany, those who had previously opposed such a move had the duty to abide by this decision. In fact, the war was extremely unpopular and thus the congressional vote did not reflect a popular mandate. Furthermore, Woodrow Wilson had been elected president in November 1916 in part on the basis of his record of keeping the United States out of the war.[17]

The leaders of the AUAM were anxious to avoid becoming targets of the Department of Justice. On May 24, 1917, shortly before registration day, Oswald Garrison Villard met with the U.S. Army's Judge

Advocate General, Enoch Crowder. Villard, acting as a representative of the AUAM, was the editor of *The Nation*, an influential progressive journal. Crowder, having been the primary author of the Selective Service Act, had been assigned the task of implementing the draft. Crowder warned Villard that any organized effort to oppose the draft "would be vigorously and relentlessly prosecuted by the Department of Justice."[18] Villard took this warning back to the AUAM and its Conscientious Objectors' Bureau, which then rejected any thought of mobilizing public opinion to oppose an extension of the draft to the postwar period. Instead, the bureau focused entirely on advising registrants of the latest interpretation of the law, while handling the complaints of abusive treatment that were sent by those imprisoned when their claims for conscientious objector status were rejected.

The Conscientious Objectors' Bureau functioned essentially as a one-person operation. Baldwin answered the many letters looking for advice or help and he also issued occasional bulletins clarifying the War Department's attitude toward those claiming an exemption from military service. With the aid of influential supporters such as Villard, Baldwin was able to meet regularly with Frederick Keppel, a civilian assistant to Secretary of War Newton Baker.

As cautious as this advocacy effort was, it catalyzed a sharp conflict within the AUAM. Lillian Wald had served as president of the American Union Against Militarism since its formation in April 1916. As registration day grew closer, she became increasingly concerned that the Conscientious Objectors' Bureau would draw the entire organization into open conflict with the Wilson administration. Wald therefore wrote to the executive committee on registration day itself, June 5, 1917, suggesting that the activities of the bureau represented "a radical change in the Policy" of the organization and that it would not be possible to further the AUAM's program, which entailed "friendly government relations," while it continued to "drift into being a party of opposition to the government."[19]

Wald was joined by Paul Kellogg in this criticism. Kellogg was the editor of *Survey*, an influential journal aimed at social workers. In a letter to Eastman, Kellogg warned that the formation of the

Conscientious Objectors' Bureau was indicative "of an aggressive policy against the prosecution of the war."[20] Both Kellogg and Wald were preparing to jettison their previous position by shifting to open support for the war effort. Their threat to resign represented a significant danger to the continued viability of the AUAM, so Eastman tried unsuccessfully to forestall their departure.

Eastman wrote to Wald that the American Union Against Militarism still viewed itself as a friendly critic of the administration, pressing Wilson to adhere to genuine progressive principles. The Bureau would continue to advise conscientious objectors while opposing arbitrary and unnecessary restrictions to civil liberties.[21]

Eastman also wrote to Professor Emily Greene Balch, another leading member of the AUAM, defending the decision to advise conscientious objectors. Balch was a professor at Wellesley College and an influential pacifist. In Eastman's view, the decision to initiate a Conscientious Objectors' Bureau was "no more an aggressive policy against the prosecution of the war" than was the effort "to save free speech, free press, and assembly from the wholesale autocratic sweep which war efficiency dictates." The AUAM was not engaged in "a policy of obstruction," but rather it sought "to lead the liberal sentiment for peace." To "avoid this danger," that is, the risk that the AUAM might be perceived as directly opposing the war effort, Eastman proposed a "reorganization" of its work, "making one legal bureau for the maintenance of fundamental right in wartime."[22]

Eastman's letter to Balch was sent on June 14, 1917. The next day, President Wilson signed the Espionage Act into law, and the entire context changed. The Espionage Act made it illegal to "obstruct" the recruiting or conscription of soldiers and sailors. Those convicted of violating this provision could be sentenced to up to twenty years in prison.

As Eastman had proposed, the Conscientious Objectors' Bureau was transformed into the Civil Liberties Bureau, handling both the cases of conscientious objectors and legal cases arising out of wartime restrictions on freedom of speech and press. Eastman sent out letters to sympathetic attorneys notifying them of the formation of the

Civil Liberties Bureau, which would "act as a clearing house" helping those being prosecuted to obtain "good legal advice." The CLB stood ready to defend "fundamental constitutional rights" that were being "endangered by the most democratic nation engaged in war."[23]

THE CIVIL LIBERTIES BUREAU

On July 1, 1917, the American Union Against Militarism issued a press release officially announcing the formation of the Civil Liberties Bureau (CLB).[24] Roger Baldwin was listed as its director, along with the same Directing Committee that had been named to coordinate the Conscientious Objectors' Bureau that May. The formation of the Civil Liberties Bureau marks the true beginning of the American Civil Liberties Union.

From the start, the Civil Liberties Bureau came under attack for its association with the AUAM and the People's Council of America for Democracy and the Terms of Peace. Throughout the month of August 1917, the *New York Tribune* printed a series of articles under the title of "Enemies Within." The *Tribune* was an influential newspaper with a sizable circulation. A wide range of left-wing organizations were denounced for allegedly aiding Germany. Although the Civil Liberties Bureau was not specifically attacked, the *Tribune* did single out the People's Council of America for Democracy and the Terms of Peace (PCA). A loose coalition, the People's Council brought together an array of organizations from around the country on a program calling for an end to secret diplomacy and a negotiated peace without territorial annexations and reparations. The *Tribune* quoted approvingly a statement from the American Alliance for Labor and Democracy, a pro-war propaganda group covertly funded by the government's Committee on Public Information, which condemned the PCA for distributing "nefarious propaganda of treachery."[25]

This article was bound to undermine the credibility of the Civil Liberties Bureau, since the Bureau functioned as a subcommittee of the American Union Against Militarism, which in turn was a participating member of the People's Council coalition. An earlier article in the series had addressed the broader issue of dissent. According to the *Tribune*, "The current institution of free speech has been occupied by the country's enemies." Those who opposed the war effort had been "touched nearly everywhere by German influence."[26] By implication, the *Tribune* was arguing that those who defended free speech rights were protecting traitors and were thus providing aid and comfort to the enemy.

These charges represented a serious threat to both the Civil Liberties Bureau and its parent body, the American Union Against Militarism. Crystal Eastman responded to the *Tribune's* charges, a clear indication of her central role in both organizations. She conceded that the CLB was "obliged" to "keep in touch" with "radical organizations from whose ranks would arise conscientious objectors, advocates of free speech and others whose liberties" were "especially imperiled in wartime." Those who "stand for freedom of speech" did "not necessarily uphold everything that every speaker says." Members of the Civil Liberties Bureau were convinced that "in a war for democracy" there was "no more patriotic duty than to keep democracy alive at home."[27]

Eastman was being disingenuous. The CLB was defending antiwar activists who were being prosecuted for making statements that most members of its Directing Committee privately held to be true. Contrary to the public image it sought to project, the Civil Liberties Bureau was not created by a group of disinterested individuals who sought to uphold the free speech rights of everyone, even those whose views they found abhorrent. In reality, the Civil Liberties Bureau was a subcommittee of a parent organization that had energetically worked to keep the United States out of the First World War, but, for pragmatic reasons, had opted to drop its opposition to the war after April 1917 and instead had determined to focus much of its efforts in defending civil liberties.

As the summer of 1917 progressed, the federal government escalated its pressure on the moderate wing of the antiwar opposition. As a result, the American Union Against Militarism found it increasingly difficult to voice even the mildest dissent to the president's conduct of the war. Over the objections of Lillian Wald, the AUAM decided to affiliate with the People's Council. This decision was the final blow to Wald, who resigned in protest, to be replaced as chair by Levi Hollingsworth Wood.[28]

On September 1, 1917, the People's Council of America attempted to convene its first national conference in Minneapolis, Minnesota. Governor Joseph Burnquist, a Republican, issued an order prohibiting the conference from being held. In the end, the PCA was only able to organize a brief rump session in Chicago, before adjourning indefinitely. The failure of the PCA to withstand the government's efforts at disruption, as evidenced by its inability to hold its national conference, forced the AUAM to reassess its relations to the broader coalition.[29]

The American Union Against Militarism had already attracted the attention of the Justice Department's Bureau of Investigation (BI), but its links to the People's Council led to even more intensive surveillance. When the AUAM convened a closed meeting of its executive committee on September 13, 1917, at the Hotel Earle in Manhattan, the Bureau of Investigation, warned by hotel management, decided to place a dictagraph, a primitive recording devise, in the room where the meeting was to be held. When the dictagraph proved to be "inefficient," hotel managers found the two BI agents assigned to eavesdrop on the meeting a nearby hiding place where they could listen without being observed. The Bureau of Investigation had not obtained a search warrant authorizing this eavesdropping, which therefore violated the Fourth Amendment of the Bill of Rights.[30]

The members of the AUAM executive committee were unaware that the Bureau of Investigation was spying on their meetings, but they were apprehensive that the government had placed the organization under surveillance. On September 5, 1917, a week earlier, BI agents had conducted nationwide raids of halls of the Industrial Workers of the World around the country. In light of these raids, the AUAM executive committee decided "to destroy or secrete important papers and records." Thus, certain "confidential" memorandums and correspondence would be removed from office files and, instead, would be kept in the homes of members of the executive committee. This decision covered the early records of the Civil Liberties Bureau and its predecessor, the Conscientious Objectors' Bureau.[31]

During the next months, the officers of the Civil Liberties Bureau would repeatedly insist to government intelligence agencies that there was no valid reason to employ intrusive measures to gather information because the CLB operated in an open and transparent manner and intelligence agents were always welcome to examine the organization's records. In reality, the bureau's officers were not being candid. Certain sensitive records were destroyed, or kept hidden in locations away from the organization's office.

Although agents of the Bureau of Investigation did not overhear which papers were to be kept secret, it is likely that the CLB was anxious to withhold correspondence from individuals seeking conscientious objector status who had made it clear that they were opposed to participating in the First World War, but were not religious. Some of the secular objectors were pacifists, but others were not, although they opposed all wars that arose out of imperialist rivalries, such as the First World War. The Bureau of Investigation would later accuse the Civil Liberties Bureau of providing assistance to individuals seeking an exemption from military service who the Civil Liberties Bureau knew were ineligible for consideration under the terms of the Selective Service Act.

During the September 13 meeting, members of the AUAM executive committee also expressed their dismay with the People's Council's failure to organize a national conference. In this context of repression and surveillance, the executive committee decided that the Civil Liberties Bureau should become an independent organization. Furthermore, to further establish the distinct and separate basis of the new organization, members of its Directing Committee were barred from holding office in other peace organizations such as the People's Council of America. (Crystal Eastman had served as a member of the organizing committee of the PCA.) Finally, the executive committee mandated Eastman to present a specific plan for launching an independent civil liberties organization at its next meeting.

As a result, Eastman drafted a lengthy memorandum outlining the history of the AUAM, along with a series of propositions to guide an independent organization. In a draft of a press release, she insisted that "during wartime" the defense of civil liberties "inevitably" became the "chief war-work" of those who had previously been the mainstays of the American Union Against Militarism.[32]

Eastman also presented a list of recommendations to the AUAM executive committee meeting that convened on September 24, 1917, once again at the Hotel Earle. Two agents from the Bureau of Investigation were once again on hand to surreptitiously eavesdrop. This time, they brought with them a stenographer to record the proceedings. Much of the meeting was taken up with a discussion of the direction the American Union Against Militarism should take in the light of the debacle surrounding the abortive conference of the People's Council of America and the intensifying government repression. The executive committee failed to reach a consensus and the AUAM soon entered into an extended period of dormancy.[33]

With the AUAM foundering, its Civil Liberties Bureau was set free. The September 24 meeting formally approved a resolution making the CLB a separate, distinct entity. A week later, the new organization, renamed the National Civil Liberties Bureau (NCLB), began functioning as an independent organization. An open letter issued by Roger Baldwin, as executive director and chief policy maker, insisted that the new organization would be "maintaining exactly the same work in behalf of constitutional liberties and the conscientious objectors" that had been previously undertaken by the Civil Liberties Bureau when it functioned as a subcommittee of the American Union Against Militarism.[34]

· NATIONAL CIVIL LIBERTIES BUREAU

On October 1, 1917, the Directing Committee of the National Civil Liberties Bureau (NCLB) convened its first meeting. A critical point confronting the newly independent organization was its relations to the People's Council of America. Baldwin reported that the PCA had "suggested that the Civil Liberties Bureau be made a department" of the broadly based antiwar coalition.[35]

The Directing Committee rejected this overture and opted instead to remain independent. The NCLB could work within the system to exert "great pressure" on the administration, while the "natural function" of the People's Council was to mobilize public sentiment for a rapid peace, that is, to raise a "clamor." The NCLB and the PCA could thus develop a friendly working relationship, with the PCA requested to "refer" civil liberties cases to the Bureau. At the same time, the two organizations would move forward as separate and distinct organizations.[36]

Soon after this initial meeting, the NCLB hired Walter Nelles as its legal counsel. Nelles had gone to Harvard as an undergraduate and then to Harvard Law School, afterward becoming a partner in a New York City law firm. While at Harvard, Nelles and Baldwin became friends. A pacifist, Nelles had become increasingly disillusioned with the war and the government's suppression of dissent. During this period, he moved leftward, briefly joining the Socialist Party in 1918.[37]

Nelles would remain as the full-time legal counsel for the National Civil Liberties Bureau and its successor, the American Civil Liberties Union, for many years. In this position, he would be at the cutting edge of civil liberties law as it rapidly evolved during the First World War and its aftermath.

CONSCIENTIOUS OBJECTORS AND THE MILITARY

The Civil Liberties Bureau, and its successor, the National Civil Liberties Bureau had two primary objectives once the United States entered the war. The first priority was the defense of the constitutionally protected right to dissent from the government's war policies, while the second focused on protecting conscientious objectors from systematic abuse within military camps. Claiming an exemption from military service as a conscientious objector was only one way of resisting conscription. Indeed, resistance was widespread and was a significant factor in leading the federal government to expand the scope of those compelled to register from those between the ages of twenty-one and thirty to eighteen to forty-five. In all, 24 million men registered for the draft and an estimated three million refused to register. Many draft resisters went underground or fled the country, with Mexico offering a safe haven.[38]

Refusing to register was only one form of resistance. Millions avoided conscription by failing the physical examination or seeking employment in an exempt industry. Furthermore, 330,000 men who registered and were inducted refused to report, about 12 percent of the total inducted. Many of them hid underground until the war ended.[39]

Thus, there were several effective methods of avoiding the draft that did not involve the certainty of a direct confrontation with the authorities in the way that filing for conscientious objector status necessarily did. Out of the millions who registered for the draft, only 64,000 claimed to be conscientious objectors. Most of these were members of religious pacifist denominations, primarily Quakers, Mennonites, and Hutterites, while roughly 10 percent were political resisters, those who refused to fight in a war that they believed was a pointless conflict between imperialist rivals.[40]

Thirty thousand conscientious objectors were called up and twenty thousand of them passed the physical examination and were inducted into the army. By the late summer of 1917, conscientious objectors were being sent to military training camps that had been established across the country to process new recruits. The Selective Service Act of May 1917 had provided that the president should determine a suitable alternative service for those claiming exemption from the military. Instead, Woodrow Wilson and Secretary of War Newton Baker refused to set the terms for alternative service, leaving thousands of conscientious objectors in limbo. Those who had filed as conscientious objectors were to be isolated from the new recruits. Enormous pressure was then brought to bear on the conscientious objectors to become soldiers.

Baker and the army high command had made it very clear to base commanders that they were expected to coerce the new inductees into becoming soldiers, although few guidelines were set. Within this broad directive, conditions in the camps varied greatly. Some camp officers limited their efforts to bullying and psychological intimidation. In other camps, the conscientious objectors were subject to physical assaults. Howard Moore, a non-religious pacifist, was assigned to Camp Upton in Long Island. Soldiers there threw bricks at him and poured cold water on him while he tried to sleep. Another conscientious objector at the same camp was beaten with rifle butts and suffered a broken jaw.[41]

In the end, the pressure on the conscientious objectors proved to be effective. Of the twenty thousand inducted, sixteen thousand agreed to join the army, with just under four thousand continuing to refuse to serve in the military.[42] This ended the first part of an extended process by which the army sought to overwhelm those claiming conscientious objector status.

The decision to delay defining the categories of work available for alternative service was done deliberately in order to create a lengthy period during which the number of those claiming an exemption from military service could be drastically reduced through intimidation and violence. It was a cynical maneuver that proved to be effective. Baker wrote Wilson that the policy of delay had "limited the number of objectors" to "those who actually entertain scruples" as religious pacifists. The president responded that he was "greatly interested" in Baker's report and that the issue would "in part solve itself" as the coercive pressure on those claiming exemption from military service was ramped upward. Needless to say, Wilson and Baker were eager to portray themselves as benevolent autocrats. Baker informed a cabinet meeting in October 1917 that conscientious objectors were being "segregated" in military training camps, but "no harm done [to] them."[43] Of course, the reality was very different. Baker was well aware of the actual conditions in the training camps, in part because of the reports he received from the National Civil Liberties Bureau.

The conscientious objectors who were viewed as incorrigible troublemakers were dispatched to Fort Riley in Kansas, where they were systematically mistreated in a concerted effort to break their will.

Once at Fort Riley, those who refused to wear uniforms, salute, or cooperate in any way, were segregated in tents in an open field with no latrines and a single water hydrant some distance away. Food was scarce and of poor quality. Soldiers threw large stones into their tents while they slept.[44]

After enduring another effort to break their determination, the conscientious objectors were moved to Camp Funston, a military training base adjoining Fort Riley. The camp commander, General Leonard Wood, had been the army's chief of staff from April 1910 to April 1914. He viewed his assignment to Camp Funston in September 1917 as a punishment for his close ties with Theodore Roosevelt, the former president and a harsh critic of the Wilson administration.[45]

The camp was located in a harsh environment with freezing cold winters and extreme heat in the summer. Conscientious objectors sent there would have confronted serious health threats in any case, but Wood was intent on making them suffer for their decision to claim an exemption from military service. The first conscientious objectors began arriving in September 1917 and hundreds more were dispatched to Camp Funston over the following months.

Wood could tolerate the religious pacifists who were willing to accept alternative service, but he detested those who refused to cooperate in any way, as well as those claiming conscientious objector status who were not religious. This was particularly true of those who resisted the draft because they believed that the war was merely a settling of imperialist rivalries. From Wood's perspective, the majority of political objectors and the absolute pacifists were either "German sympathizers or cowards." He viewed conscientious objectors as "active agents of the enemy." In a letter to the father of one of those mistreated at Camp Funston, Wood insisted that the conduct of the resisters was "reprehensible." Only by dealing "vigorously" with those targeted for punishment could the army prevent "this evil influence" from having a "far-reaching" impact on morale.[46]

Given Wood's view of pacifists and dissidents, it is not surprising that conscientious objectors assigned to Camp Funston were brutalized. During his time at Camp Funston, Moore was dragged out of bed while sleeping and forced to run around the parade grounds at the point of a bayonet. This occurred every two hours on each night for weeks on end. When the soldiers involved were questioned, they told the conscientious objectors that the orders for this calculated form of torture came directly from the camp commander, Leonard Wood. Indeed, the author of a sympathetic biographer of Wood concluded that non-religious objectors "were subjected regularly to severe beatings and humiliations at Camp Funston."[47]

Although Baker and his aides could not closely monitor the actions of camp commanders around the country, this was not the case at Fort Riley and Camp Funston. Baker knew of Wood's disdain of the antiwar opposition and he was kept informed of the brutal conditions at Funston. Eight hundred of the most resolute conscientious objectors were kept there for the duration of the war and beyond. They were constantly pressured into accepting military service, with most adamantly refusing.

Finally, in March 1918, Wilson specified that working in either the medical service or the corps of engineers would be considered as alternative service under the Selective Service Act. Religious pacifists were then offered the option of going into the ambulance service and about 1,400 agreed.[48] (Providing medical aid to those injured on the Western Front was very dangerous, at least as perilous as fighting in the trenches.)

At about the same time, March 16, 1918, Congress approved the Furlough Bill allowing draft boards to exempt farmers from military service. It took until the end of May for Crowder to advise Baker that conscientious objectors could be granted a furlough to work on a farm.[49] A board of inquiry was then established to determine which conscientious objectors were sincere in their belief and to offer those who were approved the option of a farm furlough. About half of the 2,600 who had refused alternative non-combatant service agreed to accept a furlough. Since the board of inquiry only accepted as sincere those who were members of a pacifist religious sect, political objectors were excluded from the furlough program.[50]

Conscientious objectors who refused non-combatant service, and who did not agree to a furlough to a farm, were subject to court-martial. In addition, many of the non-religious conscientious objectors were court-martialed. In all, five hundred men were brought before army court-martial tribunals and sentenced to lengthy terms of up to twenty-five years. All but a few served their sentences at the Fort Leavenworth Disciplinary Barracks in Kansas. At Leavenworth, those who refused to go on work details were beaten unconscious. Sometimes those who passively refused to cooperate with their jailers were forced to put their heads into latrine pits until they nearly suffocated.[51] This was a particularly brutal form of waterboarding, a form of torture that has frequently been used by the CIA in recent years.

The Martyrdom of the Hofer Brothers

Most conscientious objectors were healthy young men and were able to survive the cruel treatment they received from the military, but there were exceptions. Daniel, Michael, and Joseph Hofer lived in an isolated Hutterite community in South Dakota. (Hutterites held beliefs similar to those of the Amish.) The three young men were not well educated and had almost no understanding of the wider world beyond their small community of believers. All three were in their twenties when they were conscripted into the army in May 1918.[52]

The three brothers were sent to Camp Lewis, near Tacoma, Washington, for basic training. Devoutly religious, their pacifist beliefs did not permit them to contribute to the military effort in any way, either through alternative service or working on a farm producing food for the military. The three were court-martialed and given twenty-year prison sentences. At the end of July 1918, the three resisters were transferred from Camp Lewis to Alcatraz, a notorious federal penitentiary that housed some of the toughest and most violent prisoners in the system.[53]

Once in Alcatraz, the three brothers refused to cooperate in any way. Prison authorities insisted they were soldiers and were therefore required to work, salute their superior officers and wear military uniforms. The three were punished for their refusal to obey orders by being held in solitary confinement in small cells in the dungeons of Alcatraz, with no blankets, no mattresses, and no lights. For eight hours a day, they were chained to the bars of their cells. During their four months in Alcatraz, the three Hofer brothers rotated every two weeks between this barbarous regimen and one that was based on their continuously running in circles within the outside courtyard for eight hours a day.[54]

The three brothers were fit and used to hard work, but this deliberate effort to undermine their health and morale had a disastrous impact. On November 14, 1918, the three were again transferred, this time from Alcatraz to Fort Leavenworth. The train took five days to make the trip and the three brothers were kept in chains the entire time.

When the train finally arrived at 11 p.m. on November 19, the three were put on a forced march through the town and up a hill to the prison. The three again refused to wear their assigned military uniforms, so they were left outside for two hours in their underwear. Nights in Kansas in November are bitterly cold with strong winds as well. After a few hours of sleep, the three brothers were ordered to line up outside for roll call. Michael and Joseph complained of severe chest pains and were sent to the prison hospital. They never recovered. Joseph Hofer died on November 29, 1918, and Michael Hofer on December 2, 1918. Only Daniel survived the ordeal.[55]

The military command often justified its brutal treatment of conscientious objectors by insisting that this was necessary to maintain discipline in the ranks. Yet the Hofer brothers continued to receive abusive punishments even after fighting had ended and the war was over. The death of the Hofer brothers was a pointless tragedy. It reflected the intense hostility of government officials to the absolutist pacifists, an enmity that extended from the president to the army's general staff and down to the prison wardens.

WOODROW WILSON AND THE CONSCIENTIOUS OBJECTORS

The administration was well aware of the brutal treatment of conscientious objectors convicted by an army court-martial, but key decision-makers were unwilling to intervene. Baker sought to trivialize this appalling situation. The conscientious objectors being sent to the Fort Leavenworth Barracks were enjoying "a wholesome outdoor life" as they were "kept busy doing things" that were "worth doing." This for those forced to break rocks on the rock pile.[56]

The president was informed of the situation at the Fort Leavenworth Disciplinary Barracks, but he did nothing to stop the brutalities. In September 1918, the White House received a letter from the brother of one of those who had gone before a court-martial and was serving time at the Fort Leavenworth Barracks. Wilson passed the letter on to Baker with the comment that he had "little enough sympathy with the conscientious objector." This was a clear signal to Baker that Wilson supported the army's handling of draft resisters. Wilson went on to inform Baker that the military should "avoid unnecessary harshness" and "injustice of any sort."[57] Needless to say, Wood and the army command were convinced that beating and abusing conscientious objectors was necessary to maintain a rigid discipline in the ranks.

Religious conscientious objectors were finally released from Fort Leavenworth in January 1919. This left the political objectors and the non-religious pacifists. Only in November 1920 did the president sign an order providing for a universal amnesty for all conscientious objectors imprisoned during the war.[58] Thus, it was only two years after the war had ended, and only a few months before Woodrow Wilson left office, that the appalling saga of the conscientious objectors came to an end.

Neither Baker nor Wilson had any tolerance for either absolutist pacifists or political objectors. They felt that the religious objectors had been treated leniently in being allowed the option of alternative service in the ambulance corps or work on a farm, so severe punishments were justified for those whose conscience led them to refuse to cooperate with the military in any way. In any case, the president and his secretary of war placed military success over any concern for individual rights. Wilson and Baker knew what was happening at Camp Funston and Fort Leavenworth Disciplinary Barracks and yet they refused to order the officers in command to end the horrific treatment of conscientious objectors at either base. Given this, the quiet defense of conscientious objectors by the National Civil Liberties Bureau accomplished little.[59]

CONSCIENTIOUS OBJECTORS AND THE NCLB

During the fall of 1917, the National Civil Liberties Bureau focused much of its efforts on aiding conscientious objectors. At this point, the conscientious objectors were being held in army camps scattered around the country. Baldwin traveled frequently from New York City to Washington to meet with Frederick Keppel, one of Baker's civilian assistants.[60] After one such conference, held on October 17, Baldwin reported that he and Keppel had reviewed the correspondence sent by conscientious objectors to the War Department. Many of these letters had come from individuals who had previously contacted the NCLB for advice. According to Baldwin, reports of brutality or undue coercion were "handled personally" by one of Baker's civilian assistants, usually Keppel. In many cases, these situations were brought "personally to the attention of Secretary Baker."[61]

Keppel admitted that there were credible reports of "coercive treatment in some of the camps," but he assured Baldwin "that the department had moved at once to stop any such practices." When Baldwin pressed Keppel to urge Baker to issue a public statement codifying the War Department's commitment to the humane treatment of conscientious objectors incarcerated by the military, Keppel spurned the idea. Indeed, "The Secretary of War was probably not going to announce any definite public policy for dealing with conscientious objectors."

In return for these cozy chats with someone near the seat of power, Keppel made it plain that he expected Baldwin and the NCLB to refrain from publicizing the horrendous conditions actually confronting conscientious objectors. Baldwin agreed to this condition and even justified it to those looking to the NCLB for assistance. On November 1, two weeks after his meeting with Keppel, Baldwin sent out a bulletin stating that "the attitude of the War Department toward the conscientious objector" was "liberal and sympathetic." Although some reports of "coercion and mistreatment" had been received, "on the whole the situation" was "encouraging." For this reason, the NCLB had "not sought any general publicity" exposing the army's treatment of conscientious objectors. Indeed, "nothing could be gained for the cause now by public agitation."[62]

On the same day, November 1, Baldwin prepared a report to the members of the American Union Against Militarism describing the activities of the newly independent National Civil Liberties Bureau. Baldwin reported that he was "in constant touch with the War Department." Furthermore, the "situation at most of the camps" seemed "as favorable as could be expected." Although Baldwin conceded that "every kind of pressure" was "brought to bear to prevent men maintaining their stand," he still viewed the overall situation in a favorable light. Baldwin concluded that "although a few cases of coercion" had "been reported from some of the cantonments, the War Department" acted "at once to have any injustice corrected."[63]

During the initial period in the fall of 1917, the army had focused on efforts to pressure conscientious objectors into accepting military service. From that point onward, the emphasis shifted to imposing punitive measures on those who continued to resist military service.

By the winter of 1917, the most steadfast of those claiming an exemption from military service had been transferred to Fort Riley and Camp Funston. Wilson and Baker were fully aware of the situation in Camp Funston and fully supported the policies set by General Wood and other commanding officers. The administration became increasingly irritated by the National Civil Liberties Bureau and its reports of abuse and torture, so reports of mistreatment were totally ignored.

As the authorities became increasingly hostile to its activities, the NCLB stepped up its efforts to mollify them. Hollingsworth Wood, as chair of the NCLB, sought to justify the organization's policy to a key Justice Department official handling Espionage Act cases. He insisted that the bureau had undertaken "a real patriotic service to explain to the War Department the position of the Conscientious Objector, and to bring to the attention of the authorities the failure of any of the over-enthusiastic subordinates to carry out the Department's instructions."[64]

In the end, the NCLB had virtually no impact on the government's policies toward conscientious objectors. Organizing regular meetings between Keppel and Baldwin did little more than provide cover for the War Department, thus making it easier for progressives eager to support the war effort to persuade themselves that the administration was genuinely concerned with human rights and civil liberties.

Furthermore, by the spring of 1918 the administration had changed its stance toward the NCLB from one of bemused tolerance to outright hostility. The NCLB's continued defense of conscientious objectors was one factor underlying this shift in policy, but even more important was the willingness of the National Civil Liberties Bureau to provide assistance to the legal defense of the Industrial Workers of the World.

The NCLB and the Fourteen Points

For the first four months of its existence, the National Civil Liberties Bureau managed to work within the system as a quiet advocate. The NCLB did not entirely escape the government's scrutiny, as Bureau of Investigation agents eavesdropped on confidential meetings and the post office obstructed the delivery of its pamphlets through the mail. Nevertheless, the NCLB remained relatively insulated from the harsh reprisals being imposed on thousands of radicals and antiwar activists.

This situation changed dramatically in early 1918, as the NCLB became entangled in the government's suppression of the IWW. The Industrial Workers of the World was a federation of industrial unions led by radicals that had succeeded in organizing effective strikes among Arizona's copper miners and lumberjacks throughout the Pacific Northwest. During the summer of 1917, the Wobblies were growing rapidly, so the administration came to view the union as a significant threat.

The Justice Department, with the president's express approval, proceeded to launch a total assault on the union. On September 5, 1917, Bureau of Investigation agents raided union halls around the country. Two weeks later, 165 of the IWW's leaders were indicted in Chicago for allegedly violating the Espionage Act. Once initiated, the attack on the IWW was unrelenting, as halls were repeatedly raided, newspapers banned from the mails, and dozens of Wobblies were rounded up and jailed.[65]

Stunned by the ferocity of the federal government's onslaught, the IWW shelved workplace organizing and devoted its resources to raising money for attorneys and legal fees. The government responded by making every effort to hamper and obstruct the union's legal defense. Solicitations for the legal defense fund, the General Defense Committee (GDC), were waylaid by the post office. Lists of donors were seized in raids on union halls. In California, key members of the General Defense Committee were jailed and charged with violating the Espionage Act.

The NCLB made little effort to argue that the IWW's actions in organizing peaceful, but militant and effective, strikes in vital war industries were constitutionally protected. Instead, the NCLB focused its criticisms around the demand that everyone, even the IWW, had the right to present a legal defense without government interference. This led to a further intensification of government pressure on the NCLB, with the threat of prosecution used as leverage.

Events in early 1918 led the government to move from wary suspicion and distrust of the NCLB to open hostility. Initially, the NCLB believed there had been a breakthrough making it more possible for progressives to rally behind the president. In January 1918, President Wilson presented his Fourteen Points as a basis for a fair and equitable peace, once Germany had unconditionally surrendered. The moderate antiwar opposition, organized in the People's Council of America, had been calling for the United States to declare its war aims. The Fourteen Points provided the outline of such a policy, using many of the fine-sounding phrases previously advanced by the progressive opposition to the war.[66] As a result, Baldwin was eager to mediate an agreement that would allow progressives to support the war effort, while enabling the federal government to respond by curtailing its campaign of repression.

In late January 1918, Baldwin sent a memorandum to Edward House, the president's most influential advisor, with the hope that he would send it on to the White House. Baldwin suggested that "liberal and radical forces" were "now, for the most part, [ready] to back the President's war aims."[67] This glossed over a critical question. Peace advocates had been urging the United States and its allies to immediately open negotiations with Germany and its allies to bring a rapid end to the war on the basis of a policy of "no annexations, no reparations." Woodrow Wilson had accepted in theory the principle of no forced annexations, but he insisted that the war had to be continued until Germany was totally defeated and ready to unconditionally surrender. This was a crucial difference, and Baldwin's willingness to accept the president's position is indicative of how far he and those close to him in the American Union Against Militarism were prepared to go to avoid a confrontation with the government.

Still, Baldwin understood that progressives would not be willing to rally to the president merely on the basis of the Fourteen Points. The administration would have to modify its "policy of aggression," and restrain "over-zealous officials," if the conflict were to be overcome. President Wilson would have to "indicate clearly" his willingness to tolerate dissenting views, that is to demarcate "the lines in his mind" dividing issues "which can be fully discussed and those which cannot." The administration was unwilling to do this. On the contrary, the Department of Justice preferred to retain its discretionary power to define the nebulous phrases of the Espionage Act and it had no intention of ceding this power by providing a detailed explanation of its interpretation of wartime laws.

Baldwin also argued that the Justice Department should instruct U.S. attorneys "not to proceed" with indictments unless there was "a deliberate and direct incitement to law-breaking." In fact, the War Emergency Division made an effort to limit prosecutions to those cases in which there was a direct and credible threat from an effective and organized opposition to the war. Nevertheless, this left considerable space for targeting dissident opinions.

Baldwin's attempt to mediate an agreement between the government and the moderate antiwar opposition failed to gain traction because the government was unwilling to relax its repressive apparatus until the president was convinced that those who had dissented were prepared to provide uncritical support for the war effort. On the other hand, progressives distrusted the administration and were wary of the commitment of the Allies to the signing of an equitable peace. This impasse could not be broken and the stalemate continued until the war came to an end in November 1918.

Military Intelligence Investigates

By February 1918, the National Civil Liberties Bureau was established as a priority target for the intelligence community. Both the U.S. Army's Military Intelligence Division (MID) and the Bureau of Investigation (BI) were active participants in an ongoing investigation of the NCLB. Since indictments of the NCLB would have been initiated by the Justice Department for alleged violations of the Espionage Act, the Bureau of Investigation would have been the logical agency to spearhead the investigation. Instead, the MID acted as the lead agency. Initially, the NCLB had come under scrutiny because of its work in support of conscientious objectors, a matter of special interest to the War Department. Both intelligence agencies tracked the activities of the NCLB, but the MID pushed harder to have it suppressed.

The New York office of the Military Intelligence Division acted as the focal point for the campaign to harass the NCLB. Over the years, intelligence agencies have frequently been staffed by those coming from elite backgrounds, the CIA being a well-known case in point, but the New York office of the MID provides an excellent example from the early days of the U.S. intelligence community. Nicholas Biddle, its chief, came from a family that epitomized old money—the Biddles had been prominent figures in banking for generations. Although Biddle did not inherit great wealth, he did have excellent connections. Prior to his tour in the Military Intelligence Division, he had supervised the real estate interests of Vincent Astor, one of the wealthiest individuals in the United States. Biddle served as an unpaid deputy police commissioner of the New York City Police with overall responsibility for its intelligence activities. Thus, even before the United States entered the war, he had established close connections with UK intelligence operatives stationed in the United States. As head of the New York office of the Military Intelligence Division, Biddle "cooperated in the most energetic way" with UK intelligence.[68] He also recruited young men from Ivy League schools and elite backgrounds who were looking for a safe but interesting alternative to the horrors of trench warfare.

Although Biddle was granted considerable leeway in pursuing the investigation of the NCLB, he reported directly to Ralph Van Deman, the chief of the Military Intelligence Division and a career officer. This was no rogue operation. Biddle also worked closely with the New York office of the Bureau of Investigation.

Once the Military Intelligence Division had determined that the NCLB represented a significant threat to the war effort, it became a priority target for surveillance. Van Deman therefore sent a memorandum to MID offices around the country warning that the NCLB was distributing literature with "the obvious intent to disrupt American patriotic sentiment."[69] The memorandum constituted an implicit order from Van Deman to heighten surveillance of the Bureau.

With the National Civil Liberties Bureau based in New York City, it was up to Nicholas Biddle and the New York office of the Military Intelligence Division to implement this directive. Biddle reported to Van Deman that he had "endeavored to plant" one of his officers, Charles Lloyd, "in the office of Mr. Baldwin as a publicity agent." Lloyd posed as a journalist ready to perform "publicity work." Baldwin was suspicious of this overture and initiated "rather a careful investigation of Mr. Lloyd," asking one of his friends if he had heard if Lloyd had become a government agent.[70]

Stymied by Baldwin's check into Lloyd's background, Biddle turned to Van Deman for advice. Van Deman ordered Biddle to terminate the operation since it would be "disastrous" if Baldwin were to uncover an informant within the NCLB office. Nevertheless, Van Deman had "no objection to getting some other agent in there." It is unclear if Biddle undertook a further effort to place an agent within the NCLB's office.[71]

This rebuff did not stop Lloyd from participating in further covert actions. He reported to Biddle: "On two occasions our men have been through his [Baldwin's] office at night in his absence." During the second of these surreptitious entries, "We took copies of Baldwin's correspondence with F. D. Keppel of the War Department."[72]

Needless to say, these nighttime break-ins were in direct violation of the Constitution's Fourth Amendment,[73] since MID agents were searching the NCLB office without the authority of a court-ordered search warrant. Ironically, the MID spent its limited time inside the NCLB office copying the correspondence between Baldwin and Keppel, a high-ranking civilian official in the same government agency, the War Department, to which the Military Intelligence Division reported. Of course, Keppel had advised the MID of his conversations with Baldwin, but the MID could not be certain that it was being kept fully informed. Thus, the illegal entry allowed the MID to spy not only on the National Civil Liberties Bureau, but also on a civilian assistant to Secretary of War Newton Baker.

Baldwin was unaware of the extent of these clandestine operations, but he did understand that the NCLB was coming under intensive scrutiny by government intelligence agencies. In early 1918, probably February 1918, the Inspector General of the army summoned Baldwin to a meeting to caution him of the government's growing displeasure with the bureau's activities.[74] It is unclear if a specific warning was transmitted to cease certain activities, such as fundraising for the IWW's legal defense fund, but Baldwin understood that the MID had decided to target the NCLB.

Baldwin turned once again to Keppel for help. To allay the MID's suspicions, Baldwin offered to "place the books and papers in his office" at Biddle's disposal. Baldwin followed up this offer by writing to Biddle stating that the Bureau's correspondence with conscientious objectors was "entirely at the disposal of any official of the War Department." Baldwin insisted that the sole purpose of the Bureau's activities in this regard was the securing of "just and humane treatment" of those claiming conscientious objector status and that it sought the "cooperation" of the War Department in achieving this goal. Van Deman ordered Biddle to examine the NCLB's records and "to report fully on the entire situation."[75]

Soon after Baldwin's meeting with Keppel, Van Deman prepared a lengthy memorandum on the National Civil Liberties Bureau, in which he warned Keppel that "some of the bulletins from this organization come very close to being seditious." Still, Van Deman understood "how difficult" it would be "to suppress the activities of such an organization such as the National Civil Liberties Bureau." Indeed, a harsh, punitive approach would "be apt to throw them into the martyr class, and, therefore, help the German agent." Instead, the War Department, through Keppel, should intensify pressure on Baldwin to ensure that his activities "should only take certain lines" lest he be considered "unpatriotic." Van Deman concluded that the federal government "should only resort to compulsion as a last resort."[76]

Baldwin was being given a final opportunity to bring the NCLB into compliance with the demands of the War Department before confronting the legal consequences. Soon after his meeting with Keppel, Baldwin was questioned by Biddle, who reported to Van Deman that Baldwin made "a good impression" and yet "people associated with him" had "very unsavory reputations." (Biddle was probably referring to Crystal Eastman. In addition to being a socialist, Eastman had lived with her second husband before divorcing her first husband.)[77] Biddle had reached the conclusion that the National Civil Liberties Bureau served "no good purpose and that their activities should be stopped."[78]

After their encounter, Baldwin realized that Biddle remained an implacable foe. He informed Harold Rotzel, a Boston Protestant minister and NCLB supporter, that "the situation between the War Department and the Civil Liberties Bureau" was "critical." The MID remained convinced that the bureau's "propaganda" sought "to manufacture conscientious objectors." In Baldwin's view, this left the NCLB with two alternatives. It could go to the radical and pacifist press and present the difficulties of the situation confronting the NCLB, "with the likely result of our being soon indicted and put out of business," or the bureau could agree to "modify" its "tactics." In this context, conscientious objectors writing from army camps were told to "hold out," that is, to remain quiet for the time, with the understanding that those who rejected this approach, and refused to cooperate with the military in any way, would be subject to court-martial and given long terms in an army penitentiary.[79]

Baldwin tried once again to deflect the hostility of the MID and the War Department. On March 30, 1918, he wrote Biddle enclosing a copy of the latest issue of the bulletin issued by the NCLB for the information of conscientious objectors. Baldwin then reassured Biddle: "As you know, we have no sympathy with soft-backed fellows who are only looking for an easy way to save their skins."[80]

This is a very disturbing statement on several levels. First, Baldwin was himself a conscientious objector. He would soon spend nine months in jail for refusing to serve in the military. It seems most inappropriate for a person resisting the draft to denigrate the actions of others in a similar predicament. Second, Baldwin was addressing a key official in the War Department's intelligence service as a spokesperson for all conscientious objectors. His comment could only reinforce the MID's conviction that its repressive activities were aimed at stamping out the devious efforts of slackers too cowardly to serve in the army. In reality, millions of young men were deeply morally opposed to fighting in a war they believed served no other purpose beyond an inter-imperialist squabble to divide the world's resources. Finally, the principal representative of the NCLB, the foremost organization defending constitutional rights, should not be making comments to a government official that could only undermine the civil liberties of a group especially vulnerable to government repression.

This message to Biddle was followed by a letter to Keppel that specifically addressed the Bureau's work with conscientious objectors. Since both the Military Intelligence Division and the Bureau of

Investigation had raised doubts as to the legality of the NCLB's efforts to aid conscientious objectors, Baldwin suggested that the "only reason that these efforts" were "not to be construed to be in violation of the Espionage Act" was that they were "carried out in cooperation with the War Department."[81] After all, Baldwin had met regularly with Keppel, who was well aware of the activities of the Conscientious Objectors' Bureau.

Baldwin followed up this dubious argument with a specific offer in yet another letter to Keppel. If the MID continued to "take exception" to the bureau's activities, Baldwin offered to meet with Van Deman to work out an acceptable arrangement. Furthermore, "from the beginning" the NCLB had offered "to modify any" of its "activities involving conscientious objectors in accordance with suggestions" from Keppel and the War Department.[82]

These attempts to mollify hostile agencies within the government were once again spurned, and during March and April of 1918, the Military Intelligence Division, with the support of the Bureau of Investigation, pushed to find the evidence needed to convince administration decision-makers that the NCLB should be prosecuted under the Espionage Act. Nevertheless, the issue remained open. The MID hierarchy drafted a memorandum calling for immediate action. It was sent to Bruce Bielaski, the chief of the Bureau of Investigation, who passed it on to the War Emergency Division of the Department of Justice. As usual, the immediate determination was made by Alfred Bettman, its deputy director. Bettman was not convinced by the MID dossier, concluding that the NCLB's statement of purpose was "not only lawful, but a good one." Since, "under the stress of war," super-patriotic organizations had arisen demanding "the undue suppression" of constitutional rights, it was proper and appropriate to initiate the formation of organizations such as the bureau that were committed to free speech.[83]

Bettman was cautious in his approach. If the NCLB strictly limited its scope to the defense of civil liberties, and did not "indulge in any unlawful propaganda," repressive action would not be "warranted." Still, Bureau of Intelligence agents should "keep in close touch" with the NCLB to ensure that it continued "to feel that it must be careful to avoid any antiwar or obstructive propaganda."

Bettman represented one strand of thought within the Wilson administration. These officials believed that a combination of co-optation and pressure could keep the NCLB, and the wider circle of progressives that it represented, within permissible limits. This would allow the NCLB to remain a friendly critic, one that could be largely ignored and yet whose existence allowed the United States to maintain some semblance of credibility when it claimed to be fighting a war for democracy.

Defending the IWW

The NCLB as initially formed had two primary points of concern: defending conscientious objectors and defending free speech rights. In the fall of 1917, the government's assault on the IWW emerged as a critical issuue. As dozens of IWW leaders languished in jail awaiting trial for violating the Espionage Act, and the Bureau of Intelligence repeatedly raided union halls around the country, Baldwin understood that the government was intent on destroying the organization. Furthermore, the Wobblies could not rely on the courts to protect their rights. A political response was needed, bringing together a coalition of progressives who would attempt to intercede with the administration.

Baldwin understood that this project went well beyond the scope of the NCLB as an organization committed to the defense of civil liberties. He and Albert DeSilver, a NCLB attorney, therefore created a "special group" specifically devoted to the defense of the IWW. In theory, this group operated strictly "outside of the Bureau."[84]

Baldwin needed to recruit influential progressives who had given their wholehearted support to the war effort. Clarence Darrow and Frank Walsh had both been vocal in their defense of the president's policies, but both were concerned that the administration was being too draconian in its suppression of those who opposed the war. Darrow was the foremost defense attorney of the time, while Walsh was an attorney who had chaired the U. S. Commission on Industrial Relations. A meeting of this secretive group in Washington took place in January 1918, but no action was taken when neither Darrow nor Walsh attended.[85] It is not clear if this unofficial committee held further meetings, but there can be no doubt that the aim was to coordinate an informal coalition that would extend well beyond the NCLB and that could launch a sustained effort to convince the federal government to enter into negotiations with the IWW leadership.

At the end of February 1918, Baldwin wrote directly to the president. The National Civil Liberties Bureau proposed that the indictment of the IWW leaders be quashed and "the whole matter [should] be turned over to the Department of Labor as an administrative problem."[86] Baldwin enclosed a memorandum detailing the NCLB's assessment of the situation. The government's brutal assault on the Wobblies was "already producing considerable labor unrest in the West." Furthermore, the union's defense attorneys were planning on presenting a multitude of witnesses who would attest to the harsh conditions confronting workers on the shop floor and in the mines. This testimony, and the resulting "widespread publicity," would fuel discontent within the working class.[87]

The National Civil Liberties Bureau argued that the IWW was being unfairly persecuted. Its leaders were being tried for organizing strikes and yet such activities were "the essential operations" of the union "as a labor organization." In this way, the NCLB claimed, the IWW and the AFL were similar. At times, both organized strikes to win improved wages and working conditions for their members. In reality, the two union federations were very different. During the First World War, AFL unions called brief strikes that were hastily ended with negotiated agreements. On the other hand, the IWW organized strikes in key industries that often lasted for months. Gompers and the AFL leadership were eager to stifle strike actions that could interfere with the war effort, while the IWW viewed the economic boom caused by military spending as a rare opportunity to organize workers into the union.

This memorandum was followed by a series of personal interviews with influential government officials. Baldwin and the NCLB hoped to negotiate a deal under which the IWW would forgo strikes during the war and the government would ease its coordinated assault on the union. In addition to John Lord O'Brian, head of the Justice Department's War Emergency Division, and Bruce Bielaski, director of the Bureau of Investigation, Baldwin met with Joseph Tumulty, the president's personal secretary and de facto chief of staff. Baldwin presented the same argument as that formulated in the memorandum to the president. The IWW cases should "be dropped," since the union was not interested in opposing the war effort and was only organizing strikes to improve the wages and working conditions of its members.[88]

At about the same time, early in 1918, Baldwin participated in a private meeting with Secretary of Agriculture David Houston and Francis Caffey, the U.S. Attorney for the Southern District of New York. Once again, Baldwin urged the government to drop its prosecution of the IWW leadership and, instead, to seek an implicit truce for the duration of the war. Caffey and Houston made it clear that the government was determined to suppress the IWW and was not prepared to enter into informal discussions that could lead to the dropping of any of the criminal charges. The federal government "could not tolerate the organized opposition to the war by men with the power to sabotage it."[89]

MILITARY INTELLIGENCE ACTS

Unable to convince the federal government to modify its total assault on the IWW, the NCLB stepped up its efforts to raise funds for the IWW's legal defense. Leland Chumley was sent to New York from Wobbly headquarters in Chicago to raise funds for the General Defense Committee. Baldwin prepared a "specially selected list" of contributors to the NCLB that Chumley then used to solicit funds.[90]

In April 1918, the National Civil Liberties Bureau published a brochure that collected comments from several experienced obervers of the IWW. In the introduction to *The Truth About the IWW*, the NCLB insisted that the IWW was "entitled" to "a fair trial." Still, it was "not to be inferred" that the Bureau was "in agreement with the principles and methods of the I.W.W."[91]

In general, the tone of the pamphlet suggested that the government had overreacted since the IWW had a small membership and thus was of little importance. Furthermore, the union's ideology, and its opposition to war, were "inconsequential trimmings" to its valiant, if ineffectual, efforts to improve the conditions of the powerless and the oppressed.[92]

The NCLB's pamphlet accurately reflected the liberal response to the IWW, a dismissive arrogance, but one section went even further. George West, a journalist who had covered the Wobblies for the *San Francisco Examiner*, held that "the situation last summer [1917] called for some action by the Department of Justice to suppress a few extremists, and to generally sober the organization." Still, the government's repression of the union should have been "more discriminating."[93] West's comments are a disturbing statement in a brochure published by an organization intent on upholding civil liberties. It reduces the issue to one of tactics rather than principle. West was suggesting that the federal government had been justified in prosecuting IWW leaders under the Espionage Act, but that, instead of a mass trial involving dozens of defendants, only a few of the union's leaders should have been singled out and made an example.

In spite of the pamphlet's cautious approach, the federal government acted to limit its distribution. As soon as it appeared, William Lamar, the solicitor at the post office, wrote to the Chicago postmaster to inform him that "*The Truth About the IWW*" was "nonmailable under the Espionage Act." Lamar was one of the most ardent proponents of repression within the federal government. The Department of Justice followed this up by issuing an order to private express companies forbidding them to transport copies. The NCLB was convinced that the government had also "otherwise hampered" the circulation of its pamphlet on the IWW. In spite of these efforts to restrict the circulation of the NCLB's pamphlet, the head of the Chicago office of the Bureau of Investigation complained that the city was "being flooded" by copies and that these were "very prejudicial" to the government and its efforts to convict IWW leaders of violating the Espionage Act.[94]

These public efforts in support of the IWW's legal defense led the Military Intelligence Division to adopt a position of open hostility. On May 15, 1918, Van Deman informed Keppel that there was credible evidence demonstrating that the NCLB was "willing to help anybody and everybody to evade the draft, irrespective of any conscientious objections." In addition, the bureau had "associated itself" with the IWW by "financing them."[95]

Shortly after receiving this assessment, Keppel conferred with Baker. Keppel then informed Baldwin that the War Department had decided that "it would not be in the public interest" to continue "to cooperate in any way with the Civil Liberties Bureau."[96] In spite of its repeated efforts to placate government officials, the NCLB had lost access to the Wilson administration and would soon become a priority target of repression.

Baldwin must have believed that the NCLB's sustained effort to aid the IWW would be accepted by the administration as yet another misguided, if well intentioned, attempt to soften the harsher edges of government policy. This time Baldwin and the National Civil Liberties Bureau had gone too far. The president had already determined that the Industrial Workers of the World had to be crushed and he did not take kindly to any move that would deflect the impact of government repression. Pressure on the NCLB was significantly intensified, as intelligence agencies went from intense surveillance to raids and threats of indictments.

RAIDS AND SMEARS

On June 1, 1918, Marlborough Churchill replaced Ralph Van Deman as chief of the Military Intelligence Division. This shift did not diminish the MID's determination to disrupt the NCLB. On June 2, Churchill queried Lamar for information on the post office's refusal to permit the NCLB's pamphlet on the IWW to be sent through the mail. Churchill approved of this decision, convinced that publication of the pamphlet and its assistance to the IWW's legal defense fund demonstrated "conclusively the dangerous character of everything the bureau" was "identified with."[97]

Churchill was so incensed by the NCLB's activities that he attempted to interrupt its supply of paper. In a letter to an executive of a paper company, Churchill charged that the AUAM and the NCLB "identified with every pacifist movement" in existence. Programs implemented by these organizations had caused the MID and the Department of Justice "a great deal of annoyance." To counter this perceived threat, Churchill advised the paper company to stop selling supplies to both organizations.[98]

At this point, intelligence agencies were using covert actions to disrupt the NCLB, but the government had still not moved to open repression. This restraint was lifted when the NCLB openly assisted the IWW's legal defense in the Chicago conspiracy trial by bringing together several leading progressives in support of an appeal for funds that appeared as an advertisement in the June 22, 1918, issue of *The New Republic*.[99] The funds solicited would be deposited in an account administered by Albert DeSilver, an attorney affiliated with the NCLB.[100]

Under the title "Never Mind What You Think About the IWW," the ad made no effort to defend the union or its activities. Instead, it insisted that the IWW defendants were "entitled to a fair trial." Funds were required to make it "possible for the defense to present fully the industrial evils underlying the IWW revolt." The conspiracy trial was expected to last several months and cost in excess of $100,000 in legal fees and attorney fees. This sum, upward of two million dollars in current terms, could not be raised by the IWW without the financial assistance *"of those Americans who believe in the right of a fair trial, even for the IWW."*[101]

The ad made it very clear that those soliciting funds did not agree with the IWW, but were only intent on ensuring that its leaders received a fair trial. Indeed, the Justice Department and the jury could "be relied upon" to deal with "any criminal acts that may be disclosed." In small print, readers were advised that further information could be gleaned by reading "*The Truth About the IWW.*" Dignitaries such as John Dewey, Helen Keller, and Thorstein Veblen signed the ad as sponsors of the defense fund.

The editors of *The New Republic* had enthusiastically supported the decision of the United States to enter the First World War. Furthermore, one of its leading contributors, Walter Lippmann, was then serving as a civilian assistant to Newton Baker, the Secretary of War. Nevertheless, Herbert Croly, its editor, was warned by an agent from the Bureau of Investigation not to reprint the ad "under threat of getting into difficulty with the law." He was informed that future issues of *The New Republic* containing the ad would be banned from the mail. Croly immediately capitulated.[102]

This incident demonstrates how the scope of government repression ripples outward when constitutional guarantees are scuttled. *The New Republic* was an integral element of the political mainstream. It published articles supporting the war and praising Woodrow Wilson. Still, even Croly and his cohorts were dismayed by the harsh and pervasive policies employed by the federal government to suppress anyone who challenged the government's war policies. When *The New Republic* began questioning the erosion of civil liberties, it too became a target of repression. It was not necessary to jail everyone who questioned authority. Threats, even threats that involved the loss of second class mailing privileges, often worked as effectively as a lengthy term in a penitentiary.

The actions of the NCLB in publishing the pamphlet on the IWW and raising funds for the union's legal defense convinced the MID that the NCLB had to be suppressed. On June 26, an internal MID memorandum suggested that Keppel "be advised of the fact that Roger Baldwin" was "assuming more potential danger" than before, when the NCLB had focused most of its efforts in aiding conscientious objectors. By helping the IWW raise funds for its legal defense, Baldwin and the Bureau were "becoming much more of a menace." Secretary Baker and his assistants had to be convinced that it was not enough "to give Baldwin the cold shoulder," but rather to push beyond this "to take all necessary steps to suppress him."[103]

THE GOVERNMENT RAIDS THE NCLB

By the summer of 1918, the NCLB was growing increasingly desperate as it became obvious that the Justice Department was preparing to
prosecute the leadership of the bureau. In a last-minute effort to avoid
a confrontation, Baldwin wrote to Van Deman that the NCLB found
itself in an "embarrassing and difficult situation." Although the NCLB
had already offered "to discontinue efforts which the Secretary of
War" found "not to be helpful," the MID still had not specified "what
activities" were "considered improper."

Baldwin was still hoping to meet with Baker to resolve the problems,
but the Military Intelligence Division and the Bureau of Investigation
were ready to move. The MID sent its dossier on the National Civil
Liberties Bureau to Rayme Finch, the Bureau of Intelligence (BI) agent
in charge of the investigation. Finch informed Biddle on August 30,
1918, that search warrants had been obtained and the NCLB offices
were to be raided.[104]

On the morning of the next day, August 31, a Saturday, ten armed
BI agents raided the offices of the National Civil Liberties Bureau.
Several intelligence officers from the New York office of the MID
joined in the raid. They acted on the basis of a warrant signed by
a federal magistrate that authorized the government to seize every
document found during the search.[105]

The raid took place at a time when most of the staff was absent.
Those who were there tried to quickly contact the bureau's attorneys.
Nelles was the first to arrive. He insisted that the search warrant
was not valid since it failed to meet the requirements set by the U.S.
Constitution. The Fourth Amendment in the Bill of Rights requires
a specification of "the person or things to be seized" during a search.
The fact that the warrant was defective, and thus probably invalid,
would influence the course of events during the following weeks.
When Nelles continued to protest, Finch pointed a revolver at his
head and ordered him to step aside.[106]

The combined force of agents from the Bureau of Investigation
and the Military Intelligence Division proceeded to occupy the

NCLB office for five days. During that time, agents from the Bureau of Investigation ransacked the office and carried away all of its files. Three weeks afterward, Vincent Rothwell, an assistant U.S. attorney, interrogated Ray Berman, Baldwin's personal assistant. Rothwell was certain that the National Civil Liberties Bureau served as a cover for the American Union Against Militarism, allowing the core group of activists to "keep on doing the same things under another name." He warned Berman to leave her job with the bureau because "it was a sure thing that the organization would not be permitted to continue." Should the NCLB ignore this warning, "everybody would go to jail."[107]

BALDWIN AND THE SEIZED FILES

During the first weeks following the raid, both sides operated under an interim "voluntary agreement."[108] The NCLB did not go to court to immediately contest the search warrant and to insist that the Bureau of Intelligence vacate its office. In return, the issue of a grand jury indictment targeting the NCLB was held in abeyance. Baldwin also agreed to assist the BI agents as they sought to bring order to the seized files.[109]

The files seized from the NCLB's office were voluminous. Sorting through them would prove to be a mammoth undertaking. Presumably part of the jumble was caused by the chaos created by the raid, as agents carted away files without keeping track of their order. Part of the problem probably also arose from the filing system used by the NCLB. Baldwin would have been particularly helpful in explaining to the Bureau of Investigation agents the logic behind the office filing system.

One reason the Justice Department had authorized the raid was a belief that the NCLB files would assist in the surveillance of radical organizations. Thus, Baldwin was helping the federal government to suppress the antiwar opposition. This was in direct contradiction to the bureau's primary purpose, defending the rights of dissidents.

Baldwin helped the Bureau of Intelligence to sort the seized documents even though he had his doubts. Many of the letters in the files came from conscientious objectors held in military camps and prisons. They had written to the NCLB in the belief that their complaints would be kept in confidence. Instead, the NCLB entered into an agreement that left its files in the hands of the government and then helped intelligence agents to bring order to the files so that they might be more easily used.

In September 1918, Baldwin wrote to Keppel seeking assurance that the letters from conscientious objectors would not be used as justification for punishments. Still, Baldwin was ready to agree that if letters were "found expressing disloyal sentiments" or a "defiant attitude" that "the writer would be held fully responsible" for these comments.[110]

Thus, a person held in a military prison for refusing to serve in the army who sent a letter to the NCLB expressing his continued opposition to the war and his belief that the conflict arose out of imperialist rivalries would not only find that his letter was in the hands of the military, but that the bureau would have no objection to his being punished for these dissident views.

Of course, Keppel was glad to provide Baldwin with a nebulous reassurance. There was "no reason to fear" that any conscientious objector "requesting a proper solution" to a difficulty arising out of his treatment as a military prisoner would be penalized for a letter of complaint sent to the National Civil Liberties Bureau.[111]

In a later interview, Baldwin made light of his efforts to bring order out of the seized files. He had agreed because "orderly files would prove our complete innocence."[112] Still, the issue was not an amusing anecdote. The federal government believed the files could be useful in the prosecution of other individuals and organizations on the Left and Baldwin knew it.

THE PROPAGANDA SECTION

The sorting of the seized files by Bureau of Investigation agents and Baldwin was just the first step in the government's examination of these records. Once this was finished the files were turned over to

Archibald Stevenson and his Propaganda Section. Stevenson had accompanied the Bureau of Intelligence agents on their raid of the NCLB's office.[113]

A corporate attorney who enthusiastically supported the decision to enter the war, Stevenson soon discovered that popular dissatisfaction was widespread, especially in New York City. He became convinced that there was an organized far-flung conspiracy to obstruct the war effort, a conspiracy that encompassed everyone from radicals to progressive critics of the administration and on to pro-war liberals who were dismayed by the administration's draconian suppression of free speech.

Stevenson was obsessed with the potential danger posed by this supposed conspiracy, but similar views were held by many within the corporate elite. Stevenson was a member of the exclusive Union League Club. Located in a palatial mansion in midtown Manhattan, the Union League Club enrolled the most powerful bankers and industrialists in the country, among them J. P. Morgan and John D. Rockefeller. Only white males were allowed to join, while women, Jews, and people of color were excluded. Catholics were also largely barred from entry.[114]

The Union League Club provided a private place for the wealthy to mingle and make deals, but this was only part of its purpose. For years, the Club had served as the driving force behind political campaigns designed to counter Tammany Hall's hold over New York City politics. Once the First World War began, the Union League Club issued calls for the most draconian measures to be employed to crush the antiwar opposition.

With the backing of members of this powerful elite, Stevenson convinced the Justice Department in the summer of 1917 to establish a special unit that would closely monitor radical publications, primarily in the New York City area. This task required a team of translators. With their assistance, Stevenson and his staff, many of them recruited from the Union League Club, collected a large collection of clippings from left-wing newspapers and periodicals. This was information that would prove to be useful to the Justice Department in prosecuting newspapers and organizations for allegedly violating the Espionage Act. Yet Stevenson and the Propaganda Section did not stop there. A set of files was created that contained cross-referenced index cards that purported to show the underlying links between all of those who challenged the administration's policies.[115]

After the initial sorting by Baldwin and Bureau of Investigation agents, the huge haul of documents was passed on to the Propaganda Section, which then began the time-consuming process of examining each of the documents and compiling them in a way that could be useful to the federal government.

The Propaganda Section was transferred to the Military Intelligence Division in October 1918, a few weeks before the war came to an end. Those in command of the MID shared Stevenson's view that the liberal Left was an integral component of a widespread conspiracy to overthrow the government and thus needed to be ruthlessly suppressed. They were therefore happy to approve the transfer. Stevenson's unit carefully examined the NCLB files and then wrote reports to MID officers on influential progressives. Although the Propaganda Section was dissolved in January 1919, the files seized in the raid on the NCLB office are still not available for public scrutiny.[116]

Secret Negotiations

The initial interim agreement between the Justice Department and the NCLB did not resolve the key issues in dispute. Negotiations were required for a more far-reaching settlement. Both sides had pressing reasons to come to an understanding.

The federal government was determined to keep control of the seized files and yet the warrant issued to authorize the raid was defective. This left the Justice Department in an awkward position. Churchill, as the head of the MID, wrote to Biddle explaining that there was "grave doubt" of the legality of the search warrant, so there was a credible possibility that a court might dismiss the charges and order the destruction of the files.[117]

This was one reason that the government was willing to negotiate with the NCLB. In addition, it would have been politically embarrassing to prosecute respected progressives such as Levi Hollingsworth Wood for violating the Espionage Act. After all, Woodrow Wilson liked to present the image of a steadfast progressive.

On the other hand, the raid made it clear that the Justice Department was seriously considering convening a grand jury to indict the leaders of the NCLB for allegedly violating the Espionage Act. This left the organization with a difficult choice. It could continue to pursue the path of open defiance demonstrated by Nelles during the raid. There was a reasonable likelihood that attorneys could have the government's prosecution under the Espionage Act thrown out of court on the basis of the defective search warrant. Still, the risks were considerable. A conviction was still a significant possibility. This could lead to the leadership of the National Civil Liberties Bureau spending years in a high-security prison. Furthermore, the federal government would be likely to respond to a defeat in court by escalating its harassment of the NCLB, leading to more break-ins, intensive surveillance, and the genuine possibility of further indictments under the Espionage Act.

Given this choice, the NCLB sought to mollify the government. This was a dangerous decision that was bound to lead the organization into a compromising position. The day after the raid, Wood wrote to John Lord O'Brian that the bureau was prepared to restrict its activities where they "could be shown" to be "prejudicial to the country's interests."[118]

At the same time, Roger Baldwin's situation was still unresolved. Baldwin would have been a key individual in an indictment of the NCLB, but he also faced the immediate prospect of being conscripted. A pacifist morally opposed to all violence, Baldwin had no intention of serving in the U.S. Army. At the age of thirty-four he became eligible for the draft in September 1917, when the age limit was lifted from thirty to forty-five. Although Baldwin had decided to refuse to register for the draft, contrary to the advice offered in the public statement he had signed in May 1917, once the NCLB office was raided he opted to register. He thereby obtained a postponement of four weeks in order to help the bureau cope with the emergency. Part of this time was spent helping the government to sort through the files seized during the raid on the NCLB's office. In early October, Baldwin refused to appear at an army medical examination and turned himself into the authorities. Later that month, he appeared before Judge Julius Mayer in federal district court, who opted to retain jurisdiction, rather than transferring Baldwin's case to a military court. Baldwin was sentenced to one year in prison for resisting the draft, to be served in a minimum security jail.[119]

Thus, in the period following the raid, it was already obvious that Baldwin would not be serving as the NCLB's director during the next period. Still, the conditions under which he could return to the bureau would have been one factor in any negotiations with the federal government. In fact, Baldwin would eventually spend six months on an extended leave of absence before returning to his post after serving his prison sentence.

With Baldwin preparing to leave his position, the NCLB opted to employ George Gordon Battle in an effort to negotiate an agreement with the government. Battle was an influential corporate attorney who provided legal advice to Tammany Hall. He also supported the war effort and worked for charities raising funds to support the soldiers. An influential figure in New York City politics, Battle could gain a friendly hearing from administration decision makers.[120]

Battle was paid $1,000 by the NCLB, a hefty fee at the time, but the question went far beyond the usual plea-bargaining that characterizes the criminal justice system. Negotiations lasted for months before a final arrangement was made and proceeded through several stages. At first, the discussions took place between Battle and Francis Caffey, the U.S. attorney for the Southern District of New York.

At this level, the arrangement seems to have focused on a deal whereby the government would drop charges against the leaders of the NCLB and, in return, the bureau would not contest the seizure of its files. Beyond this, the NCLB would stop its efforts to aid conscientious objectors who were being mistreated in army bases or military prisons.

Within weeks of the raid, reports of a tentative agreement reached the Military Intelligence Division. Since the New York office of the MID had been instrumental in the intensive surveillance of the bureau, Biddle was disturbed by rumors that the Justice Department would not pursue indictments. In a letter to Churchill, Biddle pressed for more details of the arrangement. After all, his office had "spent [a] tremendous amount of work investigating the activities of the National Civil Liberties Bureau."[121]

According to Churchill, Caffey and Battle had reached "a quasi-agreement." Battle had agreed that if all criminal charges were dropped he "would guarantee that the men financing" the NCLB "would withdraw all further subscriptions." Furthermore, Battle "gave his personal assurance" that the NCLB "would go out of business."[122]

The NCLB had arisen out of the Conscientious Objectors' Bureau and one of its primary purposes had been to advocate for them within the military system. By agreeing to halt its counseling of conscientious objectors, the Bureau was agreeing to stop performing one of its major functions.

Negotiations between Caffey and Battle took place in September and early October of 1918. Still, the matter was too sensitive to be fully resolved at this level. Attorney General Thomas Gregory had to sign off on the deal and he insisted that Battle provide him with a memorandum more fully detailing the willingness of the NCLB to cooperate with the government.[123] These were very sensitive issues and it is therefore very likely that Gregory would have discussed the situation with the president before a final deal was put into place.

Neither Battle's memorandum nor a written version of the agreement can be found in the public record, but its general outline can be gleaned from correspondence that has been declassified, as well as the course of later events. The line between the National Civil Liberties Bureau and its clients would be more firmly drawn. There would be no more cases such as the IWW's where the NCLB, or its successor the American Civil Liberties Union, helped an organization targeted for federal prosecution to raise funds for its defense so that it could hire its own attorneys. Instead, the NCLB provided attorneys to defend those under attack. In this way, the NCLB would control the strategy pursued by the defense, emphasizing legal issues rather than broader political issues. Furthermore, Albert DeSilver, who replaced Baldwin as director, was generally more cautious in his approach. The NCLB assisted in the postwar effort to obtain a general amnesty for those prosecuted because of their opposition to the war, but it generally remained in the background.

This left the question of Baldwin's return to civil liberties work. The Justice Department remained suspicious of him, especially his ties to the IWW. Although the Wobblies had been greatly weakened by the government's sustained assault, they still had a significant base in a few industries. The Wilson administration was determined to finish its decimation of the union, despite that the wartime emergency was coming to an end.

Thus, it seems likely that the final version of the deal, as negotiated by Battle and Gregory, guaranteed that Baldwin would only be able to return to the NCLB when he was willing to distance himself from the IWW. This pledge may have included a willingness to cooperate with the government as it responded to demands for an amnesty that would include the IWW prisoners. The course of events suggests that this was a part of the agreement between the NCLB and the government.

In return for these concessions, the public record seems to indicate that the government agreed not to file charges against the NCLB's leaders. Furthermore, government officials refrained from leaking to the press the details of Baldwin's personal life, leaks that would have damaged his personal reputation.

Smearing Roger Baldwin

Churchill understood that the "quasi-agreement" did not constitute a final resolution of the question and he therefore warned Biddle that the leaders of the National Civil Liberties Bureau were "still persons of great interest to the MID."[124] With the end of the First World War, the Department of Justice stopped initiating prosecutions under the

Espionage Act. Although the NCLB no longer risked prosecution for its activities, the Military Intelligence Division continued its clandestine operation to pressure the bureau. As a result, it launched a smear campaign targeting Baldwin, an effort that ultimately involved the president.

In the summer of 1918, during the period immediately prior to the raid on the NCLB's office, the MID wiretapped the bureau's telephones. Furthermore, the telephone of Baldwin's fiancée, Madeleine Doty, was also tapped so that Baldwin's personal discussions could be overheard.[125] Once again, this was done without a search warrant issued by a judge and was therefore in direct violation of the Fourth Amendment. The wiretaps lead to a further incident when George Foster Peabody, a wealthy investment banker and a major donor to the Democratic Party, wrote Woodrow Wilson asking him to release Baldwin from jail by granting a pardon. The president's secretary, Joseph Tumulty, passed this request on to Attorney General Thomas Gregory.

Gregory responded with a letter to President Wilson urging the president to reject Peabody's request. Most of the letter was drawn from a report from a "most valued assistant," a Justice Department official with access to the Bureau of Investigation's surveillance reports. The investigation had demonstrated that Baldwin was "genuinely disloyal" and that the NCLB had been "working to create conscientious objectors" by providing advice to those who were not total pacifists, or who were pacifists but who were not religious, and yet sought an exemption from military service.[126]

The report went on to specifically note that Baldwin's telephone calls were being intercepted. These conversations had "shown that instead of being a person of high morals, as many of his friends" believed, he was "not leading a moral life." Based on this report, Gregory concluded that a one-year sentence for resisting the draft was "exceptionally light." He warned the president that Baldwin was "one of a very dangerous class of persons," a category of troublemakers that Gregory feared would be heard from "a good deal in the future."

There is no doubt that Baldwin led an unconventional personal life. In 1918, he was engaged to be married, but he and Doty had agreed to an open marriage. Baldwin had short-term relations with several other women during this period. He also appears to have been bisexual, engaging in relationships with younger men.[127]

Peabody refused to give credence to the government's deliberate effort at character assassination. Tumulty forwarded Gregory's letter to the president, including a large section of the confidential report, to Peabody on November 11, 1918, the day the war finally came to an end. Two weeks later, on November 26, Peabody insisted in a letter to Tumulty that Baldwin came from "one of the unusually fine families in Massachusetts" and that the charges against him were "absolutely without basis." Peabody followed this rejoinder with another one that declared that Gregory was "under [a] serious misapprehension," and that Bureau of Investigation agents had "drawn inferences without justification" from surreptitious interceptions of Baldwin's telephone calls.[128]

In the end, Baldwin survived this covert attack on his personal life. He served nine months of his jail sentence, most of it in a minimum security county jail in Newark, New Jersey. Upon his release in July 1919, Baldwin spent five months traveling around the United States, some of it working in blue-collar jobs. He returned to his post with the NCLB in December 1919.[129]

Launching the American Civil Liberties Union

Baldwin and the other members of the Directing Committee had come to the conclusion that there was an urgent need to reorganize the National Civil Liberties Bureau. With the war ended, Baldwin sought to turn a new leaf, to transcend the disagreements that had divided progressives. This would facilitate renewed support from those who had been integral to the initial group that had created the basis for a civil liberties organization, but who had resigned to become enthusiastic proponents of the war effort. Furthermore, Baldwin was eager to bring in eminent liberals who had not been associated with the American Union Against Militarism and who had avidly defended the president's decision to enter the war.[130]

With this in mind, Baldwin, along with Wood and DeSilver, sent out letters to a long list of influential progressives announcing the dissolution of the NCLB and the formation of a new organization that would be attractive to "every believer in industrial democracy" and "every champion of free expression of opinion."[131]

In January 1920, the American Civil Liberties Union was officially launched, with Baldwin as its executive director. He would hold this post for the next thirty years. Most members of the new organization's executive committee had been in the core group of the NCLB, but the ACLU also featured a large national committee that included well-known individuals who had wholeheartedly supported the war effort from the start, such as Felix Frankfurter, thus providing the ACLU with a mainstream credibility that its predecessor had never achieved.[132]

THE IWW PRISONERS

The question of the IWW prisoners continued to pose difficult, but crucially important, issues for the reconfigured ACLU. As long as Woodrow Wilson remained president, every effort to free the imprisoned Wobblies was summarily rebuffed. Only after Warren Harding was inaugurated in March 1921 did the situation begin to change. Harding soon announced that he would only consider granting clemency to any of the wartime political prisoners after the war had come to an official end.

In September 1921, Congress finally passed the relevant legislation bringing to an end the declaration of war of April 1917 and the administration began to consider the clemency appeals of IWW prisoners. Initially, the IWW and the ACLU participated in the Political Amnesty Committee, a loose coalition of progressive organizations seeking a general amnesty for all of those convicted under wartime legislation.

Harry Daugherty, the new attorney general, made it clear that the Harding administration would not issue a blanket amnesty. Almost all of the wartime political prisoners still incarcerated in 1921 were

IWW activists. More than 140 Wobblies had been sentenced to lengthy terms as a result of three mass trials conducted in Chicago, Sacramento, and Wichita. All of the IWW prisoners were incarcerated in Leavenworth Federal Penitentiary, the high-security prison in Kansas. Some of those who had been found guilty had received five-year prison sentences, but by 1921, these prisoners had been released, having served their sentences with time off for good behavior. Most of the IWW prisoners had received longer sentences, usually ten or twenty years, and still had several years to serve before they were scheduled to be released. Thus, a presidential commutation of their sentences was their only hope of gaining freedom.

At first, the Harding administration insisted that each prisoner had to individually apply for clemency and that these appeals would be processed through the usual channels within the Department of Justice. Accordingly, a few of the prisoners were summoned before the parole board, where they were told that their cases would not be considered unless they admitted their guilt and promised to remain law-abiding citizens when released.[133] These conditions were similar to those imposed on federal prisoners convicted of serious crimes who submitted requests for presidential clemency.

The American Civil Liberties Union responded positively to the administration's proposed procedure by encouraging each of the IWW prisoners to submit individual petitions asking for a review of his case. In June 1921, the ACLU was permitted by prison authorities to circulate a letter to the IWW prisoners urging them to apply for a commutation of their sentences on an individual basis.

The government's initial proposal requiring prisoners to apply for a commutation as individuals and to accept the conditions set by the pardon board sparked a rancorous dispute among the prisoners incarcerated in Leavenworth. Most of the IWW prisoners rejected these terms as humiliating, and refused to participate. Twenty-four prisoners did file an individual clemency appeal and most, but not all, were quickly released from prison.[134]

The majority of the IWW prisoners strongly condemned those who sought clemency in accordance with the procedure set out by the government. They were convinced that all of the prisoners should act together, rather than each individual determining his own course. Furthermore, they were certain that the Harding administration was manipulating the pardon process to divide and demoralize the prisoners and the IWW as a whole, as indeed it was.

Of the ninety-six IWW prisoners in Leavenworth in May 1921, seventy signed a public statement explaining their reasons for refusing to submit individual applications for a presidential commutation of their sentences. Those who had agreed to this process had undercut the position of the majority by implying that "the remaining defendants" were "guilty" as charged. The seventy also refused "to accept the restricted freedom" set out in "the terms laid down by the government for offenders." The prisoners who signed the public statement insisted that the government deal with them as a single unit, instead of determining the release of each individual prisoner on the basis of the alleged facts in that particular case. In the view of the seventy IWW prisoners, all of those imprisoned at Leavenworth, including those convicted at the Sacramento trial who were being categorized as particularly dangerous, were "innocent of the charges and should be immediately released without conditions in a blanket amnesty."[135]

Most of the IWW prisoners were incensed at the ACLU's intervention. Forrest Edwards, the former secretary of the IWW's Agricultural Workers' Industrial Union #400, wrote that the ACLU's encouragement of individual pardons "would hurt the movement for a general amnesty." Baldwin responded that the discharge of some of the prisoners by way of a presidential reprieve would increase the pressure for the release of all of the prisoners.[136]

Once the initial flurry of pardon submissions had been filed, the process ground to a halt as the remaining IWW prisoners refused to submit individual applications requesting a commutation of their sentences. In the early summer of 1922, fifty-two of the IWW prisoners, most of those still incarcerated at Leavenworth, signed an open letter to President Harding that the IWW published. They insisted that they would "stand together as a group" and thus they would not agree to submit individual applications for a presidential commutation since this procedure allowed the pardon attorney to "select" which Wobblies "shall remain in prison."[137]

Baldwin and the ACLU decided to propose a new set of guidelines for the pardon process that met some, but not all, of the objections set out in the open letter of the fifty-two IWW prisoners. By the summer of 1922, popular pressure to release all of the Wobblies had greatly increased. Even those who had enthusiastically supported the war had come to the conclusion that it was time to heal the divisive bitterness engendered during the conflict. As a skillful politician, Harding realized that he had to move further toward an amnesty. Thus, his administration was willing to act on the ACLU's proposal for a new set of guidelines for the pardon process.

On July 19, 1922, the president met with delegation of prominent progressives, including Baldwin. The delegation presented a petition with one million signatures calling for a total amnesty of those convicted under the Espionage Act. (Although it had urged the IWW prisoners to submit individual requests for a commutation, the ACLU's official position argued that the president should issue a general amnesty covering all wartime political prisoners.) Harding responded that he was willing to commute the sentences of those IWW prisoners who had not advocated "the destruction of Government by force."[138] This was a clear signal that only some of the prisoners would be considered as eligible for early release.

Three weeks later, Baldwin and two ACLU supporters returned to the White House to meet with George Christian Jr., the president's personal secretary. The delegation urged the administration to consider a new procedure that would speed the process by which IWW prisoners were released. Christian suggested that the delegation submit a brief detailing their suggested guidelines.[139]

The brief, written by Baldwin, proposed that the pardon attorney review each case to determine whether the prisoner had actually advocated the "unlawful destruction of property." This proposal was immediately tabled because the Justice Department insisted that the Sacramento mass trial had definitively proven that the California Wobblies in Leavenworth had engaged in arson and sabotage.[140]

The delegation's other proposal was seriously considered. Instead of individual petitions for presidential clemency, groups of prisoners would be able to collectively submit a set of cases, which would then be submitted to the pardon attorney by the ACLU "on behalf of the prisoners."[141]

James Finch, the Department of Justice's pardon attorney, accepted Baldwin's proposal, but he also insisted that all those who signed the collective petition would have to agree beforehand that they would accept clemency on the conditions offered, that is, they would pledge to remain law abiding once released. Furthermore, although the applications for clemency would be submitted by a group of prisoners, the president, acting on the advice of the pardon attorney, would "consider each case individually." Finally, the IWW activists convicted at the Sacramento trial continued to be excluded from any consideration of a commutation of their sentences.[142]

Once the Justice Department and the ACLU had agreed on the terms of the new procedure, the new plan was implemented. Baldwin was permitted to enter Leavenworth Penitentiary and conduct private interviews with the IWW prisoners covered by the terms of the agreement.[143] These private discussions were designed to convince the prisoners to join with others in signing a collective petition for clemency that would not be sent directly to the White House, but rather would be given to Baldwin, who would then transmit the petition to the federal government.[144]

This was an extraordinary arrangement. Leavenworth inmates had very limited and closely scrutinized visitation rights. Attorneys could meet with prisoner clients on legal issues involving appeals and close family members could make infrequent visits. Baldwin fit neither category and yet he was given the right to meet with dozens of prisoners on a confidential basis. Obviously, the Justice Department had a great deal of confidence that Baldwin would actually carry out the agreed upon plan and would not use this unique opportunity to stir up resistance among the prisoners.[145]

All of the IWW prisoners still refused to sign a group petition requesting clemency. The great majority of the prisoners emphatically rejected the ACLU's proposal in its entirety. A minority group adopted a slightly revised version of the plan initiated by Baldwin. Twelve prisoners signed a joint statement requesting clemency and agreeing to abide by the prison board's terms. The statement was drafted as a public letter rather than as a request to the president. Of the twelve, two of them, Walter Nef and Benjamin Fletcher, were among the most influential of the IWW prisoners. In October 1922, Harding issued a commutation order covering most of those who had signed the collective petition. The IWW prisoners were released on the condition that they would "not encourage" or advocate "lawlessness in any form."[146]

The new pardon process initiated by Baldwin and the ACLU significantly deepened divisions among the IWW prisoners. Years later, Baldwin still defended his actions. Those prisoners who had signed the collective petition had "sacrificed no principle." Nevertheless, he had to concede that his plan had led to "bitter strife" among the IWW prisoners.[147]

Many of the prisoners were kept in Leavenworth for another year. Finally, in December 1923 all of the remaining IWW prisoners were unconditionally released by Calvin Coolidge, who had become president following the death of Harding in August 1923.[148]

The federal government was intent on destroying the IWW as a viable union. It therefore deliberately exacerbated divisions among the IWW prisoners as one aspect of a coordinated campaign of repression that had begun during the war. Baldwin was well aware of this and yet he and the ACLU actively participated in the manipulation of the pardon process that led to further deepening of the divisions among the prisoners. Baldwin justified his role on the basis that each successive set of guidelines for commutation facilitated the release of another batch of prisoners. Still, one has to wonder.

In an oral history recorded in the 1950s, Baldwin continued to insist that he did "not reject" the effort to convince the Wobblies to sign the collective clemency petition, despite the discord it had caused and that a whole category of prisoners had been excluded from consideration. Baldwin also maintained to the end that he was not told of the specifics in the secret agreement made by George Gordon Battle with Attorney General Thomas Gregory in 1918.[149] One has to consider the possibility that Baldwin's willingness to act at the government's behest in its relentless drive to divide the IWW prisoners was tied to the deal Battle had made earlier with the federal government, a deal that had kept Baldwin and his associates from becoming incarcerated in Leavenworth themselves.

Summary

Woodrow Wilson viewed the Left as a credible threat to his war policies, so he was determined to crush any organized resistance. The federal government had no hesitation in blatantly disregarding the fundamental liberties guaranteed by the Bill of Rights in its unrelenting drive to suppress dissent.

In response, progressives sought to defend basic rights by forming the first significant and continuing civil liberties organization in the United States, the National Civil Liberties Bureau. In 1920, this would become the American Civil Liberties Union. Although the NCLB tried to remain above the fray, insisting that it did not necessarily agree with the viewpoint of those it defended, influential segments of the federal government were convinced that the bureau was deliberately disrupting the war effort. Threats were made, its office was raided, and telephones were tapped. The government sought to intimidate the NCLB into being less forthright in its defense of those who were being prosecuted for their opposition to the war. Unfortunately, the leaders of the National Civil Liberties Bureau failed to meet this challenge. Secret deals were made and the organization entered into arrangements with the federal government that were very questionable. Indeed, Baldwin cooperated with the Harding administration in devising amnesty procedures that could only further divide and demoralize the IWW prisoners.

Although the political situation in the United States a century later is very different, public opinion has become increasingly polarized. Should a similar situation arise, that is, a government that finds itself confronted by an organized opposition with widespread popular support, we can expect a similar assault on fundamental rights. One target of this campaign of repression is likely to be civil liberties organizations that defend those under attack. The lessons learned from the experience of the National Civil Liberties Bureau should provide a warning to contemporary organizations to be ready to cope with government repression.

4

Quashing the Socialist Party and Targeting Eugene Victor Debs

The Socialist Party of America (SP) is a unique phenomenon in U.S. history. It remains the only nationwide independent party on the Left to become a significant force over a sustained period of time.

From its founding in 1901, the party grew rapidly, establishing strong locals around the country. In the period prior to the First World War, it gained significant electoral victories as socialists were elected mayor in cities from Bridgeport, Connecticut, to Milwaukee, to Berkeley. More importantly, the party's membership exceeded 100,000 at its zenith in 1912. This was a party rooted in the working class, with a substantial base in several unions affiliated with the American Federation of Labor, including the International Ladies Garment Workers' Union and the United Mine Workers' Union. At the same time, the party's left wing developed close working relations with the Industrial Workers of the World.

Eugene Victor Debs, the Socialist Party's presidential candidate in four consecutive elections from 1900 through 1912, was one of the most respected and popular personalities of the era. Indeed, Debs was far more popular than the Socialist Party itself. Debs was beloved because of his steadfast efforts to organize railroad workers into an industrial union, as well as his unpretentious and warm personality. Although the Socialist Party was a profoundly divided organization, with the more moderate elements in the majority at the national level, Debs was a forthright radical who was in general agreement with the party's left wing. Nevertheless, he still received the enthusiastic support of the rank and file, no matter what their political perspective.

The divisions within the Socialist Party had always run deep, but the First World War greatly accentuated the acrimony within the organization. The two wings had drastically different perspectives on how to address the issues arising out of the U.S. decision to enter the war. Radicals insisted that the war was the logical outcome of imperialist rivalries. When the war came to an end, new wars would ensue as imperial powers sought to expand their empires, while hoping to block the expansion of their rivals. Thus, only a global socialist revolution could create the basis for a durable peace. This analysis followed from an even more fundamental tenet, that capitalism could not be reformed or regulated and therefore a socialist transformation was an urgent necessity if disaster was to be avoided.

Radicals in the left wing of the Socialist Party and the Industrial Workers of the World therefore sought to organize against the war by linking peace protests to a broader anti-capitalist critique. Since a genuine antiwar movement required the growth of a conscious movement toward socialism, it was essential to emphasize the need for a militant resistance to the war and to conscription as well. Of course, radicals understood that this strategy would make them priority targets for government repression. Indeed, the administration of President Woodrow Wilson deployed a range of repressive agencies to suppress any attempt to organize militant protests against the war and the draft. In its unremitting campaign to suppress the left wing of the Socialist Party, as well as any others who organized as radicals in opposition to the war, the federal government acted in flagrant disregard of fundamental civil liberties. These repressive actions were left unchecked by the judiciary, which thereby abdicated its responsibility to defend the U.S. Constitution and its Bill of Rights.

The moderate reform wing of the Socialist Party started from very different assumptions. They were convinced that socialism was the inevitable outcome of capitalist development. The transformation to a socialist society would come through a series of incremental reforms, many of them embodied in legislation. This emphasis on the importance of social reform led moderate socialists to forge alliances with progressive reformers in order to organize campaigns around specific issues.

Although the moderates within the Socialist Party viewed the First World War as a clash between imperialist rivals, they also saw the possibility of an international body that could provide the framework for a peaceful resolution of conflicts. This was a perspective also held by progressive reformers. Once the United States entered the war in April 1917, the Socialist Party's moderate leaders were eager to join with progressives on the basis of a common peace program. In their view, it was essential to create a broad coalition based on a minimal program in order to pressure the Allies into initiating immediate peace negotiations leading to a rapid end to the war and to a just peace based on the formula of "no annexations, no reparations." The result was the People's Council of America for Democracy and the Terms of Peace.

As the federal government widened the scope of repression to encompass even the most cautious dissenters, many progressives abandoned the peace movement. They looked forward to the time when the war had ended and the liberal coalition could again work within the mainstream parties to bring about social reforms. Many ceased to be politically active, while others limited their activities to the defense of civil liberties.

As a result, the Socialist Party was left isolated and vulnerable to government repression. The federal government used a variety of means, both open and covert, to pressure the party into reversing its previous policy and supporting the war effort. Eager to forestall even harsher repressive measures, and to avoid jail, the party's leaders sought to soften the organization's position in order to mollify the president. Still, they found it difficult to entirely jettison any criticism of the war. In the end, the Socialist Party kept diluting its opposition to the war and yet it never convinced the government to ease its policy of repression.

Debs identified with the radical, anti-capitalist critique of the war, although he briefly vacillated in the spring of 1918, moving closer to the antiwar position held by the party's moderates. His decision to speak out in militant opposition to the war in June 1918 led to his incarceration and brought an end to the efforts to coerce the Socialist Party into conforming to the administration's war policies.

DEBS ON WAR AND MILITARISM

When the First World War erupted in August 1914, the Socialist Party was one of the few members of the Second International of socialist parties to continue to uphold an antiwar perspective. From the start, the SP insisted that the war was rooted in a dispute between imperial rivals. In a statement issued in December 1914, the party's National Executive Committee (NEC) argued that the "fundamental causes" of the conflict stemmed from the push for overseas markets for "surplus products." As disputes intensified for spheres of influence, the entire world became "involved in a deadly struggle for the capture and control of the world market." Thus the rivalry of imperial powers "inevitably leads to war."[1]

Still, the party's leadership looked for a path toward a general peace within the constraints set by a global capitalist system. The NEC statement called for immediate negotiations leading to a general peace based on a program of "no indemnities" and "no transfer of territory except upon consent and by vote of the people within the territory." In addition, the statement also demanded an end to secret diplomacy and the creation of an international agency to maintain the peace once the current war had come to an end. These points corresponded to the peace program advanced by progressive reformers.[2]

Debs started from a very different perspective, insisting that militarism and war could only be abolished through a revolutionary transformation that established a socialist society. He rejected the call of patriotism, holding that "the workers have no country to fight for. It belongs to the capitalists and the plutocrats." Thus, any "military establishment" would be "controlled by the ruling class and its chief function will be to keep the working class in slavery."[3]

In the fall of 1915, Woodrow Wilson proposed to Congress that the United States dramatically increase its spending on military forces.[4] Historically, the United States had refrained from either financing a large standing army or the construction of a large flotilla of armed ships for its navy. The president's preparedness program broke with this tradition and represented an important first step in the projection of the United States as a global military power.

Most Socialist Party members adamantly opposed the preparedness campaign. By referendum, members voted by an overwhelming majority to make opposition to the preparedness campaign the party's official position, binding on all officers and candidates.[5] Nevertheless, a few of the party's most renowned members, authors and intellectuals, publicly endorsed the preparedness program. Charles Edward Russell, a prominent muckraking journalist, had been a prime candidate to become the socialist presidential candidate in 1916 until he declared his support for increased military spending. In an address to a convention of the Intercollegiate Socialist Society, Russell argued, "America ought to be prepared to defend itself as the last bulwark of democracy."[6]

Debs sharply criticized Russell's position in a letter to a mainstream newspaper, insisting that a large standing army "means a military autocracy" and that the American people should "not be surprised if other nations treat" the preparedness program "as a challenge to war, and if they themselves are conscripted to fight and die to maintain plutocratic supremacy in the United States."[7]

The St. Louis Resolution

By March 1917 it had become apparent that the United States was preparing to enter the war. Debs spoke before a crowd of two thousand at the Cooper Union in New York City, where he expressed his total opposition to the war. He insisted that the working class should organize "a general strike and paralyze" the economy if Congress approved a declaration of war, a statement that was met with enthusiastic applause. Debs went on to pledge that he would "rather be lined up against the wall and shot down as a traitor to Wall Street, than fight [and thus become] a traitor to myself."[8]

Responding to the urgency of the situation, the Socialist Party's National Executive Committee convened a special emergency convention in St. Louis. The week-long convention began on April 7, 1917, the day after the United States declared war on Germany. Its proceedings were dominated by the party's left wing, with most delegates prepared to defy the government in organizing a mass movement of resistance. The resolution passed by the convention, and approved by membership referendum by an overwhelming majority, held that the war was the result of the imperialist rivalries of "contending national groups of capitalists" and was "not the concern of workers." In its efforts to resist the slaughter, the Socialist party would organize "continuous action, and public opposition to the war through demonstrations" and "all other means" within its power. The Party also pledged its "unyielding opposition" to conscription. Should the draft be instituted, as it would be a few weeks later, the Socialist Party would respond by committing its support to "all mass movements in opposition to conscription."[9]

After years of stress and constant travel, Debs was physically and emotionally exhausted. Diagnosed with back pain, exhaustion, and a dilated heart, Debs was restricted to his bed in the spring of 1917. In August, he was transferred to a sanitarium in Boulder, Colorado, for treatment for depression and life-threatening heart problems.[10]

Too ill to attend the emergency convention, Debs sent an open message to the convention delegates. In this critical moment, there could be "no fear, no evasion and no compromise." The Socialist Party of America had "to stand squarely against every war save and alone the war against war." The war effort, along with the government's determination to crush dissent, had to be "denounced and resisted to the limit, if every jail in the land is choked with radicals and revolutionaries."[11] Debs was not engaging in empty rhetoric. He would soon be one of those languishing in jail for resisting the war, along with many others.

Writing soon after the conclusion of the emergency convention of April 1917, Debs lauded the antiwar resolution endorsed by the emergency convention. He was pleased that there had been "no cowardly compromising spirit" at the St. Louis emergency convention.[12]

The Socialist Party Divides

Although the great majority of the Socialist Party opposed the war, a small minority quit to become vocal defenders of the war effort. Debs harshly condemned these defectors. Among this group were the editors of the *Appeal to Reason*, a mass circulation newspaper closely linked to the Socialist Party, which had previously featured articles written by Debs. When Debs learned that the *Appeal to Reason* had shifted its position and become a defender of the war, he wrote to its editor, Louis Kopelin, rescinding his subscription. Debs warned Kopelin that the *Appeal* had "committed suicide." Furthermore, the socialist movement would "have no use for a so-called socialist paper that becomes a capitalist war organ."[13]

Debs had a more difficult time dealing with the leadership of the Socialist Party. In the months following the St. Louis convention, the party became a primary target of government repression. The passage of the Espionage Act in June 1917 provided the Department of Justice with the legal basis to jail opponents of the war. Party halls were raided, newspapers banned from the mails, and Socialist Party meetings were violently disrupted by vigilantes in locations throughout the country. Hundreds of socialist speakers were arrested and many were sent to prison for publicly opposing the war.[14] The Socialist Party was totally unprepared to cope with these draconian measures; it was left reeling from the blows.

New York City Election for Mayor

Still, opposition to the war continued to increase as illustrated by the

November 1917 election for mayor of New York City. The incumbent, John Purroy Mitchel, a reform Democrat standing as an independent, was an ardent supporter of the war effort. His official Democratic opponent, John Francis Hylan, a Brooklyn municipal court judge, maintained tight links to Tammany Hall and avoided any discussion of the war.[15] This left Morris Hillquit, one of the most influential figures in the Socialist Party, as the sole candidate advocating an immediate peace.

Hillquit's campaign attracted the enthusiastic support of a wide range of New Yorkers, extending well beyond the party's traditional base of support in the Jewish neighborhood of the Lower East Side. Large crowds came to hear Hillquit call for "a speedy and a general peace," one that would not necessitate the "mean humiliation" of any of the combatants. Hillquit pointed to the peace proposals of the Petrograd soviet in Russia, which emphasized the need for a peace treaty "without punitive measures or forcible annexations."[16]

Hillquit made it clear that he was not a pacifist. He was prepared to use force when necessary, but when it came to "a war of mutual destruction" into which the workers of the United States had been "forced by the ruling classes," that when socialists were "asked to endorse or to support such a war," they became the "most embittered pacifists."[17]

By presenting the critique of the war being advanced by the progressive opposition, Hillquit attracted widespread support. Needless to say, the White House was dismayed by the possibility of a Hillquit victory. The president was especially angered when Hillquit responded to a journalist's inquiry by publicly stating that he had not, and would not, purchase Liberty Bonds. He added, "I am not going to do anything to advance the war."[18]

Woodrow Wilson realized that the course of the New York City election represented a major rebuff to his war policy. A few days before the election, he wrote to Attorney General Thomas Gregory concerning the "recent outrageous utterances" made by Hillquit. Although the president recognized the danger of "assisting" Hillquit by "making him a martyr," Wilson still urged Gregory to seriously consider the grounds for an indictment under the Espionage Act.[19]

Gregory informed the president that Hillquit had "been very close to the line a number of times." Still, prosecuting him "would enable him to pose as a martyr." Agents of the Bureau of Investigation were monitoring "the situation rather carefully," and, when the time came, Gregory would proceed to prosecute Hillquit with "a great deal of pleasure."[20]

In the end, Hillquit lost and John Hylan, the candidate of the Democratic Party machine, was swept to victory. Still, Hillquit did very well, winning 21 percent of the total vote, nearly matching Mitchel's poll.[21] Hillquit's vote total was particularly impressive given the long history of Tammany Hall and its use of fraudulent voting practices. The New York City election for mayor convinced the federal government of the need to intensify its pressure on the Socialist Party.

THE SOCIALIST PARTY APPROACHES THE GOVERNMENT

Socialist Party leaders understood that the federal government was targeting them and they began looking for a way out of this dilemma. In December 1917, an influential socialist approached President Woodrow Wilson with a plan that would enable the party to drop the stance it had taken at the emergency convention in return for a promise that the federal government would end its concerted campaign of repression. Seymour Stedman, a prominent attorney, spoke with Senator James Hamilton Lewis, an Illinois Democrat and an ardent supporter of the war and the administration. Stedman informed Lewis that he had been given the "authority" from Eugene Debs to undertake this initiative. (Stedman was a personal friend of Debs, although not a political ally.) According to Lewis, Stedman claimed that if the president would "send for Debs and ask Debs to aid in support of the war," then Debs would go to the White House and "oppose all socialists who were using socialism as [grounds for] opposition to the nation's war."[22]

Although Lewis did not recommend this proposal, he did pass it on to the White House. Still, Lewis was concerned that the president would be embarrassed if he were to publicly issue an invitation to

Debs, only to have it spurned. Lewis, therefore, advised Wilson to not invite Debs to the White House until a reliable "friend" of the administration approached him and confirmed "his *sure* course."[23]

Wilson understood how sensitive this issue was and thus the need for secrecy. He therefore wrote an informal note to Joseph Tumulty, the president's secretary and de facto chief of staff, stating that he did not "like to answer this in writing" and that Senator Lewis should be informed of the White House response by telephone. The president had decided he did "not think it would be wise" to "send for Debs." Wilson did not trust the outcome of such a publicly held meeting, in part because of the divisions within the Socialist Party. The result could be "serious embarrassments" as the president became involved in internal disputes among socialists. In the end, Thomas Brahany, Tumulty's assistant, read the president's note to Lewis over the telephone and the initiative went no further.[24]

In fact, Debs would never have agreed to publicly support the war effort and he would not have agreed to meet with the president under the restrictive conditions being proposed. Stedman's initiative reflected the eagerness of the Socialist Party's leadership to reach an agreement with the federal government to forestall further repression. Moderates such as Stedman and Hillquit realized that the rank and file would not agree to drop the party's open opposition to the war as long as Debs continued to publicly condemn the war effort. Although the initial approach made by Stedman was quickly derailed, a shift in the SP's position on the war remained a credible possibility.

Fourteen Points

The problems confronting the party were made even more difficult by the twists and turns of the global conflict. In November 1917, the Bolsheviks overthrew the provisional government of Alexander Kerensky and announced that they were prepared to negotiate with the German government. The Bolsheviks followed up their call for peace by publishing the secret treaties that had been signed by the UK, France, and Italy in agreement with tsarist Russia. The treaties conceded all of Poland to Russia, while also granting France the disputed territory of Alsace-Lorraine and the occupation of a significant section of Germany.[25] The publication of the secret treaties and the Bolsheviks' call for an immediate end to the war were received with popular acclaim throughout the world. This forced the United States and its allies to respond.

In December, Woodrow Wilson answered the Bolsheviks in his State of the Union speech to Congress. The president continued to insist that German militarism "must be crushed," but he also conceded that the war should "not end in vindictive action of any kind." He also took notice of the demand advanced by advocates for an immediate peace based on the principle of "no annexations, no reparations." Wilson found this formula to be "crude," but he was willing to consider it as the kernel of a "just idea."[26]

The president followed this speech with an address to a joint session of Congress on January 8, 1918, laying out the Fourteen Points that should guide the delineation of a peace treaty and the creation of a different postwar world. The speech was carefully crafted. Wilson supported the concept of an international organization to arbitrate disputes, the future League of Nations, and he called for mutual disarmament by all the major powers. He also promised that "the day of conquest and aggrandizement" had "gone by." Furthermore, there would be "henceforth no secret understandings of any kind." These points represented, in principle, the outlines of part of the program advanced by progressives to provide an equitable basis for a negotiated peace.[27]

Within these generalities, the president outlined the terms of a possible peace treaty. Several of these points required Germany to divest itself of all territory gained during the war. Belgium would be restored as an independent nation and Poland would become an independent state. Germany would also have to cede Alsace-Lorraine to France, an area of mixed ethnicity that had been controlled by Germany since the war of 1871. The Turkish Ottoman Empire would be dismembered and the nationalities within it granted "unmolested development of autonomous development."

There was no way that the Fourteen Points could become the starting point for a negotiated peace, since its terms required the total defeat of the Central Powers. Still, the Left was offered another basis for hope. Wilson demanded that Germany accept "the evacuation of all Russian territory." Furthermore, the United States had "a heartfelt desire and hope" that it could "assist the people of Russia to attain their utmost hope of liberty and ordered peace."

Wilson's speech left the opposition in disarray. Since the U.S. decision to enter the war, progressives had urged the president to delineate the war aims of the United States and to pursue a democratic peace. The president had outlined his war aims and had accepted, in part and in the most general terms, the progressive program for a future without wars. In addition, he had offered to provide aid to the Soviet Union, under certain conditions, and demanded the withdrawal of German troops. For radicals in the United States who fervently supported the soviets, this seemed a ray of hope to a beleaguered regime.

Nevertheless, the speech offered little to those who sought a rapid end to the conflict. The president made no effort to address the question of reparations, an issue that would prove to be crucial in determining the ultimate impact of the war. Furthermore, the German government would never agree to cede Alsace-Lorraine to France without any effort to determine the will of that region's populace. The terms outlined in the Fourteen Points would never be acceptable to Germany or its allies. Furthermore, Wilson was clear that the United States intended to continue the conflict to the finish, that is, the total defeat of the Central Powers.

Although the president's speech caused confusion within the ranks of the Socialist Party, developments in Russia were even more telling. The Russian delegation to the peace negotiations, led by Leon Trotsky, soon discovered that the German government was intent on driving a hard bargain, forcing the Soviet government to cede much of the territory seized by a series of Russian tsars. In January 1918, as peace talks stalled, the Germans resumed their attacks along the Eastern Front, driving rapidly into Soviet territory. Convinced that they had no choice, the Bolsheviks agreed to sign an unfavorable separate peace. In March 1918, the German and Russian governments signed the Brest-Litovsk Treaty, under which the Soviet Union relinquished much of Poland and the Ukraine, but retained power in Russia itself.[28]

Sentiment within the Socialist Party of America had been overwhelmingly favorable to the Bolshevik Revolution from the start. Even moderate leaders such as Morris Hillquit lavishly praised the new Soviet government. This uncritical enthusiasm was more fervently felt among the Socialist Party's left-wing radicals, Debs included.

The German invasion of Soviet territory in early 1918 incensed the radical wing of the Socialist Party. Defense of the Soviet Union was seen as a paramount objective. To many on the Left, Germany became the primary enemy, and opposition to the U.S. war effort receded in importance.

SOCIALISTS AS OVERSEAS PROPAGANDISTS

In the aftermath of the president's Fourteen Points, the Socialist Party's leadership felt even more isolated. Eager to reach an accommodation with the government, the party publicly moved even further from its initial stance of militant resistance to the war. In private, key leaders looked for a strategy that would conciliate the administration, but that would not require an uncritical endorsement of the war effort.

In early March 1918, Hillquit gave a speech in which he argued that the president had aligned himself with the fundamentals of the socialist peace program and thus was "standing behind the Socialists." Hillquit understood that this formulation would not be sufficient to satisfy the Wilson administration. He went on to suggest that the workers of Germany and Austria were becoming increasingly restive and were demanding a rapid end to the war. He then argued that socialists were "better equipped" than anyone else to formulate and present convincing propaganda to the working class of the Central Powers.[29]

Upon reading a report of this speech in the press, Adolph Germer, the party's national secretary, wrote to Hillquit agreeing that the Socialist Party "ought to change" its policy and "follow a course such as that outlined" in the speech. Accordingly, "We ought to make it very clear that we are heartily in favor of encouraging unrest in the Central Empires, and that we would like to have the government open its channels for such activity in charge of the Socialist Party." Germer, along with Hillquit, insisted that in engaging in such activity the Socialist Party would not be acting "as agents of the government," but rather as the "organized body representing the socialists of the United States."[30]

This was a proposal made out of desperation. Unbeknownst to the leadership of the Socialist Party, the government had already come to the conclusion that former socialists could best communicate with the dissident socialists of Germany. Frank Bohn, who had been a leading figure in the left wing of the Socialist Party in the period immediately prior to the First World War, had been sent to Switzerland to engage in exactly the type of propaganda activities proposed by Hillquit and Germer.[31] Bohn had resigned from the SP in protest of its stance on the war in order to become an enthusiastic proponent of the administration's war policies and an uncritical booster of the president. There was no chance that the government would delegate such a sensitive project to those who continued to hold reservations concerning the administration's war policies.

Contrary to their protestations, Hillquit and Germer were suggesting that the Socialist Party become enmeshed in psychological warfare operations. Bohn traveled to Switzerland as a paid agent of the government's Committee on Public Information, where he worked closely with French military intelligence operatives. Needless to say, Bohn publicly insisted that he was in Europe in a private capacity and that he was being funded by private benefactors through a pro-war split from the Socialist Party, the Social Democratic League.

Had the Socialist Party been able to convince the administration of its unequivocal "loyalty," those sent to Europe would have become entangled in the intelligence networks of the Allied Powers. Hillquit and Germer were not naive newcomers to socialist politics. They should have understood the implications of their proposal. In any case, the offer was rebuffed by the government and the Department of Justice continued to prosecute Socialist Party activists for allegedly violating the Espionage Act.

Operation Ricker

All of these events set the context for one of the most sensitive covert operations of the First World War. The federal government, working through a few prominent socialists who had become avid advocates of the war, sought to coerce and cajole the Socialist Party into open support for it. This project was implemented in great secrecy and, even now, many of the details remain uncertain.

Allen Ricker was at the center of this clandestine operation. Born in Iowa, Ricker studied to be a minister before becoming a farmer. He was drawn into populist politics in the 1890s, standing as a candidate for Congress as a Populist in 1898. With the collapse of the Populist Party, Ricker moved into the moderate wing of the Socialist Party. After working as a party organizer in Nebraska, he was hired in December 1902 as an editorial writer for the *Appeal to Reason*. Ricker soon clashed with the management of the *Appeal* and, by the outbreak of the war, he had become the publisher and business manager of *Pearson's*, a left-wing populist magazine edited by Frank Harris, an Irish immigrant and a well-known author.[32]

Ricker opposed the drift toward war, but he rapidly altered his position once the United States entered it in April 1917, though remaining a member of the Socialist Party. Underlying Ricker's shift in his position on the war was an understanding that publications printing articles critical of the war effort would be barred from the mails. Shortly after the United States declared war on Germany, Ricker spoke with George Creel, the director of the government's Committee on Public Information (CPI) and a key presidential advisor. Creel and Ricker had known each other as progressive journalists during the prewar period. Ricker promised Creel that the editorial policy of *Pearson's* "would be conducted in conformity with the law." This conversation was followed up with a letter in May 1917 in which Ricker wrote Creel that he had come to accept the war "as inevitable" and that he wished to "cooperate" with the government.[33]

Still, Ricker realized that most of those on the Left vehemently opposed the decision to enter the war and that *Pearson's* would lose its credibility if it backed the administration. Since the magazine would "have lost three-quarters" of its readers by advancing a pro-war position, it sought a middle ground that would align it with the moderate wing of the peace movement and yet would not thoroughly antagonize the Wilson administration. This tactic would prove to be a fruitless maneuver.[34]

Ricker generally remained in the background with Harris writing the bulk of the articles in *Pearson's*. Although Harris tried to avoid provoking the post office, he also made it clear that he hoped that the president would enter into speedy negotiations to end the war. A July editorial suggested that it would "be wiser and better" if Wilson were "to use his enormous power to bring about peace." A short note in the following issue also announced the formation of the People's Council of America with its call for a rapid end to the war.[35]

Even this cautious policy was viewed with hostility by the Wilson administration. The post office began delaying delivery of copies of the magazine, bringing it to the point of bankruptcy. *Pearson's* responded by attempting to mollify the government by avoiding any discussion of the war. Ricker followed this up with a letter to Postmaster General Albert Burleson asking him to cease disrupting deliveries since *Pearson's* had abandoned even the mildest criticism of the administration's policies. Ricker enclosed this letter in a further note to Creel in which he wrote that "the bulk of the Socialist Party" was "realizing that point of view." An official shift in policy by the Socialist Party along these lines would be "helped by a spirit of tolera-tion and understanding at Washington."[35]

This was the first indication that Ricker was offering to help bring the Socialist Party into alignment with the government's policy. Although Creel agreed to help Ricker "as far as he could," the project remained in limbo.[36]

The Russian Revolution of November 1917 drastically shifted the context and brought the implicit truce to an end. As the Bolsheviks demanded an immediate end to the war and released the secret treaties signed by the UK and its allies, Harris became an enthusiastic supporter of the Soviets. His articles in the January issue of *Pearson's* would draw the ire of Burleson and the administration.

The January issue was written and published in mid-December 1917, a little more than a month after the Bolshevik Revolution. Harris lauded Lenin and the Soviet Union for their efforts to bring about an immediate end to the war. He followed this with an editorial in which he regretted that those who called for a total victory "by trampling their enemies under their feet" continued to hold on to power. In his view, this policy had "no end and no good can come" of it. Finally, Harris condemned a proposal being considered in the British Parliament that would have stripped conscientious objectors of the right to vote. In this context, he argued that "peace lovers" were "worse treated in England and America" than "in any of the despotisms."[37]

Emboldened by the Russian Revolution, Harris had placed *Pearson's* in a very risky situation. On December 19, 1917, the *New York Times* printed an article warning that federal authorities were closely examining the January issue to determine if its publication had violated the Espionage Act. In particular, articles critical of the war effort could be considered to be willful efforts to "obstruct" the recruiting of soldiers and sailors into the military by undermining confidence in the administration and its war policies. For a journal nearing insolvency, this was a threat that could prove to be disastrous. In the February issue of *Pearson's,* Harris responded by trying to downplay his criticisms of the Wilson administration by claiming that his comment on the mistreatment of conscientious objectors had referred to the vigilante violence of prowar mobs and not to the actions of the federal government.[38] This was hardly convincing. Harris was floundering.

From the perspective of the administration, the warning issued through the *New York Times* had gone unheeded. William Lamar, the solicitor of the post office, decided that the February issue of *Pearson's* was "non-mailable under the Espionage Act" and that local post offices should "destroy all copies." Furthermore, Burleson "personally examined" the February issue and decided to initiate the process leading to the revocation of the journal's second-class mailing privileges.[39]

Ricker understood that *Pearson's* would soon be forced to cease publication unless an understanding could be reached with the administration. Until this point, Ricker had used Creel as his sole channel to Woodrow Wilson, but he opted to contact an even more trusted presidential advisor. Frank Harris had many connections and friends, among them Edward House.

After meeting with Ricker, House contacted Burleson, who responded that recent issues of *Pearson's* had contained "a number of flagrant violations" of the Espionage Act. House then informed Ricker that he needed to "make some satisfactory agreement" with the post office and the administration.[40]

The choice was clear. Either *Pearson's* reversed its previous position and endorsed the administration's war policies or it would go out of business. The president's speech of January 1918 outlining the Fourteen Points for an equitable peace treaty provided Ricker with a serendipitous opportunity to shift from being a target of state repression to a vocal supporter of government policies.

In March 1918, Ricker issued a public statement calling upon socialists "to join in support of the war aims of President Wilson." The president's guidelines for peace, along with the overthrow of the Russian government a year previously, had transformed the situation. Indeed, Ricker argued, the war had become "a war by Democracy, of Democracy and for Democracy." He therefore called upon the Socialist Party to repudiate its previous position and to publicly support the war effort.[41]

This statement was followed by an editorial in the April issue of *Pearson's* providing the administration with unqualified support for its war policies. Ricker began speaking to groups of SP members, urging them to aid the effort to reject the St. Louis resolution and to press the party to adopt a position of uncritical support for the war effort.

A transcribed speech Ricker gave to a group of pro-war Socialist Party members appeared in the *New York Globe,* a newspaper aligned with the Democratic Party. It provides the clearest expression of his decision to give unequivocal support to the administration. Any nation engaged "in a most serious war" could "not afford to tolerate" an organized opposition to its policies. Instead, "support for President Wilson's policies in the war" could "save the Party from destruction."[42] Thus, Ricker was openly defending the administration's prosecution of SP members and leaders.

According to Ricker, Germany had "entered upon the war" for the "purpose of conquest." It was therefore the "supreme task" of the Allies to defeat Germany and the countries allied with it. Furthermore, the March revolution in Russia had brought to power a government eager to bring a quick end to the war. This had "forced America into the war" as a necessary means of "preventing a complete German victory." It was therefore essential for the Socialist Party to "support President Wilson's policies on the war, not grudgingly but heartily."

Ricker was not the only prominent socialist to switch from opposition to enthusiastic support for the war during the first months of 1918. Nevertheless, he was in a unique position. His access to House and Creel meant that he could act as an intermediary between the federal government and the Socialist Party. On April 20, 1918, Ricker informed House: "It would not be a difficult matter to put the whole radical movement of America behind the President on the basis of his war aims and peace terms." Four days later, Ricker met with House to propose that "the administration make a truce with the liberals and forgive their indiscretions of the past and get their united support" for the war effort.[43]

During this informal discussion, House urged Ricker to write a memorandum fully presenting his perspective. The next day, Ricker sent House a lengthy paper that House then passed on to the president. Ricker emphasized that Wilson had only won reelection in 1916 by a narrow margin. The Socialist Party's presidential candidate, Allan Benson, had received 300,000 fewer votes than Debs had received in 1912, in part because many socialists had cast their ballots for

Woodrow Wilson as the peace candidate. (The Wilson presidential campaign used the slogan "He kept us out of war.") Ricker believed that the "President owes his election to the votes of radicals, progressives, members of organized labor [and] organized farmers."[44]

Ricker conceded that most socialists and progressives had vehemently opposed the decision to enter the war. As a result, they had become Wilson's "severest critics" and the administration had responded with a crushing array of repressive measures. Still, the president's speech of January 1918 presenting the Fourteen Points as a basis for peace had dramatically altered the situation, so that many of those on the Left were ready to support the war effort. Progressives and radicals "now see clearly" that their "REAL enemies" were the bankers and business executives who funded the Republican Party. Radicals, by which Ricker meant those in the moderate wing of the Socialist Party, had come to understand that the president was their "real friend."

Thus, it was time "to get together and stop prosecutions and persecution." Accordingly, "the attitude of the administration toward the radicals should be modified. That's all that is needed to bring them in line." No public statement from the White House was required. A quiet signal that the government's policy had shifted could be sent to Ricker, who was "in a position to interpret this effectively" to those in the Socialist Party.

In relaying this memorandum to the president, House wrote, "I believe what Ricker says is largely true." Reassured that the president intended to push for a peace treaty based on the Fourteen Points, as well as the promise of a reassessment of prosecutions targeting socialists, Ricker moved forward with his plan to cajole the Socialist Party into abandoning the St. Louis resolution.

Ricker was not making idle promises. He was, indeed, intent on reversing Socialist Party policy. To underscore the impact of his efforts, Ricker sent House a letter he had received from Scott Nearing, a leader of the People's Council of America and a member of the Socialist Party. Nearing contended that the president could only implement his peace program "with the support of the liberal and radical elements of this country." The Left was anxious to support the war effort, but only if the post office stopped suppressing socialist newspapers, and if there was a "letup" in the Justice Department's repression of dissidents.[45]

Ricker made public speeches urging the Socialist Party to support the war, but most of his campaign was done more quietly and more subtly. Ricker worked closely with Carl Thompson, an influential member of the party's moderate wing. Thompson had served one term in the Wisconsin legislature. In 1916, he had sought election as the party's national secretary, only to be defeated by Adolph Germer. By 1918, he was working in Chicago for a nonprofit organization that promoted municipal ownership of the utilities.

In April 1918, Thompson wrote Ricker that he hoped to persuade "the Socialist Party to come out definitely and honestly for the war now." Thompson prevailed upon his local, which was based in one of Chicago's thirty-four wards, to endorse a resolution calling upon the Socialist Party to repudiate the St. Louis resolution and, instead, to support the war. He then went to the National Executive Committee (NEC) with the demand that a membership referendum be held on whether to adopt the Chicago local's resolution as the party's official policy. The NEC refused, arguing that the circulation of documents opposing the resolution, and favoring the St. Louis statement, could, in itself, be considered a violation of the Espionage Act and could thus open the party's leaders to prosecution.[46] Undaunted, Thompson continued to press the National Executive Committee for a referendum vote, soliciting other locals to endorse the Chicago resolution and the call for a referendum.

Behind the scenes, Ricker coordinated the effort to prod the Socialist Party into jettisoning its opposition to the war, working closely with Thompson. When Thompson wrote an article for a small journal, *Christian Socialist*, praising the war effort, Ricker requested a copy of the typescript, with the promise that 5,000 copies would be printed and then mailed to members of the Socialist Party. In addition, Ricker urged Thompson to provide him with a complete and up-to-date list of state secretaries so that he could mail a circular letter to all of them arguing for the arty to reject the St. Louis resolu-tion and provide unconditional support for the war effort.[47]

Needless to say, all of this required significant sums of money. Ricker had none, indeed *Pearson's* was struggling financially. It seems likely that the source was the secret National Security and Defense Fund, personally controlled by the president. This was already the source for another covert operation in pro-war propaganda aimed at molding domestic public opinion, the American Alliance for Labor and Democracy.[48]

Thompson had every reason to believe that Ricker was being covertly funded by the government. Ricker informed Thompson that he was "in close touch with Col. House." Specifically, House had given "the most positive assurances that Wilson will stick by the line laid down in his public addresses." The president was "striving to get hold of the military situation so that when the right time comes he will be able to make peace in accordance with his publicly declared position."[49]

Woodrow Wilson and his advisors were giving similar assurances to a variety of groups and individuals. In their view, all progressives should give their wholehearted support to the war effort, with the goal of forcing Germany to unconditionally surrender. The president would then make certain that the resulting peace was based on the principles embodied in the Fourteen Points. These nebulous assur-ances were of little or no value, but they came with vague promises of a narrower, and more benevolent, interpretation of the Espionage Act and were, therefore, alluring to some of those on the Left.

Ricker sent a copy of his letter to Thompson to House, but House was irked that his role in this clandestine operation was being brought into the open. House indicated his displeasure to Ricker, who prom-ised that he would no longer cite House as the source of assurances from high government officials. Ricker asked for another meeting with House, and the two met again on May 16, 1918. Ricker brought House up to date on the implementation of "his plan of bringing the socialists in line with the President's policy in the war." Ricker also reiterated his pledge to keep his ties to House a secret.[50]

Ricker was not only acting under the direct supervision of House, but he was also sending reports directly to the president. On May 15, 1918, Ricker wrote to Wilson that "a number of us" had "entered upon a determined campaign to change the policy and attitude of the Socialist Party."[51]

At first, Ricker's initial effort to cajole the Socialist Party into abandoning its opposition to the war seemed to be gaining considerable support. Ricker approached Hillquit to urge him to use his considerable influence to lead the Socialist Party into endorsing the war effort. Although Hillquit was unwilling to "say much" in public, he still "confided" to Ricker that he was "in sympathy" with his position.[52]

DEFENDING THE SOVIET UNION AND SUPPORT FOR THE WAR

Ricker's initial campaign to convince the Socialist Party to endorse the war effort coincided with the period when the party's activists were most conflicted in their attitude toward the war. Ricker was convinced that his plan would work, and that a pledge by the government to "go slow" in prosecuting dissidents would enable the United States to be "able to present a united front" to Germany and its allies.[53]

Indeed, the terms of debate within the Socialist Party had been substantially modified. In early May, Germer sent a message to the National Executive Committee reporting that he had received letters from local and state secretaries supporting a new statement on the war superseding the St. Louis resolution. Germer reported that there was "a difference of opinion as to just how far the Party should go." Some of those calling for a new statement held that it should be limited to a demand for "democratic war aims," while others insisted that the Allied Powers were "conducting the war for democratic principles" and thus the Socialist Party "should pledge" its uncritical "support to a successful prosecution of it."[54]

Germer was not just synthesizing the opinions coming from the Socialist party's membership. In a letter to Debs written in April 1918, Germer argued that the Party's adherence to the war effort could only occur when the Allied Powers formulated "clearly defined Democratic aims." There was no possibility that the Allies would move beyond the nebulous promises embodied in Wilson's Fourteen Points and Germer certainly understood this. He went on to state that given the arrests of socialist activists around the country, as well as "the merciless suppression of the [party's] press," there was no way that the Socialist Party could "consistently support" the Wilson administration.

Under pressure from the government, Germer and the leadership of the Socialist Party were clearly edging to a renunciation of the St. Louis resolution and a conditional support for the war. Nevertheless, they wanted the administration to initiate concrete measures to demonstrate that socialists would no longer be prosecuted under the Espionage Act and that the party's press would be allowed to publish.

DEBS WAVERS

Ricker understood that neutralizing Eugene Debs was essential if his plan were to succeed. On April 30, 1918, he wrote House that he intended to visit Debs. Winning Debs to a pro-war stance was crucial because only two people in the United States had "a bigger personal following," Woodrow Wilson and Teddy Roosevelt. According to Ricker, "The radicals will follow Debs as they will follow no other man. I believe I can swing Debs over."[55] House passed this letter on to the White House and Wilson then sent it to Postmaster General Albert Burleson, with the comment that "it would look as if these men" were "really in earnest."[56] Nevertheless, this high-level effort to pressure Debs into supporting the war ultimately failed.

Debs had not been persuaded by the president's Fourteen Points and he was not intimidated by the government's intensified attack on the Socialist Party. On March 9, 1918, Victor Berger, Adolph Germer, and three other party leaders were indicted by a Chicago grand jury for violating the Espionage Act. The indictment had been issued five weeks earlier, but it had not been publicly announced until finally approved by Washington decision makers. Shortly after the indictments were announced, Debs wrote an article condemning the government's assault on civil liberties, while maintaining his total opposition to the war. In his view, prosecutions under the Espionage Act were "pure despotism and dictatorship."[57]

For the entire eighteen months following the U.S. entry into the war, Debs remained staunchly committed to a policy of militant resistance. The president's Fourteen Points did not convince Debs to waver from this position. Only the evolving situation in Russia led Debs to question this policy. For Debs, as well as for most revolutionaries in the United States and elsewhere, the defense of the Soviet Union was of paramount importance.

Relations between the German government and the newly formed government of the Soviet Union were often contentious. Negotiations for a separate peace treaty began on December 22, 1917, but soon stalled. On February 8, 1918, the Germans signed a treaty with the Ukrainian Rada that pledged German support for the Rada's effort to regain power. Troops allied to the Soviet Union had recently defeated troops backing the Rada, as the Bolsheviks sought to regain control over territory that had previously been integrated into the tsarist Russian Empire.[58]

Shortly after this, talks between Germany and the Soviet Union broke down. On February 18, 1918, German troops resumed their advance eastward. Russian troops had become entirely demoralized and German troops moved rapidly, occupying Estonia and Latvia. At this point, the Bolsheviks reluctantly agreed to sign the Brest-Litovsk Treaty on March 3, 1918. The treaty required the Soviet Union to withdraw its claim to the Ukraine and Finland and to cede other territory as well.[59]

The signing of the Brest-Litovsk Treaty seemed to indicate that Russia had finally left the war. In spite of this, the war continued. German troops allied with the Rada steadily advanced through the Ukraine, as troops allied with the Bolsheviks slowly withdrew. The occupation of Ukraine by German troops was completed by the end of April 1918.[60]

In early April 1918, German troops landed in northern Finland in support of White forces battling Soviet troops. By the end of that month, troops allied with the Soviet regime had been forced to withdraw from Finland.[61] The situation seemed dire with German troops only a few miles from Petrograd. During these weeks, it appeared that the German government was intent on toppling the Bolsheviks from power.

In this context, Debs wavered. Sensing the opportunity to bring the Socialist Party into the pro-war camp, Ricker and his allies were seeking to pressure Debs into openly endorsing the war effort. Thompson wrote Debs that the St. Louis resolution "was absolutely impossible, unworkable," even "unsocialistic and wrong." From the beginning, Thompson had harbored misgivings that "the St. Louis resolutions were a mistake," but the renewed German invasion of the Soviet Union and the territorial concessions codified in the Brest-Litovsk Treaty had convinced him to call openly for a new, revised position.[62]

Debs continued to oppose the war, but he did indicate a willingness to substantively revise the St. Louis resolution. In a letter written to Germer on April 8, 1918, Debs held that it "would be a colossal blunder" to continue to stick closely to the St. Louis resolution. Indeed, the resolution was "flagrantly wrong," and it would "not do at all."[63]

Debs particularly emphasized Germany's "ruthless invasion" of the Soviet Union as justification for the proposed revision in the St. Louis resolution. He pointed to the resolution that had been recently issued by the Inter-Allied Labour and Socialist Conference, held in London in February 1918. The conference had issued a memorandum declaring that the people of Europe had a "common interest" in bringing the war to an end "as soon as possible." It also called for the "abandonment of any form of imperialism" and rejected a peace treaty that included the forcible annexation of territories.[64]

These fine-sounding phrases in the first section were undercut by the specific demands included in later sections. The conference memorandum demanded that Germany pay reparations "for all the damage" done to Belgium. This would require Germany to assume primary responsibility for starting the war. On the disputed territory of Alsace-Lorraine, the memorandum held that a peace treaty should include a provision declaring "null and void the gains of a brutal conquest." France would gain Alsace-Lorraine, although it would be bound to hold an ill-defined "consultation" with the populace before a final resolution of the issue.[65]

No German government would agree to such demands short of total defeat. In spite of the insertion of vaguely worded calls for a quick end to the war, the British Labour Party and the French Socialist Party, the social democratic parties that controlled the conference, were committed to supporting the war effort until Germany unconditionally surrendered.[66]

Debs focused on the vaguely worded phrases in the first section and ignored the specific demands found in the later sections. Eager to see an immediate cessation of hostilities, and thus a rescuing of the Soviet Union from what appeared to be the dire threat of a German military occupation, Debs found himself "wholly in accord with" the report of the conference, In fact, he argued that the Socialist Party "should at this time make a similar declaration." Due to these exceptional circumstances, Debs urged Germer to call for a special conference of the Socialist Party as soon as possible. Indeed, "the necessity for action" was "urgent and imperative."[67]

Debs was pushing for immediate peace negotiations, leading to a rapid end to the war and the signing of a treaty that avoided a humiliating defeat for either side. This had been the essence of the program raised by those in the moderate opposition throughout the war, including the leadership of the Socialist Party. Still, Debs's position continued to significantly differ from that of the administration. The president insisted that the war had to be carried to its final conclusion, that is, the total defeat of Germany and the Central Powers. Furthermore, his Fourteen Points fell far short of the call for a just peace treaty as supported by opponents to the war.

An article printed in the May 1918 issue of a journal linked to the left wing of the Socialist Party, but almost certainly written that April, sheds further insight into Debs's stance at this juncture. Debs again called for the convening of a special conference, reiterating that the Socialist Party could "no longer stand on the St. Louis platform." Although this resolution had been "sound and satisfactory" in its essential premises, "some of its phrasing was unfortunate." Indeed, their mere circulation had become "criminal offenses" under the Espionage Act. Debs concluded that those statements within the St. Louis resolution that had "been outlawed should be eliminated."[68]

In addition to the government's repression of the antiwar opposition, there had been "extraordinary and unexpected developments" during the intervening year. The German government had sought "to annihilate social democracy in Russia and reduce that great people to a nation of vassals." Furthermore, Debs argued, the German people showed no signs of organizing a revolt to topple the Kaiser. Debs left open the appropriate response to these developments. Although it was "absolutely necessary" to formulate a new position on the war, he did not "propose to state what the attitude and declaration of the party should be."

DEBS REAFFIRMS HIS MILITANT OPPOSITION

Just as it appeared that Ricker would be able to cajole the Socialist Party into supporting the war effort, the context changed once again. On May 13, 1918, the German ambassador to Russia, Wilhelm von Mirbach, informed the foreign ministry in Berlin that "any further advances" by the German army "might drive the Bolsheviks into the arms of the Entente." That same day, Richard von Kuhlmann, the German foreign minister, met with General Erich Ludendorff to set war policy. Kuhlmann informed Ludendorff that the Allied Powers were making "promises" to the Soviet government to convince them to return to the war. Kuhlmann suggested it would "be very much" in the interests of Germany "if it could be announced" that military "operations in Russia were definitely finished." Ludendorff pledged that "this was now the case." The Germans immediately halted all military operations against Soviet troops. This ceasefire was soon followed up by talks between Germany and the Soviet Union, leading to an agreement supplementing the Brest-Litovsk Treaty under which the Soviet Union would pay the German government a substantial indemnity for property seized during the Russian Revolution. The end of the armed conflict between Germany and the Bolshevik regime that had been mooted for some months now became a reality.[69]

Thus, by the end of May 1918, the possibility of shifting the Socialist Party's position on the war had considerably diminished. Nevertheless, Ricker was still "proceeding along the lines" that had been previously determined. He continued to hope that "by the end of the summer" he would "have things wound up." Once the Socialist Party had been pressured into supporting the war, the post office would not have to "watch over the socialist press." A few weeks later, shortly after Debs gave his speech in Canton, Ohio, Ricker was still trying to pressure the Socialist Party into reversing its position. In a report to Wilson concerning his continuing effort, Ricker stressed his "unqualified" support for the president and the war effort.[70]

As it became clear to U.S. socialists that Germany was not intent on overthrowing the Bolsheviks, Debs returned to his previous position of militant resistance. Nevertheless, the pressure on the Socialist Party to endorse the war effort continued to intensify. In this context, pro-war forces within the Socialist Party were utilizing Debs's recent statements suggesting the need to reassess the St. Louis resolution to spuriously claim that he would soon announce his unequivocal support for the president's war policy.

Initially, Debs made his renewed determination to a militant opposition to the war clear to his immediate friends. In late May 1918, Debs responded to an inquiry from one of his closest friends, Stephen Reynolds, by insisting that he had "simply been lied about by the capitalist press" and that he had "not changed in regard to the war." Although the current situation was "a trying ordeal for us all," he "would not change" his position "to be popular or because of threats or intimidations."[71]

DEBS AND DISINFORMATION

Debs understood that he needed to clarify his views, especially since reports in several newspapers had deliberately misrepresented his position. Of course, this has frequently been a problem for dissenting voices, but in this case there are significant indications that there was a concerted and covert effort to distort Debs's views to make it appear that he had totally renounced the St. Louis resolution and that he was prepared to give enthusiastic support to the war effort.

The government understood that cajoling Debs into dropping his opposition to the administration's policy was essential if the Socialist Party was to be coerced into open support for the war. One element in the government's covert operation directed at Debs was the planting of deliberately distorted articles in local newspapers. Although the Committee on Public Information under George Creel had the primary responsibility for providing pro-war propaganda and overseeing the mainstream press, this clandestine campaign of disinformation probably originated with the army's Military Intelligence Division. One subsection of the MID, MI10, was devoted to counterintelligence. Their activities included covert operations directed at antiwar organizations such as the Socialist Party.

Debs was well aware that the mainstream press was deliberately misrepresenting his views so as to make it appear that he had abandoned his previous position and that he was now supporting the administration's policies. Misleading articles on Debs appeared in several newspapers during the first months of 1918. One of those articles appeared in February 1918 in the *Terre Haute Tribune*, Debs's hometown newspaper. The article claimed to be a distillation of an editorial Debs had recently written for a left-wing journal. According to the *Tribune*, Debs had written that the Kaiser was motivated by an "insane dream" to "conquer and militarize and rule the world." This was similar to the propaganda formulas pumped out by the government's Committee on Public Information as justification for the president's policy of refusing to negotiate a peace treaty with Germany.[72]

In fact, Debs never wavered in his belief that the war was a horrific disaster and that it should come to an end as quickly as possible. In his editorial in *Social Revolution,* he had actually called for German socialists to "hurl the Hohenzollern and Hapsburg monsters from power."[73] Socialists in the United States had always been vigorous opponents of Prussian militarism. The *Tribune* omitted any mention of another section of the editorial in which Debs lauded the Bolsheviks, who were in the process of negotiating a separate peace with Germany.

The *Tribune* article was only one among several examples of this campaign of misrepresentation. In June 1918, Debs toured Indiana both before and after his speech in Canton, Ohio. In reporting one of his speeches prior to Canton, the Marion *Leader-Tribune* reported that Debs had spoken of "the mad man who is ruling Germany, of his dream to rule the world."[74] The similarity in wording with the article from four months earlier is striking and could hardly be coincidental. Debs never used this argument, not in his articles, nor in his speech in Canton, nor in his personal correspondence. On the other hand, advocates of the government's policies frequently claimed that Germany was a militarized autocracy and that the German government, as embodied in the Kaiser, was intent upon conquering the world.

Following the speech in Canton, and while the government was considering whether to seek an indictment, Debs spoke to a large crowd in Indianapolis. An article in the *Indianapolis News* claimed that Debs had insisted that his speech had been "grossly misrepresented" in reports of the Canton speech and that he stood "with the government in the prosecution of the war."[75] Of course, the federal government would soon be in court arguing that Debs had been so strident in his opposition to the war that the Canton speech constituted a violation of the Espionage Act.

DEBS RESPONDS

The campaign of disinformation against Debs was intended to confuse and disorient rank-and-file socialists and thus to make it easier for Ricker and his supporters to push the Socialist Party into reversing its previous position and endorsing the war effort. Debs was incensed by the deliberate efforts to misrepresent his views, but he did not decide to openly challenge the spurious articles in the press until after Germany had reached a lasting agreement with the Soviet Union.

It was not a simple task for Debs to make his true position known. The mainstream press was closed to any antiwar opinion, while the socialist press was being harassed and its editors prosecuted for allegedly violating the Espionage Act. Nevertheless, on June 4, 1918, Debs issued a public statement that was ignored by the mainstream media and was only carried by two small newspapers allied with the left wing of the Socialist Party. He vehemently denied that he had "come to realize the error" of his previous position and that he had become "a pro-war advocate and [was] appealing for the support of the administration in the prosecution of the war to the bitter end." These reports were entirely false and had "no other purpose than to create dissension in the Socialist ranks."[76]

Instead, Debs reiterated his belief that "the working class had no interest in the wars declared and waged by the ruling classes of the various countries upon one another for conquest and spoils." Many Socialist Party members had been prosecuted for advocating this same point of view. Although the government had accused them of being traitors, Debs insisted that they had remained "true to our cause."

Debs further argued that there was an urgent need to convene a special convention of the Socialist Party to review the issues arising from the war. Some parts of the St. Louis resolution had set forth proposals for action that were "now impossible" and this had placed it in an embarrassing situation. At its emergency convention in April 1917, the Socialist Party had promised to organize "continuous, active and public opposition to the war through demonstrations and mass petitions." It had also pledged its "unyielding opposition" to the draft and to "the support of all mass movements in opposition to conscription."[77] In fact, the federal government had moved quickly to suppress all demonstrations against the war and had prosecuted anyone who in any way spoke or organized against the draft. A revision of this resolution in light of the unrelenting repression of the antiwar movement would have made sense. Still, even holding such a special convention would have been difficult.

Debs was convinced that it was so important that the Socialist Party clarify its position and publicly reaffirm its commitment to a total opposition to the war that he was willing to risk an organizational schism. A special convention "may result in a split of the Party," but it was still needed. The Socialist Party was being "put to a severe test," but it was essential to "remember that we are Socialists and stand our ground."

The segment of the Socialist Party press that aligned itself with the moderate wing of the national office refused to reprint Debs's statement, fearing the legal repercussions. The left-wing papers that did print it were banned from the mails. Debs could have been prosecuted under the Espionage Act, but the federal government hoped to isolate and marginalize him without making him a symbol of the antiwar resistance.

THE CANTON SPEECH

Debs's decision to give a public speech denouncing the war can only be understood in this context. Debs realized that his credibility as a radical leader had been seriously damaged by the equivocating comments he had issued during the spring of 1918. Furthermore, false and misleading articles in the mainstream press had claimed that Debs had become an uncritical supporter of the war effort. The federal government had no intention of permitting him to utilize the press to clarify his actual position. Giving public speeches allowed Debs to bypass the mails, permitting him to make his adamant opposition to the war known to Socialist Party members, as well as to the broader antiwar movement. His arrest would only further reinforce his solidarity with those who had defied the government's repressive apparatus.

In May 1918, Debs let it be known that he would soon launch a speaking tour of the Midwest, with a highlight being a speech at the annual convention of the Ohio Socialist Party, to be held in the middle of June in Canton. This would be the first extensive speaking tour undertaken by Debs since the United States had entered the war in April 1917, primarily for health reasons. Thus, the Canton speech was widely publicized weeks before it occurred.[78]

The Ohio Socialist Party had long been a mainstay of the left wing of the party. Its leadership had been instrumental in prodding the party to adopt the St. Louis resolution and several of its leaders had been imprisoned for speaking against the draft. State and federal authorities continued to target the Ohio SP, dispersing rallies and harassing social events.

The decision to hold a state convention in June 1918 was in itself an act of defiance. Law enforcement agents swarmed around the meeting area. Leslie Marcy, a leading figure in the publication of the *International Socialist Review*, a theoretical journal aligned with the left wing of the SP, was arrested during the convention for distributing antiwar literature.[79]

In this climate of intense repression, everyone understood that any radical speaking out against the war or the draft would likely be prosecuted under the Espionage Act. The platform adopted by the delegates during the first day of the convention avoided any mention of the war.[80]

An open-air rally in a public park, featuring Debs, was scheduled for Sunday, June 16, 1918, as the final event of the state convention. Merely holding such a rally represented yet another act of defiance. Three leading members of the Ohio Socialist Party, Charles Ruthenberg, Alfred Wagenknecht, and Charles Baker, were serving one-year sentences at the Stark County Workhouse for antiwar speeches given the previous year. Nimisila Park was across the street from the jail and the audience listening to Debs could see the jailhouse behind him. Debs's decision to speak at the Ohio Socialist Party convention was a direct challenge to the president and his war policies and the government treated it as such.

While still at his hotel, Debs was interviewed by Clyde Miller, a reporter from the *Cleveland Plain Dealer*. Miller was an enthusiastic supporter of the war, so Debs had every reason to be cautious in his answers. Nevertheless, he told Miller, "I am against the war with every drop of blood in my body." When asked his current opinion of the St.

Louis resolution, Debs reiterated that he had not altered his position: "I approved the spirit and substance of that platform at the time of its adoption." Still, he had come to "favor a restatement of the Party's attitude in the light of recent developments." Debs praised the Russian Revolution of November 1917, arguing that the Party's revised position would have to take the impact of that revolution into account.[81]

Debs proceeded from his hotel to the Stark County Workhouse, where he briefly visited with the three Ohio socialist leaders imprisoned there. His discussions at the jail reinforced his intention to challenge the government. The prisoners informed Debs that, as political prisoners, they had refused to do custodial work, cleaning the bathrooms and the like, and had been severely punished for this act of defiance. As Debs later told the assembled crowd, the three prisoners had "had their hands cuffed together, and their bodies strung up for 8 hours at a time" for refusing to do "menial, filthy services that were an insult to their dignity."[82] This form of torture, handcuffing a prisoner to the bars of the cell with arms raised and feet barely touching the ground for hours at a time, was frequently used in federal penitentiaries, as well as state and county prisons, during this period. Still, it was torture and it was a cruel, if not unusual, form of punishment.

Debs then crossed the street and joined the rally. Several speakers preceded Debs, state and local leaders who called for unity and criticized the repressive actions of the government. Marguerite Prevey, an activist from Akron, Ohio, and one of the most prominent members of the party's left wing, acted as chair of the rally.

Debs then addressed the crowd of between 1,200 and 3,000. As he spoke, several Bureau of Investigation agents and Canton police officers observed. Volunteer agents from the American Protective League, a corporate-sponsored organization of pro-war zealots working as an auxiliary to the Department of Justice, circulated throughout the crowd demanding that every male of draft age present his registration card. Fifty-five men were arrested and detained for not having a draft registration card, or refusing to show one.[83]

Debs understood that he had to be careful in how he phrased his opposition to the war. Any statement that directly challenged conscription, or urged socialists to demonstrate in opposition to the war, might well lead to police officers and federal agents forcibly dispersing the crowd and immediately arresting Debs.[84] Debs understood that this was a historic moment and he wanted his views on the record and in full.

The speech was long, more than two hours, but it was received with enthusiastic applause. Two stenographers were paid to record the entire speech. One had been retained by the Bureau of Investigation, while the other had been employed by the Socialist Party.[85] Debs's speech covered a wide variety of issues from the fundamentals of socialism to the need to defend the right of free speech during wartime and the critical role of dissidents throughout U.S. history. In an incisive comment, he rejected the entire myth of the American dream of social mobility. Debs assured his audience that he had "never had much faith in leaders" and that he stood "with the rank and file every day of the week." Indeed, "When I rise, it will be with the ranks and not from the ranks."[86]

Only a small part of the speech related to the war. Debs carefully phrased his formulations, totally avoiding the most sensitive topic, conscription. Nevertheless, his terse comments were compelling. They would provide the Department of Justice with the evidence it required to prosecute Debs under the Espionage Act. Debs insisted that he had "no earthly use for the Junkers of Germany, and not one particle more use for the Junkers in the United States." He urged his listeners to join the Socialist Party and to work toward a better world. Those in the working class had to know that they were "fit for something better than slavery and cannon fodder."[87]

Debs then came to the core of the issue. The Bolsheviks had recently published the secret treaties signed by the Allied Powers prior to the entry of the United States into the war. These treaties divided up the Ottoman Empire between Great Britain and France, gave all of Poland to Russia and part of Germany along the west bank of the Rhien to France. Even after the treaties were made public, the British government refused to repudiate them. Ultimately, the secret treaties would create the framework for the Treaty of Versailles signed by the victorious powers at the conclusion of the war. Debs was convinced that the secret treaties demonstrated that "the purpose of the Allies" was "exactly the purpose of the Central Powers," Germany and its allies, that is, imperial conquest.

The Canton Speech in Perspective

The Canton speech remains a turning point in U.S. history. Some historians have argued that Debs did not expect to be arrested. In his initial report to Washington, U.S. Attorney Edwin Wertz informed Attorney General Thomas Gregory that Debs had been "very careful not to violate the law." Indeed, Debs remarked during the speech that he had to "be extremely careful and prudent in choosing what to say and how to say it."[88]

Nevertheless, Debs had seen many of his comrades jailed for making comments similar to those he used in the course of the Canton speech. Debs was careful because he wanted to be able to complete the speech, not because he hoped to avoid arrest.

Debs made this very clear when he spoke in early June 1918, prior to the Canton speech, to Noble Wilson, his manager during his 1916 congressional campaign. He was now ready to openly challenge the war effort: "Of course, I'll take about two jumps and they'll nail me, but that's all right." In a later interview with David Karsner, a Socialist Party journalist and personal friend, that was held in the Atlanta Federal Penitentiary, Debs made his decision crystal clear: "I elected to go to prison. The choice was deliberately made."[89]

Another argument that has been frequently advanced holds that Debs gave the Canton speech because he was seeking martyrdom. At times, Justice Department officials made this assertion, although it directly contradicts the claim that Debs had carefully worded his speech to avoid arrest. In any case, the argument is false. The United States entered the war in April 1917, fourteen months prior to the Canton speech. Throughout that time, Socialist Party members were being imprisoned for their resistance to the war effort. Debs could have forced the issue earlier if he had been eager to be thrown into jail and thus be made into a martyr.

Finally, historians have argued that Debs gave the Canton speech while unsure of his own position on the war. Debs had softened his position during the spring of 1918, moving toward the position held by the moderate wing of the Socialist Party. He did this at a time when it appeared Germany was intent on overthrowing the Soviet regime. Nevertheless, by June 1918 Debs had returned to his previous perspective of unwavering resistance to the war. By giving a speech at a mass rally at the convention of the Ohio Socialist Party, Debs was forcing the government to respond, thereby undercutting the deliberately misleading newspaper reports suggesting he was ready to publicly support the war. Debs was not seeking martyrdom, but he was stiffening the resolve of the Socialist Party, ensuring that it would rebuff the covert effort of the federal government to co-opt and intimidate it into submission.

Debs made this explicitly clear in his Canton speech. He cited articles in the mainstream press that had suggested he now supported the war, having "undergone a marvelous transformation" and thus had become "a patriotic socialist." This was a "deliberate misrepresentation" of his views, whose "purpose was to sow the seed of dissension in our ranks."

A letter written by Theodore Debs, Eugene's brother and close confidant, confirms this point. Shortly after the Canton speech, Allen Cook, an attorney and a leader of the Canton Socialist Party local, wrote to Debs seeking further information. Theodore responded for his brother, as he often did, insisting that Eugene's position had "been misrepresented," and that "his attitude" had "not changed in the slightest." Indeed, it was "for this" that Eugene Debs had come "under indictment" after making the Canton speech.[90]

The government understood that Debs had made the Canton speech in order to clarify his views to the wider public. In March 1919, Judge David Westenhaver, who had presided over Debs's trial in federal district court for allegedly violating the Espionage Act, responded to a request from the Justice Department for his opinion on a possible commutation of Debs's prison sentence. Westenhaver argued that a commutation should not be granted to Debs. Prior to the speech, there had been rumors that "Debs and his followers [had] repudiated the antiwar program of the Socialist Party." Westenhaver was convinced that "a large part of his endeavor" had been undertaken "to convince his following that he and they should do everything in their power to carry out the antiwar policies" formulated in the St. Louis resolution.[91]

INDICTMENT

From the start, there was a general understanding that the decision to initiate judicial proceedings against Debs far transcended the narrow issue of his alleged violation of wartime statutes silencing dissent. Of course, officials of the Department of Justice had to carefully evaluate the legal questions as well. Edwin Wertz, as the U.S. attorney for the Northern District of Ohio, was convinced that the easiest and most straightforward rationale for prosecuting Debs involved charges under the Sedition Act, the statute amending the Espionage Act that had been enacted in May 1918. Specifically, Wertz argued that Debs had made statements that tended "to bring the form of government of the United States into contempt" and tended "to incite, provoke, and encourage resistance to the United States," thereby violating the Sedition Act.[92]

Although Wertz had addressed the initial letter informing the Justice Department of Debs's speech to Attorney General Thomas Gregory, it was passed on to John Lord O'Brian as head of the War Emergency Division. O'Brian focused on the legal issues raised by the Canton speech, generally avoiding the broader policy questions. O'Brian and the Justice Department had not been enthusiastic when Congress had widened the scope of the original Espionage Act to include a ban on seditious utterances and this is reflected in his advice to Wertz.

O'Brian rejected Wertz's legal arguments and instead suggested that he concentrate on constructing the case that Debs had violated the

Espionage Act of June 1917. Wertz had earlier concluded that it was "probable that he [Debs] did not violate Section 3 of the Espionage Act as it read before it was recently amended," that is, his speech did not constitute an effort to obstruct the recruiting of soldiers ito the military.[93]

It was this conclusion that O'Brian challenged. He pointed to several sections of the speech in which Debs had indicated that the war was being fought in the interests of the capitalists and not in the interests of working people, or to promote democracy. As O'Brian correctly observed, Debs had made use of several phrases, including one that referred to soldiers as "cannon fodder," that were similar to "many expressions on which successful prosecutions have been based under Section 3 of the original Espionage Act."[94]

O'Brian urged Wertz to use caution before filing charges. The case was "by no means a clear one" and was "not without serious doubts." Indeed, the Department of Justice did not feel strongly convinced that a prosecution "was advisable."[95]

In spite of these initial words of caution, O'Brian later gave his support to the decision to prosecute Debs on both legal and policy grounds. He realized that the policy issue would be decided by the president and the attorney general, but once made, he was convinced that "the prosecution met with the entire approval of the Department." Many years later, O'Brian remembered the summer of 1918 as "one of the most critical and discouraging periods of the war." Mounting casualties from intensive trench warfare created the need for a vast increase in the number of soldiers to be drafted. Although the Socialist Party had been greatly weakened by government repression, thus undercutting Debs's stature and influence, O'Brian believed that the Canton speech could have undermined morale and could, therefore, seriously impact the war effort.[96]

The issue divided the War Emergency Division. Alfred Bettman, O'Brian's deputy charged with the operational responsibility for determining who was prosecuted under the Espionage Act, was convinced that the government should ignore the Canton speech. Bettman did not doubt that Debs would be convicted if prosecuted, but he questioned whether Debs's speech had made a significant impact given the government's intensive repression of the Socialist Party. In February 1919, eight months following the speech and while the case was still on appeal, Bettman wrote that his "own feeling" had "always been that, as a leader, Debs was on the decline and that the prosecution" had "given him an influence and importance which his own attainments would never have given him." Bettman further doubted "whether the speech was effective in influencing anybody."[97]

Although Wertz's letter was sent to the War Emergency Division for legal advice, the ultimate decision rested with Attorney General Thomas Gregory and the president. Wertz had pointed out to Gregory that Debs was "a man with a national reputation" and that "there was a question of policy involved" that administration decision makers had to "pass upon" before charges could be filed. Wertz also observed that Socialist Party members were "anxious to appear in the role of martyrs."[98]

The ultimate decision on filing charges was too sensitive to be left in the hands of the War Emergency Division. Unfortunately, correspondence on this issue at the highest level of government has disappeared from the public record. Nevertheless, Clyde Miller was shown a secret cable from Attorney General Gregory to Wertz advising Wertz not to move precipitously so as not to "make a martyr" of Debs. (Miller made the contents of this cable public many years after Debs's trial.)[99]

In the end, the government decided that the risk posed by Debs was too great. Debs had made it clear that he would continue to speak out against the war, thereby becoming a rallying point for a revived antiwar movement that could hinder conscription and thus could potentially impact the course of the war. Given Woodrow Wilson's adamant opposition to granting Debs a pardon after his trial, it seems very likely that the final decision to file charges was made by the president himself.

On Saturday, June 29, 1918, Debs was indicted by a federal grand jury sitting in Cleveland. The indictment listed ten alleged violations involving several provisions of the Espionage Act, as well as some sections of the more recently enacted Sedition Act. Thus the interchange between Wertz and O'Brian led the government to utilize both approaches. Ultimately, O'Brian was proven correct in that the charge in the indictment that was upheld by the Supreme Court related to an alleged violation of the Espionage Act.

The following day, a Sunday, Debs was scheduled to appear at an open-air rally in Cleveland sponsored by the local branch of the Socialist Party. Federal agents arrested him at the park, just as he was going to speak. After spending the night in jail, he was arraigned before Judge Westenhaver, one of two judges presiding in the federal judicial district covering northern Ohio. Westenhaver released Debs on $10,000 bail, while ordering him to remain within the judicial district, or at home in Terre Haute. Westenhaver also insisted that Debs make sure that any speech he gave while on bail remained within the law. Surety for the bond was provided by Marguerite Prevey, who pledged her house as collateral.[100]

THE PARTY'S LEADERSHIP ADRIFT

By the spring of 1918, the leadership of the Socialist Party was adrift, searching for a new policy on the war that would be acceptable to the membership and yet would not leave the party as a target for government repression. In May 1918, Job Harriman, an influential member of the moderate wing of the Socialist Party, wrote to Hillquit outlining a possible plan of action. Harriman had opposed the St. Louis resolution from the start, and generally supported the war effort. Harriman proposed that "twenty-five or thirty men" should "draft a resolution stating our position in [the] most general terms." This resolution would then be adopted as the official policy of the party, supplanting the St. Louis resolution. Harriman apparently had in mind a resolution on the war that would abandon the party's previous official stance of uncompromising opposition to the war, but would still not provide uncritical support for the president's policies.[101]

It took Hillquit six weeks to reply, during which time Debs gave his speech at Canton. Hillquit pointed out that a meeting of state secretaries had been called for August. Although he saw the virtue of that body approving a new resolution on the war along the lines suggested by Harriman, he did "not have much faith in the success of such an attempt." The situation was too fluid, "full of uncertainty and contradictory features," leading to such a "wide divergence of views" within the Socialist Party that any effort to rewrite the St. Louis resolution was likely to fail.[102]

DEBS AND THE AUGUST CONFERENCE

In general, Debs refrained from directly violating the conditions set for bail, but he did travel to Chicago in August 1918 to attend the conference of Socialist Party state secretaries. Delegates at the emergency convention of the Socialist Party held in St. Louis in April 1917 had amended the party's constitution to provide for an annual conference of state secretaries as a policymaking body.[103] Debs took the considerable risk of traveling to Chicago to make sure that the state secretaries held firm and did not repudiate the St. Louis resolution.

Debs spoke on the second day of the conference, August 11. His speech was not publicized as a major event, but the conference of state secretaries was open to the public and members of the press attended. One of those covering the event, a journalist from the *Chicago Examiner*, was also a trained stenographer. He shared his notes on Debs's speech with the Bureau of Investigation. Joseph Triner, an agent of the Office of Naval Intelligence assigned to work with the Justice Department's Bureau of Investigation, accompanied the *Examiner* reporter and also observed Debs's speech.

The August speech was concise and sharply drawn, ten minutes in length. In many ways, it is a more effective speech than the one given in Canton. Debs began by observing that the Socialist Party had "been passing through what may be called a fiery ordeal." A small minority had quit to become ardent supporters of the war effort, but Debs dismissed these "desertions" as unimportant, since their departure had rid the party of "those who did not properly belong here."[104]

Debs then addressed the critical question confronting the conference. He fervently hoped that there would "be no thought on the part of any of the comrades here to change the Party's attitude toward the war." Indeed, the working class "had no place in a capitalist war." Furthermore, there was "but one war in which" Debs had "any interest" and that was "the war of the workers against the masters." Debs was "prepared to sacrifice" his freedom in the class war, "but never in any war waged by the ruling classes upon one another." Debs concluded, "We will not weaken, we will not compromise, we will not retreat an inch."

In fact, the Socialist Party had already substantially retreated from the position of militant resistance to the war it had adopted at the April 1917 Emergency Convention in St. Louis. Nevertheless, Debs's speech stopped any effort to further weaken, or even reverse, the Party's stance on the war. Debs would have been sent to jail for the Canton speech in any case, but his speech before the conference of state secretaries made it certain that the president would refuse to grant a commutation of his sentence. There would be no amnesty while Woodrow Wilson remained president. Debs would spend several years in a maximum-security prison, wasting away.

TRIAL

With few exceptions, Debs remained at his home in Terre Haute during the latter part of the summer of 1917, awaiting his trial in federal court. He was permitted to speak in northern Ohio, but most of these speeches had to be cancelled because of the pandemic spread of influenza. Thus, the federal government effectively succeeded in silencing Debs after the Canton speech.

On Monday, September 9, 1918, Debs came to trial in the Cleveland courthouse for the federal district court for Northern Ohio, with Judge Westenhaver presiding. Westenhaver was a fervent supporter of the war. Prior to becoming a federal judge, he had been a partner in a law firm with Newton Baker, the secretary of war. The first order of business was the selection of a jury. Federal district courts were allowed to set their own methods of jury selection within very wide parameters. Women did not have the right to vote in federal elections and were thus automatically excluded. In the northern Ohio federal district court, the court clerk chose the jury panel from a selected list of registered voters provided by county judges.[105] This method of jury selection was bound to exclude most Socialist Party members, or, indeed, anyone with radical or progressive views. It also screened out most blue-collar workers and farm laborers. Since the trial was expected to be lengthy, the jury was weighted toward those who had retired from the workforce.

In the end, almost all of the thirty-six men in the jury panel came from rural areas or small towns. The average age reached seventy, with the average value of assets owned estimated at between $80,000 and $100,000,[106] or about two million dollars in current prices. Thus, the jury completely failed to reflect a cross-section of the populace. On the contrary, it was a jury deliberately drawn from those predisposed to find Debs guilty.

Debs understood that the trial was not a genuine legal proceeding, but rather a political show trial, providing a spurious facade to cover the government's decision to suppress dissent. Although he refused to present a defense to the prosecution's case, which was based on a reading of the stenographic copy of the speech, he did address the jury before their deliberations.[107] Debs insisted that there was "not a word in that speech to warrant the charges set out in the indictment." His speech was "justified" under "the laws of the land," that is, the Bill of Rights of the U.S. Constitution. Debs believed that that "the right of free speech" held "in war as well as in peace."[108] Judge Westenhaver derided this opinion as the simplistic claim of a novice who knew nothing of the law and yet judicial decisions in recent years have generally upheld Debs's position.

Debs argued that the First World War resulted from inter-imperialist rivalries, as did most wars. Indeed, it was the "ruling classes that make war upon one another, and not the people." Debs was therefore determined to oppose the war. In doing so, he was "perfectly willing" to be branded "a disloyalist" and, if necessary, to "end my days in a prison cell." In sum, "I have been accused of obstructing the war. I admit it."

This was a powerful speech that boldly stated the case for unrestricted free speech in wartime. The prosecution and Judge Westenhaver generally adhered to the then prevailing position on the limits of free speech. As summarized by Westenhaver in his charge to the jury, it was not necessary to prove that Debs's speech actually affected anyone's conduct. All that was required was a showing that Debs had "attempted" to encourage his listeners to resist the war and the draft. A statement that had the "natural and reasonable probable effect" of obstructing the war effort was illegal under the Espionage Act. Furthermore, Westenhaver informed the jurors that they could conclude that Debs had "wilfully intended" to encourage resistance to the war if the "reasonably probable consequences" of his speech encouraged "disloyalty."[109]

The proceedings in the Cleveland federal court can only be understood in the context of the intense wartime hysteria generated by the government and the corporate media. In his closing argument to the jury, Wertz claimed that Debs had done "more damage to the cause of the United States than any spy Germany" had infiltrated into "the military forces of this country." Westenhaver reinforced this paranoia by admonishing the jury that it was important to weigh the evidence dispassionately, although it was "only natural that one should have feelings of righteous indignation during a time of war against any and all forms of disloyalty or seditious conduct."[110]

In this context, the verdict was a foregone conclusion. The jury came back with a guilty verdict on September 13, 1918. The next day Judge Westenhaver ordered Debs to serve a sentence of ten years.

AFTERMATH

Debs's decision to defy the government and risk prosecution undermined any chance that the Socialist Party would endorse the war effort. There was, therefore, no possibility of a secret understanding with the federal government. Nevertheless, Germer and the national leadership were careful to avoid providing government prosecutors with opportunities for additional indictments.

Shortly after the trial in the Cleveland federal district court, the Socialist Party considered a plan to distribute thousands of copies of Debs's Canton speech. An article in the Canton newspaper provided a grandiose version of these plans, reporting that "millions of copies" would be distributed.[111]

Socialist Party leaders were well aware of the risks involved and were eager to minimize them. As the party's national secretary, Germer had an edited version of the Canton speech prepared, which he then sent to Hillquit for review. (Hillquit was a prominent attorney, as well as a leading member of the party's moderate wing.) Germer advised Hillquit that the editors had "eliminated what might be considered objectionable." Nevertheless, Germer asked Hillquit to carefully examine the proposed pamphlet and to highlight any wording that was "not entirely safe," so that further excisions could be made.[112]

At this point, October 1918, with the war coming to an end, Debs intervened. He would only agree to publication of the Canton speech if it was printed in full. Since the Supreme Court had ruled that the speech was "seditious" and it therefore could not be sent through the mails, it was "impossible to circulate" and publication would have to wait until the war ended. Debs also insisted on the correction of a "number of errors in the stenographic report" prior to publication.[113]

William J. Burns, the noted detective then heading his own private detective agency, provided Joseph Tumulty, the president's secretary, with a garbled version of this debate within the Socialist Party. He had "learned from an authentic and confidential source" that the Socialist Party would be distributing copies of the Canton speech "in the hope that it would bring about their arrest and conviction, and thus fill and overcrowd" the jail system.[114]

This message was sent on to the Justice Department's War Emergency Division, which was charged with developing a strategy to meet this threat. Alfred Bettman, who had initially questioned the decision to prosecute Debs, was placed in charge. He notified his immediate superior, John Lord O'Brian, that Socialist Party meetings would be "covered throughout the United States," that is placed under intensive surveillance by intelligence agents. Still, he doubted that there would be "a sufficient number" of SP members willing to risk prosecution "to cause any serious overcrowding" of the prisons. Just to be sure, Bettman was preparing to stifle this threat of peaceful civil disobedience by "prosecuting the leaders." If necessary, he was also prepared to arrest and detain anyone circulating Debs's speech, even if this required holding them in detention camps.[115]

Intimidated by the threat of prosecution, the Socialist Party refrained from circulating the speech during the last weeks of the war. It was some time after that a complete version of the Canton speech finally appeared. Debs permitted David Karsner to include extracts of the Canton speech in a book that appeared in the latter part of 1919. (Karsner, a member of the Socialist Party and a journalist at the *New York Call*, became a close friend of Debs.) In October 1920, Debs authorized the Socialist Party to reprint the entire speech, with the proviso that it include a foreword informing readers that he had "never had the chance to go over it" and that the version produced by the stenographer hired by the Ohio Socialist Party contained "some minor errors and inaccuracies" but was nevertheless "substantially correct."[116]

While the Socialist Party hesitated, the federal government acted quickly to silence Debs. Anxious to see Debs in jail, where he could not make any public appearances and where his ability to communicate through the press would be sharply limited, government prosecutors appealed to the U.S. Supreme Court to take the case directly, bypassing the Circuit Court of Appeals. On January 27, 1919, the Supreme Court heard oral arguments, a little more than four months after the district court trial in Cleveland. Six weeks later, on March 10, 1919, the Supreme Court issued a unanimous ruling, written by Oliver Wendell Holmes Jr., upholding the guilty verdict.

On the same day, Debs issued a statement denouncing the Supreme Court decision. The case involved "the fundamental right of free speech." Furthermore, he insisted that he stood "by every word of the Canton speech." On the verge of being sent to prison, Debs stood firm. He despised the Espionage Act and he defied "the Supreme Court and all the powers of capitalism to do their worst."[117]

SUMMARY

The Wilson administration was intent on silencing the Socialist Party as an organized force critical of the war. Initially, the government attempted to pressure the SP's leadership into abandoning its opposition to the war. Working through two influential members of the moderate wing of the Socialist Party, Allen Ricker and Carl Thompson, the government hoped that it could sway the party by vague promises of an equitable peace and a more tolerant stance toward dissidents.

The government understood that the Socialist Party would not shift its position as long as Debs continued to stand firm in his opposition to the war. Thus Debs became a target of a clandestine operation that involved a number of tactics. These ranged from newspaper reports that deliberately falsified his position to efforts by Ricker and Thompson aimed at convincing him to modify his views. By the summer of 1918, Debs had concluded that it was necessary to publicly assert his continued resistance to the war effort. His speech in Canton, Ohio, was a definitive signal that the administration's campaign to coerce Debs had failed and that the Socialist Party would not be pressured into drastically altering its stance toward the war.

The federal government then used the Canton speech as the basis for prosecuting Debs for allegedly violating the Espionage Act. Sending an individual as well respected as Debs to prison was a powerful signal that anyone who opposed the war could wind up in jail. Debs was already old and frail when he was first incarcerated. The effort to gain his freedom would become a major issue of controversy in the postwar period.

5

The Struggle to Free Eugene Victor Debs

A century ago, Eugene Debs was one of the most celebrated figures in the United States. Even his political opponents praised his personal integrity and his willingness to sacrifice his own interests to a broader cause. This was one factor that made the campaign to gain his freedom such a popular cause. There was also the very real possibility that Debs would die while still in prison. At first, the Socialist Party dominated the amnesty campaign, but as it became clear that Woodrow Wilson would summarily reject any effort to free Debs, the campaign gained momentum and included a broader circle of supporters.

In spite of the increasing support for Debs's release, Wilson adamantly refused to budge. Debs was still in prison when Warren Harding came to power in March 1921. Harding stalled as he tried to spin the issue to his advantage. The amnesty campaign continued to build as mainstream politicians joined with activists from the Left in demanding that Debs be released immediately. Finally, Harding commuted Debs's sentence in December 1921, two and a half years after he had first been imprisoned.

The campaign to free Debs is particularly interesting because it highlights the gap between those who believe that victories are won in the street and those who believe that gains are won by persuading those in power by quietly lobbying them. The Socialist Party was clear that Debs could only be freed if public opinion was mobilized through petitions and demonstrations. On the other hand, Samuel Gompers and the leadership of the American Federation of Labor were eager to protect their access to Washington decision-makers. Thus Gompers actively opposed every effort to build public pressure on the government to release Debs.

A Respite Denied

Once the U.S. Supreme Court upheld Debs's conviction by a unanimous vote on March 10, 1919, the question of a presidential pardon became urgent. Even before Debs was sent to prison, the campaign to free him had begun. In the spring of 1919, Woodrow Wilson was in Versailles negotiating the peace treaty that concluded the First World War. Nevertheless, he found that the *Debs* case could not be ignored. The newly appointed attorney general, Alexander Mitchell Palmer, understood that he would soon be pressed to recommend a pardon for Debs, so he immediately asked Judge David Westenhaver, who had presided at the initial trial, for his confidential recommendation. Although Westenhaver conceded that Debs had limited his remarks to "guarded expressions which were obviously intended to avoid punishment," still Debs had been intent on furthering "the action program of the Socialist Party" as adopted at the Emergency Convention in April 1917.

Westenhaver was incensed by Debs's politics and believed this provided an appropriate basis for his incarceration. Debs had shown himself to be "a revolutionary internationalist" who was determined to reject his "patriotic obligation to the United States." Indeed, "the only natural tendency and effect of his conduct" was "to produce social and economic revolution by violent force." Yet Westenhaver had to reluctantly concede that Debs denied any intent to bring about a socialist transformation "by other than peaceful means."[1]

Westenhaver's letter to Palmer is indicative of how dangerous the "natural and reasonable consequences" doctrine was to the right of dissidents to freely express their views. Although Debs was indicted for obstructing the draft, and not for his commitment to a socialist future, the judge who presided over the trial remained focused on his political perspective.

Westenhaver's letter was passed on to Alfred Bettman, the deputy director of the Justice Department's War Emergency Division, who was in the process of reviewing all prosecutions undertaken under the Espionage Act. Although Bettman made it clear that he still doubted the utility of imprisoning Debs, he also believed that the "question of clemency" in this matter was "a political question." Thus, he declined to present his own views on the issue.[2]

As the date for Debs's incarceration came closer, Joseph Tumulty, the president's personal secretary and chief of staff, was bombarded with requests that Debs be pardoned. Tumulty decided to pass on one of the more salient requests to France. Charles Edward Russell had been one of the most prominent members of the Socialist Party to quit in protest of its anti-war stance. He then became a vocal proponent of the war effort and a vitriolic critic of the Socialist Party. In his view, those who criticized the administration's war policies, and who were "talking this most peculiar peace stuff," were either "ignorant of the effect of their work" in demoralizing public opinion or "conscious traitors" and should be prosecuted.[3]

Russell was joined by Allan Benson and Frank Walsh in making a plea to the president for Debs. Benson had been the Socialist Party presidential candidate in 1916, although he had left the party in order to support the war effort. Walsh was an influential progressive who had chaired the U.S. Commission on Industrial Relations. The three of them wired the White House urging Wilson to grant a "respite," thereby postponing the day when Debs would be imprisoned. In sending this cable on to Paris, Tumulty pointed out that Russell had been a valued "friend" to the president during the war and that he had "done much to stem the tide of Bolshevism in this country."[4]

As busy as Woodrow Wilson was at the peace negotiations, he realized that this was an issue that could not be dismissed. Instead, he passed the nominal responsibility on to Palmer, while at the same time making his own position clear. Two days after receiving Tumulty's cable, Wilson wired Palmer with the gist of the initial cable from Russell, Benson, and Walsh. The president was "willing to grant a respite" if Palmer requested it, but he also stated his "doubt [as to] the wisdom" of granting clemency to Debs.[5]

Palmer understood that the president had made his intentions evident and he responded accordingly. He therefore sent a message to the White House that he was "opposed to granting any respite" to Debs. Palmer insisted that Debs had been "given an eminently fair trial," a highly doubtful argument. Furthermore, Debs had denounced the Supreme Court's decision upholding his conviction, while continuing to insist that his case involved "the fundamental right of free speech." Palmer insisted that this attitude of "defying the administration of the law" made "it imperative" to deny the request for a respite or pardon "at the present time." Tumulty forwarded Palmer's message with his own comment stating that he agreed with the attorney general's advice.[6]

DEBS IN PRISON

On April 12, 1919, Debs received a telephone call from Edwin Wertz, the government prosecutor at his trial, ordering him to report to Cleveland the next day. Upon arriving at the main train station the following morning, Debs was placed under arrest by Bureau of Intelligence agents, who took him to a small train station on the outskirts of Cleveland. The BI agents were to escort Debs to the West Virginia State Penitentiary in Moundsville. Since Justice Department officials were worried that mass protests would be organized at railroad stations along the way, the agents took a circuitous route using regional trolleys and trains to avoid large cities. David Karsner, a sympathetic journalist, had accompanied Debs to Cleveland. He then followed Debs and the agents as they went to the train. Karsner then boarded the train and held discussions with Debs throughout the long trip.[7]

Debs told Karsner that if the president offered him an

unconditional pardon he would "refuse to accept it." It was essential that a pardon be immediately extended to all of those in prison for allegedly violating the Espionage Act, most of whom were IWW activists. Unless this general amnesty occurred, Debs pledged that he "won't come out."[8] Karsner's article based on this interview was widely distributed and read. Woodrow Wilson had no intention of releasing Debs under any circumstances, but the issues raised by Debs would become more critical after Warren Harding entered the White House in March 1921.

The next day, April 13, 1919, Debs arrived at Moundsville, a maximum security prison holding men convicted of serious felonies such as murder and rape. The prison was overcrowded with two, and sometime three prisoners confined to five-foot by seven-foot cells. Rules were strict and prisoners were granted few visits. Mail was strictly limited in terms of both letters sent and received.[9]

When first incarcerated, Debs was sixty-three years old and in poor health. His time in Moundsville could have been disastrous, but he developed a friendship with the warden, Joseph Terrell. He was assigned light duty in the prison hospital and was given his own small room. Terrell gave Debs special permission to receive the many letters sent to him. Once a week, he was allowed to send a brief letter to his brother Theodore, with scribbled notes outlining a response to the letters sent to him. In a sharp break with usual practice, Terrell permitted Mabel Dunlap Curry to visit the prison and spend an hour with Debs alone in the prison office. Curry came from Debs's hometown, Terre Haute, Indiana, where she was active as a suffragist and feminist. Curry and Debs had been in an intimate relationship since 1916, although both remained nominally married.[10]

At first, Terrell had been fearful of an armed attack on the prison, either by sympathizers seeking to forcibly free Debs or vigilantes intending to summarily punish him. In response, Terrell hired more guards and installed additional floodlights along the prison walls. Needless to say, no raids materialized and the prison remained quiet. West Virginia authorities requested an additional $500 a month from the federal government to defray the costs of the added security.[11]

Just as Debs adjusted to his new situation, the federal government ordered his transfer to the Atlanta Federal Penitentiary. Unofficial reasons given for this move ranged from concerns that the Moundsville prison would be stormed and the additional costs of heightened security that this required to the opening of a new wing at the Atlanta facility.

The transfer to Atlanta, which took place on June 14, 1919, caused a significant deterioration in Debs's prison conditions. Debs had no doubt that the Wilson administration was punishing him for his determined refusal to submit. He told one of his visitors, Joseph Sharts, an Ohio attorney, that "Woodrow Wilson and his political crowd" had ordered the transfer from the Moundsville prison in order to either "kill or break" him. Indeed, Debs expected to die in the Atlanta Federal Penitentiary and he nearly did.[12]

Frederick Zerbst, the warden in Atlanta, was a strict disciplinarian. Although he respected Debs and did not want him to die while incarcerated, he was far less willing than Terrell to bend the prison rules. Upon his arrival, Debs was placed in a cell with five other prisoners. He ate the usual prison food, cheap, starchy, and unhealthy. Furthermore, he was confined to his cell for fourteen hours a day from 5 p.m. to 7 a.m. Debs was granted one concession—he was assigned light clerical duties in the prison clothing store.[13]

These were harsh conditions and they would have been difficult to endure for any elderly person with severe health problems. The intense summer heat and humidity acted as the tipping point. Debs spent his first three months in Atlanta at the height of the summer season. His weight plummeted from 185 pounds to 160 and he suffered from blinding headaches, with his heart rate fluctuating erratically. Not surprisingly, Debs found it difficult to adjust to his new surroundings and was frequently depressed. When Alexander Berkman, the noted anarchist, was released from the Atlanta Penitentiary in October 1919 to be deported to Russia, he told friends that Debs appeared to be "very near to death."[14]

Determined to not seek any special privileges, Debs said nothing to the prison authorities as his health rapidly deteriorated. A friend and visitor, Marguerite Prevey, spoke to the warden, warning him of the crisis situation. Zerbst understood the importance of keeping his famous prisoner alive and so in mid-August, two months after the transfer, he decided to offer Debs a light job in the prison hospital. This shift from the main prison block, as well as the advent of autumn, kept Debs from immediately dying, but his time in the Atlanta Penitentiary shattered his health. After his transfer to hospital duties, he gained weight and visitors noticed a distinct improvement in his well-being. Nevertheless, Debs's supporters believed that it was essential that he be released as rapidly as possible.[15]

Woodrow Wilson Rejects Amnesty

With Debs actually in prison, the pressure on the administration intensified. The president's adamant refusal to free Debs threatened the unity of the broad coalition that had been instrumental in reelecting Wilson in 1916. Influential progressives who had supported the war despite its unpopularity were incensed by the denial of a pardon for Debs.

At first, Palmer continued to align his views with those of the president, insisting that he could not recommend a pardon as long as Debs remained defiant. Yet by the summer of 1919 it had become clear that prestigious progressives were ready to break with the administration, even those who had supported the war effort.

During the war, several leading members of the Socialist Party had quit to become vocal supporters of the war effort. In spite of their sharp differences with Debs, these former socialists admired him for his integrity and sought his release from prison. John Spargo was the most prominent member of this group and the only one to regularly gain access to the White House. Spargo had been a central figure in the Socialist Party until 1917, when he resigned after the party's decision to oppose the war. After meeting with Wilson, Spargo had joined Gompers and the leadership of the American Federation of Labor in forming the American Alliance for Labor and Democracy. The new organization sought to counter antiwar sentiment within the working class with a propaganda blitz financed secretly from the president's National Security and Defense Fund. Spargo was then dispatched to Italy, where he served as a representative of the government's Committee on Public Information, working with pro-war socialists to quash the increasingly popular demands that Italy leave the war. While in Italy in the fall of 1918, Spargo "spent many an hour" with Benito Mussolini discussing an effective strategy to counter the rise of the Communist Party in Italy.[16]

Spargo had been one of the most vehement critics of domestic opponents of the war, including the Socialist Party of America. In a public statement issued in June 1917 justifying his resignation, Spargo denounced the Socialist Party as "unneutral, un-American and pro-German."[17] Nevertheless, even he believed that Debs should be freed.

Debs and Spargo were not close personal friends, but the two had worked together in the Socialist Party and Spargo retained a tremendous respect for Debs. In his meetings with Wilson, Spargo prodded him to grant Debs a pardon. Spargo later wrote that "on a number of occasions" he had received "almost a promise of a speedy pardon for Mr. Debs."[18]

In July 1920, Spargo wrote a personal note to the president stating that Debs's sentence had been "excessive" and that he had been "sufficiently punished" for his temerity in resisting the war effort. He also advanced a political rationale for issuing a pardon. Debs had already been nominated to be the Socialist Party's candidate for president in the 1920 election. Spargo suggested that Debs's continued imprisonment would enhance his standing as a "martyr" and would lead many progressives to vote for him as a protest vote.[19] Wilson was not persuaded and Spargo's letter went unanswered.

Clarence Darrow was another prominent progressive who lobbied behind the scenes for Debs's release. Darrow was the preeminent trial attorney of his time, having gained a global reputation, and remains an iconic figure even today, seventy years after his death. In 1894, Darrow quit a lucrative position as a corporate lawyer with a midwestern railroad line after Debs asked him to represent the American Railway Union (ARU), an industrial union organizing unskilled railroad workers. A federal district judge had issued an injunction that had the effect of breaking a strike led by the ARU. Debs defied the injunction and was sentenced to six months in jail for violating it.[20]

Darrow became the most prominent attorney defending radicals and union activists. Yet during the First World War, Darrow toured the country supporting the war effort. He was eager to continue the war until Germany unconditionally surrendered, insisting that the United States would not "stop until Prussian militarism" had "been destroyed." In a speech to a pro-war rally, Darrow argued that anyone who refused "to back the president in the crisis" was "worse than a traitor."[21]

Although he gave unstinting support to the administration's war policies, and defended the suppression of those who dissented, Darrow still could not accept the decision to prosecute Debs. By 1918, Debs and Darrow had been friends for more than twenty years. Darrow greatly admired Debs as "the bravest man" he had ever known. According to Darrow, no one was "kindlier, gentler [or] more generous" than Debs. In spite of his enthusiastic support for the war, Darrow was convinced that the case against Debs "was very weak." Thus, in July 1918, Darrow wrote to Debs that he was "sorry" to learn of the indictment. Although the two sharply disagreed on the war, Darrow understood that Debs had acted out of principle and would "always follow the right" as he saw it.[22]

A year later, in July 1919, with Debs in jail, Darrow traveled to Washington specifically to meet with Palmer. When Darrow pressed the case for a pardon, Palmer rebuffed him by questioning if he had the authority to speak for Debs. This led Darrow to travel to Atlanta, where he spent a day at the federal penitentiary in a lengthy discussion with Debs.

Upon returning to Washington, Darrow met again with Palmer stressing the urgency of the case, since Debs's health was fragile. Darrow's willingness to publicly defend the administration had been of considerable help in silencing the antiwar opposition, so his willingness to go out of his way to aid Debs carried weight. During a two-hour meeting, Palmer did not make any specific promises. Still, he began to waver. Although both Palmer and Darrow realized that the president would make the final decision, Darrow came away from the meeting with the belief that "Debs would be released very soon."[23]

President Wilson had remained in France throughout the first months of 1919, but he returned to Washington on July 8. Upon his return, he focused his energies on the effort to persuade Congress to approve the treaty establishing the League of Nations. Domestic issues were placed on hold and yet the *Debs* case kept rising to the surface.

Wilson did not convene a cabinet meeting until the afternoon of July 29, 1919, three weeks after his return from Europe. The question of granting a pardon to Debs split the cabinet and sparked "quite a discussion." Secretary of the Navy Josephus Daniels, Secretary of Labor William B. Wilson, and Secretary of War Newton Baker spoke in favor of clemency. They had the tacit support of other members of the cabinet, only Postmaster General Albert Burleson voicing his opposition. In spite of the tone of the discussion, the president remained adamant, holding that the United States "would have lost the war" had everyone acted as Debs had.[24] Only the president would decide when and if Debs was released from prison. No one else's opinion counted.

The day after the cabinet meeting, Palmer sent the White House a letter from Darrow setting out the arguments for a pardon. Darrow conceded that Debs "did violate the [Espionage] Act." The administration had accepted "a stern duty in meeting a grave emergency" when it jailed those who spoke out in opposition to the war, but the war was over and the emergency had ended. Since the danger had "passed," Debs "should be released."[25]

Darrow was articulating a position frequently advanced by pro-war progressives. During wartime, even a liberal government would be compelled to curtail the basic rights guaranteed in the Bill of Rights. Those who organized against the war or conducted strikes that impacted the war effort could justifiably be sentenced to lengthy terms in jail. Nevertheless, from this perspective the issues raised by those who only stated criticisms of the war were more complex. It

might be necessary to prosecute and temporarily incarcerate dissidents such as these, but they should be released once the war ended.
Darrow's support for an immediate amnesty for Debs was consistent
with this position.

The president's refusal to even consider a pardon for Debs left
Darrow in a difficult position. Darrow had been unwavering in his
support for the administration and its claim that it was fighting a war
for democracy. Still, the continued imprisonment of Debs for voicing
his opposition to the war demonstrated how tenuous and restricted
democratic rights actually were in the United States. As a result,
Darrow felt increasingly "embarrassed."[26]

The discussion at the cabinet meeting had forced Wilson to clarify his position. After that, every member of the cabinet, including
Palmer, understood that the president would not be swayed by popular pressure or the recommendations of his advisors. Debs would
remain in prison as long as Woodrow Wilson remained in the White
House. Palmer therefore sought to formulate a middle position that
held out hope for a presidential pardon, but postponed the decision
for some time in the future.

In sending Darrow's letter to Wilson, Palmer enclosed a memorandum presenting a revised version of his position. He was willing to
concede that Debs's "sentence of ten years" was "too long and ought
to be commuted." Still, Palmer held that Debs should not be released
until the peace treaty was "ratified and out of the way and conditions in the country have settled down." Palmer thus admitted that
Debs should be freed, but postponed the timing of his release into
the indefinite future. The president immediately answered with a note
saying that he was in agreement with this position.[27]

In response to the continuing pressure from the public and influential progressives, Palmer ordered yet another review of the case,
a review that was completed in September 1919. John Hanna, the
Justice Department attorney assigned to the review, noted that Alfred
Bettman had questioned at the time whether Debs should have been
indicted following the Canton speech. Still, Hanna concluded that the
decision to prosecute had been correct, but that the ten-year sentence

imposed by Judge Westenhaver had been excessive and should be commuted to eighteen months.[28] With time off for good behaviour, Debs would have been released from the federal penitentiary in the spring of 1920. Since Hanna's recommendation for leniency directly conflicted with the president's views, it was immediately shelved.

The Amnesty Movement Takes Its First Steps

As soon as Debs was incarcerated in April 1919, the demand for his immediate release became a focal point for public debate. Of course, the Socialist Party was committed to winning his release, but the amnesty movement spread beyond a core group of dedicated radicals and social democrats to the wider progressive Left. Over time, as the president repeatedly rejected a policy of leniency, the calls for Debs's release gained traction within the political mainstream.

Soon after Debs was imprisoned in April 1919, the Socialist Party created the National League for the Release of Political Prisoners, which called for the "immediate release of *all* political prisoners." J. Mahlon Barnes, who had served as the party's national secretary from 1905 to 1911, was named as the league's director.[29]

Although it gained the support of the National Civil Liberties Bureau, the league failed to move significantly beyond its base in the Socialist Party. Naming Barnes as its director was indicative of this narrow base of support, since Barnes had virtually no credibility among the wider milieu of progressives. In an effort to widen the support for the amnesty movement, the league organized a conference in July 1919 in Chicago, the American Freedom Convention. From this conference emerged a new organization, the Political Amnesty Committee (PAC).[30]

From the start, the PAC was convinced that the only way to achieve its goal was to mobilize popular opinion behind the call for an immediate amnesty. Accordingly, the Amnesty Committee organized a series of public protests and demonstrations. Delegations met with the president, as well as the attorney general, and appeared before congressional committees, but the focus always remained on actions, not lobbying.

Although the Socialist Party remained at the center of the Political Amnesty Committee, the new organization attracted a broader base of support. Its chair, Harriot Stanton Blatch, had recently joined the Socialist Party, but she had already become a well-known public figure as a prominent suffragist.[31] In addition, sympathetic trade union officials endorsed the call for amnesty. The Socialist Party had built a base of support in several unions, primarily in the garment trades. Benjamin Schlesinger, the president of the International Ladies Garment Workers' Union and a longtime member of the Socialist Party, joined the Political Amnesty Committee's board of directors. Still its sole staff member, Bertha Hale White, was also the assistant national secretary of the party.

The PAC was focused on the effort to convince Wilson to release Debs, but Debs made it very clear that he would only support a call for the amnesty of all of those jailed for their opposition to the war. Most of the Socialist Party members who had been prosecuted for violating the Espionage Act during the war had been released in the first months following the armistice. This left activists from the Industrial Workers of the World as the great majority of those still incarcerated for allegedly obstructing the war effort.

Although the Political Amnesty Committee placed a priority on the *Debs* case, it also worked with the IWW's General Defense Committee in the drive to free all those convicted under the provisions of the Espionage Act. This broader view of its goal, and the willingness to organize public protests, brought the PAC into conflict with Gompers and the leadership of the American Federation of Labor.

Gompers played a key role during the First World War, vocally supporting the war effort and using his authority to quickly quash any strikes by unions affiliated to the AFL that arose during the conflict. Furthermore, he condemned those who opposed the war in the harshest terms. In September 1917 he had stressed the need to "stamp out sedition" and "confound the traitors who talk peace."[32] Gompers bitterly attacked the IWW, even after the war had ended and while hundreds of Wobblies were being prosecuted for allegedly violating the Espionage Act. At the first Pan-American Labor

Conference, held in Laredo, Texas, in November 1918, Gompers attacked the IWW as those "who would destroy the only real labor movement."[33]

Although he would later claim that he was not a "man hunter," and that "every man must have his liberty,"[34] Gompers had in fact used his influence to support the government's harsh repressive measures. Nevertheless, he was eager to portray himself as a benevolent power broker, someone who could work within the system but who was prepared to use his influence to help radicals who had run afoul of the law. Gompers had already sought to assume this role in the Mooney case, a watershed moment in radical history.

THE MOONEY CASE

Tom Mooney had been falsely accused of setting a bomb at a Preparedness Day parade in San Francisco in July 1916. A radical socialist and an active member of the left wing of the Socialist Party, he became a journeyman iron molder. Mooney worked for Debs during the 1908 campaign, joining the Red Special, the train Debs took around the country on his speaking tours. In 1910, Mooney moved to San Francisco where he actively participated in the local branch of the AFL's Iron Molders' Union, a craft union organized among those working with wrought-iron. Still, he maintained close ties to IWW activists in Northern California.[35]

The Mooney case became a focal point for activists in February 1917 when he was sentenced to death after being convicted of first-degree murder. The date of his execution was set for May 17, 1917. The movement to support Mooney soon gathered strength, with rallies held in cities throughout the United States and Europe. In New York, two thousand heard Debs denounce the trial as a sham.[36]

The Mooney case was becoming an acute embarrassment to Woodrow Wilson and his administration just as the United States entered the war. On April 22, 1917, a demonstration was held in Petrograd, Russia, at the U.S. embassy, denouncing Mooney's conviction and demanding his release. Ambassador David Francis wrote an urgent cable to the State Department warning that the Mooney case could become a major problem.[37]

Russia was a key ally of the United States and Britain in the war against Germany, so anything that could upset relations was viewed with alarm. Russia's provisional government had been swept into power by a popular revolution only a few weeks earlier and the situation remained volatile.

Secretary of State Robert Lansing was deeply concerned, so he met with Gompers, who informed Lansing that Mooney's conviction was based on perjured testimony. Still, Mooney's innocence was a secondary issue. Both Lansing and Gompers agreed that a network of "communications between the labor organizations" was spurring these protests. The fragile "situation in Russia" linked to the "spread over a large part of the disturbed countries of the world" made the Mooney case an issue of "great importance."[38]

Lansing then sent a letter to the president urging him to send a cable to California's governor, William Stephens, urging a commutation of Mooney's death sentence. Wilson agreed with Lansing that this was a "critical and pregnant matter," so the letter was quickly sent. In the letter to Stephens, the president urged "the desirability of commuting the sentence of Mooney." Given "the situation in Russia," international relations were at a "very delicate stage," so blocking Mooney's execution would "greatly relieve some critical situations outside the United States." Wilson's cable was kept secret until August 1917, when Governor Stephens released it to the public.[39]

Gompers's role in this initial flurry of activity around the Mooney case was negligible. After the initial flurry of activity, the perceived need for taking immediate action dwindled as the legal appeal wended its way through the California judicial system. Still, Gompers played an initiating role in a development that would prove to have a significant impact on the Mooney case. The Industrial Workers of the World had organized effective strikes by Arizona's copper miners and timber workers in the Pacific Northwest. Gompers was concerned that the government's response, with its emphasis on repression, would only fuel greater discontent within the working class, providing the IWW with more recruits and further strengthening the left-wing opposition within the AFL unions. This led Gompers to propose that a special commission be formed that would tour the western states, where it would help mediate the most glaring disputes.[40] In the end, little was accomplished and the government relied primarily on force to suppress the IWW and labor militancy.

Although the Mooney case was not initially on its agenda, the president's Mediation Commission soon decided to investigate the matter. When staff members arrived in San Francisco, they quickly discovered that Mooney had, indeed, been framed. The testimony presented to convict him had been tainted. Furthermore, Mooney had gathered solid evidence providing a credible alibi as well. The commission therefore urged Wilson to use his influence to persuade Governor Stephens to grant a new trial where the evidence could be thoroughly and fairly judged. To do this, the commission suggested that Stephens commute the original conviction while at the same time Mooney would be indicted and tried on another murder charge arising from the bombing. (Ten people had died as a result of the Preparedness Day bombing. Mooney had been convicted for the death of only one of the victims.)[41]

The Mediation Commission was asking the president to alter his position. Until then, Wilson had focused his efforts on blocking Mooney's execution. Since it was unlikely that Mooney would be convicted in a second trial, the ultimate result of implementing this proposal would have been Mooney's release from prison. The *New York Times* printed a summary of the report on January 27, 1918, so Mooney knew that the commission had officially endorsed backing the call for a new trial.[42]

Mooney was not aware that the president, at the urging of Secretary Wilson, had followed up on the commission's report with a confidential letter to Governor Stephens. On January 22, 1918, Woodrow Wilson wrote to Stephens to stress that the Mooney case was of "international significance." Mooney's execution should be postponed "until he can be tried upon one of the other indictments against him."[43]

This letter would prove to be of considerable importance. It put the president on record calling for a new trial. There is no sign that Stephens took this letter seriously. No doubt he understood that Woodrow Wilson was merely passing on the recommendations of a commission he had created. In any case, this letter was kept secret for the moment.

The situation remained unchanged until March 1, 1918, when the California Supreme Court upheld Mooney's conviction and the death sentence as well. The Mooney case became again a matter of urgent priority, with international protests demanding that Mooney not be executed.

By this time, the Bolsheviks were in power, and they joined the call for Mooney's release. During the spring of 1918, the United States was still hoping to convince the Soviet Union to join the Allies in their campaign to crush Germany. Secretary of State Robert Lansing again sought the president's assistance in convincing Stephens to commute the death sentence.

His efforts were reinforced by concerns of domestic unrest. Calls for a new trial for Mooney were spreading from the radical Left into mainstream unions. Local leaders began discussing the possibility of a general strike on May 1, 1918, May Day. Such a protest strike would have been an extraordinary event in any case, but given that it would have occurred during the mobilization for a total war, the strike would have marked a sharp break with the cautious policies followed by AFL unions. The movement for a May Day strike soon gained momentum in the western states.[44]

Rank-and-file militancy was coalescing around the Mooney case, threatening the control of the AFL leadership. When Gompers met with the president on March 20, 1918, he informed Wilson of the growing support for a strike on May Day. Gompers urged Wilson to take further measures to block Mooney's execution, but the president answered that he was doing all he could.[45]

Gompers then went further in using his influence to push the president into taking a more energetic stance. This would be the only time that he would do so and he did it under the threat of a general strike organized at the grassroots level. In a letter to Secretary of Labor

William B. Wilson, Gompers stressed the need to do "everything" that could "be done to avoid an injustice as well as a very serious situation." Gompers urged Secretary Wilson "to prevail upon" the president "to go to extraordinary limits in order to prevent Mooney's execution."[46]

William Wilson had been a national official in the United Mine Workers and an ally of Gompers within the American Federation of Labor prior to his appointment as secretary of labor. He therefore raised the Mooney case at the next cabinet meeting. On the day after the meeting, President Wilson sent another letter to Governor Stephens. He again urged the governor "to commute the sentence of Mooney," pointing out that Mooney's "execution would greatly complicate" certain "international affairs." Stephens responded that the Mooney case would have his "careful consideration."[47]

The governor's office informed the press of the president's letter, although the letter itself was not released to the public. An article in the *New York Times* stated that President Wilson had requested Stephens to grant executive clemency to Mooney, a correct summary of the letter, but one that allowed for a certain ambiguity. Mooney then issued a statement claiming that the president had endorsed the call for "a just trial" where his "guilt or innocence" could be "established by the court." Mooney was engaging in wishful thinking. In fact, the president's March 1918 letter had been narrowly focused on convincing the governor to commute the death sentence, leaving Mooney in prison to serve a lengthy sentence for first-degree murder.[48]

As May Day approached, the administration became increasingly concerned. At this point, Gompers issued a statement that undercut support for the strike. Stopping work for even a day would be "repugnant" to "the interests of the workers." The strike was "unjustifiable and dangerously prejudicial" to the war effort. Furthermore, it could "only react against Mooney." This would be a recurring theme in Gompers's intervention in both the Mooney and *Debs* cases. He consistently argued that direct action not only was ineffective, but it also hurt the chances of those who were being unjustly treated by the judicial system, since it antagonized those who held power.[49]

Gompers only briefly examined the case itself. Due to the "machinations of the prosecution," Mooney had been convicted on the basis of "perjured evidence." This certainly indicated that Mooney was innocent of the bombing charge and should either be immediately released from prison or given a new trial. Nevertheless, Gompers carefully avoided specifying the appropriate remedy for this injustice. He thus avoided revealing that he was working behind the scenes to prevent Mooney's execution, not to pressure Governor Stephens into granting a new trial.

In Congress, the administration came under attack for not being harsh enough in quashing the threat of a strike. Senator James Phelan, a California Democrat, presented the administration's defense. The president authorized Phelan to release the January 1918 letter in which Wilson had endorsed the commission's recommendation that Mooney be granted a new trial.[50]

Phelan read the January 1918 letter into the Senate record.[51]

Under intense pressure and in the vain hope that Woodrow Wilson would use the president's office to ensure that he received a new trial, Mooney backed down. On April 29, with only two days to go, Mooney issued a public statement urging his supporters to refrain from going on strike on May Day. The release of the January 1918 letter had convinced him of Wilson's "interest in justice being done" in his case. As a result, Mooney had cabled local labor organizations "asking them to call off" the strike.[52]

The administration, with Gompers's active support, had sidetracked the call for a one-day general strike. Mooney had been gulled into relying on the influence of the president to cajole Stephens into granting a new trial. This was a disastrous strategic error. Mooney's only hope was a mass movement demanding a new trial. By publicly asking his supporters to refrain from direct action, Mooney had undermined any chance for an early release from prison.

Gompers's intervention in the Mooney case would bring him an important ally, Lucy Robins. A Jewish immigrant from a working-class family, Robins became an anarchist at a young age. At the urging of Emma Goldman, she soon became active in the movement to free

Tom Mooney. She was incensed by Gompers's statement prior to the planned May Day strike, with its explicit willingness to sacrifice the demand for justice to the war effort. Robins wrote Gompers an indignant note saying that it was not surprising that those on the Left had come to "despise" him. Piqued by the note, Gompers met with Robins to demonstrate to her that he had been working behind the scenes to block Mooney's execution.

Gompers showed Robins a file on the Mooney case containing summaries of his meetings with the president and his advisors on this issue as well as confidential letters he had sent Wilson and other key government officials. Based on this file, Gompers falsely claimed credit for convincing the president to bring pressure on the governor of California to stop the execution. Gompers also boasted that his influence would lead to a reopening of the case. Both claims were false.

The meeting with Gompers changed Robins's life. She fully accepted his grandiose boasting, but more important she accepted his underlying political perspective. The way to get things done was to work quietly within the system, using the influence of the American Federation of Labor, that is, mainstream organized labor, to bring about progressive change, in this case the release of the political prisoners.

Gompers convinced Robins that Mooney had been saved from execution "by the masterly hand that had pulled wires behind the scenes." Furthermore, she was also persuaded by his analysis of radical dissidents, her friends and former allies. The mass protests organized around the Mooney case "had been as futile as a childish tantrum."[53]

This was essentially the argument made by Gompers throughout the campaign to free Debs. It is hard to believe that Robins, who was hardly a novice, could be so easily persuaded and yet both sides benefited from this political conversion. Gompers got an acolyte with considerable credibility within the radical Left. Robins could be used as an intermediary, getting a hearing for Gompers's position from those who would otherwise not even listen to it. For Robins, she was now on the inside, holding private meetings with powerful government officials and having ready access to Gompers and the AFL leadership. The arrangement was facilitated because the two came from similar backgrounds—both were Jewish immigrants who had worked as cigar makers.

On May 28, 1918, Judge Franklin Griffin reaffirmed Mooney's death sentence and set the date somewhere between sixty and ninety days from this hearing. Griffin authorized Warden James Johnston of California's San Quentin Prison to fix the exact date. Johnston then set the date for the execution by hanging at August 23. Once again, Mooney's supporters mobilized to stop the execution.[54]

A few days after Griffin's decision, the president sent his last letter to Stephens urging him to commute the sentence. Wilson was "apprehensive of the consequences" should the death penalty be imposed. Indeed, there was "no one particular thing" that could cause "greater injury" to the war effort "than the execution of Tom Mooney."[55] These were strong words and they certainly made an impact on Stephens. Once again, the president emphasized the international implications of the Mooney case.

Later, in June 1918, the AFL held its annual conference, approving a resolution demanding that Mooney's execution be cancelled and that he be granted a new trial. These actions would "dispel the impression" that a "grave miscarriage" of justice was being "allowed with the knowledge of the authorities."[56]

Gompers relayed this resolution to Woodrow Wilson, who responded that although he had a "deep and sincere" interest in the case, he had "absolutely no power" to intervene. Governor Stephens had the sole authority to block the execution and he was still considering the matter. Still, the president assured Gompers that he hoped "with all of his heart" that there would "be a decision for clemency."[57] This message makes it very clear that Wilson was using his influence to pressure Stephens into commuting the death sentence, rather than seeking to persuade him to grant Mooney a new trial. There is no sign that Gompers disagreed with this decision, or that he pressed the president to use his influence to ensure that Mooney received a new and impartial trial.

Stephens could see that Mooney's execution would cause him

enormous problems. On July 27, 1918, he delayed the execution until December 13. As this final date came closer, mass protests were again organized around the country. With the war having come to an end on November 11, 1918, Stephens commuted the death sentence less than three weeks later, on November 28. In doing so, he cited the president's urgent requests and released to the public the letters from March 1918 and June 1918.[58]

Mooney was bitterly disappointed. He had mistakenly called off the May Day strike in the vain hope that Wilson would use his influence to pressure Stephens into granting a new trial. Instead, Mooney faced the rigors of incarceration in a high-security prison while serving a life sentence for a crime he did not commit. In a public statement, he demanded a "new and fair trial" or an unconditional pardon. He was ready for "a glorious death" rather than being buried in "a living grave."[59] After reading the president's March 1918 letter in the press, Mooney wrote Wilson that this had given him "greater pain and grief" than a "certain death." Mooney had been tricked. He would serve another twenty years in San Quentin before being given a full pardon in January 1939.

GOMPERS AND AMNESTY FOR DEBS

The duplicitous actions of Gompers during the effort to defend Mooney, and the willingness of Robins to defend those actions, would set a pattern that was repeated during the campaign to free Debs from prison.

For most of 1918, Robins devoted her efforts to the futile attempt to have the Mooney case reopened. This was a safe option when anti-war activists, including Robins's mentor, Emma Goldman, were being jailed for speaking out against the war and the draft. As the war came to an end in November 1918, Robins sought out Gompers to request his endorsement for a campaign to pressure the president into issuing a general amnesty that would cover Debs as well as other political prisoners. Gompers was willing to back the push to free Debs, but he had no intention of using his influence to gain the release of the

IWW prisoners. Furthermore, Gompers wanted to wait before being publicly committed on the amnesty issue.

Gompers told Robins that it was too soon to raise the issue of amnesty as a policy position of the American Federation of Labor. Too many rank-and-file members were still incensed with those who had been critical of the war effort. This was a convenient argument with little basis in fact. The war had not been popular and yet Gompers had provided the administration with enthusiastic and unwavering support. Instead, Gompers proposed that Robins start developing support for an amnesty that could include Debs by raising the issue in the more progressive sections of the AFL.[60]

Gompers made another comment to Robins that provides more insight into his reluctance to take up the amnesty issue even when the war had come to an end. According to Gompers, Woodrow Wilson "must always be right. If you disagree with him openly, you are lost."[61] Gompers valued his access to the president and he was unwilling to risk it by using his influence to gain Debs's release.

In June 1919, the AFL held its annual conference in Atlantic City. J. Mahlon Barnes, a leading figure in the opposition grouping within the Cigar Makers' Union as well as the director of the National League for the Release of Political Prisoners, introduced a resolution calling for the "immediate release of all persons" then in prison "for political opinion, industrial activities or religious belief." This resolution covered all of the political prisoners, including the Wobblies, as well as the religious conscientious objectors. Barnes's resolution did not specifically mention Debs.[62]

Gompers sent Robins to Benjamin Schlesinger to ask him to urge Barnes to withdraw the motion before it came to the floor, since it would only antagonize the delegates and make it harder to win them over to an amnesty position. Schlesinger refused and, according to Robins, insisted that he would push the resolution, "Never mind the results."[63] This quote, of dubious validity, corresponded to an argument frequently made by Gompers and Robins. Those who argued for a mobilization of public opinion to further the amnesty movement were engaging in political posturing that was undertaken for undeclared ideological reasons and which was counterproductive to a strategy based on quiet lobbying. In fact, Schlesinger was a pragmatic union official and far from an ideologue. More important, Gompers not only disagreed with the timing of the Barnes resolution, he disagreed with its substance as well. Gompers and the AFL leadership were unwilling to support a general amnesty that would include the IWW prisoners.

The convention's resolutions committee, stacked with Gompers's supporters, presented its own resolution. It urged the convention to make "no recommendation" on the issue of amnesty. There were "instances" where a commutation of the prison sentence was "warranted," but there were also "many instances" where the sentences were "fully justified."[64] Again, the resolution did not mention Debs.

When the issue was debated on the floor of the convention, Schlesinger supported Barnes's resolution. Keeping political prisoners in jail once the war had come to an end was indicative of a "feeling of vengeance." Those who opposed the resolution viewed it as an attack on the U.S. decision to enter the war. Joseph Weber, a former president of the American Federation of Musicians, condemned Barnes's resolution "as an insult to every man who wore the uniform of a United States soldier."[65]

As a member of the executive council, Gompers had helped draft the counter-resolution, but during the floor debate he went further. Stepping down from the chair, he called on the delegates to endorse the executive council's resolution "by an avalanche of pro-American votes."[66] Gompers was indirectly implying that those who supported a general amnesty were not truly patriotic. The executive council's resolution was approved and the AFL remained outside of the amnesty movement.

Gompers's unwillingness to publicly call for Debs's release only changed when the president's health rapidly deteriorated. After that, there was no risk of retribution from the White House.

WILSON REMAINS ADAMANT

Woodrow Wilson had suffered from uncontrolled high blood

pressure for several years before becoming president. By the time he took office in March 1913, he was already hampered by intense head-aches, a clear sign that the disease was entering a dangerous phase. Nevertheless, the illness was not treated and by the summer of 1919 the president was beginning to exhibit the physical and mental effects of a series of small strokes. Despite this, he carried on as usual and on most days was able to cope with the issues at hand. On October 2, 1919, while campaigning for the League of Nations treaty in the western states, Wilson suffered a massive stroke that left him paralyzed on his left side.[67]

For nearly four months, the president was entirely incapacitated. In effect, the cabinet functioned as an executive decision-making body. The president's wife, Edith Bolling Wilson, had veto power over important decisions, signing off on the relevant documents, with Joseph Tumulty, as the president's secretary and de facto chief of staff, serving as the intermediary between the White House and the cabinet.[68]

Attorney General Palmer understood that Wilson had been ada-mant in rejecting a pardon for Debs, so he continued to uphold that position while the president remained incapacitated. By the spring of 1920, Wilson had recovered sufficiently to be able to read and respond to brief reports on controversial issues requiring immediate decisions, although he remained completely isolated from all visitors.

On August 10, 1920, the president attended a cabinet meeting for the first time since his stroke. Once again, the *Debs* case became the focus of a heated debate. Positions seem to have remained the same since the previous discussion in the cabinet in July 1919. Daniels, Baker, and William Wilson, joined by John Barton Payne, the recently appointed secretary of the interior, argued for clemency, while Burleson continued to hold that Debs should remain in prison. The president realized that the prevailing sentiment within the cabinet supported clemency, but he insisted that his approval was necessary before a pardon could be approved. In his diary notes on this meet-ing, Daniels commented that the president's comments had "ended hope for Debs."[69]

Two Amnesty Organizations Diverge

The massive stroke suffered by Wilson in October 1919 had a significant impact on the amnesty movement. For the Political Amnesty Committee, the fall of 1919 was a time to extend the base of support, to gain the support of a wider segment of the progressive Left.

A year after the war had ended, with the bitterness that it had engendered cooling, and with Wilson incapacitated, Gompers began slowly moving toward public support for a limited amnesty. On October 10, 1919, a few days after Wilson's stroke, a joint meeting of the New York City Central Federated Unions of Greater New York City and the United Hebrew Trades met to form a new amnesty organization.[70] The United Hebrew Trades, representing the garment trade unions, primarily based in the Jewish Lower East Side, was closely aligned with the Socialist Party. In contrast, the Central Federated Unions brought together the craft unions supporting Gompers and the AFL's leadership.

The new organization was called the Central Labor Bodies Conference for the Release of Political Prisoners. Lucy Robins served as its executive secretary. Its first project was convincing the American Federation of Labor to adopt a resolution supporting an amnesty for political prisoners, especially Debs. Accordingly, Robins and the Central Labor Bodies sent out 36,000 circulars to locals of AFL affiliated unions asking them to endorse a proposed amnesty resolution.[71]

Although Gompers gave his tacit support to the new amnesty organization, he remained behind the scenes. Then in February 1920, with the president still incapacitated, Gompers helped to arrange a meeting with Secretary of War Newton Baker to discuss the issue of the conscientious objectors who remained imprisoned at the U.S. Army's Fort Leavenworth Disciplinary Barracks nearly a year and a half after the war had ended. Robins was joined by Hugh Frayne, the national AFL's New York City representative and a close ally of Gompers, as representatives of the Central Labor Bodies Conference.

At the end of their talk, Robins and Frayne issued a statement stating that the meeting had led to a plan of action. Baker agreed to release every conscientious objector who agreed to abide by the prison's rules for two weeks. He justified this requirement as a proof that the prisoners would abide by the nation's laws. Military prisoners were treated as soldiers and required to follow certain rules. These included wearing military uniforms, saluting officers and undertaking work that would produce articles that might be useful to the war effort. The great majority of conscientious objectors at the Leavenworth Barracks were absolutists, that is, pacifists who refused in any way to cooperate with the military. Most prisoners therefore rejected Baker's offer, although seven of them complied and were released two weeks after the meeting with Robins and Frayne. In the end, Baker finally agreed to release the thirty-three remaining prisoners in November 1920, without any conditions.[72]

This intervention by the Central Labor Bodies and the AFL in the question of amnesty for conscientious objectors is indicative of the underlying problems in their approach. Instead of highlighting the government's brutal treatment of those imprisoned for their moral objections to war, the focus was shifted to those who refused to accept a deal that might seem reasonable, but in actuality required many of those in prison to violate their fundamental beliefs. Furthermore, the deal accepted by Robins and Frayne was bound to deepen division among the prisoners at Fort Leavenworth, making it even harder for the conscientious objectors to withstand the pressures being placed on them to conform to military rules.

Although the Central Labor Bodies Conference insisted that it was aiming at the release of all "political prisoners," it was very careful in defining this term. In a letter to William Green, the secretary of the United Mine Workers' Union, Robins stressed the need for a "general amnesty" that would include the remaining conscientious objectors, soldiers jailed for petty crimes, and those prisoners such as Debs "who have violated the Espionage Act by word or writing." In a speech to the 1922 AFL convention, held several months after Debs had been released, Robins made this position even clearer. The Central Labor Bodies Conference had acted "solely in behalf of those who were imprisoned for their written or spoken expression of thought or opinion." Once the war came to an end, she argued, there was no point in continuing to detain these prisoners.[73]

Robins's formulation excluded most of those still imprisoned for their opposition to the war. Dozens of IWW members were still incarcerated in the years following the war for violating the Espionage Act and calls for their immediate release remained highly controversial. Their convictions had been based on their ability to organize successful strikes and not primarily on what they had said or written.

Debs grew increasingly disturbed by the focus on his release rather than the demand that all political prisoners, including the IWW prisoners, should be released. In July 1920, Debs wrote to Lucy Robins that he would "object emphatically to any further appeal being made" on his personal behalf. Indeed, he wished "to fare no better" than "his comrades" jailed for opposing the war. Debs concluded, "my place is here." He reiterated this point in an August 1920 article in a socialist journal. Debs "objected emphatically to any further appeal" to the White House for his release since he had "nothing to ask at the hands of the Wilson-Palmer-Burleson Administration."[74]

By the spring of 1920, it was clear that there were two distinct amnesty organizations with two distinct strategies and goals. Tensions between the two groups sharpened as the first anniversary of Debs's imprisonment drew near. The Political Amnesty Committee began planning a major demonstration in Washington on April 13, 1920, to mark the occasion. A march up Pennsylvania Avenue would culminate in a short rally, after which delegations would meet with Palmer and congressional leaders. This public protest would mark a slight escalation in tactics, a demonstration that the amnesty movement was strong enough to organize a mass rally.[75]

Gompers and Robins, as leaders of the Central Labor Bodies Conference, were strongly opposed to any organized protests and they worked hard to keep it from happening. Robins was convinced that a demonstration in Washington would "mean disaster to the amnesty movement."[76] It would interfere with the quiet lobbying of the Wilson Administration, while also causing a backlash of resentment within the wider public. Of course, Wilson had already made it clear that he would never pardon Debs.

In early April 1920, Robins was given permission to visit Debs for the first time at the Atlanta Penitentiary. She tried hard to convince Debs to pressure the Socialist Party and the PAC to call off the protests. Debs was caught in the middle. He desperately hoped to see a unified amnesty movement that could lead the way to his freedom and to the release of all the other political prisoners, including the IWW activists. He was therefore unwilling to take sides in this divisive dispute. Indeed, Debs wrote his brother Theodore that he should inform Robins that he could not "enter into any controversy of any kind" considering his "present situation."

The AFL leadership brought pressure on the garment workers' unions aligned with the Socialist Party to reject any participation in the amnesty protest planned for the first anniversary of Debs's incarceration. With Debs wavering, the momentum behind the mass action began to dissipate. At the last moment, the Political Amnesty Committee called off the rally. Instead, Socialist Party locals held meetings to call for Debs's release and to support an amnesty for all political prisoners.[77]

By the summer of 1920, Gompers was ready to see the AFL endorse a limited amnesty that would include Debs, even though this would put him in conflict with the Wilson administration. At the June 1920 AFL convention, the executive council endorsed a resolution that continued to insist that the lengthy sentences imposed on those allegedly violating the Espionage Act had been "thoroughly justified under war conditions." Still, there was no cause to be "served by detaining further" those imprisoned for the mere "expression of views." This formulation was clearly intended to provide support for an immediate pardon for Debs.[78]

With Gompers as her mentor, Robins was given the opportunity to address the 1920 convention. She avoided any mention of Debs, but she did declare that many of the political prisoners were "harmless" and "did very little."[79] Thus Robins sought to justify the call for a limited amnesty by trivializing the efforts of those who had opposed the war.

Unlike the previous year, this time the issue of amnesty did not become contentious. Schlesinger and seven other delegates who were loosely affiliated with the Socialist Party introduced a resolution calling for the release of "all prisoners whose political beliefs formed the basis of their prosecution." Their further incarceration would serve no further valid purpose since "the sole justification" of "war-time necessity no longer" existed.[80] Schlesinger's resolution was very similar to that presented by the executive council except that Schlesinger's proposal did not endorse the government's prosecution of dissidents during the war. After a minimum of debate, the executive council's resolution was approved by the delegates. The AFL had finally approved the call for a limited amnesty that would cover Debs.

Nevertheless, Gompers delayed before implementing this resolution, a point noted by those close to Debs. In July 1920, Mabel Dunlap Curry, a close friend of Debs, wrote to Robins that she "personally" believed that Gompers held "the key to Gene's release" if he were prepared "to use all his power."[81]

In September 1920, three months after the passage of the convention resolution, Gompers led a delegation of twenty-five AFL officials in a meeting with Attorney General Palmer. Gompers presented the AFL resolution and supported the idea of an amnesty as a way of healing the divisions opened during the war. Palmer responded that each case would be considered on its own individual merits, but he gave no indication that Debs would soon be released.[82]

Shortly after this meeting, Gompers wrote a letter to the president transmitting the essence of the AFL resolution and suggesting that a proclamation declaring a general amnesty for "political prisoners" would have a "general tranquillizing effect." He went on to say that he recognized that Palmer had already pointed out that such a proclamation would not negate the need for a case-by-case review for each prisoner. This undercut the whole point of a general amnesty, as Gompers well knew. The letter made no mention of Debs.[83]

The underlying tension between Gompers and Debs soon became

apparent. After his nomination as the Socialist Party's presidential candidate in May 1920, prison authorities permitted Debs to issue a limited number of statements to the press as a candidate for national office. In a statement dated October 7, 1920, Debs attacked the AFL's leadership. He warned of pervasive corruption and a willingness to negotiate contracts that left workers worse off than before. The rank and file had to "look out" for the "so-called leaders" who were "often" the "chief betrayers" of the labor movement. Furthermore, he denounced the "Gompersonian policy" of supporting candidates from "the capitalist political parties," candidates who stand for "capitalism and wage slavery."[84] Of course, Gompers, as well as most of the others on the AFL executive council, were already providing enthusiastic support for James Cox, the Democratic Party's presidential candidate.

Debs's statement reiterated comments that he had frequently made before. Nevertheless, Gompers was furious. As a result, Robins wrote Debs a letter in an effort to cajole him into softening his criticism. She insisted that radicals had to "admit that the leaders in the American Labor Movement are the leaders of the masses." In reality, the AFL organized a small segment of the U.S. working class, primarily skilled white male workers. Going further, Robins claimed that rank-and-file union members would "never tolerate antagonism upon the leaders from an outsider." This was an odd comment considering that Debs had spent many years as an official of the Brotherhood of Locomotive Firemen and then as a leader of the American Railway Union.[85]

After chastising Debs for having the audacity to challenge Gompers and the AFL leadership, Robins went on to implicitly threaten him. Gompers, wrote Robins, received inquiries "asking why he should come out so openly" for "the release of Debs when Debs continually hammers and slams him."

Gompers was using Robins to pressure Debs into remaining silent. Although Debs tried to avoid personal wrangles, this was a threat he could not ignore. Theodore Debs answered Robins for his brother. Debs "would rather stay in prison to his last day than to keep silent." There was "nothing personal" in Debs's critique of Gompers, but rather a sharp political disagreement arising from the support Gompers and the AFL gave "every time for the utterly rotten Democratic Party."[86]

In response to Robins's assertion that Debs should work with the AFL leadership, Debs, through his brother, retorted that he was only "interested in the rank-and-file and not in the leaders." This interchange of letters pointedly encapsulated the conflicting perspectives of those who remained within the orbit of the union officialdom and radical socialists who sought to organize a militant alternative to the bureaucracy.

To Robins's credit, she continued to work for Debs's release from prison despite this outspoken rebuff of her implicit threat. The same did not hold true of Gompers. In spite of the AFL resolution, Gompers did nothing to exert his personal influence to further amnesty for Debs in the weeks leading up to the 1920 election. Finally, in December 1920, he wrote a personal letter to the outgoing president.

By this time, most Socialist Party members who had been jailed for violating the Espionage Act during the war had been released from prison through a presidential commutation of their sentence, so the great majority remaining in jail were IWW leaders.

In his letter to Woodrow Wilson, Gompers suggested that all of those convicted for opposing the war should be granted a pardon except those "whose conviction and imprisonment" were the result "of moral turpitude." This qualification was aimed at the IWW prisoners who had been charged with acts of sabotage, as well as a conspiracy to obstruct the war effort. Gompers was careful to differentiate these cases from that of Debs. He was convinced that no one could believe that Debs "was a traitor to his country." The views expressed in the speech in Canton were merely "a mistaken conviction."[87] By implication, Gompers was suggesting that this was not true for the IWW prisoners.

Gompers's decision to actively petition the president was welcomed by those who were concerned about Debs's health and thus anxious for his immediate release. Nevertheless, Gompers's intervention came very late. Many progressives had been working on this cause for a year and a half, ever since Debs's appeal was rejected by the Supreme

Court. In any case, the president remained adamant and Gompers's letter went unanswered.

The fall and winter of 1920 saw a considerable broadening of support for an amnesty for Debs and the other political prisoners. This brought a critical response from those who were steadfast in their determination to crush the Left. In September 1920, the *Christian Science Monitor* printed an editorial that specifically addressed the issue of amnesty. The editors were "inclined to doubt" that Debs was a political prisoner since Debs had "declared his determination to obstruct the draft." Thus, the Canton speech could have led to "a lengthening of the war." The fact that it had not was a mere "technical" matter, not a substantive one.[88]

Upton Sinclair, the noted author and an ardent proponent of amnesty, sent a copy of the *Monitor* to Theodore Debs for transmittal to Atlanta. Gene Debs responded with a vehement denial. The claim that the Canton speech was intended "to obstruct the draft" was "an absolute falsehood." Debs pointed out that he had not mentioned conscription once in the course of that lengthy speech.[89]

Clearly the *Monitor* had incorrectly represented the gist of the Canton speech. Yet this exchange reflected a broader question. Efforts to determine the intent of a statement from the general political perspective underlying it are bound to be fraught with difficulties. In all likelihood, Debs was telling the truth. He had not intended to obstruct the draft through his speech in Canton. Still, there is no doubt that Debs vigorously opposed the war and that young men who heard the speech might well have been more inclined to resist the draft after listening to him.

In spite of the *Monitor*, and the other mainstream media that attacked the amnesty movement, a widening circle of prominent progressives publicly pleaded for Debs to be freed even during the last days of the Wilson presidency. In March 1921, a delegation of prominent women went to the White House with a petition calling for Debs to be immediately released. The delegation included Genevieve Davis Bennett Clark, the wife of Champ Clark, the speaker of the House of Representatives, and Belle Case La Follette, wife of Senator Robert

La Follette, Sr. Although the delegation had been promised that it would be able to hand the petition to Tumulty, who would make sure that the president saw it, Tumulty did not meet the delegation and Wilson did not receive the petition. Nevertheless, the fact that the wives of leading politicians were willing to be publicly identified with the effort to free Debs is indicative of how broadly based support for his release had become.

During the final days of the Wilson administration there was a final push to resolve the issue. In January 1921, Palmer submitted an extensive memorandum, including a summary of a letter from Judge Westenhaver dated October 1920. Westenhaver still believed that the verdict of guilty had been "justified," but he was now willing to concede that the ten-year prison term he had imposed was a "heavy sentence." Furthermore, he revealed that he had determined on this lengthy sentence as a deterrent to others who opposed the war. At this point, two years after the trial, Westenhaver was ready to agree that a two- to five-year sentence would have been appropriate and that a "decision to commute the sentence proportionately" would be in order. Westenhaver's shift toward a position endorsing a speedy pardon is a further indication of the widespread support for Debs's release.[90]

Palmer also included his own position on the issue in the memorandum. Debs had been properly convicted of violating the Espionage Act and the severe sentence could be justified because he was "a man of influence and with not an inconsiderable following." Still, other members of the Socialist Party who had received lengthy sentences had been released after serving two years or so in prison. Debs would soon have spent one year and eight months behind bars. Palmer suggested that Debs be released a month later, on February 12, 1921, as a farewell act of clemency. To insist that he remain imprisoned would make Debs a martyr and would "invite criticism of a discriminatory character."

Wilson's response was short and to the point. Palmer's plea for a last-minute pardon was "denied." The president told Tumulty that he would "never consent to the pardon" of Debs because Debs had been continually "sniping" at the government's policy during the war, and had, thus, been a "traitor to his country."[91]

This final action by the president rejecting the recommendation of his attorney general brought an open retort from Debs. In a public statement issued by Samuel Castleton, a sympathetic attorney who frequently visited the Atlanta Penitentiary, Debs answered that he did not want to be "indebted" for his "liberty to Woodrow Wilson," who was "the most pitiful figure in history."[92]

Wilson was incensed. Debs was ridiculing the president of the United States and thus had to be punished. Debs was not allowed to receive any visitors, cut off from all mail and newspapers and not permitted to send any letters from prison. His brother wrote that he had been "shut off from the outside world." This vindictive reprisal was only partially rescinded after Wilson left office.[93]

The bitter feelings between Debs and Wilson did not diminish once Wilson left the White House. Tumulty recounted the president's response to Palmer's memorandum in a book he wrote after Wilson left office. Extracts were printed in major newspapers around the country in December 1921, prior to publication. After reading the section concerning the rejection of Palmer's request for his pardon, Debs wrote a sarcastic commentary in a private letter. The rationales advanced for his continued imprisonment were "brilliant reasons" formulated by a president who could "not look the workers in the face whose sons he [had] sent to slaughter." Woodrow Wilson was merely "a cadaver—a corpse still twitching by malice, hate and revenge" on those who, "unlike himself, did not sell out their country" for the "profit and glory" of his "Master's, the Profiteers."[94]

For his part, Wilson remained certain that Debs should have served the entire prison sentence imposed upon him, even though this would have led, in all likelihood, to his death while still incarcerated. In May 1922, the former president and his wife invited Ida Tarbell, a noted muckraker, to an informal lunch. Wilson still suffered from the effects of the stroke that had totally incapacitated him for several months. Nevertheless, during the brief discussion with Tarbell he criticized President Warren Harding for commuting Debs's sentence. In Wilson's view, "Debs was one of the worst men in the country." The former president still believed that Harding should have rejected the calls for amnesty and that Debs "should have stayed in the penitentiary."[95]

HARDING AND DAUGHERTY PLAY GAMES

Woodrow Wilson's successor, Warren Harding, understood that the issue of releasing Debs would be one of the first major decisions he confronted as president. During the 1920 presidential campaign, Parley Christensen, the Farmer-Labor Party candidate, had issued a public statement calling for a general amnesty for those who had opposed the war, with special reference to Debs. Christensen had cabled Harding requesting him to join in this call. Harding responded that he was in favor of a "general amnesty for political prisoners," but that he would also review each individual case on its merits. This proviso negated the underlying principle of a general amnesty. Harding then stated that until this review had been completed, he would make no further comment on the *Debs* case.[96]

This constituted the sole public remark that Harding would make on the issue of amnesty prior to becoming president. Yet as an astute politician he was well aware of the growing popular support for Debs's immediate release from prison. On the day before his inauguration, March 3, 1921, Harding and his wife informally met with the Speaker of the House, Champ Clark, and his wife. Genevieve Clark later wrote that she had asked Harding to quickly pardon Debs and that the incoming president had answered that "he would give the matter his earliest consideration."[97]

Indeed, Harding spent a considerable effort in considering the *Debs* case. At first, he ordered Attorney General Harry Daugherty to review the question, sending voluminous files from the White House to the Department of Justice. This was a most unusual transfer of sensitive documents. Daugherty told the press that he would be personally reviewing all of the files on the case before reporting back to the president. This was also highly unusual, since normally it was the pardon attorney who compiled a report on each prisoner whose sentence was being considered for presidential clemency. According to

Daugherty, Harding held "a human being's and a technician's interest in the case of Gene Debs."[98]

This review process led to an extraordinary incident, unique in U.S. history. Daugherty, with Harding's approval, ordered Debs to come to Washington, for a personal interview. Debs then took a train from Atlanta to the capital alone, unaccompanied by guards. No reporters were permitted to interview Debs during this trip and Debs was pledged to silence on the details of his discussion with the attorney general.

The trip was highly unusual. Debs was a convicted felon serving a lengthy sentence in a high-security prison. Presumably he had been convicted and sentenced because the judicial system had determined that he posed a direct threat to society. Furthermore, Wilson had to grant an amnesty after the war had ended, again because Debs was considered a threat to peace and order. Nevertheless, the president authorized Debs to travel as if he were a free person while he was still serving his prison sentence.

Once in Washington, Debs was met at the train station by Jesse Smith, Daugherty's closest confidant. Smith held no position in the Justice Department and yet he occupied an office near Daugherty's. Smith and Daugherty also shared an apartment in an expensive hotel. Smith would become the unofficial leader of the Ohio gang, an assortment of Daugherty's friends engaged in a variety of corrupt deals involving influence peddling.[99] It is difficult to envision two more different people than Eugene Debs and Jesse Smith, but then the entire situation was somewhat bizarre.

Smith escorted Debs from the train station to a hotel. The following day, March 24, 1921, Smith took Debs to the Justice Department and after the interview there brought Debs back to the train station. Debs met with Daugherty and his chief assistant, Guy Goff, for more than three hours, beginning in the morning and continuing in the afternoon after a lunch break. Obviously, more than pleasantries were exchanged.[100]

Debs did not directly comment to the public on this meeting, but he did make it known that "he had nothing to take back, nothing to recant." In a book written some years later, Daugherty confined his account to generalities. The two had discussed the merits of socialism, agreeing to disagree. Daugherty concluded that Debs was "sincere" and a "charming personality."[101]

The specifics of the lengthy meeting between Daugherty and Debs remain unknown, but the general outline is clear. Daugherty pressed Debs to publicly declare that he had, indeed, violated the Espionage Act and that his trial had been fairly conducted. In addition, it is likely that Daugherty pushed Debs to agree that once freed he would soften his criticisms of the government and refrain from supporting a militant resistance to capitalism. Debs was well aware that Harding and Daugherty had the power to keep him imprisoned for many years. Given Debs's frail health, a refusal to grant a speedy release from prison was likely to be a death sentence.

Debs pressed Daugherty to review the cases of the political prisoners, most of them IWW activists. Daugherty promised that he would carefully examine the cases presented by the political prisoners, but of course he reneged on that promise.[102] In spite of the sharp differences between them, Debs and Daugherty seem to have held a cordial discussion. Debs returned to Atlanta Federal Penitentiary, again without any guards. He seems to have believed that there was a reasonable chance that Harding would promptly begin releasing the political prisoners, including himself. He would soon discover that he was engaging in wishful thinking.

The Amnesty Movement Divides

Reports of a speedy release that circulated in the aftermath of the trip to Washington deepened the split within the amnesty movement. Lucy Robins and her AFL-backed committee had remained aloof from the Political Amnesty Committee, the broad coalition led by the Socialist Party. For months, the coalition had been gathering signatures on a mass petition demanding the release of all of the political prisoners, including both Debs and the IWW prisoners.

The petition organizers gathered more than a million signatures and by the spring of 1921 they were preparing to present the petition to Congress. In addition, the coalition was ready to start picketing the White House until all of the political prisoners were released from prison. Robins and the AFL vehemently opposed this strategy. Robins insisted that the only way to gain Debs's freedom was to remain quiet and rely on lobbying by influential figures such as Gompers.

Debs was caught in the midst of this bitter dispute. Initially, he tried to develop a middle position. On March 28, 1921, three days after returning from Washington to the Atlanta Penitentiary, Debs wrote to Otto Branstetter, the national secretary of the Socialist Party, urging a "temporary postponement" of any demonstrations. This would provide the new administration with "a reasonable time" to "act of its own volition."[103]

Branstetter then traveled to Atlanta, thus becoming the first outside visitor permitted to see Debs since his privileges had been rescinded by the previous administration for calling Woodrow Wilson a "pitiful figure." The two agreed that the picketing of the White House would be held "in abeyance," but Branstetter also convinced Debs that the plan to present the mass petition to Congress should proceed.[104] This compromise did little to end the bitter dispute between the two amnesty groups.

A few days later, Branstetter wrote to Debs that the plans to present the petition were moving forward, but that Robins, with the support of Gompers, was "actively working against" the Socialist Party by urging other groups not to work with the Political Amnesty Committee. This pressure was being particularly felt within AFL-affiliated unions that were led by those close to the Socialist Party, especially those in the garment trades. Furthermore, Robins was insistent that amnesty could only be gained through the quiet lobbying of Gompers "or some other influential personages" and that the coalition should "be absolutely quiet."[105]

Branstetter emphatically rejected this strategy. He insisted that Harding's decision would be primarily determined by "political expediency" and that the Socialist Party and other leftists had to "make their own fight" and not rely on influential personalities. Indeed, socialists could not expect "anything but the most bitter antagonism" from Gompers.

Debs responded to Branstetter through his brother. Even though his decisions were based on political expediency, Harding had shown "a decent disposition toward political prisoners." It would thus have been a "sound strategy to postpone" all public protests. Nevertheless, the plans for the presenting of the petition had been set into motion and it was too late to abandon the project. Debs still hoped to mediate the dispute between the amnesty groups. He insisted that there should be "perfect cooperation" among those calling for amnesty despite the "small differences" between them.[106] Unfortunately, this was wishful thinking.

On April 12, two hundred progressive leaders representing a wide range of organizations presented the mass petition to Congress. Twenty-one thousand signatures, virtually the entire adult population, came from Debs's hometown of Terre Haute. Small delegations met with Harding, Daugherty, and Vice President Calvin Coolidge. These delegations were informed that the administration was considering the question of an amnesty, but that each case, including that of Debs, would be considered individually.[107]

Shortly after the petition had been presented to Congress, Harding issued a statement that he would not review the cases of any political prisoners "before a technical peace" had gone into effect. Congress rejected the Versailles Treaty in March 1920, leaving the United States without a formal closure to the war.

Harding's position made little sense. Woodrow Wilson had commuted the sentences of scores of prisoners convicted of violating the Espionage Act, many of them members of the Socialist Party. The excuse of an unsigned peace treaty merely provided Harding with a convenient rationale to stall before deciding on a controversial issue.

Support for a General Amnesty Grows

Popular pressure to release Debs continued to build, but most of those rallying to this cause voted for Democrats or were aligned with the

Socialist Party. On the other hand, many of Harding's staunchest supporters, steadfast Republicans, vehemently opposed any move to free Debs. The American Legion repeatedly voiced its resolute opposition to an amnesty. Leading newspapers were also quick to condemn those calling for presidential clemency. The *New York Times* printed several editorials denouncing Debs and insisting that he should remain in jail as a threat to the public order. In one editorial, the *Times* denounced Debs as a "dangerous criminal" who, as an "unrepentant enemy of the Government," should be made to serve all of the lengthy jail sentence that he "deserved."[108]

Furthermore, the issue divided the Harding administration. Daugherty was hostile to Debs and opposed his release from prison. Harding was reluctant to override his chief legal advisor and yet he was also an astute politician who saw the advantage of appearing as a benevolent alternative to Woodrow Wilson.

For months, the issue seemed to have reached a stalemate. Although the administration repeatedly issued statements that Daugherty was studying the issue of an early release for Debs, nothing happened. Even after Congress declared an end to the war on July 21, 1921, and authorized a separate peace treaty with Germany, Debs remained in jail. He realized that his March meeting with Daugherty had been a publicity stunt. His hopes for an early release having been dashed, Debs concluded that Branstetter had been correct and that only popular pressure could convince Harding to issue a pardon. Theodore Debs, acting for his brother, wrote to the president condemning his refusal to even consider an amnesty for the political prisoners until a peace treaty with Germany went into effect as "not only silly and disgusting, but cowardly."[109]

GOMPERS AND DEBS MEET

Although Debs was now ready to repudiate the policy of quiet lobbying being advocated by Gompers and the American Federation of Labor, he did not break off his relations with Lucy Robins. She continued to be one of his most frequent visitors at the Atlanta Penitentiary.

Debs was generally cut off from visitors, but Robins was the exception. She was given special permission to regularly meet with Debs.

In September 1921, Robins joined Gompers in traveling to Atlanta. This was a significant gesture for Gompers, given the profound differences in political perspectives between Debs and Gompers. Nevertheless, the demand for amnesty for Debs was becoming a popular cause, one that even the AFL had officially endorsed. Gompers used the annual conference of the Amalgamated Association of Street and Electric Railway Employees as a convenient excuse to go to Atlanta.[110] Shortly after attending the conference to give a keynote speech, he would also visit the nearby federal prison.

Thus, on September 16, 1921, Gompers and Robins met for a short time with Debs in the warden's office. Afterward, Robins sought to present this visit as a time when Debs expressed his support for her in the continuing battle with the Socialist Party and the Political Amnesty Committee. According to Robins, Debs and Gompers met on the friendliest terms, exploring reminiscences of "boyhood days." Robins also reported that Gompers had informed Debs of his disagreement with socialist efforts to put pressure on the Harding administration. Gompers found he "could not work with" the PAC since its militant tactics only "hindered" the amnesty effort. Robins then went further, claiming that Debs had responded, "I fully understand and I do not blame you."[111]

Robins was putting words into Debs's mouth. It is highly unlikely that Debs would criticize the Socialist Party to Gompers, a person he had publicly derided for decades. Gompers was far more circumspect in describing the Atlanta meeting in his autobiography. According to his account, Debs had modified his views, so that "the perverting twist" given by radical politics "seemed to disappear."[112]

In a conversation with David Karsner shortly after his release from prison, Debs limited his comments on this meeting to the observation that it had been "very brief." In talking to a reporter, he merely characterized his discussion with Gompers in prison as "frigid."[113] Debs was reluctant to reopen the bitter disputes that had taken place among those demanding amnesty.

A more revealing report can be found in a letter from Gompers to Harry Lang, the labor reporter for the *Forward* and a political ally. (Lang would later marry Lucy Robins.) In his account of the meeting in Atlanta, Gompers wrote that he took the occasion to "whisper a word of encouragement" and to convey "hope" for Debs's "liberation."[114] Gompers's description of this brief encounter has the ring of truth. Needless to say, it bears no resemblance to the description given by either Robins or Gompers in his autobiography.

HARDING AND STEFFENS MAKE A DEAL

For months, the issue of an amnesty for the political prisoners of the war remained deadlocked as Harding adamantly refused to move until an official peace treaty with Germany was signed and went into effect. Debs became increasingly bitter in his attitude toward Harding and his stalling tactics. Theodore Debs wrote to a friend of rumors that Harding might soon act and yet he could "no longer enthuse." There had been a time when Harding might have "received credit for righting a grievous wrong," but that day was "long past."[115]

Finally, on November 15, 1921, the U.S. peace treaty with Germany came into effect and the logjam finally began breaking. That same day, the American Civil Liberties Union and the World War Veterans, an organization formed as a counter to the jingoism of the American Legion, picketed a meeting of an international conference to limit armaments held in Washington demanding an amnesty for all political prisoners. Debs strongly approved of this demonstration. He pointed out that an earlier picket of the White House by those supporting women's suffrage had been attacked by thugs, but this time the presence of "a husky soldier or marine" had ensured that the amnesty pickets were "not insulted or assaulted."[116]

A few days after the signing of the peace treaty, a delegation from the Political Amnesty Committee briefly met with Harding. The delegation, which included Roger Baldwin from the American Civil Liberties Union, left a written message with the president stating that

Debs "had no wish to receive executive clemency" that was not also extended to "others convicted under the same wartime laws."[117]

Debs had made it clear that he would not apply for a pardon, admit his guilt, recant his views, or accept any restrictions on what he would say once released. Harding was willing to accept Debs's position on his previous actions, but he still hoped to cajole Debs into a promise that would limit Debs's attacks on the administration, at least in the period immediately following his release from prison. An article in the *New York Times* reported that the administration was considering the speedy release of Debs contingent on "a pledge to abstain from public expression of his views."[118] Although the government publicly claimed that this would not be a condition for his release, it is clear that Debs was being told that Harding might delay his release unless he agreed to such a pledge.

One of the important prerogatives reserved to a president is the issuing of pardons. Most presidents have compiled a list of Christmas Day pardons to mark the holiday season.[119] By the end of November 1921, the question of including Debs on this list was becoming a matter of urgent priority. At a meeting held on November 22, 1921, Harding asked each member of his cabinet to express his views on the issue of an amnesty for political prisoners. Half of the meeting was spent in discussing this issue.[120] Harding also held several lengthy meetings with Daugherty trying to forge a coherent policy.

The entire question of amnesty for those jailed for opposing the war effort could no longer be dodged. Although the release of the IWW prisoners remained a controversial issue, the president understood that the "*Debs* case" would "come first." Once again, unofficial reports were circulated that "an offer of freedom" would be extended to Debs "provided he would exercise discretion in expressing his views."[121]

Debs had already indicated that he was not prepared to make such a commitment as a condition for his release. Instead, the president and his coterie devised a shrewd and devious plan. Harding was coming under intense popular pressure to release Debs while the hard-liners within the Republican Party continued to insist that Debs serve his entire prison sentence. The president sought to gain all of the possible plaudits from the granting of a pardon by having Debs come to the White House upon his release, with the assurance that he would not immediately condemn Harding for his adamant refusal to release the IWW prisoners.

Harding worked through Will Hays, a politically connected attorney who had managed Harding's presidential campaign and who was awarded with the cabinet position of postmaster general. On December 4, 1921, Hays traveled to Chicago and met with Lincoln Steffens, the most famous of the muckraking journalists. A few weeks prior to the Chicago meeting, Steffens had written to Hays arguing that Harding should issue a "general amnesty" that would include not only Debs but "the broadest, most generous" pardon ever declared.[122] Steffens was eager to follow up this letter with a personal meeting with the president.

Hays had an offer to propose to Steffens. He would arrange for Steffens to meet with Debs in the Atlanta Penitentiary and then afterward Steffens could return to Washington and meet with Harding. During the last months of his prison term, Debs was only permitted to see visitors approved by the warden.

Hays certainly made it clear that Harding would be more likely to release Debs if he agreed to refrain from attacking the administration. It seems clear that Harding and Hays were pressuring Debs to mute his criticism of the administration once he was freed, but there was also a specific focus on the immediate period following his release from the Atlanta Penitentiary. Steffens got the message and told Hays that he would advise Debs "not to come out and talk hate, but rather would speak for Russian relief." Steffens was an enthusiastic and uncritical admirer of Soviet Russia, which had recently emerged from a brutal civil war and was in dire need of foreign aid to feed its people. Hays responded, "Just what we want." He then indicated that Debs had a good chance of being on the Christmas list of pardons.[123]

It took some time to arrange for Steffens to visit with Debs. He first went to Washington and met Hays for a further discussion, before taking the lengthy train ride to Atlanta. On December 16, 1921,

Steffens had a two-hour discussion with Debs within the prison walls. Steffens's account of this meeting focused on a vigorous debate the two had concerning Soviet Russia.[124] Debs was already becoming disaffected with the Soviet regime while Steffens unreservedly defended the Bolsheviks. In the end, Debs agreed to solicit funds for Russian relief since the Russian people were in desperate need.

Obviously, this discussion was held in the context of Steffens's attempt to persuade Debs to limit his remarks to Russian relief and to avoid any condemnation of the Harding administration. No doubt, Steffens also told Debs of his upcoming visit to the White House and his hope that he could convince Harding to release the IWW activists and the other political prisoners. From the indications given by his future actions, Debs agreed to refrain from attacking Harding in the period immediately following his release, thus making it easier for the president to gain a positive popular response for commuting his sentence. Debs had no intention of being muzzled after this initial period and he would have been certain to make this clear to Steffens. It would seem from later events that Debs was told that he would be expected to go to Washington upon his release from prison. In addition to a meeting with the president, Debs was also promised another meeting with Daugherty, where he could again press for the immediate release of all of the political prisoners.

As Steffens traveled to Atlanta and back to Washington, Harding was making the final decisions on the Christmas list. On December 17, Daugherty advised Harding that Debs was "an habitual violator of the laws of the country" who had demonstrated a "chronic disregard for his country." In spite of the unceasing pressure and his failing health, Debs had continued to voice his radical politics. As retaliation for Debs's continuing criticisms of the Harding administration, Daugherty urged the president to reject a commutation of Debs's sentence.[125]

Later that same day, December 17, 1921, Harding fulfilled his promise and met with Steffens. In reporting on his meeting with Debs, Steffens indicated that Debs was prepared to accept the proposal presented by Hays. The president accepted this arrangement, but he also directly rejected the proposal of a general amnesty for political prisoners. Harding also showed Steffens a memorandum from the Justice Department arguing that IWW prisoners should be required to sign a statement admitting their guilt and pledging to remain law-abiding once freed as a prerequisite for being considered for executive clemency. Steffens responded that these conditions were humiliating and that he would not have agreed to sign such a statement had he been one of those in jail.[126]

Steffens had to admit that he had totally "failed" to move Harding on the question of a general amnesty. Still, his actions had facilitated Debs's release. On December 20, Harding convened another meeting of his cabinet. The Christmas list was one of the featured items on the agenda. Daugherty again expressed his opposition to releasing Debs and his reluctance to free any of the IWW prisoners. Nevertheless, the president confirmed that Debs would be receiving "an out-and-out pardon."[127]

Debs understood from his meeting with Steffens that there was a good likelihood that he would soon be released. In a letter to his brother Theodore, written on December 19, Debs mentioned that it was "highly possible" that he would soon be free. He sarcastically concluded that his release would be granted because Wall Street bankers had determined that "we traitors should now be treated with clemency and granted a pardon."[128]

DEBS FREED

On Christmas Day, December 25, 1921, Debs left the Atlanta Federal Penitentiary, his sentence having been commuted by Harding. He was immediately greeted by a small party of friends including his brother and Lucy Robins. Debs stood briefly outside of the prison complex waving his hat as 2,300 prisoners bellowed their support for him.

Debs sent a cable to his wife describing his immediate plans, referring to a "necessary trip to Washington."[129] Surrounded by reporters upon his release and on the train, Debs declined to comment. The reporters understood that Debs was acting in accordance with a confidential agreement made with the administration. The correspondent from the *Indianapolis Star* noted that there was "no doubt but that a condition of release" had "been imposed," silencing Debs for at least the duration of the trip to Washington. When queried on this point, Debs responded that "he could say nothing."[130]

Debs did inform the reporters that he would not use the Pullman car berth that had been ordered and that the money saved would be given to Russian relief. This seems to fit with the scenario previously agreed upon by Debs and the administration as mediated by Steffens.[131]

Once in Washington, Debs had a thirty-minute meeting with Daugherty. After the meeting, Daugherty issued a statement declaring that "no unusual conditions" had been "attached to the commutation" of Debs. From the Department of Justice, Debs walked with his brother to the White House and a thirty-minute meeting with the president. Harding did not issue a statement concerning this meeting.[132]

Initially, Debs avoided meeting with reporters while in Washington. Finally, just before returning home to Terre Haute, Debs participated in a full interview with a group of reporters. Even then, he was cautious in his statements. Debs carefully noted that he had been "received very cordially" at the White House and that both Harding and Daugherty had assured him that his "release was unconditional." He also stated that he had found the president to be "a most gracious and charming gentleman."[133]

Still, Debs made it clear that he was committed to making every effort to free the remaining political prisoners, especially the IWW members who refused to recant their views and who had thus been declared ineligible for a pardon. Debs emphasized that he had an "obligation" to "every political prisoner" to insist on their immediate release and that he would tour the country for this cause.[134]

Clearly, Daugherty and Debs had agreed that the substance of their second conversation would remain confidential, as had the first. Still, Theodore Debs later provided some insight into what had occurred during the meeting in a letter to Roger Baldwin. Daugherty and Debs had reviewed the cases of the political prisoners, most of whom were

IWW activists. The attorney general had then promised Debs "to do the best he could in each case."[135] It was with this promise in mind that Debs had agreed to remain silent as to his conversations with Harding and Daugherty and to remain circumspect in his interviews with reporters while in Washington.

Of course, Daugherty had again deliberately misled Debs. In his confidential memoranda to the president, Daugherty had consistently opposed the release of most of the IWW prisoners, although Harding had opted for a more devious policy of pitting one group of Wobbly prisoners against another. In any case, Daugherty's promise to Debs was worthless.

Having fulfilled his obligations in Washington, Debs returned to Terre Haute where he was met by 50,000 jubilant supporters in a joyous celebration of his release. Again, Debs kept his remarks general, only advising that he had no "bitterness or rancor" in his "heart against anyone."[136] Thus, throughout the days following his release from prison, Debs avoided any sharp criticisms of the Harding administration, although he did affirm his support for the political prisoners who had not been freed and his willingness to tour the country on their behalf once he had sufficiently recuperated.

Debs's health had been severely damaged during his incarceration, and for months after his return home he remained in bed, unable to actively participate in any political activity. Debs also spent lengthy periods in a sanatorium in a Chicago suburb. His treatment there did little to cure his ailments, but he was able to rest and gain distance from the pressures to return to political activity.[137]

Debs felt a strong obligation to speak out for the IWW prisoners who remained incarcerated. His brother wrote that Debs would "leave nothing undone" in the effort to free those "comrades still in jail."[138] His total collapse prevented him from fulfilling this pledge for several months.

By the summer of 1922, Debs was feeling somewhat better. From this point until his death, he did not hold back in his public statements. His criticisms of the government and the corporations were trenchant and were made in the same spirit as those he had made prior to his imprisonment. Debs must have believed that the terms of his tacit agreement with Harding had been met and that he could now freely express his criticisms of both the capitalist system and the administration. He also realized that Harding and Daugherty had no intention of a speedy release of the IWW prisoners.

During the first months of 1922, railroad workers organized a nationwide strike. For Debs, who had first been politicized as a leader of a drive to create an industrial union of railroad workers, this strike held a special importance. As the government clamped down on the strikers, with state militias mobilized and federal troops on call, Debs issued a furious denunciation. His statement of July 17, 1922, insisted that it was essential for the working class to "cut loose once and for all from the rotten parties" of their "masters." Workers had rallied behind the government as it waged a pointless imperialist war, gulled by the argument that their situation would improve once the war came to an end. Instead, the government was preparing "to shoot you down like dogs."[139]

This was a strong statement, but Debs was even more caustic during his first personal appearance after his release from prison. On November 26, 1922, five thousand gathered in Chicago to hear Debs speak. He denounced the Harding administration's refusal to release those who had opposed the war and he reiterated that he had "nothing to regret" for his own actions as a dissenter. Indeed, Debs proclaimed that he would not be intimidated and that he would continue to "despise and defy their laws." This was a clear challenge to the authorities to jail him again for his beliefs. Illinois had passed a criminal syndicalism law and members of the newly formed Communist Party were being sent to prison under its terms. Implicitly referring to the Harding administration's efforts to coerce him prior to his release, Debs insisted that he would "rather be in jail" with his "self-respect than on the street with a gag" stuffed in his mouth.[140]

Debs never recovered his health. In the years after his release from prison, he suffered from lengthy spells during which he was confined to his bed. He was therefore never able to tour the country in defense of the IWW prisoners.[141] The last of the Wobbly prisoners were only released from Leavenworth Federal Penitentiary in December 1923 by action of President Calvin Coolidge. Harding had refused to sign a general amnesty covering all of the IWW prisoners until his death in August 1923.

Debs died in October 1926 of heart failure.[142] He had met the challenge. Both Woodrow Wilson and Warren Harding had used every means to muzzle him and coerce him into silence. Debs persevered, holding to his radical politics, but the cost had been high.

Summary

When Debs left the federal penitentiary in Atlanta on Christmas Day 1921, it was the culmination of a lengthy campaign to gain his freedom. Nevertheless, the two and a half years in jail had taken a tremendous toll on his health. Debs never recovered and he remained in ill health for the rest of his life. He had paid a huge price for his opposition to the First World War.

Woodrow Wilson's stubborn refusal to free Debs came as an enormous disappointment to progressives, including some of those who had supported the war effort. The struggle to free Debs became a popular movement mobilizing a wide range of sympathizers. It was very hard for many to understand how the United States could have been fighting a war for democracy while it harshly condemned those who dissented. The amnesty campaign continued to build during the Harding administration as the president stalled for months before finally releasing Debs.

The American Federation of Labor was one of the organizations that joined the amnesty campaign well after it had initially formed. Samuel Gompers was cautious in lending his support to the drive to free Debs. Furthermore, once the AFL began calling for an amnesty for those who had spoken out against the war, Gompers and the AFL's leadership used their influence to discourage any effort to organize a public protest. Gompers insisted that the only way forward was quiet lobbying and that protests only alienated those who held power. The split in the amnesty campaign left Debs in a difficult position, although he eventually came down on the side of the Socialist Party which was calling for a mobilization of public opinion.

The debate within the amnesty campaign a century ago is still reflected within current social movements. Thus, the debate around the push to free Debs is still relevant today.

SECTION II

THE MILITARY AND THE SUPPRESSION OF DISSENT

6

Traitors, Spies, and Military Tribunals

The question of whether judicial bodies controlled by the military can claim jurisdiction over civilians has been a repeated point of contention since the United States was founded. The issue was indirectly debated at the constitutional convention in 1789. As a result, the sole fundamental civil liberty incorporated into the U.S. Constitution was the right to obtain a writ of habeas corpus, that is, a guarantee that the government could not arbitrarily detain an individual for an extended period of time, but rather the person had to be turned over to a civilian court as rapidly as possible and charged with a specific offense. This basic right provides an implicit assurance that civilians cannot be tried in a military court. Thus, the issue of when the president or Congress can suspend the writ of habeas corpus has been of critical importance and has led repeatedly to heated debates.

The question of the scope of military tribunals usually becomes acute during times of war, when those in power are eager to sacrifice basic rights to the expediency of the moment. Military tribunals do not provide defendants with basic rights guaranteed to defendants in civilian courts. For instance, instead of being tried by a jury of one's peers, the judges in a military tribunal are officers appointed by those in command.

A critical episode in this continuing controversy came during the First World War, when the federal government launched a sustained campaign to suppress all organized opposition. As a result, fundamental civil liberties were trampled upon in the rush to jail radicals, pacifists and militant trade union activists.

In the midst of this wartime hysteria, influential members of Congress, with the support of military intelligence and legal advice from a high official within the Department of Justice, pushed hard to have the writ of habeas corpus suspended. They were intent on expanding the jurisdiction of military tribunals to include those who opposed the war. Those prosecuted would be charged with a crime that could subject them to the death penalty if convicted. Important figures in the business community endorsed these plans, eager to see the federal government adopt an even more draconian stance toward those who criticized the war and the corporate system. In the end, President Woodrow Wilson blocked the move and dissidents continued to be prosecuted within the civilian judicial system. A close examination of this debate can help us to better understand the dangers inherent in more recent debates that have occurred since the tragic events of September 11, 2001.

The Espionage Act and the Defence of the Realm

Charles Warren stood at the center of the First World War–era controversy concerning military tribunals. A Harvard graduate and a descendant of a prominent colonial family, Warren had been involved in Democratic Party politics before joining the Justice Department in 1914 as an assistant attorney general, where he specialized in enforcing the Neutrality Act.

In the spring of 1917, Warren was given the responsibility of drafting the Espionage Act, the statute under which opponents of the war were sentenced to lengthy prison terms. While writing the Espionage Act, Warren leaned heavily on the British experience.

Warren worked closely with William Wiseman, who led the U.S. operations of the Secret Intelligence Service, and MI6, the UK equivalent of the Central Intelligence Agency. In January 1917, three months before the United States declared war on Germany, Wiseman began "working with federal authorities" on legal strategies to counter and disrupt the antiwar opposition. In doing so, he not only gained access to detailed information on the activities of U.S. intelligence agencies, but he was also able "to some extent [to] influence their actions." Wiseman quickly discovered that "various state and federal police authorities" were "at loggerheads, and without proper cooperation." He therefore "drafted a report showing [the] necessity for cooperation and much fuller powers."[1]

According to Wiseman, this report convinced the administration to formulate a "Conspiracies Bill" for congressional approval. Wiseman also provided Warren and the Department of Justice with a complete copy of the Defence of the Realm Act, including the many regulations that had been issued to enforce it. He reported to his superiors that U.S. authorities had then "based their bill on it." Wiseman was not engaging in idle boasting.[2]

In October 1917, Warren sent a copy of the Espionage Act as enacted by Congress in June to Rufus Isaacs, Lord Reading, who had recently visited the United States as a special emissary of the British government. Warren pointed to the Espionage Act as a key indication of how "far this country has gone in the direction of your Defence of the Realm Act."[3]

Title I, Section 3, of the Espionage Act provided the federal government with the legal grounds to incarcerate hundreds of antiwar activists and radical union militants during the First World War. Those convicted of violating this section could be imprisoned for up to twenty years. Its provisions closely followed key sections of the Defence of the Realm Act.

The most frequently used provision of Title 1, Section 3 of the Espionage Act provided that anyone who "shall willfully obstruct the recruiting or enlistment service" of the armed services during wartime would be in violation of the law. This wording is patterned on Regulation 27 of the Defence of the Realm Regulations as promulgated in November 1916. That regulation made it illegal to "spread reports" that were "likely to prejudice the recruiting of persons" into the armed forces of the United Kingdom.[4] The wording was deliberately designed to be both broad and vague, thus enabling the UK and U.S. governments to shift the parameters of permitted speech without having to take any formal action.

In 1918, dozens of IWW leaders received sentences of ten to twenty years in maximum-security federal prisons upon being convicted of violating this provision of the Espionage Act. As justification, government prosecutors pointed to editorials printed in the union's newspaper, *Solidarity*, criticizing the draft.

The Supposed Inadequacies of the Espionage Act

Although Warren had drafted the Espionage Act, and had initially supervised its enforcement, he soon decided that the statute provided an insufficient basis for the total suppression of radical dissidents and antiwar activists. In spite of the administration's relentless enforcement of the Espionage Act, Warren remained convinced that key flaws in the judicial system would undercut government efforts to suppress dissent and thus make it possible for the peace movement to emerge as a credible threat to the war effort.

Warren was furious that those charged with violating the Espionage Act could be released on bail pending final disposition of their legal appeals. In fact, federal district judges usually set such high bail terms that the great majority of those charged were held in prison while waiting their trial or appellate reviews. Still, a few well-known figures, such as Eugene Debs, Bill Haywood, and Victor Berger, were released on bail even after being convicted at the district court level and remained free for months before their appeals were concluded. Cases such as these dismayed Warren.

More important, Warren was convinced that radical activists would not be deterred by the lengthy prison sentences being imposed on those convicted under the Espionage Act. Dissidents would risk lengthy prison sentences in the belief that they would be granted presidential pardons once the war ended. In the end, most political prisoners did not serve their full sentences, although many IWW leaders remained in Leavenworth Federal Penitentiary, a brutally rigorous high-security prison, for more than four years after the war had ended. Many of them never recovered from the harsh treatment they received as prisoners.

In Warren's view, only the death penalty could deter radicals from engaging in activities that might obstruct the war effort. Furthermore, death sentences needed to be carried out quickly, while the war was still being fought. There could be no presidential pardon once the war ended for those who had already been executed. Warren was convinced that a few summary executions would provide a signal warning to everyone who was thinking of joining an antiwar group.

Warren's objections to the existing system of judicial trials under the Espionage Act required two distinct changes in the government's push to suppress dissent. First, those charged with opposing the war had to be charged with an offense that carried the death penalty. This was initially a political problem, although it soon led to a series of complex legal issues. Congress had already approved the Espionage Act providing twenty-year sentences for obstructing the war. This legislation could have been amended by Congress to call for the possibility of the death penalty, and yet this would have aroused widespread popular opposition since few believed that merely criticizing the war effort should be punished by death. Thus Warren sought to find a way to include opposition to the war among the actions covered by a charge that normally carried the death sentence. He came up with two possibilities, treason and acting as a spy.

Still, this was not enough. Warren had to provide a basis for moving civilian dissidents into the scope of military tribunals, a shift that would have required the suspension of the writ of habeas corpus. Military courts did not permit bail for those charged with serious crimes. Furthermore, the military judicial system moved far more quickly than civilian courts, so a defendant sentenced to death could be quickly executed.

Warren proposed two possible legal justifications for a suspension of the writ of habeas corpus. One argument held that the constitutional

requirements for a suspension of the writ were met in the distinct circumstances of the First World War. The other justification argued that
those opposing the war were acting as spies and were thus subject to
military tribunals.

The debate concerning Warren's justifications for expanding the
scope of military courts thus raised a series of troubling questions
that operated at different levels. Nevertheless, had Warren's suggestions been implemented, the result would have been the execution of
individuals for either expressing their opposition to the war or conducting peaceful strikes. This would have been a devastating blow to
civil liberties that would have established a disastrous precedent for
the future.

TREASON

In the summer of 1917, Warren formulated a novel legal strategy to
meet the supposed failings in the Espionage Act. He started by proposing that those who actively opposed the war, organized militant
strikes, or engaged in sabotage were guilty of treason and, once found
guilty, could be executed. His original brief supporting this argument
does not seem to have survived, but other sources, including a law
review article, provide the essential points.

Charges of treason were frequently hurled at anyone who opposed
the war. Sensationalized articles in the tabloid press spuriously
claimed that those opposing the war were funded by the German government. These arguments were even made by members of Wilson's
cabinet. Postmaster General Albert Burleson categorized the antiwar press as "traitorous," thus defending his decision to bar socialist
newspapers from the mails.[5] Nevertheless, Warren was going much
further, arguing that dissidents should be prosecuted as traitors and,
once convicted, executed.

Treason is the only crime specified in the U.S. Constitution, with
the wording derived from a British parliamentary statute of 1351.
The English statute had several sections, but the two key ones held
that those providing "aid or comfort" to the enemies of the king or

"levying war" against the monarch were guilty of treason and could be punished by the death penalty.

Initially, treason was narrowly defined. In his codification of the common law, Blackstone held that a charge of providing "aid and comfort" required an "overt act" such as providing secret intelligence to an enemy nation or "selling them arms." These actions could also constitute treason when furnished to those "in actual rebellion at home."[6]

In the nineteenth century, English courts went even further by creating the crime of "constructive treason," which made it possible to try those who criticized the government as traitors. Any opposition to the government could be treated as a threat to the life of the monarch and was thus considered to be an act of treason.[7]

The authors of the U.S. Constitution were concerned that the charge of treason could be misused to suppress legitimate dissent. Article III, Section 3, of the United States Constitution narrowly defines treason as either the "levying of war" against the federal government, that is, armed revolt, or "adhering to their enemies, giving them aid and comfort." Furthermore, this provision specified that a person could only be convicted of treason on the basis of two witnesses who would testify that the defendant had committed an "overt act" to further the conspiratorial plot.

Throughout U.S. history, very few individuals have been convicted of treason. Indeed, the federal courts have narrowly limited the scope of the actions that can be prosecuted as treason under the provisions of the Constitution. Already in 1807, Chief Justice John Marshall, sitting as a trial judge in a case that involved Aaron Burr, a former vice president charged with conspiring to send a military force to separate a part of the western frontier from U.S. rule, had written that treason "should not be extended by construction to doubtful cases." Specifically, Marshall had ruled that the "overt act" required for a conviction does not include those who merely "advise" the key figures in a conspiracy and do "nothing further." Instead, "crimes not clearly within the constitutional definition should receive such punishment as the legislature in its wisdom may provide."[8]

By enacting the Espionage Act of 1917, Congress had done exactly what Marshall suggested, that is, making opposition to the war or to the draft a federal crime. Warren had drafted this legislation and yet he sought to vastly expand the scope of the treason charge to cover a wide range of activities already made illegal by the Espionage Act.

The charge of treason had been devised to deter the citizens of a combatant nation from providing assistance to the government of an enemy nation and to punish those who participated in organized efforts to use violence in a deliberate effort to overthrow the government. During the period from the start of the First World War in August 1914 to the U.S. entry into it in April 1917, German agents carried out an extensive program of sabotage directed at facilities in the United States that were producing goods for the UK's war effort. German agents also initiated rather feeble attempts to finance pro-German propaganda and to incite strikes in factories producing munitions for the UK. Once the United States declared war on Germany, U.S. authorities, with the aid of UK intelligence agents, quickly rounded up and detained as enemy aliens most of those suspected of cooperating with German agents.

Warren's belief that the Espionage Act was insufficient did not stem from his fear of the activities of German agents or those who cooperated with them. Instead, he focused on the activities of the Industrial Workers of the World. In the summer of 1917, the federal government felt threatened by the IWW, which had organized militant strikes in the timber camps of the Pacific Northwest and the copper mines of the West. In a letter to Attorney General Thomas Gregory on August 6, 1917, Warren denounced these strikes as "treasonable."[9]

The federal government viewed the IWW as a significant obstacle to the war effort because it had shown its ability to coordinate effective strikes involving tens of thousands of workers. Since prosecutions initiated on this basis would have caused a major political embarrassment, the Department of Justice pointed to alleged acts of violence that had caused property damage to recalcitrant corporations. Over the years, the IWW had been vocal in its support for sabotage as a valid tactic in the class struggle, although it had refrained from specifically defining this tactic. Once the United States entered the war, and the Wobblies had become a primary target of government repression, the union publicly disavowed the use of sabotage. Furthermore, there is no credible evidence that the IWW committed significant acts of sabotage during either the timber strike that spread throughout the Pacific Northwest in the spring and summer of 1917 or the strike of copper miners in Arizona.[10]

Still, government officials insisted that the IWW continued to engage in acts of sabotage, so one of the charges its leaders confronted under the Espionage Act was a conspiracy to commit acts of violence. Warren understood that bringing a charge of treason against IWW leaders could not succeed unless he could counter the guidelines established by Marshall in the Burr case. He therefore argued that the destruction of property needed "for the successful prosecution of the war may equally constitute treason and giving aid and comfort to the enemy." Such actions were covered when "performed with the intent" of aiding the enemy. Warren went on to claim that in determining intent a defendant "must be held to intend the direct, natural and reasonable consequences of his own act."[11]

Under the "natural and reasonable consequences" doctrine the government did not have to demonstrate that a defendant intended to breech the law. Instead, the prosecution could focus on the possible harmful consequences of the acts and then argue that the defendant should have been aware of these consequences before committing the acts in question. In this case, the destruction of property of a corporation producing goods for the war effort, as virtually every corporation did during the First World War, was bound to help the Germans by curtailing the power of the U.S. military. Thus, acts of sabotage or violence initiated during a strike with the aim of limiting the production of goods by strikebreakers could be considered as providing aid and comfort to the enemy and therefore treason and could be punished by death. Of course, the logic of this argument would have led the federal government to prosecute as treason destructive acts committed during strikes organized by AFL unions, something the Department of Justice would have never considered, given the AFL's close ties to the Democratic Party.

Warren was making use of a legal standard of proof that allowed the government to gain convictions on the basis of a minimum of evidence. The natural and reasonable consequences argument is rooted in British common law in relation to seditious libel. A person could be prosecuted for statements uttered or printed that have the "tendency" to encourage listeners or readers to violate the law. In his codification of English law, Blackstone had written that those who publish "what is improper, mischievous or illegal he must take the consequences." The government can punish those responsible for "any dangerous or offensive writings" the authorities believe is of "a pernicious tendency" as "necessary for the preservation of peace and order."[12]

Seditious libel laws permitted the government to suppress any dissident opinion it saw as a threat to its authority. Free speech had no legal standing and depended on the good will of those currently holding office. Until the 1920s, U.S. courts generally followed Blackstone's guidelines. Debs was indicted for allegedly violating the Espionage Act on the basis that one could voice opposition to the war or the draft "unless the natural and reasonable tendency and effect" of a speech would have "consequences forbidden by law."[13]

Warren was stretching the net cast by the natural and reasonable consequences argument even further than previously. He was proposing that defendants be convicted of treason, that is, of assisting the enemy, because their actions objectively aided the German cause. Thus, the prosecution did not have to prove that defendants intended to help the enemy, or even that their actions had any significant impact, as long as the government could establish the "natural and reasonable consequences" of these actions. Warren was prepared to infer a link between those charged with treason and the German government on the basis of the possible results of the defendants' actions, even when no evidence of such a link existed.

In this case, the natural and reasonable consequences doctrine led to a conclusion that was not only tenuous but directly contrary to the facts of the case. Even making the false assumptions that the IWW received funds from Germany and that it engaged in acts of sabotage, the union engaged in strikes to advance the wages and working conditions of its members. Any efforts that were made to hinder production were not undertaken to further the German military effort, but rather to put pressure on recalcitrant employers.

Warren had a difficult time finding any precedents for such a vast expansion of the scope of the charge of treason in U.S. case law. Instead, he turned once again to the British legal precedent. Specifically, he cited a ruling by Rufus Isaacs, who had presided as Lord Chief Justice over the trial of Roger Casement, an Irish nationalist involved in the Easter Uprising in Dublin in April 1916. Isaacs had held that any British subject who commits an act that "strengthens or tends to strengthen the enemies of the King in the act of the war against the King" is thereby giving "aid and comfort" to the enemy and is, therefore, guilty of treason.[14] Casement had been executed on the basis of this ruling. The wording provides such sweeping grounds for prosecution that virtually any opposition to the war, or any strike, could be considered an act of treason.

Warren was unable to find a single precedent in U.S. law to support his argument. Instead, he turned to a most unusual source for validation. In 1894, soon after his graduation from Harvard Law School, Warren was one of the three founders of the Immigration Restriction League (IRL), becoming its first secretary as well. The league called for limits in the numbers allowed to immigrate to the United States at a time when this was unrestricted, with the exception of those from China and Japan. Yet this would only be the first step. The Immigration Restriction League was concerned that too many of the immigrants came from the "inferior races," that is, they were not white Anglo-Saxon Protestants. Thus, the league mixed xenophobia with racism, a combination that remains potent to this day.

One of those who joined the IRL was Madison Grant, a leading zoologist and a proponent of eugenics. Grant brought Charles Stewart Davison, one of his closest friends, into the league. A New York City corporate lawyer, Davison had connections with powerful financiers. During the First World War, he became the chairman of the American Defense Society, an organization which zealously supported the war effort, while chastising the federal government for not doing enough to suppress the antiwar opposition.[15]

Davison wrote a tract on treason that appeared in the *New York Tribune* in 1917 and was then reprinted in several other newspapers around the country. In Davison's view, articles questioning the government's war policies would be sufficient foundation for a "finding" that the author was "giving aid and comfort" to the enemy. Such a finding would have been equivalent to being found guilty of treason, for which one could be executed. The charge would hold whether the statements presented were "true or false," since the writings might "tend to diminish" the effectiveness of the armed forces.[16] Davison made no effort to cite legal precedents for this argument. His position constituted a virtual nullification of the First Amendment.

Warren cited this tract as support for his argument. He praised Davison's contribution as a "thoughtful" pamphlet.[17] His praise of this diatribe was most unusual. When his article appeared in the *Yale Law Review* in January 1918, Warren was still an assistant attorney general. The article defended a legal argument that had already been rejected by the Justice Department and, implicitly, by the president. Furthermore, the American Defense Society was made up of stalwart Republicans. Its relations with the Wilson administration were frequently strained, so citing an article by Davison was not likely to persuade government decision makers. Still, both Warren and Davison were convinced that the need to mobilize the entire society for a total war rendered the Bill of Rights inoperative. Legal precedents that went counter to this argument were simply swept aside.

Attorney General Thomas Gregory was prepared to expand the range of the treason charge to cover sabotage in certain instances, holding that "the destruction of human life or property for the purpose of aiding the enemy" constituted in itself an act of treason.[18] This was a very dubious argument. The government had prosecuted IWW leaders under the Espionage Act on the basis that they had allegedly conspired to commit acts of sabotage in order to obstruct the armed forces and the war effort.[19] There was therefore no compelling reason to expand the scope of the treason charge.

The federal government had repeatedly attempted to demonstrate that the IWW was receiving funds from the German government, but no evidence to support this charge was uncovered.[20]

Furthermore, under the guidelines set by Marshall's opinion the "overt act" required to sustain a charge of treason entailed direct participation in that act. Many IWW leaders who were indicted for conspiracy were located in Chicago, thousands of miles from the timber strikes and the strikes of copper miners. Finally, these strikes were remarkably peaceful. The IWW relied on mass action and avoided acts of sabotage.

In spite of the evidence to the contrary, Gregory was convinced that the IWW was secretly funded by the German government and that it deliberately engaged in a campaign of sabotage. Furthermore, he believed that civilians committing certain acts of sabotage in time of war could be prosecuted for treason, an argument of dubious validity. Nevertheless, although Gregory accepted a significant part of Warren's argument, he still rejected a critical point. Gregory did not believe that intent could be inferred but rather that the intent underlying an act of sabotage had to be demonstrated by the specific targets of the action and by evidence establishing the motivation behind the act.

Gregory concluded that the charge of treason failed to provide an effective basis for "dealing with the willful destruction or injury of war supplies or war industries." Treason was such a serious crime, and the penalty for its commission "so severe," that "the hostile intent" had to be "clearly demonstrated."[21] This represented an implicit rejection of Warren's argument that intent could be inferred from the "natural and reasonable consequences" of an allegedly treasonous act.

Spies engaged in sabotage picked out targets that were of vital importance to the war effort, a bridge or a plant making explosives. Timber corporations accused the Wobblies of spiking trees or cutting board to the wrong lengths. Evidence to support these accusations was meager, but in any case these are not the acts of sabotage that would be carried out by agents of the German government.

Gregory realized that Warren's argument would not withstand scrutiny, so the proposal to levy the charge of treason against IWW leaders and antiwar activists never moved beyond an internal debate within the Department of Justice. The administration believed that the death penalty was not needed and would prove to be unnecessarily provocative. Thus, IWW activists as well as other opponents of the war continued to be prosecuted under the Espionage Act throughout the duration of the war.

THE NEED FOR MILITARY TRIBUNALS

Although Warren was interested in convincing the Justice Department to prosecute dissidents as traitors, he was primarily concerned about moving these prosecutions into the realm of the military judicial system. A military court would be more likely to impose the death sentence on those convicted of a serious felony than a civilian court. Furthermore, a military tribunal was far more likely to accept the argument that an opponent of the war who was charged with sedition or sabotage was a traitor than a civilian judicial court following the guidelines already established by Marshall in the Burr case of 1807.

Indeed, in the century following Marshall's decision there were virtually no prosecutions for treason brought to the civilian judicial system, even during the Civil War. A few cases involving civilians were heard in military courts, but one case, not cited by Warren, is of special interest. In April 1862, a Union naval flotilla gained control of the Mississippi River, leading the Confederate military command to withdraw its troops from New Orleans. On April 25, Admiral David Farragut ordered the city's officials to pull down the Confederate flags flying over public buildings and replace them with U.S. flags. A contingent of marines enforced this order, leaving a U.S. flag flying over the federal mint. As the sailors retreated to their ships, a crowd led by William Mumford, a local gambler and an ardent Confederate sympathizer, defied the marines by tearing down and shredding the U.S. flag being flown over the mint. Mumford was charged with treason for this act of defiance, tried before a military commission and found guilty and hanged in June 1862.[22]

This vindictive act certainly sent a chilling message to the white inhabitants of New Orleans, but it was also a travesty of justice. Mumford was not guilty of treason under the definition explicitly set forth in the U.S. Constitution. His death provides a disturbing example of the risks inherent in establishing a system of justice based on military tribunals.

Warren believed that the federal government needed to create the same sense of threat during the First World War that the occupying troops of the North believed to be necessary as they moved into Confederate territory during the Civil War. By the summer of 1917, Warren had already come to the conclusion that the "Army should deal with enemy activities to a very large extent." In Warren's view, "the only effective way" to quash dissent was "trial by court martial," that is, trial by a military tribunal, since the "methods of criminal courts" were "inadequate." In particular, dissidents "must be *promptly* punished."[23] Trying opponents of the war in military tribunals would permit the government to prosecute them as traitors. Warren believed that dissent could only be effectively suppressed if "the law of treason" was "*vigorously* enforced."[24]

In conjunction with his plan to widen the scope of the charge of treason, Warren proposed that Congress impose martial law throughout the United States. Those accused of treason would therefore be tried by military tribunals and could be executed upon conviction. Within the military judicial system, a defendant has far fewer rights and appeals to a higher authority are quicker. At the time, defendants could be convicted of crimes carrying a possible death sentence by a two-thirds vote rather than the unanimous verdict of a jury in a civilian court. In addition, those charged with "serious offenses" were not eligible for bail prior to their trial. In general, the judges in a military tribunal are not independent of the prosecution, but rather are officers reporting to the same commanding officers who are overseeing the prosecution's case.[25]

THE WRIT OF HABEAS CORPUS

A declaration of martial law, as proposed by Warren, would have nullified the fundamental right to obtain a writ of habeas corpus. A writ of habeas corpus, when issued, is an order to the military, or the police, to physically hand over a prisoner for trial within the civilian judicial system. A public hearing is then held at which the prosecution has to provide credible proof that the accused has committed the crimes specified. If a judge agrees, a trial is then held in which those charged with a crime have the full rights guaranteed by the due process clause in the Constitution.

The right to request and receive a writ of habeas corpus in a court of law is a fundamental right in a democratic society. The writ enables the judicial system to assert its authority over agencies acting for the executive, at the federal level the president. It prevents the government from holding a person indefinitely without bringing them to trial and it also, by implication, prohibits the government from trying a civilian in a military court.

The right to obtain a writ of habeas corpus is rooted in English common law and its implementation was an important step in restricting the arbitrary actions of the monarch and his or her deputies. It was codified in a statute signed by Charles II in 1679 which guaranteed that a person detained without charges would be brought before a judge "within three days of service" of a writ of habeas corpus. Only those charged with treason or another crime carrying a possible death sentence were exempt from the provisions of the Habeas Corpus Act.[26]

In 1776, when the colonists in North America revolted against British rule, one of their foremost grievances was the belief that the imperial authorities acted at their whim to harshly punish those who dissented and that these repressive measures should be subject to an impartial judicial review. Officials often suspended the writ, claiming the urgent necessity to quell popular discontent. As a result, the right to seek and obtain a writ of habeas corpus was viewed as a crucially important safeguard from dictatorial rule. This fundamental right was included in the U.S. Constitution, where Article I, Section 9, holds that the writ of habeas corpus can only be suspended "in cases of rebellion or invasion" when "the public safety may require it." No exemptions were made for those charged with treason or any other crime. Although the constitutional provision did not specify a time limit beyond which a person could be detained without charges, the authors of the U. S. Constitution would have been well aware of the seventeenth-century English statute, so it seems reasonable to assume that a similar time span was implied.

THE *MILLIGAN* CASE

A declaration of martial law by the president, endorsed by Congress, would have granted the armed forces enormous powers, while depriving citizens of fundamental rights. Fortunately, both Attorney General Gregory and President Wilson were wary of moving in this direction. Soon after the United States entered the war in April 1917, Gregory commissioned a respected outside attorney, James M. Proctor, to examine the precedents and evaluate the current situation within that context.[27]

Proctor concludes that the conditions prevailing in the United States in 1917 precluded the possibility of a declaration of martial law, either through a presidential order or through legislation approved by Congress. In reaching this conclusion, Proctor relied heavily on the majority opinion issued by the U.S. Supreme Court in a key case arising out of the Civil War, the Milligan case.

During much of the Civil War, martial law prevailed in Indiana, even though the state was at peace most of the time. The *Milligan* case arose at a time, the military claimed, when Indiana "was constantly threatened to be invaded." In July 1863, a contingent of more than fifteen hundred Confederate cavalry troops had crossed into Indiana. They skirmished with Union troops before moving into Ohio and then retreating southward. Interestingly, Confederate soldiers were met with widespread hostility by Indiana's residents, even in districts where the war was unpopular.[28]

Lambdin Milligan was an attorney and a Democratic Party stalwart in Indiana, a border state in which a significant section of the populace was eager to see the Civil War come to a rapid conclusion. Milligan had sought the Democratic nomination for governor but failed to obtain it. Although Milligan did not support slavery, he believed that each state had the right to determine this issue. Milligan despised the abolitionists and he was fearful that Lincoln was establishing an autocratic state. In working within the Indiana Democratic Party to push for an immediate truce, Milligan worked alongside Harrison Dodd.[29]

Dodd was not satisfied with openly organizing in opposition to the Lincoln administration's war policies. He covertly met with a Confederate agent who gave him $10,000, a sizable sum at the time. The money was to be used primarily to bolster the peace wing of the state Democratic Party, but Dodd also purchased a batch of rifles with a portion of the money. He also created a secret organization, the Sons of Liberty, which seems to have been little more than a paper structure. Furthermore, he named Milligan as one of the leaders of this shadowy group, although Milligan later insisted that he had not known of this appointment and had no interest in pursuing it.[30]

Dodd had nebulous plans for an uprising and he tried to recruit leading members of the Indiana Democratic Party as sponsors, with no success. By now, Dodd's floundering effort had come to the attention of the authorities. Governor Oliver Morton, a Republican and a staunch supporter of the administration, was worried that he might not be reelected in the fall of 1864. He urged Brigadier General Henry Carrington, the commander of the Union troops in Indiana, to detain Dodd and other "peace Democrats" for trial by military tribunal. Carrington saw no reason to do this, since the civilian courts were functioning and grand juries were considering indictments naming those who might be conspiring with Confederate agents. Morton succeeded in having Carrington replaced by Brigadier General Alvin Hovey. In September 1864, Hovey issued an order that Dodd should be detained for trial before a military tribunal.[31]

Dodd succeeded in escaping from detention and then fleeing to sanctuary in Canada. Incensed, Hovey ordered the detention of Milligan and several other peace Democrats. They were tried before a military tribunal in October 1864 on the charge of providing "aid and comfort" to the enemy, that is, treason. Milligan and two other defendants were convicted and sentenced to death. Lincoln stopped the executions and his successor, Andrew Johnson, commuted the death sentences to life in prison. Thus, Milligan was still being held in detention when the war came to an end.[32]

It is highly questionable whether Milligan was actually guilty of treason. Dodd was certainly guilty of engaging in criminal activity by conspiring with a Confederate agent, but it is doubtful that his actions reached the level needed to convict a person of treason. Furthermore, the link between Milligan and this plot was weak. Milligan and Dodd shared a political perspective, one that the Confederacy was eager to promote, but it is far from clear that Milligan was actively involved with Dodd's ineffectual efforts to organize an uprising. The case became a legal test of the limits of the military judicial system in the midst of a wartime emergency.

In addition to the threat of invasion, government prosecutors pointed to the Confederate secession as an act of rebellion justifying the suspension of a writ of habeas corpus and the declaration of martial law. In September 1862, Lincoln issued a proclamation giving military commanders "throughout the country" the right to declare martial law. This proclamation was reinforced by one issued in September 1863 along the same lines. Earlier, in July 1861, Lincoln had justified the summary detention of Confederate sympathizers by holding that the southern states were engaged in a "rebellion" and thus "the public safety" required "the qualified suspension of the privilege of the writ."[33]

In effect, Lincoln was arguing that in a time of total war, when the entire country was being mobilized to defeat the Confederate States, the rebellion in the South justified a drastic suppression of fundamental rights in every other section of the country. With the nation's unity at stake, the actions of dissidents in the Northern states could directly hamper the military operations being mounted against Confederate troops many miles away.

The government thus claimed that the terms of the constitutional provision authorizing the suspension of the writ of habeas corpus were being met in that there was an ongoing rebellion and Indiana was threatened with invasion. Nevertheless, in March 1866, the U.S. Supreme Court ordered the military to release Milligan from detention. In a decision issued that December, the judgment of the military tribunal was overturned by a unanimous vote.[34] Justice David Davis went further, using the opportunity to issue a sweeping decision guaranteeing the right of civilians to be tried in a civilian court even during a wartime emergency. His opinion, supported by a majority of the Supreme Court, held that military tribunals established in areas "in which the federal courts were open" and in "unobstructed exercise" of their operations "had no jurisdiction" to try civilians from states that had not joined the rebellion for "any criminal offense."[35]

Davis explicitly rejected the justifications presented by government prosecutors. On the issue of quashing a rebellion, Davis held that only in a "theatre of active military operations where war really prevails" and "no power is left but the military" would the authorities be "allowed to govern by martial rule." Furthermore, if martial law remained in effect after peace had returned and the civilian courts were "reinstated," there would be "a gross usurpation of power."[36]

On the issue of a possible invasion, Davis held that "martial law cannot arise from a threatened invasion. The threat must be actual and present." This is crucially important wording and should hold for any government effort to undercut basic rights. All too often, the government relies on nebulous threats to public order to justify an erosion of essential liberties. There can be no doubt that Lincoln and the Union Army had a difficult set of problems to overcome, but silencing opponents of the war by summary detentions and military trials of civilians was not the correct way forward.[37]

The Proctor Memorandum and Martial Law

With Davis's ruling in the *Milligan* case in mind, attorney James Proctor, in his advisory opinion to the Justice Department, concluded that it was "impossible" to declare martial law given the existing situation. Although the United States was then engaged in fighting a total, global war, the country itself was peaceful, with "neither invasion, nor threat of invasion, nor any interference with the administration of law by the courts." Thus, the question was not "whether Congress or the President" had the authority to suspend the writ of habeas corpus, since the Constitution granted neither of them that power. In the situation prevailing throughout the United States during the First World War, U.S. citizens charged with treason, or any other alleged criminal activity, could not be brought before a military tribunal, but rather should be brought promptly before a civilian judge who would ascertain that the government had sufficient evidence to bring the defendant to trial on specific charges.[38]

In Proctor's opinion, the majority opinion in the *Milligan* case had "held that martial law was only permissible when there was a real rebellion or invasion." This is not exactly what Davis had written. He had conceded that the government could authorize military tribunals to try civilians when a specific section of the country was threatened by an imminent invasion. Needless to say, the United States was not threatened by invasion in 1917 and thus neither Congress nor the president "had any authority to put martial law in force."

Proctor proceeded to specifically address the issue raised by Warren. Even when someone was "charged with an offense against the United States, even treason," the right of a court to issue a writ of habeas corpus remained in effect. This meant not just a "perfunctory" hearing in which an official representing the government declared that the person being detained by the military was being held on the authority of the president, but rather "a judicial hearing" in which the government would have to specify the offense being charged and to provide sufficient evidence "warranting holding him."

Proctor's memorandum is compelling. It provided the legal rationale for the administration's refusal to declare martial law as a prerequisite to expanding the scope of military tribunals to include the prosecution of dissident civilians.

WARREN'S REBUTTAL

As assistant attorney general, Warren would have received a copy of

Proctor's memorandum. He therefore would have known that the administration had already determined that the Milligan decision precluded the possibility of the president's declaring martial law in the circumstances then prevailing. Undeterred, Warren sought to counter this argument by insisting that the First World War posed a set of challenges to government authority that were significantly greater than those posed by the Civil War. Indeed, "under the new organization of warfare introduced by Germany," which involved "enlisting the services of hosts of civilians" to "cause all the injury possible by undermining propaganda" or committing acts of sabotage, "the question arises whether the whole country has not become a part of the zone of operations of the war."[39]

In a total war, Warren argued, the economy of the entire country is mobilized to produce the munitions, armaments, and supplies required to supply an army of millions of soldiers. Any activities that could possibly restrict output, whether by organizing strikes or distributing literature criticizing the government, provided a direct threat to the war effort and must be stopped. The imposition of martial law, followed by the execution of targeted dissidents, would crush the opposition and ensure that the war effort continued without disruption.

Warren's argument is not persuasive. The Civil War was also a total war, albeit not a global one. Furthermore, Confederate agents engaged in sabotage throughout the North. They also funded activists within the Democratic Party who argued for the nomination of a presidential candidate who, if elected, would agree to an immediate truce and initiate talks leading to a negotiated settlement. Yet Davis had explicitly rejected Warren's argument in his opinion in the *Milligan* case. His ruling held that the right to obtain a writ of habeas corpus remained intact throughout the United States even in the midst of the Civil War. Logically, this remained true during the First World War as well.

Gregory was not swayed by Warren's brief and Proctor's memorandum continued to set the parameters for federal policy throughout the First World War. Warren responded by attempting to circumvent the Department of Justice by winning the support of key members of Congress. In January 1918, Senator Robert Latham Owen, an Oklahoma Democrat, an ally of the administration, and a zealous supporter of the war effort, wrote to the president suggesting that Attorney General Gregory draft "a law authorizing the trial by court-martial" of "citizens of the United States detected in conspiracies involving treason."[40]

Woodrow Wilson firmly rejected Owen's suggestion as "a very serious mistake." Such a move would undercut the civilian judicial system by giving "the impression of weakness," thereby sending an implicit message of no confidence in the courts.[41] Although the president's emphatic rejection of a proposal to expand the jurisdiction of military tribunals to include civilians was made in the context of the charge of treason, he would maintain a similar position when Warren advanced a new rationale for bringing antiwar activists before military commissions.

SPIES

By August 1917, Warren had abandoned his effort to widen the range of actions covered by the charge of treason for a new legal theory. Even members of Congress who were sympathetic to Warren's views were not eager to give the military the total authority it would gain under a declaration of martial law. Bypassing the touchy questions of treason and martial law, Warren argued that those who opposed the war, or committed acts of sabotage, were engaging in espionage. Warren understood that this represented a vast expansion of the traditional scope of acts covered by the charge of spying. He again pointed "to changes in the conditions of modern warfare," specifically the efforts made by Germany "to attack and injure the successful prosecution of the war" by a variety of covert means as a rationale. In Warren's view, anyone charged with violating any section of the Espionage Act in wartime should be tried by a military tribunal as a spy and could be sentenced to death upon conviction.[42]

In drafting the Espionage Act, Warren had already equated opposition to the war to spying. Title 1 of this statute was headed

"Espionage" and its first two sections targeted the usual activities of spies, obtaining secret military information and transmitting it to an enemy nation. Section 3, on the other hand, contained several broadly phrased prohibitions, clauses that were used to prosecute a wide range of radicals and antiwar dissidents.[43]

If Warren's purpose had been solely to ensure that those convicted under this section could be punished by the death penalty, the arbitrary revision of the definition of spying would have been unnecessary. Congress could have passed legislation amending Section 3 of the Espionage Act by including the death penalty as a possible sentence. Warren wanted to drastically expand those who could be charged with espionage because those caught spying during wartime were normally tried by a military court and then executed. This was the exact scenario Warren sought to institute for those who opposed the war effort.

Warren argued that Congress had already broadened the scope of those who could be charged with espionage and thus it could extend the scope of this charge as it saw fit. In particular, he argued that anyone violating the expansive provisions of Section 3 of the Espionage Act could be tried as a spy and executed, once convicted. This would have meant that anyone who sought to "obstruct" the war effort by vocally opposing the war or the draft could be tried as a spy. In Warren's view, the U.S. Constitution gave Congress "the power today to subject to court-martial civilians who commit acts just as injurious to the members of our army and navy" as those who spied on military fortifications.

Indeed, Congress had altered the terms under which a person could be tried as a spy by a military tribunal during times when the country was at war. In 1775, the Continental Congress had agreed that those who did not hold allegiance to the rebellious states and who were found "lurking as spies" in the vicinity of military installations were subject to the death penalty if convicted by a military tribunal. In 1806, Congress incorporated a similar provision into the Articles of War of the newly founded country. Under this provision, "all persons not citizens of the United States" who were found "lurking as spies" in the vicinity of military installations could be tried by military tribunal and executed if convicted.[44]

The Civil War saw Congress significantly change this wording. In March 1863, Congress had rewritten this section of the articles of war. The revised section extended the scope of the charge to include those caught spying "elsewhere" and not just in the vicinity of a military installation. Furthermore, the charge of spying would include "all persons" found "lurking" near fortifications or engaging in espionage, not just those who were not U.S. citizens.[45]

Thus, Congress both expanded the geographic scope of actions that could be prosecuted as espionage and widened the range of individuals who could be charged as spies; U. S. citizens, as well as those serving in the military forces of an enemy nation, could be brought before a military tribunal. This would seem to give credence to Warren's argument, though a closer examination of the record shows the fallacies in his argument.

The congressional intent in revising the articles of war was to provide guidelines for soldiers fighting in the border states or acting as forces of occupation in states that had been aligned with the Confederacy. The articles of war were designed to set policies for military units in war zones where martial law operated out of necessity. Union armies in these areas were often engaged in combat with paramilitary units who fought in civilian clothes and even sometimes disguised themselves by fighting in the uniforms of the Union Army. Those caught delivering messages or spying on Union troop movements, even when these actions took place at a distance from an army fort, could be tried by military tribunals as spies under the amended provision of the articles of war.

Contrary to Warren, both Congress and Lincoln realized that this revision in the articles of war had no relevance to the question of trying civilians in the Northern states before military courts on a charge of espionage. On March 3, 1863, Congress approved several statutes in an effort to clear its slate before adjourning. At the same time it approved a revision in the articles of war, Congress also enacted legislation specifically authorizing the president to declare martial law in any part of the country during the rebellion of the Confederate states.[46] Lincoln had already issued a proclamation to this effect in September 1862, so Congress was acting to validate that earlier decision.

There had been widespread objections to the president's decision to authorize a declaration of martial law in states far from the war zone without a specific mandate from Congress. In September 1863, Lincoln decided to issue another proclamation along the lines of the earlier one, but specifically citing the March 1863 statute concerning martial law as support for his action. As president, Lincoln had determined that "public safety does require" that the writ of habeas corpus "shall now be suspended throughout the United States," since the "rebellion" was "still existing." Those covered by this proclamation who could be detained indefinitely or subjected to trial by a military tribunal included "spies" as well as those acting as "aiders and abettors of the enemy."[47]

Lincoln's 1863 proclamation totally undercuts Warren's argument. The president was prepared to bring those caught spying before military tribunals even in the Northern states, but he did so as part of a broader program that placed the entire country under martial law. He then authorized the military commander of a specific region to detain and prosecute those allegedly engaging in espionage as well as others seen as a threat to the war effort. Contrary to Warren, Lincoln understood that the only way the federal government could expand the jurisdiction of military tribunals to include civilians was to declare martial law.

Thus, the Civil War experience does not validate Warren's argument. Congress expanded the scope of jurisdiction of military tribunals to cover civilians charged with spying but it did so to provide guidelines for soldiers fighting guerrilla units in a war zone, an area where martial law was already in force. Furthermore, Lincoln understood this was the intent of Congress. In an effort to bring civilians charged with spying in the Northern states under the jurisdiction of a military court, he suspended the writ of habeas corpus throughout the United States and authorized military commanders to declare martial law in their region.

There remains the more general question as to whether the president has the right as Commander in Chief of the military to suspend
the writ of habeas corpus and override the Constitution's guarantee of
this fundamental right. In general, Lincoln sought to justify his right to
authorize a declaration of martial law by claiming that the existence of a
civil war created the conditions required in the Constitution, that is, "in
cases of rebellion or invasion" when "the public safety may require it."

Since the majority opinion in the Milligan case specifically rejected
Lincoln's argument, Warren searched for an alternative. Lincoln came
close to formulating an argument along the lines proposed by Warren
in defending his decision in the Vallandingham case, but in doing so
he defended his decision to authorize a declaration of martial law in
any part of the country.

In the spring of 1863, former congressman Clement Vallandingham
was prosecuted before a military tribunal in Ohio for delivering
speeches attacking Lincoln's war policies and calling for an immediate
truce leading to a negotiated peace. Vallandingham was an influential
leader of a significant wing of the Democratic Party. A blatant racist,
his argument was wrong at every level. Nevertheless, he was presenting one perspective on a controversial issue of public policy.

Vallandingham was convicted by a military tribunal and sentenced
to prison for the length of the war. Lincoln approved the judgment
of the military tribunal, but modified the sentence to exile. After his
transfer to the Confederates, Vallandingham traveled to Canada and
then slipped across the border and returned to Ohio. Wisely, Lincoln
decided to ignore Vallandingham for the last months of the war.

Lincoln's decision to exile Vallandingham was denounced by those
aligned with the Democratic Party. In Albany, New York, Democrats
called a public meeting and a resolution was sent to Lincoln decry-
ing the government's erosion of fundamental rights. Erastus Corning
acted as chair of the meeting and Lincoln sent his reply to him.
Although Corning was active in the Democratic Party, he generally supported the war effort. As president of the New York Central
railroad, Corning was a person who held wealth and power. It was
therefore difficult for the government to ignore his protest.

Lincoln's open reply to the Albany resolution was widely circulated. It has been considered his most detailed defense of his administration's repression of dissent. Lincoln justified his suspension of the writ of habeas corpus by insisting that "disloyal persons" were "not adequately restrained by the ordinary processes of law from hindering" the war effort. Thus, "aiders and abettors" were "affording aid and comfort" to the Confederacy by "discouraging volunteer enlistment" into the army or by encouraging resistance to conscription. Those viewed as a threat to the military could be indefinitely detained and could be "subject to martial law and liable to trial" before a military tribunal.

Lincoln's argument provided a rationale for the government exercising a sweeping power to suppress dissent during wartime. The Justice Department would make a similar argument in defending its prosecution of dissidents during the First World War. Any statement that criticized the government's war policies could encourage men of draft age to refuse induction. Yet Lincoln and Wilson pursued significantly different strategies. Lincoln was worried that prosecutions made on the basis of such an argument would fail to convince juries. Wilson, on the other hand, rejected military tribunals and found that most juries were willing to convict those who opposed the war on the flimsiest of evidence.

Lincoln based his argument on the powers given to the president as "Commander in Chief of the Army" as codified in Article 2, Section 2, of the Constitution. This would seem to reinforce Warren's argument, but the two arguments were quite different. Warren believed that the president or Congress had the authority to ignore the constitutional guarantee to a writ of habeas corpus in wartime once a war was officially declared and thus there was no need to impose martial law. Lincoln understood that the right to suspend the writ of habeas corpus did not automatically occur once war was declared. Instead, he contended that the specific circumstances that characterized the Civil War met the requirements set in the Constitution for a suspension of the writ.

This was a significantly more restrictive argument than Warren's and yet it was specifically rejected in the majority opinion in the

Milligan case. Davis declared that history had shown that the United States would not "always remain at peace." Furthermore, the country had "no right to expect that it will always have wise and humane rulers." The authors of the Constitution "foresaw that troublous times would arise" when rulers would "seek by sharp and decisive measures to accomplish ends deemed just and proper." Indeed, "unlimited power, wherever lodged" would prove "hazardous to freemen."

Spies and the Law

Throughout the Civil War, Confederate officers were tried by military tribunals for spying and a few were executed. Some of the accused spies were caught near a military base, but others were found carrying messages containing military secrets. Some of those charged with spying were actually engaged in paramilitary operations, blowing up railroads or covert attacks on military fortifications. The Confederacy funded a Secret Service Bureau that implemented a coordinated campaign of sabotage and covert political warfare. Its officers, posing as civilians, were tried as spies by military tribunals if caught.

One case became a matter of public controversy. John Yates Beall was a soldier engaged in covert paramilitary operations under orders from the Confederate Secret Service Bureau. Based in Canada, he forayed into the adjoining states to engage in clandestine missions. In December 1864, Beall was caught trying to derail a passenger train carrying captured Confederate soldiers. He was tried as a spy by a military commission and executed in February 1865. Lincoln refused to commute the sentence despite a considerable outcry.[48]

Still, the charge of espionage was strictly limited in scope during the Civil War. Those charged with spying who were not directly involved in relaying military secrets to the enemy were also Confederate soldiers acting under the direct orders of its military command. Furthermore, all of the acts that could lead to a charge of spying were undertaken by those who were engaging in military activities in Union territory who disguised themselves in order to give the appearance of peaceful civilians.

Lincoln was quite clear in this. In October 1862, he reviewed the case of Jose Rivas, a Confederate soldier caught by Union forces surveying a military base in New Mexico. Lincoln reversed the death penalty imposed by a military commission since Rivas had not been "shown to have been" in Union territory "in disguise, or by false pretence, except by hearsay testimony." Although Rivas had admitted to being a "spy," he had not understood the "technical" definition of this term. Lincoln concluded that Rivas had been acting as a "scout of the enemy" and therefore, once captured, must be treated as a "prisoner of war."[49]

Thus, Lincoln specifically rejected the idea that the government could arbitrarily extend the definition of who was a spy. The term had a clear meaning that necessarily involved the use of deception and disguise. Needless to say, those who opposed the war during the First World War, or who organized strikes during this period, did so openly and without disguise.

Warren was being disingenuous in arguing that during the Civil War Congress had broadened the definition of who could be tried as a spy and thus could arbitrarily include political dissidents in a further expansion of the category. Both Congress and Lincoln had been quite careful in revising the acts that could be ascribed to a spy.

Lincoln also had to deal with civilians in the North who acted as spies for the Confederacy. Although the proclamation of martial law had allowed the military to try anyone charged with espionage in a military court, this does not seem to have taken place. Instead, the government relied on detentions and exile as punishments.[50]

Congress and Military Tribunals

Warren understood that the *Milligan* case would be cited in opposition to his new proposal. Although Warren recognized that the U.S. Supreme Court's ruling in the *Milligan* case had limited the times when martial law could be imposed, he insisted that the ruling did not "necessarily limit" the "application of military law to civilians." The right to impose martial law arose "out of strict military necessity," while the authority of Congress to institute military tribunals derived from a very different source, the U.S. Constitution.[51]

The first article of the Constitution had authorized Congress to "declare war," "provide for the common defence," and "make rules for the government and regulation of the land and naval forces." From these general guidelines, Warren argued that Congress had the power to override the basic rights guaranteed to citizens of the United States in the Bill of Rights when it determined that the risk to the armed forces of "the inherently dangerous effect" of certain acts "upon the military situation" required such legislation. Thus, he concluded, the Milligan decision had not limited the "power of Congress to legislate under Article 1, Section 8, of the Constitution."

In 1919, after the First World War had come to an end, Warren wrote a law review article defending the proposition that Congress could authorize military tribunals to try civilians as spies for acts of sabotage, thereby greatly restricting the range of actions included in his previous argument. This time he implicitly agreed that opposing the war effort did not provide a sufficient basis to prosecute someone as a spy. Instead, he focused on sabotage. Warren insisted that the Constitution had given Congress the authority to permit military tribunals to punish "the acts of the destructive enemy agent." After all, saboteurs might prove to be "more dangerous than spies."

Once again Warren pointed to the experience of the Civil War. According to Warren, Lincoln had used his authority as Commander in Chief of the armed forces to deliberately override the individual rights guaranteed by the Bill of Rights. Yet Lincoln had been very clear that military tribunals could only try civilians when the writ of habeas corpus had been suspended and that this could only be justified in exceptional circumstances during the course of a rebellion or an invasion. Furthermore, he recognized that the charge of spying was strictly limited in scope and did not cover those who opposed the government's war policies.

The argument that the *Milligan* decision did not limit congressional authority to extend the jurisdiction of military tribunals to civilians during wartime is tenuous at best. The decision to overturn the conviction of Milligan could have been made on narrow grounds, but Justice Davis had used the opportunity to write an opinion intended to establish broad guidelines on the entire issue. His opinion held that "it is the birthright of every American citizen when charged with crime to be tried and punished according to law." The controversy concerning the jurisdiction of military tribunals is grounded in "the struggle to preserve liberty and to relieve those in civil life from military trials." Furthermore, the Constitution "is a law for rulers and people equally in war and peace." The argument that the fundamental rights embodied in the Bill of Rights "can be suspended during any of the great exigencies of government" is "pernicious," and "leads directly to anarchy or despotism." Although the *Milligan* case arose out of a trial before a military tribunal held under martial law, Davis was making arguments that were designed to restrict the power of military trials to try civilians at any time and whatever the legal rationale.

Had the federal government accepted Warren's original argument classifying opponents of the war as spies and trying them before military tribunals, the Justice Department would have been marginalized in the effort to stifle dissent during the First World War. Neither Attorney General Gregory nor President Wilson was prepared to move in this direction and the issue soon led to a tense confrontation between the president and members of Congress.

CONGRESS THREATENS TO INSTITUTE MILITARY TRIBUNALS

Warren did not just develop a legal theory justifying the use of military tribunals to prosecute civilians as spies for opposing the war and the draft, he sought to bypass the Department of Justice in order to win congressional approval for his plan. In August 1917, Warren met with Senator Paul Husting of Wisconsin and Wheeler Bloodgood, a corporate attorney. Bloodgood represented the Wisconsin Defense League, which would be renamed the Wisconsin Loyalty Legion in the following month.[52] Husting was eager to have antiwar activists tried by military courts. Wisconsin had a large population of German heritage, while Milwaukee was a bastion of the moderate wing of the

Socialist Party of America. Husting and Bloodgood were incensed that the *Milwaukee Leader*, the newspaper of the Socialist Party of Milwaukee, was still being printed two months following the passage of the Espionage Act.[53]

Victor Berger, the editor of the *Leader* and the leader of the moderate wing of the Socialist Party, criticized the war as an imperialist venture and yet he also urged his readers to obey all the laws, to register for the draft, and even to buy Liberty Loan bonds to fund the war.[54]

Husting and Bloodgood realized that the war remained extremely unpopular in Wisconsin. They were worried that Berger's cautious critique could still present a threat to the war effort and thus were anxious to establish a repressive apparatus to silence the *Leader* and dismantle the Socialist Party.[55] Warren proposed his new legal theory under which opponents of the war would be tried as spies in military tribunals as the solution to this problem. Convinced, Husting and Bloodgood persuaded Warren to write a memorandum providing the legal rationale underlying the proposed legislation.[56]

Warren was undermining administration policy on an important and sensitive issue, while continuing to occupy an influential position of responsibility. Attorney General Gregory was quick to respond. In mid-September 1917, he met with John Lord O'Brian, a prominent attorney in upstate New York with close ties to the Republican Party. As a result, a new division of the Justice Department was created on October 1, the War Emergency Division. As head of this new division, O'Brian supervised and coordinated the entire array of programs within the Justice Department aimed at suppressing radicals and disrupting the antiwar opposition. Warren was displaced, confined to prosecutions targeting those companies that continued to indirectly trade with Germany and were thus violating the Trading with the Enemy Act.[57]

Obviously, Warren had been demoted in retaliation for his persistent advocacy of a policy that would have stripped the Justice Department of its leading role in the suppression of antiwar activities. Nevertheless, he remained an assistant attorney general and he continued to promote the ideas formulated in his memorandum.

The issue finally came to a head in the spring of 1918. Once again, events in Wisconsin provided the spur to the conflict. A year earlier, soon after the United States had entered the war, Bloodgood had approached Daniel Hoan, the mayor of Milwaukee, who had been elected on the ticket of the Socialist Party, to assess his support for the war effort. Hoan reassured Bloodgood that he "did not favor" the antiwar resolution that the Socialist Party had recently passed at an emergency convention in St. Louis. Hoan pledged that he "was ready to assist the Defense Council" in its work and, indeed, Bloodgood reported, Hoan had provided "active and very helpful assistance" along these lines. In public, Hoan dodged the issue of the war, but with municipal elections approaching in April 1918, Hoan, under pressure from Berger, signed on to the Socialist Party's platform criticizing the U.S. entry into the war, while calling for a quick end to hostilities and a negotiated peace.[58]

At the same time as Milwaukee's municipal elections were scheduled, a special statewide election was called to fill the seat vacated by the death of Senator Husting, who had been accidentally killed during a duck hunting trip in October 1917. Berger stood as the candidate of the Socialist Party on a platform urging immediate negotiations to draw up a peace treaty based on the principle of "no annexations and no reparations." His election would "have a greater effect in shortening this bloody war than anything else." As a result, Berger attracted supporters throughout Wisconsin, moving well beyond the Socialist Party's Milwaukee stronghold. His campaign demonstrated the widespread conviction that the war should be brought to an end as quickly as possible.[59]

The administration was deeply worried that Berger might be elected to the U.S. Senate. On March 9, 1918, the government made public a grand jury indictment of Berger and four other Socialist Party leaders, including Adolph Germer, its national secretary, for allegedly violating the Espionage Act.[60]

Bloodgood was convinced that prosecuting Berger for violating the Espionage Act would not serve as a sufficient deterrent to those who opposed the war. He therefore returned to Washington shortly after

Berger's indictment was announced. Bloodgood met with members of Congress and with Warren. In Warren's view, only the death penalty, quickly administered, could successfully intimidate the antiwar opposition and thus safeguard the war effort. He insisted that "the moral effect of one man arrested and tried by court-martial was worth a hundred men tried by the Department of Justice in the criminal courts." Warren suggested to Bloodgood that Congress enact legislation mandating the army to "deal with enemy activities."[61] Specifically, Warren proposed that opposition to the war be included under the charge of espionage and that military tribunals try civilians under this charge.

At Bloodgood's urging, Warren began circulating a memorandum presenting this position. The memorandum was soon in the hands of Senator George Chamberlain, an Oregon Democrat and the chair of the Senate Military Affairs Committee. Chamberlain then asked Warren to draft a law that would bring antiwar dissidents before military tribunals on a charge of espionage.[62]

Warren understood that the proposed statute could not be passed unless it had the support of congressional Republicans. He thus sent his memorandum and draft statute to Henry Cabot Lodge, the leader of the Senate Republicans. Chamberlain and Lodge were enthusiastic recruits. They initiated a debate on the issue of military tribunals on the Senate floor on April 5, 1918.

Lodge began by referring to Berger and his campaign for the vacant seat in the U.S. Senate from Wisconsin. According to Lodge, Berger was so eager to see the war come to an end that he was for peace "at any price practically." This position was "so disloyal as to border on treason." Berger's views were one of several "dangerous expressions" that had spread to "different parts of the country." Those who uttered seditious comments could be "dealt with by lynch law," but it would be better to extend the jurisdiction of military tribunals to cover civilian dissidents. Peace activists and radicals, indeed anyone who opposed the war, should be treated as German spies and tried by court-martial. Once convicted, the military authorities should "shoot them." Lodge was convinced that "the tender way" the government had been handling dissenters had not deterred them from continuing to make trouble.[63]

Chamberlain agreed with Lodge's argument, arguing that the military code should be "amended" to cover civilians who opposed the war. Senator Lee Overman, another prominent Democrat, bolstered these arguments. In his view, additional legislation was needed to broaden the scope of military tribunals so that it provided "for a court-martial to hang these people."[64]

Lodge, Chamberlain, and Overman were three of the most influential members of the Senate and it is likely that their position represented the majority opinion. Senator William Borah, a progressive Republican, was one of the few willing to speak out for civil liberties. He pointed out that the wartime hysteria had already led to the lynching of an innocent person. In the early hours of that same day, April 5, 1918, Robert Prager, a German immigrant and a socialist, had been hanged by a mob in the town of Collinsville, Illinois.[65] This grisly incident did not faze Lodge, who countered that the laws suppressing dissent should be strictly enforced so "as to really strike terror" into the "hearts" of those who questioned the war effort.

On April 16, Senator Chamberlain filed the proposed legislation, claiming that the United States had been "allowing treason to run riot."[66] He then proceeded to hold hearings on the bill before his committee. (Chamberlain may have been particularly eager to sponsor a bill extending the jurisdiction of military tribunals because Oregon had felt the impact of an IWW strike of timber workers that had drastically curtailed production in 1917.)

Initially, Chamberlain received the support of a majority of the Senate Military Affairs Committee for his bill. Those who backed the bill cited the popular support given to Victor Berger in his campaign for a seat in the Senate as a primary reason that a more draconian repression was essential. The proposed legislation specifically mandated that those charged in military tribunals under its provisions would be denied bail. According to Chamberlain, "the privilege of bail" had "been used in furthering spy plots."[67]

The Chamberlain Court-Martial bill, as drawn up by Warren, established a wide definition of espionage in time of war. Anyone who violated the Sedition Act, amendments to the Espionage Act that would be signed into law by the president a few days after the Chamberlain bill was introduced, could be charged with espionage. In addition, a provision of the bill barred the "spreading [of] false statements and propaganda." This replicated the Espionage Act, but Chamberlain's bill went further by holding that those who printed and distributed literature that undermined the morale of those in the armed forces or that "oppose the cause of the United States" in the war were spies, and, thus, came under the jurisdiction of a military tribunal. Those convicted of any provision of the bill would "suffer death."[68]

Warren testified in an executive session during the first days of the committee's hearings, voicing his dissatisfaction with the methods being used by the Department of Justice to suppress opposition to the war. This closed session was followed by a series of open hearings. Bloodgood appeared before the committee, expressing his dismay with the situation in Wisconsin. Colonel Ralph Van Deman, the chief of the U.S. Army's Military Intelligence Division (MID), testified that it was essential to have tribunals that could "give quick and summary action" to quell those who opposed the war. Since civil criminal courts were "tied up with forms and red tape and law," that is, guarantees of due process, military courts were necessary.[69]

Van Deman did not refer to one aspect of the proposed legislation. MID agents tended to view liberal critics of the war as at least as much of a threat to the government as the IWW and the radical left wing of the Socialist Party. As a result, John Lord O'Brian and the attorneys at the War Emergency Division generally disregarded these reports as unreliable.[70] If military tribunals, operating under the auspices of the War Department, supplanted civil courts, the Military Intelligence Division, and Van Deman, would largely determine who would be prosecuted for their opposition to the war and progressive activists would be included as targets of repression.

The President Responds

Van Deman's willingness to openly testify in favor of legislation in blatant contradiction to administration policy is telling. It is hardly likely that he would have agreed to appear in public without the support of his superior officers. Woodrow Wilson understood that his authority was being directly challenged, and he moved quickly to meet the challenge. Warren was forced to resign from the Justice Department on April 19, 1918, only days after his testimony in a closed, executive session. Van Deman was replaced as chief of the Military Intelligence Division in early June 1918 and then transferred to General Pershing's headquarters staff in Paris. This shift was a severe blow to Van Deman's career as a military officer although he remained in the army until 1929. His replacement, Marlborough Churchill, followed similar policies, but he did so more discreetly.[71]

Clearly the administration was embarrassed and angered by the committee hearings on the Chamberlain Court-Martial Bill. It therefore moved forcefully to prevent the Chamberlain bill from being further considered by Congress. Attorney General Gregory sent an open letter to Representative William Gordon, a Democrat from Ohio who was a member of the House Military Affairs Committee, categorizing the bill as "exactly contrary" to the policy adopted by the Department of Justice. Furthermore, Gregory insisted that Warren had sent his brief and the proposed bill to Congress "without the consent or knowledge of the Attorney General," and without his approval.[72]

On April 20, President Wilson sent his own public letter to Senator Overman, insisting that he was "wholly and unalterably opposed" to the Chamberlain Court-Martial bill. The bill was "unconstitutional" and its passage "would put us upon the level of the very people we are fighting and affecting to despise." Confronted with the imminent threat of a presidential veto, Chamberlain reluctantly withdrew his bill from consideration. Warren's drive to vastly expand the scope of military tribunals had finally been thwarted.[73]

In the end, the Justice Department retained the primary responsibility for prosecuting antiwar dissidents. The federal government did not lessen its efforts to quash dissent, but, in general, it acted within the formal procedures set by the judicial system. Indeed, the Espionage Act provided the basis for prosecuting hundreds of activists for their opposition to the war, or for initiating strikes. Many of those prosecuted, including dozens of IWW activists, served lengthy sentences in high-security federal penitentiaries.

Summary

The assault on basic rights was more drastic during the First World War than in any other period of this country's history. Nevertheless, as severe as the repression became, influential voices sought to make the repressive measures even harsher, to greatly expand the role of the military in suppressing domestic dissent. Only President Wilson's intervention blocked the passage of legislation greatly widening the jurisdiction of military tribunals.

Yet the president was willing to use the army to quash a peaceful strike. In doing so, Wilson authorized military detentions that necessitated the suspension of the writ of habeas corpus.

7

The IWW and the Suspension of the Writ of Habeas Corpus

The right to obtain a writ of habeas corpus is fundamental, one that is guaranteed by the Constitution. In most cases when the writ has been suspended, martial law was in force. Still, there have been rare instances in which the writ of habeas corpus has been suspended without martial law having been declared. One of these instances occurred in the midst of the First World War when President Woodrow Wilson dispatched federal troops to break a peaceful strike of timber workers organized by the Industrial Workers of the World. As the strike spread through the Pacific Northwest, the federal government escalated its repressive tactics by detaining hundreds of strikers in makeshift bullpens. This flagrant violation of basic rights needs to be remembered.

HABEAS CORPUS AND MARTIAL LAW

The writ of habeas corpus can be suspended in two different ways. A declaration of martial law transfers all power over law and order to the military. This necessarily involves the suspension of the writ by giving the military the authority to detain a citizen for an unspecified period of time without a detailing of charges or a trial before one's peers. Martial law also permits a military commander to bypass civilian courts and to try specified persons in a military tribunal. Yet the writ of habeas corpus can be suspended even though martial law has not been declared. In this situation, military commanders can detain civilians who are viewed as dangerous for an indefinite period of time as they deem necessary.

The imposition of martial law is the more drastic action since it provides military commanders with a wider set of options. Under martial law, civilians are ruled by military authorities and can either be detained indefinitely during an emergency or tried in military courts. On the other hand, with a suspension of the writ of habeas corpus without a declaration of martial law the government can detain a civilian for an indefinite period, but only as long as the crisis situation continues. Still, those detained in these circumstances are not informed of specific charges and have no chance to defend themselves in a hearing of any sort.

In every case, the president has to authorize the military to engage in drastic actions that undermine fundamental rights. Article 1, Section 9, of the Constitution sets strict limits on when the writ of habeas corpus can be suspended. Only when an invasion or an armed rebellion has led to a situation in which civilian courts have ceased to function and the civilian police are not able to cope with disorder and lawlessness can the military intervene by detaining civilians or bringing them before a military court.

The decision as to which option to choose is essentially a political one. The imposition of martial law is a public admission that the existing system has failed to function. A president may decide that he or she does not want to publicly concede such a failure, or the president may be reluctant to turn over so much power to the military command. In such a situation, the president can simply suspend the writ of habeas corpus by executive order or by authorizing the military to indefinitely hold suspected troublemakers.

In the midst of the Civil War, Lincoln was prepared to impose martial law in every section of the country, viewing this as a necessary measure to preserve the Union. Woodrow Wilson rejected this option, but he was willing to authorize the military to indefinitely detain those engaged in a peaceful strike that had spread throughout the Pacific Northwest. His action blatantly violated the Constitution.

THE CIVIL WAR AND HABEAS CORPUS

The question of when the writ of habeas corpus can be suspended did not come to the forefront until the Civil War, when the Confederate states were in rebellion against the federal government. In April 1861, Lincoln suspended the writ of habeas corpus for the area lying along the railroad line from Philadelphia to Washington, D.C. Three months later, Lincoln extended the area covered to include the line from New York City to Washington. Soon afterward, he authorized military commanders in every region of the country to suspend the writ of habeas corpus in order to indefinitely detain those civilians who were viewed as a threat to the war effort.[1]

Military commanders were authorized to detain those suspected of having links to Confederate agents or engaging in acts hostile to U.S. military forces. Soon, the net spread wider as newspaper editors and leading proponents of a peaceful settlement were detained in military prisons. Those held were not charged with specific crimes or tried before a tribunal of any sort where they could present a defense. Although the detentions began in Maryland at a time when that state was troubled by riots and efforts to block Union troops from passing through its territory, the detentions soon spread to New York and other Northern states where order prevailed and the civilian courts were functioning. Many of those detained were released after a short stay, but some were incarcerated for up to seventeen months. Lincoln drew considerable criticism for these arbitrary detentions and by November 1862 the last detainees were released.[2]

Instead, Lincoln turned to military tribunals. Certain border states were in a state of wartime chaos in which the civilian judicial system and the local police had ceased to function. In Missouri, a bitter war between guerrilla units and the Union Army flared up shortly after the Southern states seceded. All of Missouri was placed under martial law in August 1861 and military commissions began trying civilians by September 1861.[3]

In September 1862, Lincoln authorized military commanders in any part of the country to institute martial law.[4] Soon, military commanders in Northern states where peaceful conditions prevailed were establishing military commissions to prosecute those suspected of treason and or disloyalty. Lincoln's willingness to extend martial law to any northern state led to the crucial legal decision of the Civil War, the *Milligan* case, in which the majority of the U. S. Supreme Court ruled that military tribunals could not try civilians where peace prevailed and civilian courts still functioned.

RECONSTRUCTION

Since the end of the Civil War, there have been few cases in which the writ of habeas corpus has been suspended and even fewer that did not involve the imposition of martial law. During Reconstruction, in the aftermath of the Civil War, military commissions were established to try civilians in Southern states where the paramilitary operations of the Ku Klux Klan rendered the courts and the police ineffectual. In February 1867, Congress approved legislation creating five military districts covering all of the Confederate states. President Andrew Johnson was authorized to appoint a commissioner for each district to supervise the military forces stationed in that district. With the abolitionists in control of Congress, the statutes became law when the president's veto was overridden. Ulysses Grant, as Commander in Chief, submitted nominations for the five districts and Johnson approved them.[5]

Military rule was instituted in order to end armed resistance to federal authority and to ensure that the recently freed slaves were treated fairly. Throughout the South, organizations such as the Ku Klux Klan were organized to ensure white supremacy by creating a climate of terror. Federal troops responded by rounding up those suspected of committing acts of violence against African Americans. In Wilmington, North Carolina, the local army commander refused to accept a writ of habeas corpus issued by a federal district judge that would have freed one of those detained. His refusal was endorsed by his commanding officer, Major General Daniel Sickles, who had been appointed commissioner for North and South Carolina. Sickles defended this decision by holding that he was acting in accordance with the mandate of Congress. Sickles was soon removed from office by President Johnson. Nevertheless, his replacement, Brigadier General Edward Canby, continued to detain those suspected of involvement in terrorist acts.[6]

The majority opinion in the *Milligan* case had held that the writ of habeas corpus could only be suspended, and civilian courts bypassed, when law and order had broken down and civilian courts had ceased to function. These conditions prevailed in the former Confederate states in the aftermath of the Civil War. While Congress debated the creation of five military districts, Justice Davis wrote a private letter making it clear that his majority opinion in the *Milligan* case was not intended to negate such an option.[7]

The aftermath of the Civil War was a time of turmoil in the United States. Congress had every right to sanction military rule in the South. The dire situation in the former Confederacy required a drastic response to restore order and protect the rights of former slaves. Fifty years later, Woodrow Wilson would suspend the writ of habeas corpus in very different circumstances and without any credible justification.

THE IWW ORGANIZES LUMBERJACKS

During the First World War era, fundamental civil liberties came under sustained attack from the federal government. In the spring of 1917, federal troops were sent to crush a strike of lumberjacks organized by the Industrial Workers of the World. The strike soon spread throughout the Pacific Northwest. Soldiers detained Wobbly activists and held them without charges. Army officers acted under the authority of President Woodrow Wilson. Nevertheless, no official order suspending the writ of habeas corpus was ever issued, nor was martial law declared in the region. IWW organizers were held for up to two months, a serious violation of fundamental constitutional rights. Normally, prisoners appear before a civilian judge within a few days after their arrest. In general, the federal government sought to avoid court challenges to these arbitrary detentions, relying on stalling tactics and a compliant judiciary.

The Industrial Workers of the World organized a wide variety of workers during its heyday in the war era, but it had not made a concerted effort to organize lumberjacks in the Pacific Northwest until the fall of 1915. At that point, organizers were sent to the forests and began signing up new recruits.[8] Lumberjacks were eager to join the Wobblies in order to improve the deplorable conditions in the timber camps.

Food was cheap, unappetizing, and unhealthy. Men were crowded into poorly insulated bunkhouses with eighty timber workers living in a bunkhouse designed for less than half that number. Lumberjacks slept on straw mattresses, with two lumberjacks often forced to sleep in the same bed. Beds were frequently rife with bedbugs. There were few shower facilities and no hot water. Primitive outhouses swarming with flies were the norm. In general, timber workers provided their own bedding, although in some camps management supplied blankets ridden with lice. Ten-hour days, six days a week, were the norm, with lumberjacks receiving $3.50 or less for a workday. Timber camps were often miles from the site where trees were being felled. Travel time was unpaid, so lumberjacks would walk long distances, work for ten hours, and then walk back to their camp.[9]

Bringing down large trees was hard, dangerous work and the corporations did little to provide a safe workplace. A scholarly study of the Pacific Northwest timber industry concluded that "it was cheaper for the lumber industry employers to keep replacing killed and maimed men with more men [rather] than put money into safety devices."[10]

Lumberjacks were ready to act. The founding conference of the newly chartered Lumber Workers' Industrial Union #500 (LWIU) was convened in Spokane, Washington, in early March 1917. With the United States moving toward a declaration of war against Germany, the delegates approved a resolution calling for the IWW to organize a general strike should legislation establishing conscription come into force.[11] This resolution was soon shelved by the LWIU's leadership. Still, its adoption reinforced the Wilson administration's belief that the IWW was not a genuine trade union, but rather a group of radicals primarily intent on disrupting the war effort.

The founding conference was primarily focused on organizing lumberjacks into a militant industrial union. Plans were set for a general strike of timber workers in the Pacific Northwest to begin that June. When the Lumber Workers' Industrial Union was formed, it had enrolled about three thousand members.[12] This was a considerable number, but the delegates were convinced that it was necessary to consolidate the union in camps across the region before initiating a strike.

The delegates also elected James Rowan as the union's secretary and authorized him to begin planning for a strike, to start that summer. Rowan was thirty-eight when elected. Born in Ireland, he had emigrated to the United States in 1898. Rowan moved to the Pacific Northwest in 1911, where he found work as a lumberjack. He joined the IWW in 1912 while living in Spokane. Badly beaten by sheriff's deputies while organizing solidarity demonstrations during a strike of shingle weavers in Everett, Washington, in August 1916, Rowan's courage in returning to the fray had marked him as a leader. At the time of the conference, Rowan was in the field organizing timber workers into the union.[13]

The March 1917 conference of the Lumber Workers' Union adopted a list of demands that included the eight-hour day, with double time for Sundays, and with no reduction in pay for the workday. The eight-hour day would prove to be the key demand that rallied workers to the new union. River drivers, who guided the logs down the river in the spring, were to receive $5.00 for an eight-hour day. As the strike continued, timber workers demanded that the companies pay for the time it took to walk to work if it exceeded two and a half miles.[14]

In addition, the list included demands for "good food," as well as the provision of quality bedding and a warm dormitory room for sleeping. As the strike spread, additional concerns were included. Timber workers also insisted on shower facilities and a limit of twelve men sleeping in a small bunkhouse. Although the issue of safety was not directly addressed, the union called for free hospital care for those injured on the job.[15]

The union demanded an end to a payment system based on piece-work. It also called for an end to another system under which those who exceeded the quota received a bonus. These wage systems were designed to encourage workers to compete against one another. Furthermore, timber workers hoping to push output to the limit were more likely to ignore safety measures.[16]

Finally, the union hoped to end the system in which new workers were recruited in cities such as Spokane by "sharks" from private employment agencies. This frequently led to scams where lumberjacks had to pay the employment agency to get a job. Quite often the fee, $1.00 for a job, was shared with foremen at the timber camp. This encouraged foremen at the sites to quickly fire new workers so that a new group could be hired and the additional fees could be pocketed by the same foremen.[17]

Instead of employment agency sharks, the Lumber Workers' Union demanded that employers hire through union halls, although an exception was made for employers to hire directly at the timber camp, as long as this was done without discriminating against IWW members. Few lumberjacks were hired on the spot since timber camps were usually located deep within forests, miles from any town and with only trails and rivers providing access. Instead, most lumberjacks were hired in the towns and cities closest to the timber camps, with Spokane serving as the most important employment center.[18]

These were not revolutionary demands, but a contract along these lines would have led to a significant improvement in the life of the region's lumberjacks. Furthermore, instituting an employment process that resulted in most workers being hired at an IWW hall would have marked a substantial shift in power at the workplace. The forests of the Pacific Northwest outside of those within national parks were largely owned by a few huge corporations. The Weyerhauser

Corporation, along with the railroads, owned much of the timberland in Washington and Oregon, while the Anaconda Mining Corporation owned many of the timberlands in western Montana.[19] These powerful corporations had no intention of negotiating with the IWW's Lumber Workers' Industrial Union, so a long, bitter strike was a certainty.

LUMBERJACKS GO ON STRIKE

Although the founding conference of the LWIU had planned for a period of several months of low-key organizing before initiating a strike, timber workers began moving on their own. Throughout the winter months, lumberjacks cut down trees around isolated camps. In the spring of 1917, the rivers began thawing, so the trees harvested during the winter months could be sent to timber mills. With little in place in the way of roads that could carry heavy loads, logs were floated down rivers to the mills for processing. The spring thaw brought a surge of water in the streams running past timber camps. This was a brief and critical moment in the yearly cycle of the timber industry. River drivers, skilled workers who waded in the streams with long rods to guide the logs and break up logjams, brought their demands for a five-dollar wage for an eight-hour day to the local bosses and then started walking out when their demands were rejected. The lumberjacks who cut the timber and the mill workers who processed the logs soon joined the strike, as work in the timber forests came to a standstill.[20]

The initial cluster of timber camps to go on strike were located along the Fortine Creek in the far northwestern corner of Montana near the Idaho border. On April 12, 1917, a week after the United States declared war on Germany, the first spontaneous strikes began with a walkout of river drivers who refused to pilot logs down the Fortine to the Eureka Lumber Company's mill in Eureka, Montana. Lumberjacks soon followed and the camps were shut down. An informal base camp was soon established in a field a mile west of the village of Fortine, where strikers assembled and then sent pickets to discourage strikebreakers from entering the timber camps.[21]

Soldiers Police the Strike

At first, the timber companies sent private guards to intimidate the strikers, but this proved ineffective. Charles Weil, the manager of the Eureka Lumber Company, then sent an urgent message to Governor Samuel Stewart requesting "military assistance." Executives at the Great Northern Railway also wrote Stewart with the plea that soldiers be dispatched to disperse the pickets. Upon receiving these urgent messages, Stewart, a Democrat, called on the federal government to send troops to the timber country. National Guard reserve units in all of the northwestern states had been integrated into the U.S. Army on March 25, 1917, so Stewart could not dispatch Montana's Guard units to lumber camps shut down by the strikers. In order to provide a flimsy rationale for intervention by the federal government, Stewart informed Secretary of War Newton Baker that the Great Northern Railway (GNR) was concerned that "bridges and other property [were] endangered" by the strike. The GNR was the only transcontinental line through the northern part of Montana and Idaho and thus, according to Governor Stewart, it was essential that the railway be protected by federal troops. In a message to Montana's Senator Thomas Walsh, a Democrat and an ally of Woodrow Wilson, Stewart was more candid, insisting that federal troops were needed "to overawe and suppress lawless agitators," that is, the IWW. After talking with Walsh, Baker directed General Thomas Barry, the commander of the U.S. Army's Central Department, to dispatch "whatever troops" were needed.[22]

One hundred and forty soldiers were dispatched from Fort Missoula, Montana, on April 20. They arrived in Eureka the following day and immediately began dispersing Wobbly picket lines along the Fortine Creek.[23] Another unit of 150 soldiers was quickly sent, so that soon there were nearly three hundred soldiers patrolling the picket lines of striking timber workers in northwestern Montana.

The IWW and Violence

From the start, federal troops were sent to the timber country with the goal of breaking the IWW strike. Soldiers frequently used violence to break up picket lines and disrupt meetings. As the Wilson administration implemented a coordinated policy aimed at crushing the strike of timber workers, the government sought to justify these authoritarian actions by repeatedly claiming that the Wobblies were deliberately using violence to achieve their ends. Yet the government knew full well that this was totally false. This was made explicitly clear during the 1918 Chicago conspiracy trial of IWW leaders; the government called Sheriff Jack Metcalfe of Flathead County, located in northwestern Montana, as a prosecution witness. Metcalfe testified that the strike had halted timber production within his jurisdiction, thus hampering the war effort.

The lead attorney for the IWW, George Vanderveer, took the opportunity to question Metcalfe about the conduct of the striking timber workers. He queried the sheriff as to whether any property damage occurred during the strike. Metcalfe responded, "None whatsoever." Indeed, there had been no disorder of any kind. When Vanderveer sought to probe Metcalfe further on the issue, Frank Nebeker, the chief prosecuting attorney, objected that this line of questioning was irrelevant and immaterial. Judge Kenesaw Landis sustained the objection. Both judge and prosecutor were in agreement that the IWW neither used violence against strikebreakers nor did it encourage sabotage to curtail production.[24]

A Strategy of Nonviolence

Lumber Workers' Industrial Union #500 implemented a strict policy of nonviolence on the picket line. This was both the official policy of the union and one it actually put into practice. IWW leaders understood that the government would use any violent confrontation as an excuse to further escalate the level of repression, thus making it easier to suppress the entire IWW. Striking timber workers were warned that covert agents hired by both the government and the corporations were urging strikers to engage in violent actions. The Strike Committee of the LWIU warned its members of provocateurs "who advocate violence."[25]

Still, this was not the entire reason behind the policy of nonviolence. The union also sought to dissuade strikers from any use of liquor. Alcoholism was a major problem for workers living several months at a time in harsh, isolated conditions. The IWW leadership believed that the union was creating the basis for a new, cooperative society. This meant viewing the class struggle as a means of forming the consciousness needed to build a new society. Organizing a disciplined, nonviolent strike during which the timber workers remained sober was seen as an important step toward the revolution.

Rowan set out this policy in a public statement issued in June 1917: "We do not believe in violence in strikes." Indeed, "the bosses want violence" as "an excuse to call for troops." In the same statement, Rowan also urged striking timber workers to avoid alcohol.[26]

In addition, gaining a reputation for inciting violence was bound to make it more difficult to organize timber workers into the union. The tabloid press ran sensationalizing stories portraying the Wobblies as bloodthirsty terrorists and the lumber corporations played on this spurious reputation.

In Dover, Idaho, a small community in northern Idaho, the Dover Lumber Corporation distributed flyers accusing the IWW of resorting to violence and sabotage to win its demands. The local branch responded by insisting that "direct action does not mean arson or murder." Furthermore, the IWW did "not advocate such methods."[27]

The union's denials that the strike depended on violence to discourage strikebreakers were confirmed by confidential reports sent to Attorney General Thomas Gregory. In August 1917, Burton Wheeler, the U.S. Attorney for Montana, asked county attorneys in the northwestern section of the state to file complete accounts of the impact of the strike. Although these county officials were hostile to the IWW the reports were full of praise for the disciplined behavior of the striking timber workers.

T. H. MacDonald, county attorney for Flathead County, reported that Joseph Ratti in his role as IWW organizer had directed "that the strike should be conducted in a lawful manner." In addition, Ratti had advised strikers "to keep away from the saloons to keep from getting drunk." MacDonald also reported that the Lumber Workers' Union had attempted to get "all rivermen to join the union," but that these efforts "were made by moral suasion only."[28]

This memorandum was supplemented by one made by Wade Parks, the county attorney for Sanders County. Located just to the west of Flathead County along the border with Idaho, Sanders County was timber country. Parks had discussed the strike with representatives of the timber companies who had agreed that the Wobblies were "quiet and law abiding." Strikers avoided the use of alcohol and the union took its cards "from men who became unruly and drunken."[29]

Parks went further than MacDonald in his praise of the Wobblies. He had interviewed several Wobblies who had informed him that the union had taken "especial pains to see that NO law" was "violated." Strikers had been instructed "that if any of the men were insulted or assaulted" that "it was a point of the IWW discipline to quietly withdraw from the scene without offering to even defend themselves."

These reports from Montana county attorneys completely undermine the argument that federal troops were sent to suppress the timber strike to prevent violence. There was no violence on the part of the Lumber Workers' Industrial Union and the Justice Department was well aware of this fact. An examination of these reports underscores the belief that the actions taken by federal soldiers in suppressing the timber strike represented an unconstitutional and autocratic abuse of power. The Wilson administration was intent on destroying the IWW because of its radical politics and because of its ability to organize effective, disciplined strikes that relied on mass action, not on violence.

The Detentions Begin

The officers directing the federal troops in Montana were quick to expand the scope of the army's actions. Soon, troops were moving beyond the protection of railway stations and the escorting of strikebreakers into timber camps. Soldiers broke up the informal camp near Fortine that had been set up by strikers as a base from which to send Wobblies to picket lines at nearby timber camps.[30]

These repressive actions hampered the ability of the LWIU to maintain an effective strike in the Fortine area. Still, army officers felt that a more decisive action was required. Soldiers raided the union's office in Fortine and insisted that the IWW's red flag be taken down and replaced by a U.S. flag. Fred Hegge, the union's organizer for the area, refused to cooperate. Once the soldiers left the union's office, the U.S. flag was taken down and the red flag of the IWW was again displayed.[31]

On May 2, 1917, Hegge was detained by a unit of troops armed with a machine gun and held without charge. Soon after, Hegge was transferred to Whitefish, Montana, a nearby town in which the troops sent to suppress the strike had established their headquarters. Although he was kept in the city jail along with civilian prisoners awaiting trial or serving short jail sentences, he was guarded by army soldiers.[32]

Captain Wade Gobel, who commanded the first unit of federalized militia sent to the area, sought to justify Hegge's detention to the local press by citing Hegge's unpatriotic action in taking down the U.S. flag. In addition, he pointed to Hegge's role as an organizer of the strike of timber workers.[33] Since the strike had been entirely peaceful, there was no valid basis for any criminal charges. Furthermore, soldiers had no right to order any organization to display the U.S. flag in its office. Although Woodrow Wilson had issued no formal announcement, he had, in effect, suspended the writ of habeas corpus, a fundamental right guaranteed by the Constitution.

Hegge would be the first of many IWW activists to be detained without charges by the military. He would be held fifty-eight days without any charges being specified. Two weeks after his detention, Hegge wrote to Burton Wheeler, the U.S. attorney for Montana, demanding to be informed as to the specific laws he was charged with violating. Wheeler responded that there were "no federal charges against Hegge," but that he was being held "under Federal guard."[34]

In spite of the use of federal troops to disperse picket lines set up along the Fortine River, the strike rapidly spread. One of the first locations to feel the impact was Whitefish, which was located a few miles east of Fortine. Once again, the strike proved successful, with timber camps shut throughout the area. Soldiers were soon patrolling Whitefish, but the strike held solid.

The army officers commanding the troops in Whitefish were committed to breaking the strike. At the same time, they were intent on suppressing any opposition to the war effort. As in Fortine, soldiers were sent to every store and office in the town with orders to make sure that a U.S. flag was prominently displayed. Needless to say, this enforced patriotism had no legal justification.[35]

Joseph Ratti was the Lumber Workers' Industrial Union's organizer for Whitefish. In agreement with most Wobblies, Ratti detested the war. He therefore refused to display the flag in the union hall, once again triggering a confrontation with the military. Don Sheridan, the interim secretary of the LWIU, advised Ratti to display the flag under duress, in order to avoid an unnecessary "rumpus."[36]

Needless to say, Ratti's efforts in organizing the strike in the Whitefish area, as well as his militant opposition to the war, made him a prime target of the military. On June 8, 1917, soldiers raided the LWIU's hall in Whitefish, trashing the office and destroying documents.[37]

Ratti was detained and questioned by Captain Gobel. The IWW had been organizing railway maintenance workers in the area. Several Wobblies working on the tracks of the Great Northern Railroad near Columbia Falls, Montana, had walked off the job in a spontaneous action to improve wages and working conditions. Gobel insisted that Ratti sign a guarantee that there would be no more strikes along the railroad line. Furthermore, if there were more strikes, Ratti would be held responsible. Needless to say, Ratti refused to sign, so he was detained and confined in the city jail, under military guard, along with Hegge. Both Ratti and Hegge were held for weeks without charges and without being brought before a judge in a court of law.[38]

James Wallace, an attorney from Missoula, Montana, repeatedly sought a hearing on the request for a writ of habeas corpus. Finally, on June 24, 1917, Judge T. A. Thompson of the superior court in Flathead County agreed to schedule a hearing on the issue. Four days later,

Thompson issued a writ of habeas corpus for Hegge, Ratti and five other Wobblies detained by the military in the Whitefish jail.[39]

This would be the only instance in which a judge issued a writ forcing the release of those detained because of their participation in the timber workers' strike. Hegge's case would set an unofficial limit on detentions. No IWW members being summarily detained by the military would be held for more than fifty-eight days. The Wilson administration accepted this as the implicit limit on its authority to detain dissidents without bringing them to trial. Furthermore, other judges, at the state and federal levels, tacitly abided by this unofficial limit. The result was a drastic infringement of a fundamental right. The whole point of the writ of habeas corpus was the requirement that the government turn over to a civilian court anyone it detained as soon as possible, certainly no longer than three days. Holding a person under military guard for no specified reason for nearly two months nullified this basic constitutional right.

THE STRIKE SPREADS THROUGHOUT THE PACIFIC NORTHWEST

From its initial base in northwestern Montana, the timber strike soon spread into the northern panhandle of Idaho. The small town of St. Maries became the focal point for union activity. Although the timber corporations were quick to call for the dispatch of troops, Idaho's governor, Moses Alexander, a progressive Republican, was reluctant to ask for federal intervention.[40]

In this context, the LWIU was soon able to shut down production in the lumber camps around St. Maries. After a three-day strike, several of the smaller timber companies negotiated an informal, unwritten, agreement with the union. The strikers returned to work having won an eight-hour day with no reduction in pay. In addition, river drivers were granted a pay scale of $5.00 a day, a substantial increase in their wage.[41]

The informal agreement in St. Maries was an unusual milestone in IWW history. Most employers adamantly refused to meet with IWW representatives, or to grant any form of recognition to the Wobblies as the union representing their workers. On the other hand, the IWW distrusted written contracts and refused to make any agreement that limited their right to strike during an agreement. Still, the gains won in Idaho were soon reversed. By August 1917, Governor Alexander had agreed to send federal troops to suppress the strike throughout Idaho. In December 1917, the union hall in St. Maries was closed, with Alexander's tacit approval.[42]

From Idaho, the strike spread to the state of Washington. A substantial part of the state was timber country. The LWIU was remarkably successful in coordinating strike activity throughout the Pacific Northwest from its headquarters in Spokane.

The strike was so successful because the wartime boom had greatly increased the demand for timber while the demand for labor soared. The copper mines of Butte, Montana, used wood to construct the props that kept underground tunnels from collapsing. Contractors constructing military camps around the county used wood to build barracks. Timber was vital to the war effort.

In this context, the IWW gained the solid support of the lumberjacks with its militant demands. Rowan estimated that ninety percent of all timber workers in the northwestern states endorsed the demands of the Lumber Workers' Industrial Union and were willing to go on strike to win them. This was not a rhetorical boast. Sheriff E. B. Noland estimated that more than 80 percent of the lumberjacks in Benewah County in northern Idaho supported the IWW and its list of demands.[43]

By the middle of July 1917, the strike had shut down timber production through most of Washington. According to the Lumber Workers' Industrial Union, 50,000 timber workers were on strike. This may have been an exaggeration, but there can be no doubt that the strike drastically reduced production. The *Tacoma Times*, a newspaper that regularly printed vitriolic editorials attacking the IWW menace, reported that 20,000 strikers had "practically tied up the lumber industry of the state." Clay Allen, the U.S. attorney for western Washington, informed the U.S. attorney general, Thomas Gregory, that 75 percent of the timber camps west of the Cascade Mountains were "tied up" by the Wobblies.[44]

At first, the union organized separate walkouts at each timber camp, but on June 30, 1917, Rowan called for a general strike of all timber workers in Montana, Idaho and eastern Washington. Rowan extended the strike call on July 13 to include timber workers west of the Cascade Mountains in Washington and Oregon. Reports from throughout the region flowed into the Spokane headquarters of the LWIU. Using these reports, Rowan turned out regular strike bulletins chronicling the spread of the strike throughout the region.[45]

The Federal Government Escalates Its Repressive Tactics

Even before the strike spread into Washington, state authorities were discussing the necessity of requesting federal soldiers. The Washington State defense council had assessed the situation with particular concern that the IWW might extend the strike to include migrant agricultural workers during the harvest season. Ernest Marsh, president of the Washington Federation of Labor and a member of the state defense council, joined the other members of the council in asking the governor to call in federal troops to suppress the IWW. In explaining his vote, Marsh pointed to "the fantastic principles of the organization," thus implicitly arguing that the radical politics of the IWW justified the use of soldiers to crush its strikes.[46]

In early July 1917, Governor Ernst Lister, a Democrat, agreed to accept this recommendation. Troops from federalized militia units were dispatched to Washington, where they were deployed to disperse picket lines and raid IWW halls. Soon, union activists were being detained by the military and held for lengthy periods without any judicial process. The officers directing these operations were concerned that these detentions would not be upheld when brought to the attention of a civilian court, that is, those detained would be able to obtain a writ of habeas corpus.

Francis Garrecht, the U.S. attorney for eastern Washington, toured the strike districts shortly after the federal troops began suppressing the strike. The War Department had ordered the militia units "to use every means to prevent trouble." This order had been construed by those directing operations in the field as "sufficient authority" to detain "a large number" of Wobblies.[47]

Of course, Garrecht understood that the summary detentions were in flagrant violation of the U.S. Constitution. Since the timber strike was entirely peaceful, there was "no adequate statute, federal or state" that would provide a valid basis for prosecution. Still, Garrecht endorsed the continued detention of IWW activists. Given the effectiveness of the strike and the importance of the timber industry to the war effort, he was convinced that the "courts would not interfere with the detentions." Unfortunately, his prediction proved to be correct.

In spite of the detentions and the attacks on picket lines and union halls, timber workers throughout Washington continued to join the strike. For the Wilson administration, the strike of the lumberjacks became a critical test of power, one they were determined to win. This can clearly be seen in an interview given to the press by Clarence Reames, the U.S. attorney for Oregon.

Reames was a fervent advocate of harsh repressive measures. He insisted that the federal government had obtained "conclusive proof" that the IWW was "backed by German money." This was a deliberate falsehood. Although the government maintained a considerable network of informants, it failed to uncover any evidence of German money flowing to the Wobblies. Nevertheless, Reames was certain that the union represented the "greatest menace" to the United States coming from within its borders. The federal government was about "to force the issue" in order to find out who was "boss—the government or the I.W.W."[48]

To counter the perceived threat, the federal government escalated the repressive measures being taken to crush the strike. This involved both widening the scope of the detentions and establishing even harsher conditions for those detained. An important test for these tactics took place in central Washington. When a strike began at the Cascade Lumber Company in Cle Elum, troops responded by rounding up everyone on the picket line. One hundred strikers were then detained in a hastily constructed bullpen in Ellensburg, a nearby town and the county seat.[49]

Conditions in this stockade were horrendous. In addition to over-crowding, food was scarce and the meat served was rotten. A hunger strike was started, but was soon called off when it became clear that the authorities had no concern for the welfare of those being held. One of those in the bullpen reported that his weight had dropped by nearly a pound a day during his detention. He was released after three weeks, having promised to return to work and quit the Lumber Workers' Union.[50]

This was a deliberate effort to intimidate the strikers. For nothing more than participating in a peaceful picket line, one could be held for weeks without charges in horrendous conditions that were bound to undermine the health of those detained.

The government also decided to increase the pressure on the IWW by extending the scope of those subject to arbitrary detentions by including agricultural workers as well as those employed in the timber industry. Lumberjacks were recruited into the IWW through its affiliate, the Agricultural Workers' Industrial Union #400 (AWIU), prior to the formation of the Lumber Workers' Industrial Union. The two unions worked closely together in the Pacific Northwest.

Hundreds of fruit pickers in the state of Washington had joined the AWIU. Still, the IWW was far weaker in the apple orchards than in the timber camps. Nevertheless, the federal government was deter-mined to maintain the production of food for the huge number of troops being sent to the Western Front.

Intent on preventing the spreading of the timber strike into the orchards and agricultural fields of the Pacific Northwest, troops began detaining IWW members throughout south-central Washington. This district was very different from the forests of northwestern Montana and northern Idaho. Apple orchards and hop fields pro-vided the economic mainstay of this farming area. On July 9, 1917, federal soldiers raided the union hall in North Yakima, Washington, and held eight Wobblies, including L. S. Showalter, the branch sec-retary, and Philip Mayhew, a union activist. During the next weeks, forty-four more IWW activists in North Yakima and its immedi-ate surroundings were detained by soldiers and then confined to a makeshift bullpen. The Yakima detentions would prove to be the outrage that triggered a definitive clash between the LWIU and the federal government.[51]

By detaining migrant agricultural workers, the federal government stretched even further the dubious rationale of suspending the writ of habeas corpus in order to suppress a strike in a key industry during a wartime crisis. The federal government was going even further, detaining IWW activists who might organize strikes in other industries at some undefined time in the future.

COURT CHALLENGES AND HABEAS CORPUS

The IWW repeatedly attempted to free its members from military detention by seeking a writ of habeas corpus. In general, the government sought to avoid court hearings on the constitutional questions raised by these detentions. Justice Department attorneys tried to stall proceedings and found judges generally receptive to dilatory tactics. At times, Wobblies were freed immediately prior to a court hearing, so the specific case became moot. When a hearing became inevitable, government prosecutors argued that the court had no jurisdiction since troops were acting under the authority of the president coping with an emergency situation. As Garrecht had foreseen, judges usually accepted this argument and a hearing on the substantive issues was again avoided.

A key case arose out of detentions that took place in North Yakima, Washington. On August 4, 1917, George Vanderveer, an IWW defense attorney, filed a request for a writ of habeas corpus for Showalter and Mayhew. The writ was filed in a local district court and a hearing was set for August 14, a considerable delay. Vanderveer opted to make this a test case that would lead to a clear decision concerning the army's arbitrary detentions, at least in relation to eastern Washington. After a discussion with Scott Henderson, the personal representative of Governor Ernest Lister, the two agreed that Mayhew and Showalter would be held until a hearing on the writ was held. On the evening of August 13, less than a day before the scheduled hearing, the two

Wobblies were released from detention in an obvious maneuver to avoid a ruling on the writ of habeas corpus.[52]

THE IWW CALLS A GENERAL STRIKE

Vanderveer was furious, but more important, Rowan and the leadership of the Lumber Workers' Industrial Union were finally convinced that direct action was the only way to resolve these issues. The lengthy detentions in North Yakima and the cynical way in which they were handled proved to be the flash point for a dramatic escalation of the strike, a further step in the union's response to the repressive actions of the federal government.

A month before the North Yakima detentions, on July 13, Rowan had written to Charles Knight, a Lumber Workers' Union delegate in Libby, Montana, informing him that unless union halls were "permitted to open and members released [from detention], general strike in all industries will follow."[53]

The fiasco involving the detained Yakima Wobblies finally convinced Rowan that he had to act. On August 14, the day after Showalter and Mayhew were released to avoid a court hearing, Rowan issued a call for a general strike of all IWW members in the Pacific Northwest to start on August 20. This would expand the scope of the strike beyond the lumberjacks who were already on strike to include construction workers and farm laborers, sectors in which the IWW's presence was less solidly grounded. The strike was to last until the federal government released all IWW prisoners and agreed to allow the union's branches in the area to operate without interference from either federal authorities or local police. The strike call was issued in the form of an open letter to the governors of the Pacific Northwest states. Rowan warned that the result of the strike would be that the "harvest [would] go to waste and the fruit rot on the ground."[54]

THE FEDERAL GOVERNMENT QUASHES THE GENERAL STRIKE

Rowan's call for a general strike to protest government repression moved the dispute between the lumberjacks and their employers beyond the usual terrain of collective bargaining. His call brought an immediate response from Washington's governor, Ernest Lister. Earlier that summer, Lister had been among a group of governors from the western states who had urged the president to institute a coordinated campaign to suppress the IWW. This plan included the proposal of summary detention of IWW leaders. Soon after Rowan issued his call, Lister urged the federal government to move immediately to quash the proposed general strike.[55]

Lister's plea for urgent action met with a speedy response. Federal troops had been detaining IWW activists in the field for several months, so it was easy to take the next step and detain the leaders of the strike. Although strikes had not been made illegal, unnamed officials at the Justice Department declared that they would not tolerate a general strike and would take "swift and drastic" action to prohibit it.[56]

At 3 p.m. on the afternoon of August 19, 1917, forty soldiers raided the IWW hall in Spokane. Rowan and twenty-three other union activists were arrested. The hall was occupied by the soldiers, who proceeded to indiscriminately seize union records. Everyone in the union hall was detained, even those who had merely come to learn more. George Mast, a farmer from a nearby community, had come to the hall "out of curiosity," but was still held in the raid. Another detachment of soldiers was dispatched to the Lumber Workers' Union strike headquarters, where two more Wobblies were detained.[57]

At the union hall, Rowan was dispatched by taxi to the county jail, while the twenty-three others who had been arrested were marched through the streets of Spokane, guarded by armed soldiers. Along the way, an IWW sympathizer shouted to one of those arrested that he would inform Bill Haywood and the IWW's Chicago general headquarters of what was happening. He too was detained, bringing the total for the day to twenty-seven.[58] This last arrest demonstrated the dangers of authorizing the military to summarily detain those viewed as troublemakers.

The officer in charge of the raid, Major Clement Wilkins, was in command of the federalized Idaho National Guard deployed at

Fort Wright, near Spokane. He had received orders from Colonel Clarence Dentler, commander of all National Guard units stationed in the Pacific Northwest, to lead the raid on the IWW office. Colonel Dentler had, in turn, received his orders from the army's adjutant general, Major General Henry McCain. This was a raid approved at the highest levels of government.[59]

During the raid, Wilkins made it very clear that the raid was a military operation and that the Wobblies were being detained under authority of the army command. Those held in custody were not being charged with violating any specific law. Wilkins acted with the cooperation of the local authorities and the Department of Justice. The IWW prisoners were held in the Spokane County jail, which was operated by the county sheriff, George Reid. Furthermore, Garrecht, as the U.S. attorney for eastern Washington, approved of the raid and joined Wilkins in interrogating those who had been detained. Wilkins, with Garrecht's assistance, would determine those who were "strike leaders and inciters of trouble" and who would, therefore, be further detained, and those who could be released as relatively harmless.[60]

On the afternoon of August 19, in the hours immediately following the raid on the IWW offices, federal soldiers patrolled the streets of Spokane prohibiting any assemblies or public meetings by the IWW or its supporters, apparently in fear that the IWW would initiate an assault on the jail. One person, who was not an IWW member, was slow to heed the orders of a soldier to keep moving and received a bayonet wound in his hand. By that evening, local police had resumed patrolling the streets and soldiers were limited to the duty of occupying and guarding the two IWW offices. When five hundred IWW sympathizers congregated outside of the main union hall and began heckling the soldiers, Spokane police created a cordon between the two groups and the situation was defused.[61]

Spokane's workers were infuriated by the federal government's use of troops to quash a peaceful strike. On August 20, 1917, the Spokane County trades council met to discuss the events of the previous day. Delegates to this meeting came from unions affiliated with the

American Federation of Labor, which were generally hostile to the IWW. Furthermore, several local union officials were fervent supporters of the war effort and had participated in government organized bodies promoting the war. Nevertheless, the Spokane trades council approved by overwhelming votes a series of resolutions denouncing the raid. One resolution held that the IWW had been "justified" in calling a strike of lumberjacks and that all those detained by the military should be immediately released. Another resolution urged that a "general strike of all industry be called" to "insure the observation of the law."[62]

In accordance with this last resolution, A. H. Nowaka, the secretary of the Spokane Trades Council, telegraphed the White House denouncing the arrests as an "outrage" and demanding that all of the IWW prisoners be immediately released. Nowaka also sent a cable to Samuel Gompers, a zealous supporter of the war effort, calling on him to initiate a nationwide general strike "as protest against Prussianizing America."[63] Needless to say, Gompers ignored this appeal, since he had no intention in using his personal influence or that of the American Federation of Labor to defend the constitutional rights of the Industrial Workers of the World. Nevertheless, it would have been supremely ironic if the government's drive to suppress an IWW strike had led to a nationwide general strike of a wide segment of organized labor.

The indefinite detention of Rowan in August 1917 represented a significant escalation in the scope of the government's repression. Until then, troops had been used to disperse and detain those on the picket lines. Local union halls had been raided and key activists had been held by the military. Yet throughout the first months of the strike, the union's headquarters in Spokane had been left undisturbed. By detaining Rowan and disrupting the Spokane offices, the government was demonstrating that it was seeking to destroy the union as a viable structure. This point was made even more emphatically the following month when dozens of IWW leaders from around the country were indicted for allegedly violating the Espionage Act.

Woodrow Wilson was told that the military was detaining IWW

members for long periods and without any charges being brought. As a key member of the Cabinet, Secretary of War Newton Baker remained in frequent communication with the president. Baker was furnished with a steady series of reports on the activities of military units in the field, including the mass detentions of Wobblies. Still, Rowan's call for a general strike had brought the clash to a different level.

On August 25, 1917, Baker sent the president a report filed from Washington by two mediators from the Department of Labor. He seems to have done this primarily to reassure Wilson that the draconian actions of the federalized militia were succeeding and that the strike of timber workers was being quashed. In sending this report, Baker also made sure that the White House had been informed in writing that federal troops were summarily detaining IWW leaders.

The two Labor Department mediators reported that Rowan and twenty-six other individuals were being detained and were being "held as military prisoners." Furthermore, the call for a general strike had been "a complete failure." Indeed, the actions of the military had been so successful that "fear" of the IWW was "fast declining" throughout the state of Washington.[64]

The report exaggerated the impact of the mass detentions. Nevertheless, the lengthy detentions and the brutal treatment meted to those detained did severely injure the strike. A strike that had spread rapidly throughout the Pacific Northwest as it gained in strength was placed on the defensive. The upward surge had been broken.

The Rowan Case in Court

Seventeen of the twenty-seven seized during the raid, including Mast, were released within a few days. The general strike initiated by Rowan met with little response and was quickly cancelled. Within a couple of weeks, Rowan was the only one still being detained, held in the Spokane County jail with soldiers detailed to guard him.[65]

In the end, Rowan was held for five weeks under military detention without being arraigned in a court or being provided with a specific set of charges. On September 28, 1917, more than one hundred IWW leaders, including Rowan, were charged with conspiracy to violate the Espionage Act. Rowan remained in the Spokane County jail until November 1917, when he was transferred to Chicago to await trial on a charge of conspiring to violate the Espionage Act. After a trial that lasted several months, Rowan and dozens of other IWW leaders were convicted of violating the Espionage Act. Rowan received the maximum sentence of twenty years. In December 1923, he was one of the last IWW prisoners to be released from Leavenworth Federal Penitentiary, after President Calvin Coolidge granted an unconditional commutation of his sentence.[66]

Rowan's continued detention by the military prior to his indictment was a flagrant violation of his constitutional rights. On August 21, 1917, the day after the raid, IWW attorneys filed a writ of habeas corpus in the Superior Court of Spokane County. The next day, Judge Hugo Oswald ruled that he had no jurisdiction over the matter. In rejecting the request for a full hearing on the request for a writ of habeas corpus, Judge Oswald held that Major Wilkins was acting under the authority of the president "as an officer of the United States army."[67]

Efforts to obtain a writ in federal court were also rejected. Judge Rudkin had already indicated that he was unwilling to challenge the government's arbitrary actions and there is no record of a hearing in the federal district court for eastern Washington. Indeed, no appellate court in either the state or federal judicial system was willing to schedule a full hearing on the request for a writ of habeas corpus. Rowan was therefore held in detention without any charges being filed for more than five weeks before being named in the indictment issued by a Chicago grand jury. Once again, the judicial system failed to protect a fundamental right guaranteed by the Constitution.

THE LUMBER WORKERS' UNION IN DECLINE

The intense assault on the strike left the Lumber Workers' Union in shambles. Don Sheridan, who replaced Rowan as interim secretary, opted for a less confrontational approach. The union called off the general strike and instead reverted to short impromptu strikes and local actions. Timber workers were encouraged to stop working after eight hours. New hires were urged to come to the new camp without bringing their own bindles, in order to force the timber companies to provide bedding. These and other imaginative protests were devised to put pressure on the timber companies without the calling of a strike.[68]

Clearly these tactics did not have the same impact as a widespread strike. Since the actions were brief and localized, troops could not be used to suppress them. By October 1917, most of the soldiers had been withdrawn to their bases. Even with a lower profile, the LWIU still held the support of thousands of lumberjacks and river drivers, so its actions could not be entirely ignored.

In November 1917, the federal government initiated a new plan to cope with the IWW in the timber industry. Spruce trees grew primarily in the forests west of the Cascade Mountains. Spruce was essential to the construction of the first airplanes and the United States was intent on building a fleet of planes for use on the Western Front (although in fact no airplanes were ready to be flown by the time the war ended in November 1918). The president therefore opted to bring the spruce forests in western Washington and Oregon under federal control. Colonel Brice Disque was placed in charge of this operation.[69]

Under Disque, spruce production was militarized. Those who went on strike were subject to court-martial. Disque also created a company union, the Loyal Legion of Loggers and Lumbermen, and prohibited any other union from organizing in the spruce timber camps. The federal government combined harsh repression with a few concessions. In a direct response to the IWW, Disque mandated the eight-hour day in the camps and mills under his jurisdiction starting in March 1918.[70]

The Loyal Legion "declined rapidly after 1919," becoming primarily a social service agency. Military rule came to an end and the spruce forests were returned to the previous owners, large corporations such as Weyerhauser. Within a few years, the timber companies had brought back the ten-hour day.[71]

Most of the forests in the Pacific Northwest stayed in private hands throughout the war. The large timber corporations adamantly refused to recognize a union affiliated with either the IWW or the AFL. Furthermore, in spite of pressure from the federal government, the companies refused to accept the eight-hour day.

In the face of military rule and corporate resistance, the Lumber Workers' Union maintained a significant presence in timber camps throughout the region during the postwar period. Localized actions continued to erupt well into the 1920s. On May 1, 1923, May Day, the union called a general strike in support of the IWW prisoners still incarcerated in the federal penitentiary in Fort Leavenworth. In eastern Washington, a key area during the 1917 strike, one third of the lumberjacks joined the strike for several days. Thus the IWW was able to sustain a base of support in the timber camps for more than five years after the mass strike of 1917. Only the disastrous split of 1924, a split triggered by Rowan, brought a definitive end to the viability of the Lumber Workers' Industrial Union.[72]

Ultimately, the strike of the timber workers resulted in positive changes in living conditions. The Eureka Lumber Company improved the bedding it provided for its workers. Sanitary conditions were improved and bathtubs were installed in bathrooms. Similar improvements were introduced in many timber camps throughout the Pacific Northwest.[73]

Nevertheless, the strike failed to gain the primary demands that had been raised. The ten-hour day remained the norm, wages lagged behind inflation and management refused to negotiate with any union. In order to defeat the IWW, the timber corporations relied on the brute force of federal troops. The military utilized a variety of repressive tactics to break the strike, but the one that had the greatest impact was the lengthy detention of union activists.

HABEAS CORPUS AND THE DETENTION OF THE WOBBLIES

Martial law had not been imposed on the State of Washington. Indeed, there was no rebellion and no threat of invasion. The courts functioned and the police maintained law and order. The timber camps remained peaceful with the only violence coming from the soldiers sent to suppress the strike. Woodrow Wilson had suspended the writ of habeas corpus without any justification and without any formal notice. Hundreds of IWW organizers were detained by federal troops and held illegally, many for weeks. Rowan's detention was the ultimate act in a continuing campaign of government repression. IWW activists were detained by the military for only one reason, because they were radical troublemakers leading an effective but non-violent strike. The federal government was determined to arbitrarily hold Rowan and hundreds of other Wobblies because the Wilson administration was intent on crushing the strike of lumberjacks.

In the few times when these detentions led to a court hearing, government prosecutors had a difficult time providing a plausible rationale for such a blatant violation of fundamental rights. An internal investigation by the army defended Rowan's continued detention by claiming that vigilante groups were active and that "there was a danger of their taking the law into their own hands." Furthermore, local and state authorities, including Governor Lister, "felt themselves powerless." This was an odd argument. It alleged that Rowan was confined to jail for weeks although no charges had been filed because a group of lawless vigilantes might organize a terrorist act of retribution.[74] Actually, it was the job of the authorities to arrest those who sought to forcibly prevent other citizens from exercising their constitutional rights. In any case, the argument was based on a spurious set of factual premises. The military released most of those detained in Spokane within a few days of their arrest, including several leaders of the IWW. Those released went about their daily routine without any interference from vigilante mobs.

The president's decision to send federal troops to break the IWW's timber strike by authorizing the lengthy detention of hundreds of Wobblies was in direct conflict with the constitutional right to obtain a writ of habeas corpus. The memorandum written for the Justice Department by James Proctor in April 1917 was clear on this point. It was sent to Gregory, who would have made the gist of it known to Woodrow Wilson.

Proctor declared that it would be "impossible" for Woodrow Wilson to declare martial law since there were no situations anywhere in the United States that "would permit the suspension of the privilege of the writ of habeas corpus" in accordance with the Constitution.[75] Proctor understood that the federal government could suspend the writ in two distinct ways, either through a declaration of martial law or by dispatching federal troops to an area and then summarily detaining those viewed as troublemakers. Given the existing situation where peace prevailed, the president did not have the constitutional authority to suspend the writ of habeas corpus by either method.

Proctor then proceeded to consider the specific rationale being advanced by federal prosecutors in justifying the suspension of the writ during the timber strike. The government's belief "that public safety," in this case protecting the war effort, made "such suspension advisable" was not a sufficient "warrant for the suspension." Only an actual "rebellion or an invasion" could provide a valid basis for abrogating a fundamental right.[76]

Thus, those reading the Proctor memorandum would have known that the Justice Department's own expert on the issue had already advised the administration that the president did not have the authority to order the military to detain citizens on the basis that the government believed this to be necessary for the war effort. Nevertheless, this was exactly the argument Garrecht had advanced in court in justifying the detention of IWW activists by federal soldiers. Unfortunately, most of the judges in the northwestern states, both federal and state, were unwilling to enforce the constitutional right to obtain a writ of habeas corpus, even though they were well aware of the *Milligan* decision, which upheld fundamental rights even during wartime. The judicial system failed to carry out its most essential task, the defense of the rights set forth in the Bill of Rights.

Ironically, the president specifically rejected the proposal of those who argued that the IWW should be quashed through summary detentions enforced at the national level. In July 1917, George Bell presented a five-point plan for suppressing the union to federal officials. Bell held the post of executive director of the California Commission of Immigration and Housing, but his plan was endorsed by the governors of eight western states. One point in the plan called for the summary detentions of Wobblies who acted "treasonably to hinder the operation of industries" essential for the war effort. Those held would be "interned during the period of the war" in camps "some distance" from where they resided. The detentions would "mystify and frighten" the IWW, but the sweeps would be done quietly and without any publicity.[77]

Needless to say, the implementation of this proposal would have constituted a gross and flagrant violation of fundamental constitutional rights. Woodrow Wilson accepted most of Bell's plan, but he specifically rejected the plan for the internment of IWW leaders as unconstitutional, relying on Proctor's memorandum and the Milligan decision.[78]

Nevertheless, from April 1917 to October 1917, hundreds of IWW members and activists were detained by federal troops across three different states. Many were held for several weeks without any charges being brought.[79] The president acted in direct violation of the U.S. Constitution and he was well aware of this. He went ahead despite this, adamantly determined to crush the IWW's efforts to peacefully organize lumberjacks and farm workers.

Clearly, the president distinguished between the use of summary detentions to destroy the IWW as a union and the use of detentions to break a strike. There seem two possible reasons for Wilson's decisions on these vital issues. Neither are relevant to the constitutional implications of a policy that requires the suspension of the writ of habeas corpus. First, most of the hundreds of detentions took place in obscure localities far from any likely press coverage. Wilson was sensitive to criticisms from the progressive media concerned with violations of civil liberties and he was anxious to keep arbitrary repressive measures from public attention. Rowan's detention did receive some coverage in the press, but it should be seen as the final action following upon the many detentions that had taken place over the previous months and that had gone virtually unnoticed.

The second reason concerns the length of the military detentions.

Bell's plan called for summary detentions that could last until the war ended. This would have meant arbitrarily incarcerating IWW leaders for up to fifteen months. Those detained during the timber workers' strike were held for no more than two months. Thus the government could argue that the internments in the Pacific Northwest were not punitive but rather a necessary, emergency response to an urgent crisis. This argument seems to have persuaded judges at every level of the judicial system and yet it is totally unconvincing. The provision guaranteeing the writ of habeas corpus was included in the U.S. Constitution to prevent the arbitrary and dictatorial actions of the government in a time of crisis. It spelled out quite clearly when the writ could be suspended and these conditions were not remotely met by the strike of timber workers.

Government prosecutors had no credible argument for summarily detaining IWW activists for lengthy periods of time. The detentions were blatantly unconstitutional and the president knew full well that he had no legal basis justifying his decision. These were the actions of an autocrat. In spite of this, the judicial system did virtually nothing to block the detentions. Unfortunately, the detention of hundreds of IWW activists in dismal conditions for weeks on end proved to be an effective method of crushing a peaceful strike.

SUMMARY

The U.S. Constitution guarantees citizens the right to obtain a writ of habeas corpus even during wartime except when an armed rebellion or the threat of an imminent invasion makes a suspension necessary for the public safety. A majority of the U.S. Supreme Court had ruled in the Milligan case that the writ of habeas corpus could not be suspended by a declaration of martial law in the Northern states even in the midst of the Civil War. The situation in the United States in the First World War did not approach that of the Civil War. Peaceful conditions prevailed and the civilian courts were unhampered in their functioning. In this context, neither martial law nor a suspension of the writ of habeas corpus was justifiable.

Woodrow Wilson was wary of giving the military too much power over domestic affairs, specifically the suppression of dissent. He therefore adamantly opposed Charles Warren's repeated efforts to give military commissions the authority to try civilians. On the other hand, in the spring of 1917 the president was quite willing to initiate a de facto suspension of the writ of habeas corpus by implicitly authorizing the military to indefinitely detain hundreds of peaceful timber workers in order to end an IWW strike. Wilson was ready to point to the Constitution and the *Milligan* decision as reasons to reject the use of military tribunals to try civilians, while disregarding the clear intent of these guarantees when it came to the use of the military to arbitrarily detain the leaders of a peaceful strike. As president, Woodrow Wilson deliberately and flagrantly violated the Constitution. Furthermore, the judiciary did virtually nothing to act as a meaningful check on these autocratic actions.

SECTION III

FREE SPEECH

AND LEGAL

THEORY

8

Herbert Croly, *The New Republic*, and the "Clear and Present Danger" Doctrine

New legal theories concerning free speech and civil liberties emerged out of the First World War and its aftermath. Both the "clear and present danger" doctrine of Oliver Wendell Holmes Jr. and the "balancing of conflicting interests" doctrine of Zechariah Chafee Jr. that underlies it developed out of a specific milieu. Many of the intellectuals who defended the Wilson administration's war policies became increasingly uneasy with the government's effort to quash any dissent. Most progressive intellectuals opposed the decision to declare war on Germany or kept silent once the United States entered the war. Still, there were progressives who genuinely believed that this was a war to promote democracy. They enthusiastically backed the government and were convinced that a peaceful world depended on the total destruction of Imperial Germany.

The New Republic voiced the concerns of these pro-war progressives. Its editorials supported the president and his war policies, but the journal also expressed a measured dismay with the increasingly draconian measures that the government instituted to suppress dissent. This led the editors to look for new ideas concerning the limits of free speech during wartime. Articles and editorials printed in *The New Republic* would be critical to the initial formulation of the new legal theories.

HERBERT CROLY

The central figure within *The New Republic* network was Herbert Croly. Both of Croly's parents were successful journalists. His father became the editor of the *New York World*, a newspaper with a large circulation aligned with the Democratic Party. His mother, a staunch feminist, worked full-time as an editor of *Godey's Lady's Book* and *Demorest's Monthly*. After a childhood spent in New York, Croly became a student at Harvard University in 1886. Over the next eleven years, he intermittently attended Harvard without ever graduating.[1]

In spite of his checkered record as a student, Harvard would prove to be a critical factor in Croly's career. His circle of friends and colleagues had ties to that university as either former students or current faculty members. Once having left the Boston area for good, Croly travelled to Europe before returning to the United States in 1900 to take a job as the editor of the *Architectural Record*, an architecture journal.[2]

Despite this undistinguished early career, Croly would nevertheless rapidly gain recognition as a leading ideologue of progressive thought. In 1909, he published *The Promise of American Life*. The book sold only a few copies, but it still made a significant impact. Croly greatly admired Theodore Roosevelt and, in turn, Roosevelt praised Croly's book.[3]

The book sketched out one strand of thought among progressives at the turn of the twentieth century. Croly rejected the idea that the best government was the one that did the least. He envisioned a major role for the federal government in regulating the massive trusts that were coming to dominate the economy. From his vantage point, the trusts were at the cutting edge of efficiency and innovation. Powerful corporations were "enormous machines" that were "wonderfully and indefinitely serviceable to the American people."[4]

Still, corporations needed to be regulated to ensure that they acted in the public interest. Instead of breaking them up into smaller units, the government should prevent trusts from manipulating prices and unfairly hindering competition. Legislation was also needed to permit workers to organize unions that could act as a counterforce to the power of the trusts. A similar perspective is still held by many mainstream liberals. Croly also saw the need to build a strong U.S. military in order to project a strong presence overseas. Certain countries, especially those in Asia, "may well be benefited by more orderly and progressive government." Furthermore, war had been "a useful and justifiable engine of national policy."[5]

Croly's position ran counter to the historical tradition of the United States. Popular mistrust of a large professional army had blocked large military expenditures during peacetime. Nevertheless, the goal of a centralized and effective government, both domestically and abroad, reflected the policy goals pursued by Teddy Roosevelt during his terms as president from September 1901 to March 1909.

Although Croly was focused on the need for a strong federal government, it was his views on civil liberties that would ultimately have the greatest impact. Most of his book did not deal with this question, but one topic that was covered would prove relevant. Croly wanted to see a strong and dynamic federal government, so, logically enough, he also endorsed the idea of a forceful president who would use his office to push the United States toward a more progressive society. His choice as a historical model was Abraham Lincoln. To Croly, Lincoln had utilized the power of the president to carry through to the finish the suppression of a slave owners' revolt. This had necessitated a significant restriction in civil liberties and yet, according to Croly, Lincoln had pursued this policy without vindictiveness and only to the extent required by the exigencies of the Civil War.

In Croly's view, Lincoln "treated everybody" in a "just and kindly spirit." Indeed, he had been "the most humane statesman who ever guided a nation through a great crisis."[6] This was myth-making at its most blatant. Croly provided no evidence to support these claims. Furthermore, he did not even discuss the many actions Lincoln had taken during the Civil War that had drastically curtailed fundamental constitutional rights.

Of course, Croly's argument presupposed that a president during wartime would use his power wisely. As the First World War unfolded, Croly became increasingly disenchanted with the administration's ruthless repression of those who opposed its policies.

CROLY'S NETWORK

Most members of *The New Republic*'s editorial board, as well as many of its regular contributors, were part of a social network that predated the publication of the journal. Many of them were also Harvard graduates or on its faculty. Croly was at the center of this network and yet none of the participants had been friends of his during his lengthy sojourn as a Harvard undergraduate.

One key link in the network was forged in 1908. Beginning in 1893, Croly spent the summer in a small town near the New Hampshire coast not far from the border with Massachusetts. Cornish was known as an easy-going place that attracted artists and intellectuals. Looking for a friendly environment, Learned Hand decided that he and his family would rent a house in the summer of 1908. At the time, Hand was still a young, aspiring corporate attorney. Hand met Croly in this informal setting and the two of them became close friends. Later, Croly tried unsuccessfully to recruit Hand to *The New Republic*'s staff. Although Hand refused the offer, he frequently attended meetings of the journal's editorial board.[7]

In April 1909, Hand was appointed a federal district judge for New York City. Shortly after his appointment, Felix Frankfurter sought out Hand in his judge's chambers. Frankfurter was then a promising young attorney who had just entered into a private practice. Hand and Frankfurter were both progressives and the two soon cemented an enduring friendship.[8]

In March 1911, Hand hosted a dinner in New York where Frankfurter and Croly were invited. Frankfurter had read Croly's book and was "stirred" by its vision of a progressive alternative.

Frankfurter moved to Washington in July 1911 to serve as an aide to Secretary of War Henry Stimson, who had been appointed to the Cabinet by President William Howard Taft. For Frankfurter, the move was a prime opportunity to expand his circle of influential contacts. Soon, he was boarding at the house of a friend, Robert Valentine, another progressive with a post in the Taft administration.[9] The two friends began holding a series of informal dinners with friends and mentors, a political salon that came to be known as the House of Truth. Hand and Croly attended these dinners on their frequent trips to Washington.

Frankfurter and Hand would become members of *The New Republic*'s inner circle. Indeed, Croly tried to convince Frankfurter to join the staff, but with no success as Frankfurter accepted a faculty position at Harvard Law School. Still, Frankfurter wrote articles and unsigned editorials for the newly launched journal.[10]

Another key figure in *The New Republic* was drawn from a later generation of progressives. Walter Lippmann came from an affluent family. He too attended Harvard as an undergraduate, where he was attracted to the politics of the Fabian socialists, the most moderate wing of British social democratic thought. After graduation, Lippmann served briefly as an aide to the socialist mayor of Schenectady, New York.[11]

Adrift, Lippmann spent the summer of 1912 writing a book, *A Preface to Politics*. The book reflected the influences of John Dewey's pragmatic philosophy as well as Croly's book. Although his book was not widely read, it gave Lippmann a certain credibility as a progressive intellectual.[12]

In May 1913, Lippmann sent Croly a copy of the book. Croly liked it, finding that the two authors shared a similar political perspective. Nevertheless, it was several months before Croly followed up on this initial interchange. By the fall of 1913, Croly had already assembled a core group of editors and contributors for the forthcoming journal. Still, Croly was looking for an opportunity to broaden the base of the journal beyond this small social group. In November 1913, he invited Lippmann to a working lunch at a private New York club. The two got along well and a series of discussions soon followed, leading to Lippmann's agreement to join the staff of *The New Republic*.[13]

Croly also benefited from the efforts made by Frankfurter to develop personal relationships with those who had become influential progressive elders. Through Frankfurter, Croly was able to draw these contacts into the orbit of *The New Republic* . Louis Brandeis had gained a considerable reputation as an eminent lawyer defending worthy causes even before Frankfurter graduated from Harvard Law School. The two met in a professional capacity while Frankfurter was employed as an assistant U.S. attorney, but a personal relationship developed only after Frankfurter had left this post. In June 1910, Frankfurter wrote to Brandeis in order to congratulate him on winning a case defending a law in Illinois setting a ten-hour limit on the workday of women employed in factories or laundries. Brandeis sent a cordial response, thus initiating a lengthy and frequent correspondence. Frankfurter solidified the relationship by inviting Brandeis to dinner at the House of Truth when Brandeis came to Washington.[14]

Although Croly first met Brandeis at the informal gatherings held at the House of Truth, the two only developed a friendship during the campaign to ensure Brandeis's appointment to the U.S. Supreme Court. Wilson made the nomination in January 1916, but it soon ran into stiff opposition. During the first months of 1916, *The New Republic* printed seven articles defending Brandeis and urging the Senate to confirm his appointment. Through letters to Frankfurter, Brandeis provided suggestions for possible articles to Croly and the editorial board. After Brandeis was confirmed as a justice in June 1916, he made an effort to distance himself from direct involvement in *The New Republic*, although he still maintained close ties to Frankfurter and others in its inner circle.[15]

Frankfurter respected Brandeis as a dedicated attorney, but he was in awe of Oliver Wendell Holmes Jr. Soon after Frankfurter arrived in Washington in the summer of 1911, he approached Holmes with a letter of introduction from Professor John Gray of Harvard Law School. Soon afterward, Holmes was attending dinners at the House of

Truth where he met that circle of young progressives, including Croly. Holmes was sceptical of the progressive agenda of social reforms, but he shared with them the conviction that the courts should not be engaged in adjudicating economic policy as set by Congress or state legislatures.[16]

Holmes never wrote articles for *The New Republic* and had no interest in influencing the journal's editorial direction. Nevertheless, he was an avid reader and he took seriously articles on legal issues such as civil liberties. Furthermore, during the war years, Holmes maintained a steady correspondence with Frankfurter, who remained close to Croly and *The New Republic* circle.

PROGRESSIVES AND THE 1912 ELECTION

By 1912, Croly had developed personal relationships with many of those who would later play key roles in the development of *The New Republic*. This network was further consolidated during the presidential election of 1912, a most unusual campaign. The incumbent, William Howard Taft, was challenged for the Republican Party's nomination by two leading progressives. Senator Robert La Follette Sr. had previously gained a national reputation as a crusading reformer for his record as Wisconsin's governor, but his candidacy failed to attract the support it needed within the Republican hierarchy. Teddy Roosevelt was enormously popular, but he too failed to defeat Taft for the nomination. Unwilling to accept his defeat, Roosevelt proceeded to stand as an independent candidate. This move guaranteed the victory of the Democratic Party's candidate, Woodrow Wilson. La Follette refused to back Roosevelt and indirectly indicated his support for Wilson, who presented himself as a cautious progressive.[17]

All of this would have made for a lively campaign, but it became more so as Eugene Victor Debs, the candidate of the Socialist Party, began drawing large crowds as he traveled around the country. Although Debs presented a program that was far more radical than that advanced by any of the candidates seeking the nomination of one of the mainstream parties, his enormous personal popularity enabled him to attract the support of many workers who might have other-wise voted for Roosevelt or Wilson.[18]

In this volatile situation, the kernel of *The New Republic* group gravitated toward Roosevelt's campaign. Frankfurter worked as an advisor to Roosevelt on domestic issues. Contributions of progressive intellectuals such as Frankfurter to the campaign gave it a certain credibility among progressives who might otherwise have been reluctant to support a candidate as committed to expanding the empire of the United States as Roosevelt was. Croly wrote a memorandum on antitrust policy for Roosevelt and also wrote an article lauding him. Lippmann came late to the 1912 campaign, but when he heard Roosevelt speak in Madison Square Garden, he became an enthusiastic supporter. As a federal judge, Hand could not openly enter the campaign, but privately he strongly supported Roosevelt.[19]

Plans for the launching of a new magazine began in the midst of the campaign. Clearly, the journal was intended to provide a focal point for the progressive intellectuals who had worked for Roosevelt, allowing them to continue to work together in order to influence future policy debates.

FOUNDING *THE NEW REPUBLIC*

Croly had expressed an interest in editing a journal of progressive opinion well before 1912. Although he had cultivated a wide circle of intellectuals prior to the 1912 election, the project would have never been more than a fantasy without the funds of one of the richest families in the United States. Dorothy Whitney Straight had inherited a fortune in 1904. Her father, Williams Collins Whitney, a successful financier and real estate developer, left her a bequest of seven million dollars, or roughly 200 million in current dollars.[20]

In September 1911, Dorothy Whitney married Willard Straight, a partner at J. P. Morgan, a firm of investment bankers with a global reach. When Straight returned from a stay in China in the late summer of 1912, he approached Croly, having read his book and welcoming it as a positive vision of a progressive future. Soon, Straight and his wife were meeting with Croly to develop a detailed plan to launch the new journal.[21] The Straights had a fortune and were prepared to spend a significant part of it on the journal. During the first decade of *The New Republic's* publication, from 1914 to 1924, Croly received $800,000 in subsidies from Dorothy Whitney Straight. Thus, the average annual subsidy came to $80,000, the equivalent of substantially more than a million dollars in terms of current prices.[22] This was a sizeable sum, enough to give Croly the funds to hire a staff and pay them a generous salary.

THE NEW REPUBLIC AND WOODROW WILSON

The first issue of *The New Republic* appeared in November 1914, just as the world was entering into the horrific catastrophe of the First World War. It quickly became the leading journal promoting social reforms and yet it represented only one strand of thought within the progressive spectrum. The key individuals who edited and wrote for *The New Republic* became enthusiastic supporters of the war effort once the United States opted to enter the war in April 1917.

From the start of the First World War, *The New Republic* had been sympathetic to Britain and its allies, while still endorsing Woodrow Wilson's intention to keep the United States a neutral nation. The tilt in coverage of the war became even more pronounced after the sinking of the *Lusitania* in May 1915.

The journal's path toward support for Woodrow Wilson was a hesitant one. Croly and most of the other editors had supported Roosevelt in 1912. Croly was dubious that Wilson could provide the forceful leadership he believed was required. Still, he began to view the president more favorably in the course of his first term. After all, Wilson was in the White House, while Roosevelt was reduced to sniping from the sidelines.

The New Republic enthusiastically endorsed the president's "Preparedness" campaign. A powerful military was one of the core tenets of Croly and his circle. The United States could be a force for good in international politics, but only if this was buttressed by a strong military. Thus, when Wilson began to publicly campaign for a substantial increase in military expenditures in the spring of 1916, the journal rallied to his support.

As the 1916 presidential campaign progressed, Croly moved from vacillating between the candidates of the two mainstream parties to an open endorsement of Woodrow Wilson and the Democratic Party. In an article that appeared a few weeks before the election, Croly stated that he would "vote for the reelection of President Wilson," despite his misgivings, "chiefly" because Wilson had succeeded in "transforming" the Democratic Party "into the more promising of the two major party organizations." Furthermore, "military preparation" had been "introduced into the legislative program of the administration."[23]

Lippmann was more explicit in combining his support for Wilson with his stance toward the war. In taking a position on the election, he sought to speak for that "powerful section of American opinion" which believed that "the cause of the western Allies" was "our cause." From this perspective, the president's position on the war had been "as sound as American tradition" permitted.[24] Lippmann also praised Wilson as a progressive concerned with the growing concentration of wealth and power in the hands of a few families.

Although *The New Republic* did not print an editorial officially endorsing the president, the slant of its coverage of the campaign was clear. With the election closely contested, the president and his closest advisors welcomed the assistance provided by *The New Republic* in attracting the votes of progressives. In return, the administration went out of its way to cultivate a relationship with the journal. Even before election day, Croly and Lippmann began meeting regularly with Edward House, Wilson's closest confidant.[25]

Once Wilson won a narrow victory in the election, these confidential discussions became more frequent and intense. A month later, in December 1916, Croly wrote to House that he and Lippmann were "interested in doing what little" they could "to back the President" through the pages of *The New Republic*. When Wilson delivered a speech to the Senate in January 1917 affirming the need to negotiate an end to the war that delivered "peace without victory," Croly told House that it had been "the greatest event in his own life."[26]

THE NEW REPUBLIC AND THE FIRST WORLD WAR

In February 1917, with Britain on the verge of losing the war, *The New Republic* convened a crucial editorial meeting attended by Croly, Lippmann, and Frankfurter, among others. The president was moving toward the decision to enter the war, but the question was still unresolved. Eager to see the United States enter the war, *The New Republic* jettisoned its support for neutrality and pushed for a declaration of war.[27]

Even after the United States entered the war in April 1917, House continued to meet with Croly and Lippmann on a weekly basis.[28] Obviously, at this point, the spring of 1917, *The New Republic* and the administration were closely aligned. Croly and his friends were convinced that Wilson had led the United States into the war in order to bring about a just peace, while also promoting democracy at home and abroad.

Yet even at this point, there were signs of trouble ahead. The editors of *The New Republic* wanted the United States to enter the war, but they also believed that the Wilson administration would need to resist the tendency to give in to war hysteria. Three days before the congressional declaration of war, Lippmann wrote to the president that it was "absolutely essential" that "the country be spared the worst features of the war psychology."[29] Lippmann's view was shared by Croly.

Although Croly believed that Wilson would uphold civil liberties during the war, he also thought the president would come under intense pressure from right-wing zealots who would demand the suppression of all those who opposed the war. He therefore joined with Dorothy Whitney Straight, Jane Addams, Lillian Wald, and several other prominent progressives in signing an open letter to the president. The letter urged Wilson to demonstrate his commitment to free speech even during wartime by issuing "an impressive statement" pledging to "uphold in every way our constitutional rights and liberties."[30]

Wilson was slow to respond to the open letter. Indeed, no statement directly affirming civil liberties was ever issued by the White House at any time during the war. Quietly, Wilson sent a vague, nebulous answer nearly two weeks later. He declared that the views expressed in the open letter agreed with his "own feelings and sentiments."[31]

Croly was willing to declare his support in principle for civil liberties during the war, but he was not prepared to assist an organization formed to monitor the administration's record on this issue and to engage in legal challenges as needed. In April 1917, Wald and Max Eastman met with Croly to inform him that the newly formed Civil Liberties Bureau was about to become an independent organization rather than remaining as a sub-committee of the American Union Against Militarism.[32] Although Croly was invited to join the board of directors of this new venture, he refused. In his view, there was no need to create an organization dedicated to defending civil liberties during the war. Instead, progressives had to enthusiastically support the president while counteracting the super-patriots bent on repression.

The Hillquit Campaign

In the weeks following the decision to enter the war, the administration concentrated on the German-American community. Wilson was worried that many of those who had emigrated from Germany would support their home country and would work to defeat the Allies. In reality, most of those in this community were torn between the two combatants and opted to remain silent.

By the summer of 1917, the federal government was turning its attention to radicals who were organizing in opposition to the war. The Industrial Workers of the World became the highest priority target in this campaign of repression. Wobbly halls were repeatedly raided, offices trashed and tons of documents seized. Hundreds of IWW militants were prosecuted for allegedly violating the Espionage Act and many served lengthy prison sentences. *The New Republic* made no effort to oppose this series of gross violations of basic human rights.

Croly and the editors of *The New Republic* were convinced that the focus had to remain fixed on winning the war. Any organized opposition to the war that significantly hindered the war effort had to be stopped. Indeed, an editorial lauded the government's efforts to crush the IWW since "conspiracies to harass the government by the reckless and disloyal fomenting of strikes ought to be put down with a strong hand."[33]

Little attention was paid to the marathon conspiracy trial of dozens of IWW leaders that was held in Chicago during the summer of 1917. When virtually all of the defendants were convicted of violating the Espionage Act and sentenced to lengthy terms in a high security federal penitentiary, *The New Republic* again endorsed this draconian repression. The jury had been correct in denying the union the "right to carry on a class conflict during war at the expense of America's national success."[34]

With the IWW stunned into inactivity by the ferocity of the attacks, the government began casting an even wider net. Once the United States declared war, those progressives who continued to oppose the war entered into an alliance with leaders of the Socialist Party. A new organization, the People's Council of America for Democracy and the Terms of Peace (PCA), arose from this alliance. The People's Council put forward a program calling for immediate negotiations and a rapid end to the war.

The Wilson administration was worried that the PCA could bring together a wide range of groups into an organization that would attract a significant popular base. This possibility began to become a reality in the fall of 1917 during the mayoralty election in New York City. The base of operations for *The New Republic,* New York was by far the largest city in the country, with nearly 10 percent of the total population of the United States. New York was a volatile mixture of immigrant communities. One of the largest was the Jewish community.

The Socialist Party had a solid base of support in the Lower East Side, the arrival point for Jews entering the United States. Most of them came from tsarist Russia and spoke Yiddish. Several newspapers served at this audience, but by far the most popular was the *Jewish Daily Forward,* or *Forverts.* Closely aligned to the moderate leadership of the Socialist Party, *Forverts* had an enormous influence within the Jewish community of New York City. Although the newspaper was careful in its criticisms of the administration, its editorials did condemn the government for undermining civil liberties and the paper did promote socialist candidates.

In addition to *Forverts*, the English-language *New York Call* was also closely aligned to the Socialist Party. A daily, the *Call* did not have the influence of *Forverts*, but it did succeed in serving as a counter to the tabloid press. To the Wilson administration, both periodicals were inflammatory critics that had to be silenced. Still, the suppression of these newspapers was a risky move that could jeopardize the support given by some prowar progressives to the administration. In spite of this, the growing support for the socialist candidate for mayor in the New York City election of November 1917 convinced the government that it had to move.

Morris Hillquit, a prominent voice in the Socialist Party, mixed the orthodox Marxism of the Second International with a stiff dose of cautious pragmatism. Hillquit was hardly a charismatic figure and yet his campaign was able to attract the enthusiastic backing of tens of thousands of New Yorkers, reaching well beyond the Jewish community. The incumbent mayor, John Purroy Mitchel, was an avid defender of the administration's war policies. Thus, Hillquit's effort to unseat Mitchel became a test of popular support for the war.

Of course, both *Forverts* and the *Call* gave extensive and enthusiastic coverage to Hillquit's campaign. In return, the post office threatened to cancel the second-class mailing privileges of both papers. Mailing a daily newspaper was prohibitively expensive at the regular postal rate. Sending material by second class realized a savings of 80 percent over the regular rate. Both the *Call* and *Forverts* were primarily read by those in New York City, but both also had a significant base of subscribers that went beyond the urban metropolis. The potential loss of their second-class mailing permits therefore represented a significant blow to the finances of both newspapers.

Although the Espionage Act of June 1917 had authorized the post office to entirely ban from the mails any material deemed to be "in violation of any of the provisions of the Act," the bill only remained in force during wartime. Instead, Postmaster General Albert Burleson relied on a section of a statute approved by Congress in 1879 that established the requirements for mail to be sent second-class. One of those requirements insisted that printed material had to include "information of a public character." This section was intended to exclude mail-order catalogues from second-class mail. Although journals containing criticisms of the war were engaged in a debate on matters of public policy, Burleson arbitrarily determined that such material was not of a "public character." This meant that the loss of second-class privileges was not based on a measure that was specifically limited to wartime. Some newspapers targeted by Burleson did not regain their permit until after Woodrow Wilson left the White House in March 1921.[35]

The actions taken by the post office to threaten the two socialist newspapers became the focus of intense controversy during the last weeks of the mayoralty campaign. On October 12, 1917, *Forverts* received a notice to appear at a hearing to determine whether its second-class mailing permit should be revoked. The *Call* received a similar notice setting October 15 as the date for a hearing on its permit. These two notices set off a firestorm. On October 14, 1917, the Socialist Party joined the two newspapers in sponsoring a mass rally at Madison Square Garden. The venue was filled to capacity, fifteen thousand, with another ten thousand outside trying to gain admission. Hundreds of police officers patrolled the area outside the arena. Inside, U.S. marshal Thomas McCarthy was joined by fifteen police officers, a post office inspector, and a representative of the American Defense Society. According to the *New York Times*, they were prepared to "break up the meeting if any sedition showed itself."[36]

When Hillquit was introduced, he received a fifteen-minute ovation from the audience. He insisted that newspapers aligned with the Socialist Party were being targeted by the federal government because they stood "against war and for peace." Furthermore, he warned that the post office would soon shift its attention from socialist newspapers "to all publications that dare to disagree with the policies of the administration."

John Dewey Dissents

Hillquit's campaign gained the support of an array of progressives who detested the government's efforts to stifle the *Call* and *Forverts*. Anger around this issue even extended to some of those who supported the war but were prepared to vote for Hillquit as a way of protesting the administration's crackdown.

These divisions reached into the circle around *The New Republic*. John Dewey was a celebrated scholar and educational theorist whose philosophy of pragmatism had greatly influenced Croly.[37] His willingness to write for *The New Republic* greatly enhanced the journal's credibility. Dewey supported the decision to enter the war, as well as the president's decision to reject negotiations until Germany agreed to unconditionally surrender. This placed him in sharp disagreement with the many progressives who were demanding a rapid end to the war.

Nevertheless, despite this hawkish stance, Dewey strongly disagreed with the administration's efforts to stifle all of those who opposed the war. He was fearful that these repressive measures would unnecessarily divide popular opinion, and that they also undercut intellectual freedom and the free exchange of ideas. Dewey voiced these concerns in two articles published by *The New Republic* in 1917.

In the first article, Dewey began by rejecting the idea that free speech and civil liberties were absolute values to be defended even during wartime. Thus, "some surrender and abandonments of the liberties of peace" were "inevitable" once war was declared. Furthermore, Dewey was not "specially concerned" that the immediate restriction of fundamental liberties would have an "impact in any lasting way."[38]

Nevertheless, Dewey believed that it was important to maintain a significant, if limited, scope for debate and dissent. He was convinced that there was "no evidence" that those opposing the administration's war policies had attracted an "influence" that was "great enough to hamper success." This would become a basic guideline for those advocating the "clear and present danger" doctrine. On the other hand, Dewey argued that repression had a "historically demonstrated inefficiency" as a viable means of rallying popular support for a protracted war. In addition, suppression of dissent tended to "foster general intellectual inertness." For Dewey, there was "not a tithe of the degree" of danger to the war effort from permitting dissent than from a pervasive repression that led to a populace that did "not think enough."[39]

Dewey's article provided a theoretical gloss to a pragmatic approach to free speech. It contained the seeds of the civil liberties doctrines that would emerge out of *The New Republic* milieu. His argument on this issue was very much in accord with the overall philosophy of pragmatism he espoused.

In a second article, Dewey was more specific in his criticism of the Wilson administration. The government was engaged in suppressing even the most moderate opponents of the war, actions that were not required to protect the war effort. Unless this arbitrary repression of dissent ended, many of those supporting the war effort would "be provoked" into taking drastic actions "in favor of fair play." Indeed, it was "possible" that the post office's harassment of the *Call* and *Forverts* would "mark a turning point" that could lead to Hillquit's election as mayor.[40]

LIPPMANN AND THE HILLQUIT CAMPAIGN

Dewey's willingness to consider voting for Hillquit reflected the widespread support the Hillquit campaign was beginning to attract. This led the White House to become increasingly concerned with the New York City election. Lippmann had left the staff of *The New Republic* in the fall of 1917 to serve as a civilian assistant to Secretary of War Newton Baker, though he retained his close ties to Croly and his circle. In October 1917, Lippmann traveled to New York to assess the situation and to report back to the Wilson administration.

Lippmann met with Mayor Mitchel, but he also conferred with

Dewey and other pro-war liberals who were preparing to vote for Hillquit. It is highly likely that he would have also seen Croly and met with the editorial board of *The New Republic*.

In a report to the president, Lippmann lauded the incumbent mayor, holding that Mitchel's record in office had been "extraordinarily fine." Lippmann was eager to help the mayor, so he advised Wilson that Mitchel was convinced that a presidential statement of support "would be worth seventy-thousand votes."[41]

Nevertheless, Lippmann was well aware of the considerable difficulties confronting Mitchel. The mayor's fervent defense of the war effort had inspired the formation of a broad coalition bringing together "all the pro-German, anti-British, antiwar sentiment" in New York City. As a result, his reelection was "exceedingly doubtful."

This left the president in a quandary. As important as it was to aid Mitchel, it was "more important" that the election "not be allowed to appear as a test vote" of popular support for the war. To resolve this conflict, Lippmann proposed that Wilson issue a statement endorsing Mitchel, but solely on the basis of his record as a "good government" elected official. Even with the president's public support, Mitchel was likely to lose. His defeat would "let loose pacifist feeling," but the president's effort to divert the focus of the election from the question of the war would help "to disassociate the issues." Lippmann's strategy was a shrewd one, but it failed to convince the president.

Wilson was unwilling to publicly back Mitchel. He wrote Secretary of Commerce William Redfield Cox that he would not "take any part in the mayoralty campaign" since he had "lost confidence" in the mayor.[42] Nevertheless, he was eager to see Hillquit defeated.

THE NEW REPUBLIC AND THE HILLQUIT CAMPAIGN

For Lippmann, the questions arising from the Hillquit campaign were primarily tactical. The federal government was creating an unnecessary split within the progressive community, thus making it more difficult to rally support for the administration's war policies. Croly and the editors of *The New Republic* agreed with this point, but the journal went even further. The administration had failed to stand up to the jingoists who were fanning a pervasive war hysteria.

A few days after Lippmann had sent his report on the situation in New York City, Croly wrote a lengthy letter to the president. The efforts by the post office to silence the *Call* and *Forverts* were "really hurting" support for the war and damaging Mitchel's effort to be elected to a second term as mayor. A "very considerable number" of progressives who had voted for the president in 1916 would "in all probability vote for Mr. Hillquit" if the newspapers were "suppressed." These were "all men of moderate opinions" who were convinced that "the suppression of Socialist newspapers" raised "an issue of importance scarcely inferior to that of the war itself."[43]

Instead of relying on repression, the government should engage in a dialogue with the editors of the socialist press to "persuade them to keep their agitation within certain limits." Popular support for the socialist position was growing and yet there was "no danger that this minority will prove to be of grave embarrassment to the country," as long as its members were not subject to "persecution."

Popular opinion was being polarized between those who were totally opposed to the war and those who were "irreconcilable pro-war enthusiasts." In this context, the position of those such as the editors of *The New Republic*, who "occupy an intermediate position," became "extremely difficult." They sought "to draw attention to the pacific and constructive purpose" of the administration's war policies and yet the jingoistic propaganda of organizations such as the American Defense Society made "the task of realizing the constructive purposes" that underpinned those policies "exceedingly and unnecessarily difficult."

Croly emphasized that he still supported the war policy being pursued by the president. Nevertheless, the government's repression of the moderate opposition and the "war propaganda" issued by the Committee on Public Information created the "utmost difficulty" in writing editorials "without making an expression of opposing" what the government was "trying to do."

Although Croly understood that Mitchel was not a popular choice,

The New Republic enthusiastically endorsed his reelection campaign. The journal printed a two-part series on the New York municipal election with that goal in mind. In the first part, Hillquit was castigated for allegedly advocating "an immediate peace, an immediate separate peace." William Hard, a muckraking journalist, argued that this position, and his socialist politics, made it certain that Hillquit could not be elected mayor. Thus, progressives should rally behind Mitchel, even those who were critical of his unqualified support for the war and his willingness to use the local police force to disperse street rallies.[44]

In spite of their desire to see Mitchel returned to office, the editors of *The New Republic* found themselves in an awkward position. New York was the base of the journal, drawing the bulk of its contributors from that city's pro-war intellectuals. Yet many of those in this milieu planned on voting for Hillquit as a protest against the increasingly harsh measures being taken by the administration to suppress any opposition to the war.

This delicate situation led *The New Republic* to print two letters that were contrary to the journal's editorial policy and that could have precipitated a clash with the post office. Hillquit was allowed to reply to Hard's slanted critique. Hillquit pointed out that he rejected the idea of a separate peace and that he had instead called for "a general peace, a negotiated peace for all belligerents on the basis of the familiar formula: No forcible annexations, no punitive indemnities."[45]

There is no doubt that Hard deliberately distorted Hillquit's position. Still, it is difficult to see how the United States could have pressured the British government into entering meaningful peace negotiations with the German government without a credible threat of a separate peace.

The New Republic went even further in an effort to mollify the progressive critics of Mitchel. It also printed a letter from ten prominent intellectuals endorsing Hillquit for mayor. The letter turned around the usual lesser evil argument. Since the likelihood of Mitchel's being reelected was "small," progressives should rally behind Hillquit as the only candidate who could defeat John Hylan, the candidate of the

Democratic Party who was being backed by the corrupt Tammany Hall machine.[46]

The letter also urged support for Hillquit on the basis of his support for civil liberties even during wartime. Still, the central issue of the war and the call for a negotiated peace was not entirely avoided. No thoughtful person could "take seriously" the claim that Hillquit was "disloyal and pro-German" merely because he called for "a speedy and general peace."[47]

This was a carefully worded argument. It did not commit those signing the letter to support for an immediate start to peace negotiations, but it did insist that this position was a legitimate one. The willingness of *The New Republic* to print this letter indicates the extent to which the journal's editors had begun to question the administration's repression of the moderate opposition.

As Election Day approached, *The New Republic* joined Lippmann in trying to minimize the impact on the overall war effort of Mitchel's likely defeat. Throughout the United States, the New York City election was seen as a test of popular support for the war. In an editorial that appeared only a few days before the election, the journal sharply condemned Hillquit for his refusal to promote the purchase of war bonds. His refusal indicated "a perfect willingness to have America's part in the war" end in an absolute failure.[48]

Still, *The New Republic* recognized Mitchel's lack of popular support and the likelihood of his defeat. Some of those who were ready to vote for Hillquit would do so as a protest "against the tide of intolerance," as well as the actions of the administration in arbitrarily restricting free speech. It was therefore important that it be widely understood that many of those who were voting for Hillquit still supported the war.[49] This was the message that Lippmann was privately sending to the president.

Hylan was elected mayor with nearly 47 percent of the vote while Mitchel barely polled more votes than Hillquit.[50] New York City voters were unwilling to reelect a politician who gave unstinting assistance to the war effort. Furthermore, many progressives were willing to back a socialist who spoke for peace.

In the issue of the journal following the municipal election, Croly and his editorial board tried to draw a deeper lesson from the election. Hillquit had "carefully refrained from denouncing the war" during his campaign for mayor. Still, his call for an immediate start to peace negotiations coincided with the position articulated by several socialist newspapers that had seen their second-class mailing privileges cancelled. The editorial suggested that the situation as it had evolved in New York might provide the basis for a "future agreement" between the Socialist Party and the administration. From *The New Republic*'s perspective, "both the government and the Socialist leaders" had "behaved with a creditable forbearance."[51]

Croly had moved considerably during the first months after the United States entered the war. He was becoming increasingly disillusioned with the administration's unwillingness to tolerate even the most cautious opposition to its war policies. This discontent reflected more than the tactical considerations raised by Lippmann. Croly's perspective was shared by many other pro-war progressives. They had counted on the good judgment of the president to minimize the repression of dissent to that necessary to protect the war effort. As it became clear that Wilson was vindictive and that he was intent on suppressing any organized opposition to the war, progressives such as Croly began to look to the judiciary to place a limit on the administration and the Justice Department.

The New Republic and the Socialist Party

One of the problems that arose in trying to mediate a tacit agreement between the Wilson administration and the leadership of the Socialist Party was the shifting boundary marking the line between the permissible and the seditious. Although the Justice Department had opted not to prosecute Hillquit for his public refusal to back the sale of war bonds during the municipal election of November 1917, a few months later several leaders of the SP were prosecuted for comments very similar to those made by Hillquit. This shift in the government's policy forced *The New Republic* to further define its position on civil liberties during wartime.

In March 1918, the federal government made public a grand jury indictment charging several national leaders of the Socialist Party with violating the Espionage Act. The most prominent person to be indicted was Victor Berger, a former member of the U.S. House of Representatives and a prominent leader of the moderate socialists.[52]

The New Republic implicitly disagreed with the Justice Department's decision to prosecute moderate socialist leaders. It continued to seek an agreement between the administration and the Socialist Party that would help to consolidate a broadly based progressive coalition. A lengthy editorial attempted to bridge the differences between the government and the Socialist Party. The editorial pointed out that the socialist vote had been increasing despite the administration's efforts to disrupt the party. Still, the combined effect of prosecutions and raids, along with the impact of the president's Fourteen Points speech, had changed the attitude of the Socialist Party so that "effective resistance within the party to the war" had "steadily diminished."[53]

The editorial suggested that this was a good time for both sides to reach a common position. Socialist Party leaders should "bury their grievances" and "come out actively" in support of the war. Indeed, the party should endorse liberal Democrats who backed the war and "repudiate" socialist candidates who call for "an early peace." In fact, there was no way that the Socialist Party could accept such a program since it would have required a total abandonment of its political perspective.

This was only one aspect of Croly's proposal to heal the schism within the progressive Left. The administration had made "mistakes" in countering dissidents that had led to "the stupidity of many of its measures of repression." Still, if the Socialist Party dropped its opposition to the war, thereby creating the basis for a "united liberal" Left, the federal government would be in a position to "do better" in upholding civil liberties and promoting a just peace.

DEVELOPING A NEW PERSPECTIVE ON CIVIL LIBERTIES

The New Republic became increasingly critical of the administration's repression of dissent from the spring of 1918 onward. In part, this reflected the widespread realization that the war was drawing to an end. It was therefore essential to rebuild a progressive coalition that could influence the Democratic Party while providing assistance to a campaign to defeat the Republican presidential candidate in 1920. Furthermore, Croly and his circle came to believe that the decision as to who to prosecute was not being made on the basis of safeguarding the war effort, but rather as retaliation for past transgressions.

The issue of reviving the progressive coalition was a real one. As the 1917 municipal election in New York had demonstrated, many progressives were becoming disenchanted with Woodrow Wilson and the Democratic Party. In spite of this, it became increasingly clear that the government would not bend in its determination to crush dissent. The actions of the Justice Department in the case of *The Masses* made this all too evident.

The Masses was a popular magazine aimed at progressive intellectuals. In the first months following the U.S. entry into the war, the journal printed articles and cartoons that gently criticized the war effort, while praising the courage of conscientious objectors. Harassed by the post office, *The Masses* ceased publication in November 1917.

Nevertheless, four of those involved in producing the magazine, including Max Eastman, its editor, were tried for violating the Espionage Act in April 1918. The trial ended in a hung jury. Shortly afterward, the U.S. attorney for New York City, Francis Caffey, opted to proceed with another trial. This decision was made despite the fact that Eastman had jettisoned his previous position and was now supporting the war. He and his sister, Crystal Eastman, had launched a new journal, *The Liberator*, which supported the war effort while lauding the soviet regime in Russia.[54]

The government's decision to retry *The Masses* case caused

consternation among progressive supporters of the war. Once again, *The New Republic* was placed in a delicate situation. An editorial pointed out that the editors of *The Masses* were "ready to support the President." Indeed, they had "already recanted." Eastman was now "perfectly willing to aid the government in its difficult enterprise." The decision to retry the case was yet another proof of Wilson's propensity to pursue vendettas.[55]

By the late spring of 1918, *The New Republic* was prepared to delve more deeply into the broader issues concerning civil liberties and the moderate opposition. Nevertheless, the journal's editors continued to believe that an agreement between the administration and the Socialist Party could be reached. Still, such an agreement would now require that socialists openly support the war effort in return for a relaxation of the government's coordinated effort to suppress its newspapers and jail its leaders. The administration was already sponsoring a covert operation to pressure the SP into dropping its opposition to the war. Nevertheless, government officials were only prepared to give nebulous assurances of a more lenient policy should the party reverse its stance.

In an editorial from May 1918, *The New Republic* reported on the efforts of Carl Thompson to persuade the Socialist Party's leadership to hold a membership referendum to approve a new policy of uncritical support for the war. According to *The New Republic*, Thompson's campaign was "extremely significant." Furthermore, "with the expenditure of a little tact" by the administration, socialist resistance to the war effort could "be reduced to negligibility."[56]

Even in May 1918, Croly retained excellent contacts within the Wilson administration. The editors of *The New Republic* had to be aware that Thompson's drive to cajole the Socialist Party into backing the war was one aspect of a broader covert operation. In spite of the president's record of engaging in spiteful vendettas against dissenters, *The New Republic* was still prepared to urge the Socialist Party to abandon its opposition to the war in return for the indefinite promises being made by influential advisors to the president.

THE SEDITION ACT

As *The New Republic* attempted to develop a middle position between the draconian policies of the administration and those who defended the unqualified right to dissent during wartime, the journal further refined its approach to civil liberties as Congress voted to approve the Sedition Act. This piece of legislation was not a separate statute but rather a series of amendments to Title 1, Section 3, of the Espionage Act of June 1917.

The amendments were designed to make virtually any comment critical of the official war policies a felony. In particular, "any language intended" to bring the U.S. government or the military "into contempt [or] scorn" constituted a violation of the Espionage Act.[57] It is questionable whether Debs's Canton speech actually violated the initial Espionage Act, but there can be no doubt that his speech had violated the Sedition Act. Debs was scornful of the Wilson administration and he made his position very clear in his comments.

On this issue *The New Republic* took a definitive and unequivocal position. An editorial opposed the passage of the amendments on the grounds that these provisions "fall within the prohibition of the Constitution." Even during wartime, certain statements were protected by the First Amendment's guarantee of free speech. The editorial warned that a government that relied on repression to suppress dissent was "playing with fire."[58]

This was a significant first step and yet it raised the further issue of how one could determine the protected limit of free speech during wartime. The editorial argued that "any agitation" that was "unmistakably intended to bring about American defeat and to prevent the government from obtaining the needed supplies of men and materiel must be forcibly discouraged, but such suppression should be confined to clear cases." If there was a doubt about a specific case under these guidelines, "the presumption should run against suppression."[59]

This editorial, in conjunction with other comments on the same set of issues, led directly to the new civil liberties doctrines that emerged from the First World War.

Harold Laski and *The New Republic*

It was within this context that Croly began looking toward a more active judicial review of the administration's suppression of dissent. Croly was in contact with an array of lawyers and judges, but the key contact turned out to be Harold Laski, a progressive intellectual who had been drawn into *The New Republic* network after it had started publishing. Once again, Frankfurter acted as the intermediary.

Laski was an English academic who sympathized with the British Labour Party and its social democratic vision of a welfare state. He moved to Canada in the fall of 1914 to teach at McGill University in Montreal. Norman Hapgood, the editor of a rival liberal journal, *Harper's Weekly*, met Laski while in Canada on a visit and was impressed by his erudition. Hapgood wrote to Frankfurter to tell him of Laski. Frankfurter was intrigued and in the spring of 1915 went to Montreal to meet Laski. From this first meeting came a "long and intimate friendship" that lasted until Laski's death in 1950.[60]

By the time Frankfurter and Laski met, *The New Republic* was already an influential journal among progressives. Laski began contributing articles and spent part of his summer vacation in 1915 in New York City editing the journal. In the spring of 1916, Croly went to Montreal in a vain effort to persuade Laski to quit academia and join *The New Republic* staff. Instead, Laski joined the Harvard faculty as a history instructor. Frankfurter was instrumental in getting Laski this job. During the fall of 1916, his first semester on Harvard's faculty, Laski also enrolled as a student at Harvard Law School. He only lasted a semester as a law student, but in the fall of 1917 Laski agreed to become the book review editor of the *Harvard Law Review*.[61]

Thus, Laski's ties to the Harvard Law School were considerable. He soon met Zechariah Chafee, an assistant professor at the Law School. The two shared an interest in progressive ideas. Chafee and Laski held frequent discussions on legal theory, as well as the issues of the day. Chafee specifically cited one of Laski's publications for providing insights into the philosophical underpinning of his new theory of civil liberties.[62]

The network of progressive intellectuals around Croly had reached into the Harvard Law School and found someone committed to closely examining the question of civil liberties in wartime. The result would be a new legal theory that changed the assumed basis of public discourse on these issues.

Summary

The New Republic was a focal point for progressive thought during the First World War and its aftermath. Lavishly funded, its chief editor, Herbert Croly, was able to recruit an array of talented individuals to join the editorial board and write for the new journal. For a brief while, *The New Republic* gained further cachet by closely aligning with the Wilson administration. The journal enthusiastically endorsed the entry of the United States into the First World War in April 1917. Initially, Croly and the other editors were convinced that Woodrow Wilson was zealously pursuing a just peace while being careful to minimize the negative impact on civil liberties. As the entire country was mobilized, popular resistance to the war increased. The government responded by ratcheting up its repression of dissenters. Croly and those on *The New Republic*'s editorial board became increasingly disillusioned, convinced that the administration was becoming unnecessarily repressive and that its actions were frequently vindictive and arbitrary. They began to seek an effective check to the president and to the Department of Justice.

It was in this context that Croly began looking toward the judiciary as an oversight to government prosecutors. *The New Republic* was an unusual journal. Despite its small circulation, it gained considerable influence among Washington decision-makers. One of its contributors, Louis Brandeis, was a Justice of the U.S. Supreme Court. Furthermore, two of those in its inner circle, Felix Frankfurter and Harold Laski, were friends and frequent correspondents with another Supreme Court Justice, Oliver Wendell Holmes Jr. Thus, the decision to publish an article that criticized the government's policy toward dissent, while presenting an alternative theory on the boundaries of free speech in wartime, was bound to have a considerable impact.

9

Zechariah Chafee Jr. and the "Balancing of Conflicting Interests" Doctrine

Although he is little known now, Zechariah Chafee Jr. continues to exert a profound impact on civil liberties law, both in influencing court decisions and, even more important, in setting the framework within which issues related to dissent are considered. His perspective has become the dominant discourse within which the right to dissent is determined. To understand Chafee's perspective, it is essential to place his views in their historical context, that is, the First World War and its immediate aftermath.

PERSONAL BACKGROUND

Chafee came from two of the oldest and wealthiest families of Rhode Island, the Lippitts and the Chafees. Both families could trace their family lines back to one of the early settlers of the colony. Indeed, Chafee's mother was a "descendant of Roger Williams," the founder of the colony. In 1809, two Lippitt brothers built one of the first textile mills in Rhode Island. Once the Chafees intermarried with the Lippitts, the basis for a lasting political dynasty had been laid. Indeed,

Lincoln Chafee, the governor of Rhode Island from 2011 to 2015, is a nephew of Zechariah.[1]

Thus, Zechariah Chafee was born and raised as a member of the established elite of Rhode Island. He was an undergraduate at Brown University, an Ivy League school founded in 1764. Several generations of Lippitts and Chafees had attended Brown University, so Zechariah Chafee fit in well as a student. [2]

After working for three years in the front office of the family firm, a non-union iron foundry, Chafee went to Harvard Law School and upon graduation was hired as an assistant professor in the fall of 1916. While teaching a course in torts, he began looking into the issues related to the limits of free speech. After the Espionage Act became law in June 1917, Chafee began examining the cases that arose from this statute.[3]

The New England Brahmins, the established elite, felt they knew what is best for the society as a whole. Its members, with their privileged background in the "best" schools, could take the long view, while the average person was likely to be caught up in the emotions of the moment. Of course, Chafee understood that even the rich and powerful can become trapped in the whirlwind of passions that arise in crisis situations. Judges and prosecutors, even presidents, can cease to be dispassionate observers who limit the right to dissent when it becomes dangerous, while tolerating a critical opposition when it is weak and ineffectual. Chafee was convinced that it was essential to clearly formulate the essential principles underlying the limits of dissent in order to make it less likely that those in power would vindictively persecute political opponents during a time of crisis.

CHAFEE AND THE NEW REPUBLIC

Chafee's legacy rests on two seminal books on civil liberties, *Freedom of Speech* (1920) and *Free Speech in the United States* (1941). Yet the essential principle underlying his views on free speech was already set out in two articles published in the aftermath of the First World War. The first of these appeared in *The New Republic* in November 1918.

Chafee's first semester as a teacher in the law school, the fall of 1916, coincided with Harold Laski's arrival at Harvard. Laski and Croly became friends and began discussing the civil liberties problems arising out of the wartime experience. Laski had already established close links to *The New Republic* before coming to Harvard. Thus, when Laski informed Croly that Chafee was reviewing the cases arising out of the Espionage Act, the groundwork was set for the article. In September 1918, Croly contacted Chafee to write on the issue of free speech. Chafee received $75 for the piece, a significant sum in 1918. Although the article was commissioned during the war, it actually appeared in print after the Armistice.[4]

The focus of Chafee's initial article was a consideration of the Sedition Act, which had been enacted in May 1918. The sweeping provisions of this legislation made it illegal to issue statements that brought the government into "contempt [or] scorn." Chafee pointed out that the First Amendment had been crafted by those "who intended to make prosecution for seditious utterances impossible in their country." Thus, Congress had "made a mistake under the pressure of a great crisis" in approving this legislation and it should be repealed immediately.[5]

In the course of presenting his critique of the Sedition Act, Chafee set out the basic outlines of his new legal theory. He began by stressing the importance of free speech even in the midst of a global war. It was "essential" to facilitate an "absolutely unlimited discussion" of public policy issues in order "to prepare the public for an intelligent exercise of their rights as citizens and to subject those in power to just scrutiny and condemnation." Still, the government has "legitimate purposes," including the protection of the country from foreign aggression. At times, free speech "interferes with these purposes." These are conflicting and valid purposes, so the government's interest in implementing its policies has to be "balanced against freedom of speech, but freedom of speech ought to weigh very heavily in the scale."[6]

This is the fundamental premise of Chafee's legal theory, a concept that has framed the discussion of civil liberties for decades. At its root is the belief that every right of an individual in relation to the government is relative and must be weighed against the government's interest in pursuing its policy goals. The specific context then determines how much freedom is permitted to those who oppose the government and its policies.

Chafee's principle of balancing interests represents a pragmatic perspective on issues arising out of the quest for freedom and the protection of vital civil liberties. To this point, the argument remained on the level of abstract theory. Chafee did not go far in moving from the general to a specific guideline for setting the limits of free speech during wartime. Nevertheless, he did present the beginnings of a legal theory on this critical issue.

During a time of war, a dissenting opinion should be permitted "unless it is clearly liable to cause direct and dangerous interference with the conduct of the war."[7] This formulation, which Chafee used in later works, points directly to the "clear and present danger" doctrine formulated by Holmes. Although Chafee did not analyze specific cases in his *New Republic* article, it is clear he was prepared to accept a considerable restriction on the limits of free speech during wartime.

This followed from his zealous support for the war effort, as well as the president's decision to continue the conflict until the unconditional surrender of Germany. For Chafee, the "national welfare doubtless demands that the just war be pushed to victory." Still, there should be limits on the government's suppression of dissent. After all, "pacifists and Socialists" were "wrong now, but they may be right next time."[8]

CHAFEE AND THE *HARVARD LAW REVIEW*

An article published in the *Harvard Law Review* in June 1919 gave Chafee an opportunity to present in greater detail his new theory and to review recent court decisions in the light of that theory. He began with an exposition of the balancing of conflicting interests theory that was virtually identical to that presented in *The New Republic* article. He then placed his theory in a wider context. According to Chafee, it was necessary to reject the "extreme views" that had polarized debate on the issue of free speech. Instead, the "true solution lies between" the "two extreme views."[9]

On the one hand, there were those who argued that constitutional rights were suspended during wartime. Chafee countered that the constitutional provisions on the declaration of war could "not be invoked to break down free speech." Yet he also rejected the view that the "unlimited discussion" of public policy issues could continue unfettered in the midst of a declared war.[10] Although the need to balance conflicting interests held at all times, there had to be a "natural adjustment" in times of war. Thus, Chafee argued, there was no doubt that "some utterances had to be suppressed." After all, the United States had "passed through a period of great danger."[11]

The question is of crucial importance. Although Chafee's position corresponds with that held by Holmes and Brandeis in their landmark opinions on free speech, the point is far from obvious. As Chafee pointed out in his *New Republic* article, the federal government had at its disposal "public opinion, [the] press, police, the army to prevent" dissenters from "causing unlawful acts."[12]

Chafee also directly criticized the free speech theory as expounded by Blackstone that had previously prevailed in the judicial system. According to Blackstone, the government can punish those responsible for "any dangerous or offensive writings" the authorities believe is of "a pernicious tendency" as "necessary for the preservation of peace and order."[13]

In countering this theory, Chafee cited Jefferson's preamble to an act approved by Virginia's legislature in 1786 that guaranteed religious freedom. Jefferson had warned that to allow a judge "to restrain religious views" based on "their ill tendency" was to engage in a "dangerous fallacy." A legal guideline based on this premise would "destroy all religious liberty" since a judge would "condemn" those views that seemed to "differ from his own." Chafee argued that Jefferson's critique as it relates to religious freedom would hold for the discourse on all public policy issues.[14]

The *Harvard Law Review* article was written in the months immediately following the Supreme Court's decision in the Debs and

Schenck cases. Chafee was surprisingly critical of the "clear and present danger" doctrine as set forth by Holmes in the *Schenck* case. He began by granting that this provided a "good test," one that "substantially" agreed with his own formulation prohibiting statements that were "clearly liable to cause direct and dangerous interference with the conduct of the war." Still, if Holmes's theory was "to mean anything," convictions in cases such as that involving Debs had to be reversed. Chafee pointed out that Judge Westenhaver had instructed the jurors to convict Debs of violating the Espionage Act if they believed that his "speech had a tendency to bring about resistance to the draft." Given this instruction, and the fact that Debs did not mention conscription in his speech, Chafee concluded that it was "hard to see" how Debs could be found guilty under the clear and present danger standard.[15]

Chafee understood that the decision of the Supreme Court's minority to move beyond the "pernicious tendency" argument would only be significant if it led to the justices voting to reverse guilty verdicts that would have previously been upheld. Nevertheless, he had no problem with Holmes's decision to uphold the guilty verdict in the *Schenck* case. In Chafee's opinion, the *Schenck* case was "clear," even under the clear and present danger doctrine. This was a questionable assertion. Nowadays, few would argue that Schenck did not have the right to distribute a flyer criticizing the draft, even in the midst of the First World War.

Chafee was also disturbed that Holmes had not explicitly referred to the need to balance conflicting interests even after the declaration of war. It was "regrettable that Justice Holmes did nothing to emphasize the social interest behind free speech" and "the need for balancing even in war time."[16] In a later decision in the *Abrams* case, Holmes would go far to meeting Chafee's critique as expressed in the *Harvard Law Review*.

Chafee concluded the article by providing a brief assessment of the U.S. experience during the war. Thus, "action in proportion to the emergency" had been justified, but the administration had gone too far in suppressing "speech which was very far from direct and dangerous interference with the conduct of the war." The Justice

Department had turned the Espionage Act "into a drag-net for pacifists." Furthermore, most judges had followed along with these unwarranted prosecutions. As a result, the Wilson administration had "insisted on an artificial unanimity of opinion behind the war." In suppressing those who had "advocated peace without victory," the government had stifled a discussion that could have "saved us from a victory without peace."[17]

WILSON AND THE WAR

In two books that followed the initial articles, Chafee had the opportunity to explore in greater depth some of the issues and cases that had arisen during the wartime crisis. His outlook on these issues remained remarkably consistent, although he did modify his opinion on a few specific cases.

Writing some time after the war had ended, Chafee remained an ardent supporter of the war effort and an enthusiastic admirer of Woodrow Wilson. Although the president had committed "fatal blunders" in countering the antiwar opposition, Chafee nevertheless praised Wilson for his "vision" of a global peace ensured through an international organization that could mediate disputes.[18] Of course, the idea for such an international league had been widely discussed within the peace movement several years prior to Wilson's adoption of the plan. Furthermore, the creation of the League of Nations, and then the United Nations, failed to prevent an unending series of wars and armed conflicts. Still, Chafee had faith in the president as a wise and thoughtful statesman who had, unfortunately, been swept up in the hysteria of war and had thus mistakenly authorized a policy of repression that went beyond that necessary to protect the war effort.

Chafee accepted wholeheartedly the official propaganda proclaiming that the United States had entered the war to fight for democracy and to defeat the aggressive aims of a militaristic autocracy. He was disdainful of radicals, and, indeed, of anyone who opposed the war effort and, indeed, had "no sympathy" with "the views of most of the men" who had "been imprisoned since the war for speaking out."[19]

THE INDUSTRIAL WORKERS OF THE WORLD

The Industrial Workers of the World posed the greatest threat to the smooth operation of the war machine and thus the union became a priority target for government repression. Chafee held that "the eventual disappearance of the IWW" was "highly desirable." This could be accomplished by "a vigorous suppression and punishment of sabotage" and by initiating reforms at the workplace to undercut the appeal of the union to migrant farm workers, who received subsistence wages and lived in appalling conditions as they traveled from farm to farm harvesting crops.[20]

Chafee had little understanding of the IWW and its organizing efforts. The union's executive board had repudiated the use of sabotage in the fall of 1917, a statement reaffirmed after the war came to an end.[21] Furthermore, the IWW had successfully organized copper miners and lumberjacks in addition to migrant farmworkers during the economic boom generated by the First World War. Copper miners frequently worked in the same mine for several years, while living in one urban area, unlike agricultural workers who had to travel with the harvest.

Chafee's analysis of the IWW was superficial and misleading. He had little to say concerning the many civil liberties issues raised by the federal government's coordinated assault on the IWW, although he appears to have approved of the harsh sentences imposed on the union's leaders at the conclusion of the Chicago conspiracy trial in 1918. Dozens of Wobblies received ten-year sentences, while several key leaders, including "Big Bill" Haywood, were sentenced to twenty years, the maximum permitted under the Espionage Act. Chafee held that the Chicago defendants had received the "long sentences for threats and designs of tangible obstruction to war work."[22] This is a nebulous formulation that covers all sorts of activities.

The IWW became a primary target of government repression because it organized militant nonviolent strikes that significantly reduced production in key industries, in particular copper mining and timber. Strikes were legal and the Wobblies were intent on avoiding violence, so the government sought to overcome this quandary by arguing that the strikes of copper miners and lumberjacks were only a pretense for disrupting the war effort. In essence, Chafee accepted this argument.

The government's case was specious. In April 1919, *The New Republic* printed an open letter to the president written by Alexander Sidney Lanier, who had served as a captain in the U.S. Army's Military Intelligence Division during the war. Lanier had been assigned to review the trial transcript of the Chicago conspiracy trial. Each weekday, throughout the spring and summer of 1917, Lanier compiled a summary of the testimony for the use of the MID's high command. The trial lasted for five months and the transcript ran to more than 35,000 pages.

Lanier, therefore, was an expert on the government's prosecution of the union. A conservative, he was "uncompromisingly against the IWW." Nevertheless, Lanier held that the government had failed to demonstrate that the IWW had engaged in a "conspiracy" to obstruct the war effort. Organizing militant strikes during the war was "consistent" with its activities prior to the war.[23]

The *New Republic* article was a serious blow to the government's case, and yet Lanier was even more forceful three years later when he appeared before the House Judiciary Committee. In his view, the strikes were "an expression of a legal right" and thus the "mere fact" that the war effort had been "incidentally prejudiced" did not in itself "constitute a violation of law." Furthermore, the actions of the IWW had "been consistent from the beginning" and did not change after the United States entered the war, either "in methods or purpose." Lanier concluded that had he been on the jury of the Chicago conspiracy trial he would not have "convicted a single one of them," since there was "no evidence" that the defendants "were guilty of the conspiracy with which they were charged."[24]

Chafee, as an ardent supporter of the war effort, ignored Lanier's article and thus incorrectly held that it was not legal to organize strikes "specifically planned to interfere with the war."[25] The government's determined assault on the IWW was a serious violation of fundamental civil liberties, even though Chafee refused to recognize this. Chafee was prepared to criticize the Wilson administration for suppressing dissidents who merely expressed their views, especially when there opinions were largely ignored, and for its vindictive policies once the war ended, but he wholeheartedly endorsed the administration's efforts to suppress those opposed to the war when their efforts were effective and garnered popular support.

THE SOCIALIST PARTY

Chafee had little to say about the IWW mass trials, but he spent a considerable effort analyzing questions of free speech arising out of the federal government's effort to divide and demoralize the Socialist Party of America. The *Debs* case was the most famous legal proceeding to arise from this ongoing effort. Chafee had a continuing difficulty in determining whether Debs should have been convicted of violating the Espionage Act. In 1920, with Debs still in prison, Chafee vacillated in his views. He was reluctant to criticize Judge Oliver Wendell Holmes Jr., who had written the unanimous opinion upholding Debs's conviction. Chafee argued the case had been a "close one." Yet he was also ready to admit that it was "hard to see" how Debs "could have been guilty" if Holmes had held to the clear and present danger standard that he had just formulated in the *Schenck* case.[26]

By 1941, Chafee was more willing to criticize Holmes, commenting that Holmes's opinion in the *Debs* case had been "regrettable." The prosecution had spent a great deal of time establishing Debs's political perspective as a radical socialist, although this had little to do with the charge of obstructing the draft. Chafee had to concede that Debs had been "probably convicted for an exposition of socialism."[27]

Chafee was unsure of his stance on the Debs case, but he had no doubt as to the validity of the guilty verdict rendered in the *Schenck* case. The *Schenck* case had provided Holmes with the opportunity to formulate the clear and present danger doctrine, while upholding Schenck's conviction for violating the Espionage Act.

Chafee agreed with Holmes, and went even further. In Chafee's view, "no real question of free speech arose" in the *Schenck* case. The Philadelphia Socialist Party had distributed a leaflet attacking the war and the draft. Chafee argued that the flyer was not protected by the First Amendment since some copies of the leaflet had been specifically sent to those about to be conscripted, urging them "to insist on their rights."[28] This was a feeble basis to jail someone for expressing their views on a critical issue of public policy.

Chafee also dealt in considerable detail with the free speech issues concerning Victor Berger. A spokesperson for the SP's most moderate tendency and the leader of the Milwaukee Socialist Party, Berger had been elected to the U.S. House of Representatives in November 1918. The House of Representatives refused to seat Berger and in December 1919 a special election was called to fill the vacant seat. Berger was again elected and once again he was not permitted to take his seat.[29] Chafee vigorously objected to this refusal to seat an elected official.

Still, Chafee emphatically rejected Berger's political viewpoint. As editor of the *Milwaukee Leader*, Berger was careful to avoid printing any article that could be construed as encouraging a militant opposition to the war, or resistance to the draft. He went even further by urging readers to buy Liberty Bonds to finance the war effort.[30]

Nevertheless, Berger was a critic of the president's war policy. He believed that the origins of the war lay in the imperialist rivalries of European powers as they sought to acquire new colonies and zones of influence. Furthermore, Berger continued to hold that the decision to enter the war was a mistake even after the United States declared war on Germany. He remained convinced that the United States and its allies should enter into immediate peace negotiations leading to a speedy end to the war through a peace treaty founded on the principles of "no annexations, no reparations." In a speech given in the spring of 1918, Berger stated that he wanted the United States "out of the war as quick as we can." This goal could be reached by beginning with an "immediate armistice looking forward to a general and permanent peace."[31] This was a very cautious record of dissent. Nevertheless, it still led to Berger's prosecution under the Espionage

Act, although his conviction was overturned by the Supreme Court on the basis of the obvious bias of the trial judge.[32]

Chafee came to "thoroughly detest the attitude of Berger." His position was so offensive that Chafee felt "no personal sympathy" with Berger's plight. By emphasizing the economic motives underlying the war aims of both sides, Berger sought to "sneer at the possibility of noble purposes in the conflict."[33]

Notwithstanding his distaste for Berger, Chafee sharply dissented from the decision to exclude him from Congress. In Chafee's view, the only valid ground for the disqualification of someone elected to Congress was a credible charge of treason. Berger's objections to the decision to enter the war did not provide the basis for a treason charge and thus he should have been seated by the House of Representatives.[34]

Chafee would have known of the push to have those found guilty of violating the Espionage Act prosecuted for treason and tried by a military tribunal. Although Chafee did not directly address this set of issues, it is clear from his comments on Berger that he rejected this approach. Treason involved a direct effort to provide aid and comfort to the enemy. It did not cover a situation in which one's critical comments could be considered to be helpful to the cause of an enemy nation.

BALANCING CONFLICTING INTERESTS

Chafee disdained even the most moderate opponents of the war. As an enthusiastic supporter of the administration's war policy, he sympathized with the government's efforts to suppress any effective opposition to the war, since this could hamper the U.S. military effort. At the same time, he viewed with alarm government repression that went beyond that which was necessary, thus creating the basis for a police state. Chafee was fearful that unnecessarily harsh wartime measures could lead to a drastic curtailment of civil liberties even after the war had come to an end.

In his two books on free speech, Chafee more fully developed the legal theory he had first advanced in the *New Republic* article.

In doing so, he closely adhered to the original formulation. Chafee began by holding that the "provisions of the Bill of Rights cannot be applied with absolute literalness, but are, [instead], subject to exceptions." From this perspective, statements, whether written or spoken, are not always protected by the Constitution's First Amendment, but can be prohibited in certain circumstances. On the other hand, he rejected the position that set the framework for most judicial decisions during this period, whereby speech that had the "natural and reasonable tendency" to encourage listeners to violate the law could be made illegal. Chafee insisted that words that merely have "some tendency, however remote, to bring about acts in violation of the law" were constitutionally protected, and could not be made illegal.

Chafee sought to define a middle position, one he believed presented a reasonable alternative to the polar positions he viewed as extreme. Thus, the "true boundary line" should be based on "the balancing against each other of two very important social interests, in public safety and in the search for truth."

On the positive side, Chafee believed that the expression of dissenting views was of significant value to the society as a whole. The free discussion of ideas permitted society to assess a difficult and complex situation by weighing the array of possible alternative solutions. This argument held during wartime, as it did during the calmer circumstances of peace.

On the other hand, Chafee argued, society had an interest in maintaining "public safety." that is, maintaining order through the enforcement of laws. Chafee's formulation deliberately confused two distinct issues. Most crimes involve personal violence or financial skullduggery. Everyone can see that "public safety," is enhanced when criminals are deterred from further acts of violence, or fraud, by the threat of punishment and incarceration. Laws such as the Espionage Act have nothing to do with "public safety" in the normal use of this phrase. In suppressing dissent, the government acts so that it can pursue its policy objectives, the winning of a war, for instance, without any hindrance from those in the opposition. Clearly the motivation underlying laws suppressing dissent is very different from the one underlying most criminal law.

Chafee was convinced that the basic principles determining the limits of free speech remain in force during a declared war and yet, in balancing the valid but conflicting social interests involved, it was essential that the government's interest in pursuing a military victory had to be weighed as a critically important factor. Even "in wartime freedom of speech exists" and the Bill of Rights remains in force "subject to a problematical limit." It was necessary to more narrowly limit the permitted range of opinions than those that could be expressed in peacetime because the United States was "passing through a period of danger" and thus "certain utterances had to be suppressed."[35]

In reality, the decision of the United States to enter the First World War was not a response to a threatened invasion by Germany and its allies. Woodrow Wilson had decided that U.S. strategic interests would be advanced if Germany was militarily crushed and then forced to unconditionally surrender to the Allied powers. Chafee's description of the objective situation is misleading and inaccurate, but it does reflect his uncritical and enthusiastic support for the war effort. He had no doubts that Congress had the authority to "make criminal any matter which tended to discourage the successful prosecution of the war," given the underlying limits set by the First Amendment, which required "the same method of balancing social interests" as mandated during peacetime.[36]

THE "DIRECT AND DANGEROUS" GUIDELINE

This analysis remained at a high level of abstraction. Chafee then provided his own version of Holmes's "clear and present danger" doctrine. In Chafee's view, "Conspiracies and attempts [that] constitute a direct and dangerous interference with the war [are] outside [of] the protection of freedom of speech." Still, he was convinced that government prosecutors had gone too far in suppressing dissent. Accordingly, "Action in proportion to the emergency was justified, but we censored and punished speech which was very far from direct and dangerous interference with the conduct of the war."[37]

Individual dissidents had been harassed although they represented no threat to the war effort. Several anarchists who opposed the U.S. intervention in Russia had been prosecuted during the war, although their call for a general strike was bound to be entirely futile. In the *Abrams* case, a small, isolated group of anarchists had been charged with violating the Espionage Act as amended by the Sedition Act by calling for a general strike to block the sending of supplies to U.S. troops in Siberia, where these troops were providing logistical support to military forces hostile to the Bolshevik government that ruled most of Russia.[38]

From Chafee's perspective, the federal government had acted in flagrant disregard for the Bill of Rights in prosecuting Molly Abrams and her fellow anarchists. The government had disregarded the basic right of free speech in prosecuting a "silly, futile circular of five obscure and isolated aliens."[39] Chafee's argument is very similar to that made by Holmes and Brandeis in their dissenting decisions on the *Abrams* case. This is not surprising since Chafee influenced the position taken by Holmes and Brandeis on issues related to civil liberties and, in turn, Chafee was influenced by Holmes's clear and present danger doctrine. It is interesting to see where Chafee's perspective took him, since he wrote far more extensively on the topic of free speech than either Holmes or Brandeis.

THE CIVIL WAR AND MILITARY TRIBUNALS

Chafee's first book on civil liberties was published in 1920, in the immediate aftermath of the First World War and in the midst of the first wave of anti-communist hysteria. Chafee was very disturbed by the government's vindictive attitude toward those who had been convicted of violating the Espionage Act during the war, when a peacetime amnesty seemed to be in order. He turned to the experience of the Civil War, when Abraham Lincoln had used military tribunals to quash dissent. At the same time, Lincoln argued for a policy of reconciliation once the war had come to an end.

Chafee praised Lincoln for narrowly focusing government repression on those who met the "test of direct and dangerous interference with the war" and for his generous attitude toward his former enemies as the war came to an end. This was an implicit attack on Woodrow Wilson. From Chafee's perspective, Lincoln had remained above the fray, while Wilson was petty and vindictive to those who had opposed his war policies. This vindictiveness could be seen most clearly in the case of Eugene Debs, who remained in jail for five years after the war ended. Chafee argued that Lincoln "would not have allowed an old man" to "lie in prison for sincere and harmless, even though misguided, words" once the war had ended.[40]

Chafee's argument is similar to the argument made by Croly in his 1909 book. Both men believed in a Lincoln who benevolently exercised autocratic power. Chafee, like Croly, was disappointed when Wilson used his wartime power to persecute his opponents even after the war had ended.

In praising Lincoln's policy toward his opponents, Chafee was prepared to justify Lincoln's reliance on military commissions. The majority of the U.S. Supreme Court had rejected the use of military tribunals in the *Milligan* case, a landmark in the judicial history of constitutional rights. Woodrow Wilson had relied on the *Milligan* case in rejecting demands to expand the jurisdiction of the military courts to include civilians accused of violating the Espionage Act. Chafee questioned whether it was true that military tribunals were "never justified" in trying civilians and, instead, suggested that they could be "necessary when the machinery of the [civilian] courts cannot adequately meet the situation."[41]

Chafee's formulation on this issue is far less stringent than the standard set by Davis in the *Milligan* case. Although Chafee condemned the government for its vengeful policy of repression during the postwar period, there are indications that he would have supported an even more draconian approach to dissent during the war.

In criticizing the Sedition Act of 1918 for being overly broad in scope, Chafee suggested that Congress could have enacted legislation under which those who "were really causing trouble could be tried and confined until the emergency was passed," and then released.[42] It seems probable that Chafee had in mind IWW activists, with their ability to organize effective and militant strikes in key industries.

One of the problems that Chafee cited with the administration's policy of relying on the civilian courts was that defendants could be released on bail while awaiting trial. In fact, federal district judges usually set bail for those accused of violating the Espionage Act at very high levels, so few defendants were released prior to the end of the war. Nevertheless, Chafee pointed to Lincoln's Civil War policy as a better alternative, since those tried in military courts were not eligible for bail.

Chafee would not have been aware that a similar plan had been proposed in the summer of 1917 calling for IWW activists to be quietly rounded up and interned until the war ended. Justice Department attorneys rejected this proposal, citing the *Milligan* case. U.S. citizens could not be detained without a jury trial in which due process procedures were followed at a time when civilian courts were open and functioning and order prevailed throughout the country.[43] The president accepted this opinion, and the idea was shelved. Thus, Chafee was prepared to suspend certain constitutional rights during wartime that even Woodrow Wilson believed should remain in effect.

HAMPERING VOLUNTARY ENLISTMENTS

Chafee's sharply constricted tolerance for dissent in wartime can be seen in another issue that arose during the war. He pointed out that there were already laws on the books from the Civil War era that "would have met any serious danger to the prosecution of the war." Still, he conceded these laws would not cover all of the problems confronting the government during the war. In particular, it was "not a crime to persuade a man not to enlist voluntarily." Chafee believed that the federal government should "have been content to limit itself to meeting the tangible needs" of the situation, rather than pushing for the adoption of the Espionage Act with its broadly worded prohibitions.[44]

In Chafee's view, Congress would have been justified in enacting legislation making it illegal to discourage young men from voluntarily enlisting in the armed forces. It was "normal criminal law" to penalize those who engaged in "interference with governmental functions like [the] refusal to enlist." Since the Constitution authorized Congress to declare war on an enemy nation, Congress could expedite "this task by penalizing those who actually keep men out of service, whether by starting a riot or by effectually persuading men not to register or not to enlist." According to Chafee, Congress could go further by "penalizing unsuccessful efforts to interfere, whether they are actions or words."[45]

Had Congress enacted legislation along these lines it would have greatly limited free speech during the war. Chafee held to the general principle that speech could only be prosecuted when it presented a clear and present danger to the authorities, rather than a remote possibility of a threat. Still, Chafee's proposed legislation would have meant that any organized effort to circulate literature condemning the war and the draft could have been prosecuted on the basis that young men who read these documents might be less likely to volunteer for military service.

Chafee was eager to claim that the president's war policies reflected the will of the people. According to Chafee, the American "people by an overwhelming majority believed conscription to be a necessary and just method of waging an unavoidable war."[46] Nevertheless, his argument in support of the prosecution of those whose statements might hinder voluntary enlistments indicates that he knew this argument was specious. After all, the government generated a vast flow of propaganda extolling the war while cajoling young men to volunteer. Furthermore, the tabloid press was full of spurious atrocity stories demonizing Germans. Government decision-makers were not willing to permit a counterargument to be made, even when it came from organizations with limited resources, because they understood that the war was deeply unpopular. Yet it is exactly this type of situation in which the right to dissent is of critical importance and must be defended.

Instead, Chafee was willing to sacrifice the First Amendment to protect the war effort. According to Chafee, Congress had the authority to "make criminal any matter which tended to discourage the successful prosecution of the war," within the underlying limits set by the fundamental principle "of balancing social interests." Leaflets that had the effect of discouraging men to volunteer for the military could be subject to legislation "because of the danger created by their language, and the surrounding circumstances," that is, U.S. involvement in the First World War. Although Chafee recognized that speech or writing that discouraged voluntary enlistments "served a social interest," nevertheless "this was outweighed by the pressing peril to the social interest in the enforcement of war legislation."[47]

Encouraging someone not to volunteer, whether directly or indirectly, was not inciting someone to commit a crime. During the first months after the United States entered the war, the U.S. military relied on volunteers, by definition those who were not being compelled by law to join. Thus, those urging men of draft age not to join the army were not encouraging them to violate any law. If speech along these lines was not protected by the First Amendment because it undercut the government's war policy, then the government could suppress any speech that had a significant negative impact on the military. Public debate on war policies or conscription must be protected from government repression even during wartime if the First Amendment was to be more than a fine-sounding phrase.

— 10 —

The "Clear and Present Danger" Doctrine in Historical Context

The "clear and present danger" doctrine of Oliver Wendell Holmes Jr. marked a major step in the development of legal theory around issues of free speech. Until then, courts in the United States had relied on the "natural and reasonable consequences" doctrine that was rooted in British common law. Under this legal theory, virtually any opposition to government policies could be held to be seditious and severely punished. This was particularly true in wartime, when any opposition was viewed as aiding the enemy. In the United States during the First World War, government prosecutors arguing for convictions under the Espionage Act contended that the natural and logical consequence of any statements criticizing the war or the draft was an undermining of civilian morale.

Most of the justices on the U.S. Supreme Court agreed with the government's argument and were therefore prepared to give the Justice Department full authority in determining who would be prosecuted. Oliver Wendell Holmes Jr. and Louis Brandeis were the two exceptions to this prevailing viewpoint. When the Debs case came before the Supreme Court on an expedited appeal, Chief Justice Edward White was anxious to ensure that Debs's conviction was upheld by a unanimous opinion. He therefore assigned the case to Holmes, with the understanding that all of the judges would sign on to his opinion.[1]

The Supreme Court's consideration of the *Debs* case was tied to two other cases involving convictions under the Espionage Act. Both the *Debs* case and the *Schenck* case involved the Socialist Party of America, while the Frohwerk case involved a German language newspaper that was viewed as sympathetic to the German cause. Holmes simultaneously wrote his opinions for the three cases, with the unanimous backing of the other eight justices. The *Schenck* case was heard on appeal first and it was therefore in this case that Holmes rendered his famous dictum that would set the guideline for determining free speech cases over the next decades.[2]

In rejecting the argument that Charles Schenck had been engaged in activities protected by the First Amendment, Holmes declared: "The question in every case is whether the words used in such circumstances are of such a nature as to create a clear and present danger that they will bring about the substantive evils that Congress has a right to prevent."[3]

Holmes's argument can only be understood in its historical context, beginning with a close examination of the *Schenck* case itself and then proceeding to an analysis of the *Debs* case in light of the clear and present danger doctrine. Holmes did not fully develop his argument in his first rulings. Instead, the argument evolved over several years, with both Holmes and Brandeis participating in its development.

Holmes did not initiate the clear and present danger doctrine in a vacuum. On the contrary, he was responding to a widespread belief among progressives who supported the war effort that the Wilson administration was pursuing unnecessarily harsh repressive policies. In particular, Holmes developed his perspective in a milieu created by *The New Republic* and within the underlying legal framework established by Zechariah Chafee Jr. An examination of these connections leads to an analysis of the fundamental points underlying the clear and present danger doctrine and, from there, to the formulation of a very different theory of free speech, one that directly challenges the underlying assumptions made by both Holmes and Chafee.

THE SCHENCK CASE FLYER

In his opinion in the Schenck case, Holmes devoted considerable space in an effort to justify his verdict by citing extracts of a flyer. In August 1917, the Socialist Party of Philadelphia decided to circulate a leaflet criticizing conscription. The arguments advanced in the flyer were in accord with the position taken by the Party in opposing the war and the draft, as expressed in the majority resolution approved by an emergency convention in April 1917. Nevertheless, the specific wording of the flyer was formulated by the officers of the Philadelphia local and reflected the perspective of Philadelphia's socialists.

The executive committee of the local voted to print 15,000 copies of a one-page leaflet and to distribute most of them on the streets of Philadelphia. In addition, the local executive decided to mail seven hundred copies to young men who were in the process of being inducted into the U.S. Army. The document enclosed in this mailing had two sides, with one side the original flyer and the other a message specifically aimed at those being conscripted.[4]

Charles Schenck, the secretary of the Socialist Party local, was charged with violating the Espionage Act, since the flyer was printed and circulated under his authority. He was convicted in federal district court and given a six-month prison sentence. (Elizabeth Baer, the secretary of the Philadelphia local, served a three-month sentence.) The case became a test for the many indictments of Socialist Party members under the Espionage Act.

The U.S. Supreme Court held a hearing on the case in January 1919 and the unanimous decision of the court was delivered in March 1919. Although there has been a great deal written about Holmes and the evolution of his thought on the constitutional implications of the First Amendment and the right of free speech, little has been written that examines the flyer itself and how Holmes dealt with it.

The original flyer distributed to the public was titled "Long Live the

Constitution of the United States." It was clearly written in such a way as to emphasize that it was counseling its readers to oppose the war in a peaceful manner, through the use of tactics that had been deemed lawful prior to the advent of the war. Much of the leaflet addressed the issue of conscription, which the Philadelphia Socialist Party viewed as a violation of the Thirteenth Amendment abolishing slavery. Indeed, a draftee was "forced into involuntary servitude."

This was particularly true when a person conscripted was sent "abroad to fight against his will." In 1917, there was a widespread belief that those who wrote the U.S. Constitution were steadfastly opposed to a conscripted army being sent overseas. This was an argument that resonated well beyond the socialist movement. Indeed, Senator Robert La Follette would make a similar point in a speech on the Senate floor in April 1917. La Follette argued that there was "no authority in the Constitution to raise an army by draft and send them across the seas into foreign lands."[5]

Having presented the arguments against the draft, the flyer moved on to the essential reasons that it not "go unchallenged." This was particularly true in Philadelphia, "the cradle of American liberty." Congress in legislating conscription for an army to be sent to the trenches along the Western Front was exercising "a tyrannical power in its worst form."

There can be no doubt that the leaflet was aimed at encouraging its readers to organize against the draft. Yet the flyer was clear that this opposition should be accomplished through peaceful protest. It urged those opposed to the war to join the Socialist Party, as well as to speak out and to peacefully assemble in opposition to conscription. Finally, the flyer asked everyone to sign a petition to repeal the draft.

The leaflet represented a perfectly legal expression of opinion by a significant political party discussing an important and controversial issue of public policy. Nevertheless, the Justice Department had no doubt that the original flyer violated the Espionage Act. Both Holmes and Brandeis agreed with that decision, as did Chafee.

There are several aspects to the issue, but the most critical is the one of intent. The government was convinced that printed documents containing arguments attacking the draft would necessarily convince young men who read them to resist conscription, either by refusing to register or going underground once they received induction notices. Many of those threatened with induction did just that. Still, there is nothing in the flyer that suggests in any way that the Socialist Party of Philadelphia intended to encourage draft resistance by circulating the leaflet. The initial flyer was drafted for circulation among the wider public, although copies were sent to some of those who were in the process of being conscripted.

The second side of the leaflet was written specifically for those about to be drafted. Titled "Assert Your Rights," it began by condemning the U.S. government's decision to enter the war. This decision did not reflect popular opinion since Americans had not voted "in favor of war" at the last election. (Woodrow Wilson had campaigned as a peace candidate.) Young men in the United States were being thrust "into the shambles and bloody trenches of war-crazy nations." Furthermore, the president's claim that this was a "war for democracy" was merely the "propaganda of jingoism," a propaganda phrase being used to "becloud the issue." Everyone had to decide for themselves whether they stood "with the forces of liberty and light," or war and darkness.

This section of the second page of the flyer presented a vigorous attack on the Wilson administration and its justification for bringing the United States into the First World War. Although its inclusion might have led the Justice Department to initiate a prosecution, the government's focus was on the other sections of the page of the leaflet that further condemned the draft.

The flyer sharply criticized the Selective Service Act for singling out those who belonged to Christian pacifist churches, such as the Quakers and the Amish, for preference in granting conscientious objector status. This, the flyer argued, violated the First Amendment's prohibition of any federal legislation furthering the "establishment of religion." Those who were "conscientiously opposed to war," whether they questioned the existence of a god or adhered to another religion that did not hold pacifism as a fundamental tenet, had as much right to an exemption from military service as those specifically recognized by the statute.

There can be no doubt that this section of the flyer was aimed at those who were in the process of being conscripted and that it called upon them to challenge the existing legislation. Nevertheless, the flyer did not encourage its readers to resist the draft, either by refusing to register or by going into hiding once inducted.

The Philadelphia Socialist Party's flyer did not mention either of these possibilities. Instead, it suggested that those opposed to all wars should register as conscientious objectors, even if they were not religious. This would lead to a legal test of the constitutionality of that section of the Selective Service Act.

The flyer raised a pertinent constitutional issue. If the federal government was prepared to offer young men who were Quakers or Amish the opportunity to perform non-combatant alternative service, then those with similar views on war but who were not members of those religious sects should be provided with the same option. The government was granting preferential treatment to those holding certain religious views, an egregious violation of the separation of church and state as codified in the First Amendment.

The proposition that this provision of the Selective Service Act should be challenged in court was perfectly reasonable. Indeed, the validity of the draft was contested in the judicial system and the preferential treatment given to certain religious groups was one point in the challenge. In January 1918, Chief Justice White issued a unanimous opinion upholding the Selective Service Act of 1917 instituting conscription. He noted that the point had been raised that the statute violated the constitutional mandate separating church and state. White then rejected this argument without comment, arguing that "its unsoundness is too apparent to require us to do more."[6]

Whether correct or not, the Philadelphia Socialist Party was raising an important issue of public policy. In an important case decided twenty-five years later, the Supreme Court reversed a conviction, deciding that someone with "honest motives who honestly believes a law is unconstitutional" could suggest "that the law shall not be obeyed" until "a court shall have held it valid" without "knowingly counseling" that the law be resisted.[7]

HOLMES AND THE *SCHENCK* CASE

This was the flyer produced by the Philadelphia Socialist Party that had been the starting point for a landmark case in the right to dissent. There is not the slightest doubt that it would be deemed a constitutionally protected expression of free speech by the currently prevailing judicial standard. Nevertheless, Holmes was certain that the government had properly prosecuted Schenck since the flyer presented a clear and present danger to the war effort. He never wavered from this view.

Holmes began by insisting that one cannot say anything at any time and at any place and therefore free speech rights were not absolute. In making this argument, Holmes was following the groundwork already laid by Chafee. Holmes was setting up a caricature of the position advanced by Debs and other radicals in order to knock it down. Of course there were limits on what one could say, but expressions of opinion on important issues of public policy should be given the widest possible latitude.

Holmes understood the value of a free discourse on policy issues and yet he still believed that free speech could be substantially curtailed in wartime. Thus, "When a nation is at war, many things that might be said in times of peace are such a hindrance to its effort that these utterances will not be endured." Indeed, "No Court could regard this as protected by any constitutional right."

This is a sweeping statement, one that has very dangerous implications. For those opposed to a war to create a "hindrance" is to act effectively to persuade public opinion that the continuation of the war is unjustified and should be ended as soon as possible. In other words, according to Holmes the only opposition to a declared war that is protected from government repression is one that is ineffectual. Holmes's perspective could only result in a drastic curtailment of fundamental rights.

Holmes devoted much of his opinion in the *Schenck* case to a detailed examination of the Philadelphia Socialist Party's flyer. Although he differentiated between the two sides of the flyer, he did not mention that one side had been initially written as a one-page leaflet for distribution to the wider public, while the other side had been written specifically for a mailing sent to those about to be inducted.

In citing sections from the initial page to the public, Holmes pointed out that it had condemned conscription as "a monstrous wrong against humanity." This, he wrote, was "impassioned language." Holmes was touching on a critical issue. There can be no doubt that the flyer presented a set of ideas for public debate, that is, opposition to the draft and to the war. Yet in doing so it used vivid language in an effort to make the argument more persuasive. For instance, the flyer attacked those who promoted the war as "cunning politicians and a mercenary capitalist press." The language of the flyer is often rhetorical, designed to appeal to the emotions as well as to the intellect. Of course, the mainstream press sought to demonize the anti-war opposition, using emotional language and misleading innuendo. No one doubted that these statements were protected by the First Amendment and yet when those critical of the government expressed their views, their right to do so was denied on the basis that their wording was inflammatory.

In effect, Holmes was ready to hold statements critical of the war effort that were written or spoken in a rhetorical style to a different standard than to those presented in a dry, academic style. Holmes did not formulate this position, but it is implicit in his opinion in the Schenck case. The argument is a dubious one.

Holmes was quick to set out the framework for his verdict, but this still left unanswered whether the Philadelphia Socialist Party's flyer actually violated the Espionage Act. In theory, one could agree that statements that presented a clear and present danger to the war effort were not protected by the First Amendment. Nevertheless, one could argue that the flyer had been carefully written to remain within the law, notwithstanding its rhetorical language.

In trying to justify his guilty verdict, Holmes emphasized that copies of the flyer had been specifically sent to hundreds of young men who were in the process of being inducted into the army. In his view, "the document would not have been sent unless it had been intended to have some effect" and the only "effect that it could be expected to have" was "to influence them to obstruct" the draft.

Holmes thus ignored the obvious intent of the page of the flyer specifically written to those about to be inducted. The flyer presented an alternative option to not reporting for induction and going underground. Instead, readers were urged to apply for conscientious objector status, even if they were not religious. One could argue that this was a smokescreen, although a close reading of the flyer would make this a difficult position to sustain. Holmes did not even attempt to formulate such an argument.

HOLMES ON THE *DEBS* CASE

Although the *Schenck* case provided the specific occasion for putting forward the clear and present danger doctrine, Holmes understood that the *Debs* case would be viewed as the essential marker by which to judge the new legal theory. In his opinion affirming Debs's conviction, Holmes did little more than refer to his reasoning in the *Schenck* case. Nevertheless, Holmes made several references to the *Debs* case in private correspondence that reveal more of his underlying reasoning.

Holmes wrote frequently to Harold Laski, a frequent contributor to the *New Republic*. An avid reader, Holmes was convinced that the journal had been "exactly right" in its assessment of the *Debs* case.[8] Croly was very cautious in approaching the massive incursions into fundamental civil liberties during the era of the First World War. Still, *The New Republic* printed two unsigned editorials on the *Debs* case that appear to be consistent with Holmes's approach to the case.

The editorials approached the issues raised by the *Debs* case from the perspective that the administration was missing an opportunity to win over moderate socialists by initiating an unnecessary prosecution of the party's most prominent member. Debs had enormous credibility, going well beyond those who voted for him or were members of the Socialist Party. In opting to prosecute him for the speech in Canton, the administration was making it clear that anyone who spoke out against the war could be punished with a lengthy sentence in prison.

In an editorial that appeared in September 1918, shortly after Debs had received a ten-year prison sentence for opposing the war, *The New Republic* held that Debs "was no doubt justly convicted and sentenced" according "to the letter of the Espionage Act." After all, he was an "expounder of unsound doctrines," which, "if more widely accepted," would have impaired "the country's fighting power." Nevertheless, Debs was sincere in his beliefs and widely respected. Thus, the government's power to suppress dissent "might have been employed with better discretion."[9]

A later editorial printed in April 1919, shortly after Holmes's decision affirming Debs's conviction, again held that there was "no doubt about the legality of his [Debs] conviction," since the Canton speech had "clearly violated the Espionage Act." Yet, "since the emergency which might have justified" the prosecution had "passed," insisting that for Debs to serve his sentence "would be both cruel and blind."[10]

Holmes wrote to Laski immediately after reading the second editorial, praising its approach to the case. He went on to present his opinion of Debs. Holmes "wondered if Debs really" had "any ideas." The Canton speech seemed to Holmes to be "really silly." Furthermore, Debs's speech to the jury "showed great ignorance" of the legal ramifications of the First Amendment guarantee of free speech.[11]

These comments are indicative of Holmes's personality and his political perspective. A Boston Brahmin, he scorned and disdained any ideas that challenged the legitimacy of the existing system. Debs was one of the most admired individuals of his era, a person with enormous integrity and courage. He was able to convince many of those in the working class that there was an alternative to their lives of hard work and poverty. Holmes, from his secure, comfortable vantage point on the Supreme Court, saw none of this. Debs was dismissed as a misguided fool.

HOLMES RESPONDS TO PROFESSOR FREUND

A few months after the *Debs* cases had been decided, Ernst Freund, a professor of law at the University of Chicago, wrote a critique of the Supreme Court's decision in *The New Republic*. Freund raised several issues, those specific to the *Debs* case as well as others concerning the wider issues involved in prosecutions under the Espionage Act. A regular reader of *The New Republic*, Holmes felt certain his opinion upholding Debs's conviction was consistent with the editorial line taken by the journal. He was therefore especially perturbed by Freund's critique.

Holmes drafted a response to Freund, although he never sent it for public distribution. He wrote to a friend that he had considered a public response to criticisms of his decision, so as to "shoot off my mouth," but he had opted to "keep a judicial silence."[12] Instead, Holmes enclosed the draft in a letter written to Laski. Since Laski was in contact with Croly, there is every reason to believe that Croly saw the response.

Freund's critique and Holmes's unpublished response provide further insights into the development of the "clear and present danger" doctrine. One point Freund addressed arose in Holmes's decision in the Schenck case. Holmes sought to counter the argument that free speech was an absolute right by advancing the famous hypothetical case of a person who causes a panic by falsely shouting "Fire!" in a theater.

Freund criticized Holmes for using the analogy to demonstrate his argument that free speech was not an absolute right. According to Freund, the validity of Holmes's "unsafe doctrine" was undermined by the use of such a "manifestly inappropriate analogy."[13]

The *Schenck* case was reviewed in conjunction with the Debs appeal. Holmes would have been reviewing the transcript of record in the *Debs* case as he wrote his opinion affirming Schenck's conviction. Edwin Wertz, the U.S. attorney for northern Ohio, used the same analogy in his presentation to the jury in the *Debs* case. According to Wertz, "a man in a crowded auditorium, or any theater, who yells

'Fire!', and there is no fire, and a panic" ensues has engaged in speech that is not protected by the First Amendment.[14] Implicit in this argument is the assumption that the person involved knows that there is no fire in the auditorium and is deliberately seeking to create a panic. Holmes reduced Wertz's wording to its bare essentials: "The most stringent protection of free speech would not protect a man in falsely shouting fire in a theatre and causing a panic."[15]

Wertz and Holmes did not pull this analogy out of thin air. In July 1913, the Western Federation of Miners organized a strike of copper miners in the Upper Peninsula of Michigan. The strike was still in force during that Christmas season when the union organized a Christmas Eve celebration that took place on the second floor of a hall in Calumet, Michigan. Four hundred people were crowded into an auditorium when someone yelled "Fire!," even though there was none. Seventy-five people died in the resulting panic, trying to force their way out of a narrow staircase. Although no one knows for sure who was to blame, there is good reason to believe that the person responsible deliberately sought to create a panic and that he was acting on behalf of the mining corporations.[16]

Wertz knew that the analogy would resonate with members of the jury in the *Debs* case. Holmes would have also understood its immediate relevance. Nevertheless, the analogy was spurious. In his letter to Croly, Holmes did not respond to this aspect of Freund's critique, perhaps because he realized the faultiness of the analogy. The pertinent issue was not whether one could say anything at any time and place, but whether a point of view concerning a matter of public policy could be voiced in public, no matter how distasteful that perspective was to a segment of the audience or how much the powers that be detested it.

Freund also challenged Holmes's decision by questioning whether Debs had actually violated the law even when the Espionage Act was interpreted by the guidelines of the clear and present danger doctrine. Was Debs actually in a position to actually pose a significant threat to the war effort or the draft? Was it plausible to believe that this was Debs's intent in giving the Canton speech? Freund argued that as "an experienced speaker" Debs knew that though he could "create disaffection, his power to create actual obstruction to a compulsory draft was practically nil, and he could hardly have intended what he could not hope to achieve."[17]

Freund's point goes to a fundamental problem with the clear and present danger doctrine. The assessment of the potential threat posed by a given speech or article is inherently subjective. To Holmes, it was obvious that Debs represented a credible threat to the war effort. Yet it was not only Freund who questioned this judgment. Alfred Bettman, who as deputy director of the War Emergency Division had been assigned primary responsibility for overseeing the Justice Department's administration of the Espionage Act, had opposed the decision to prosecute Debs on a similar basis.[18] Of course, neither Holmes nor Freund was aware of this fact.

HOLMES AND THE *ABRAMS* CASE

In writing the decisions affirming the conviction of Schenck and Debs, Holmes believed that he was acting in accord with the legal theory formulated by Chafee and first presented in *The New Republic*. After all, Holmes had started by holding that the fundamental rights codified in the Bill of Rights were not absolute standards, but rather could only be determined in relation to the specific circumstances as they arose. Furthermore, he had ruled that basic civil liberties could be curtailed in wartime as the state balanced individual rights with the collective need to protect the country from an external attack and to win the war.

Holmes was therefore dismayed when Chafee criticized his rulings in the *Debs* and *Schenck* cases in his article in the *Harvard Law Review*. Chafee had chided Holmes for presenting the clear and present danger doctrine while voting to affirm the guilty verdicts in three controversial cases. The initial impetus underlying the push to develop a new legal theory that could present an alternative to the natural and reasonable consequences doctrine had come from a desire to see the courts act as a check on the government prosecutors.

Chafee would not have known that Holmes and Brandeis had been willing to reverse a guilty verdict in a case involving those opposed to the war that had come before the U.S. Supreme Court prior to the *Schenck* case. In October 1918, the Supreme Court heard an appeal of a case involving a group of socialists in South Dakota who had circulated a petition calling for the repeal of the conscription statute. Emanuel Baltzer and twenty-six others were convicted of violating the Espionage Act and given sentences of one to two years in prison.[19]

Seven of the justices were prepared to affirm this conviction. Holmes then wrote a dissent, which gained the support of Brandeis, that held that an "emergency would have to be very great" before the circulation of a petition seeking a change in public policy "was an act that the Constitution would not protect." Indeed, the Bill of Rights was "still worth fighting for" and should not be arbitrarily "abridged" even during wartime.[20]

At this point, Chief Justice White brought the matter to a close. He was eager to have the Supreme Court act as a unanimous body in supporting the government's efforts to suppress the antiwar opposition. The government was persuaded to drop the prosecution of Baltzer, and Holmes's draft opinion remained hidden in the archives until it was discovered in 1991.[21]

Chafee's critique of Holmes's decisions in the *Debs* and *Schenck* cases as presented in the *Harvard Law Review* article went beyond the point that those criticizing the war effort should only be prosecuted when their views presented a credible threat to the war effort. He was insistent that free speech was crucially important in a democratic society and that the positive contribution to society of an unbridled discussion continued to be true even during wartime. Chafee believed that Holmes had downplayed this point in his rulings in the initial free speech cases. Instead, Holmes had emphasized only one pole in determining the balancing of conflicting interests by stressing the need to protect the nation's security from dissenting voices. Chafee was also concerned that Holmes had minimized the point that those who opposed the war should only be prosecuted for expressing their views when their objections posed a credible threat to the success of the war effort.

In July 1919, shortly after the publication of Chafee's article in the *Harvard Law Review*, Laski arranged for Chafee to meet Holmes. Holmes was staying in his summer home along the coast north of Boston, so the meeting was scheduled for Cambridge. Laski thought that this informal meeting would give Chafee a good chance to present his critique of the Schenck decision, and wrote to Chafee that the encounter would allow the two to "fight on it" with Holmes. The meeting was in fact brief and cordial. Holmes later reported that he had held a "few minutes' talk" with Chafee, who "seemed unusually pleasant and intelligent."[22] It is clear that Holmes viewed the meeting as primarily social and that it had not had a significant impact on his perspective.

This is not to say that Holmes was not influenced by Chafee's critique. Holmes had read Chafee's article in the *Harvard Law Review* and he thought it was "first rate."[23] Furthermore, the objective situation had changed and it was a fundamental tenet of the clear and present danger doctrine that the limits of free speech are determined by the specific context within which a statement is made.

The *Schenck* and *Debs* rulings had come before the U.S. Supreme Court only two months after the war had come to an end. As the postwar period unfolded, it became clear that the authorities at both the state and federal levels were prepared to utilize the enormous powers that the government had accrued during the war to maintain their repression of left-wing radicals. Progressives were united in their objection to the Red Scare hysteria that had been whipped up by tabloid newspapers. This critical perspective was held by virtually everyone on the Left, no matter what their position had been on the war. In a private letter, Brandeis wrote that the Red Scare reflected a "disgraceful exhibition—of hysterical, unintelligent fear."[24]

Holmes's opinion in the *Abrams* case provided, in part, a response to Chafee's criticisms as expressed in the *Harvard Law Review*. Of course, Holmes was not only responding to Chafee, but also to the views of a wide range of progressive thought in the postwar period. Brandeis joined Holmes in a dissent to a majority decision that once again upheld the prosecution of those who had spoken out against the administration's policies.

A small group of anarchists had distributed leaflets calling for a general strike to protest U.S. aid to right-wing military forces in Russia who were seeking to overthrow the Bolshevik regime. This action took place in August 1918, in the midst of the war. Needless to say, this small group had no credible likelihood of causing a significant disruption of the war effort. The *Abrams* case gave Holmes the opportunity to argue that there were limits to the government's actions in suppressing dissent, even during wartime. Furthermore, his opinion stressed the importance of free speech in the formulation of public policy. Thus, in his dissent, Holmes responded positively to both points in Chafee's criticism as formulated in the *Harvard Law Review* article.

Holmes began by minimizing the potential impact on the war effort of the anarchist flyers. The defendants were "poor and young anonymities" who held to a "creed of ignorance and immaturity." Statements advocating a certain position on a matter of controversy should only be made illegal when they "imminently threaten immediate interference" with government policies that are required to "save the country."[25]

Holmes then presented a broad argument on the importance of free speech. The Bill of Rights rested on the belief that "the best test of truth is the power of thought to get itself accepted in the competition of the market." Thus, "we should be eternally vigilant against attempts to check the expression that we loathe" unless these dissident opinions represent a direct and dangerous threat to society.[26]

HOLMES AND THE PERSECUTION OF UNPOPULAR VIEWPOINTS

In his dissent in the Abrams case, delivered in November 1919, Holmes moved beyond the points raised in Chafee's critique. His dissent provided the basis for judicial review of a government intent upon using the crisis conditions of a total war as an opportunity to launch an attack on its political enemies. Yet this point raised another set of difficult questions. Government attorneys would always claim that the decision to prosecute a dissident was solely based on the urgent need to protect the country's military forces from those who intended to disrupt them.

Holmes not only suggested that the prosecution of a tiny group of radicals under the Espionage Act represented a disproportionate response to a minimal threat. He was also arguing a more important point as well. The courts could only assume that such a prosecution was being initiated to suppress political ideologies that were considered to be hostile to the government and to the existing power structure. If you hold power, and want "a certain result with all your heart," then there is a tendency to "sweep away all opposition." In the *Abrams* case, the defendants were being "made to suffer not for what the indictment alleges, but for the creed they avow."[27] The point is very clear: anarchists and socialists were being imprisoned not because they were effectively obstructing the war effort, but because the Wilson administration was using the wartime emergency as a convenient opportunity to crush its left-wing radical opponents.

Holmes was directly countering an argument frequently made by those on the Supreme Court who defended the state's repression of radicals. They claimed that the government had the right to suppress those who raised the possibility of a revolution some time in the future because it made sense to stamp out these views before they could present a credible threat. The issue was directly addressed in the Gitlow case, decided in 1925. Benjamin Gitlow was a leader of the Communist Party. Its literature posed the possibility of a revolutionary upheaval some time in the indefinite future.

In a majority opinion upholding Gitlow's conviction for violating New York's criminal anarchy law, Justice Edward Sanford argued that a "single revolutionary spark may kindle a fire." Sanford held that the government was justified in acting to "suppress the threatened danger in its incipiency."[28]

A similar argument is sometimes raised now by those on the Left who contend that speakers representing the far Right or fascist perspectives should not be given a platform for their views. When it is pointed out that these speakers garner a small audience, the response is often made that it is better to snuff out these dangerous ideas before they spread. Yet this is exactly the same argument Sanford formulated as a justification for the government's repression of the radical Left. The fundamental basis for defending free speech is the belief that a free and unlimited discussion will lead to a positive outcome. It is a belief that underlies a commitment to the democratic process. The alternative leads to autocratic rule by an elite.

Key figures within the Justice Department agreed with Holmes that some U.S. attorneys were overzealous in prosecuting those who opposed the war. John Lord O'Brian and Alfred Bettman, as the key decision-makers in the Justice Department's War Emergency Division, tried to restrain prosecutors from bringing cases to court where the defendants did not, in their opinion, pose a significant threat to the government's war policies. In May 1918, when the Sedition Act signif-icantly widened the potential scope for the prosecution of dissenters, Bettman wrote a memorandum suggesting that a circular letter be sent to all U.S. attorneys warning them to be careful in their use of this new statute. Bettman concluded, "Undue repression of legitimate criticism and legitimate discussion of war issues is a greater evil than occasional disloyal utterances."[29]

Yet neither Bettman nor O'Brian took the further step that Holmes took in the *Abrams* case. They viewed these questionable prosecu-tions as mistakes made by U.S. attorneys in suppressing dissent. Holmes was suggesting that this was a deliberate misuse of govern-ment authority to unconstitutionally silence legitimate free speech.

Holmes was certainly correct in his analysis of the decision to ini-tiate the Abrams prosecution. Still, the U.S. Attorney's office in New York was at the center of the government's efforts to crack down on radicals using the Espionage Act, reflecting a broader decision by the Wilson administration to suppress its left-wing opponents, in par-ticular those in the Socialist Party and the Industrial Workers of the World.

Holmes was sensitive to this argument. He had been publicly chastised by prominent progressives for his decision to uphold the conviction of Gene Debs. His critics had suggested that Debs was being prosecuted for his politics, in this case radical socialism, and that Holmes was giving his approval to this act of persecution. Holmes dismissed Debs's opinions as silly, but he vehemently denied that his decision was a political one. Instead, Holmes insisted that he had affirmed the verdict of the jury solely on the evidence that the Canton speech had presented a clear and present danger to the conscription of soldiers and that Debs had knowingly intended such a result.

There is no reason to doubt Holmes's claim as to the motivation behind his decision, but the more relevant question relates to the motives of the Wilson administration. There were significant disputes within the Justice Department concerning the decision to prosecute Debs. In the end, the decision was made at the highest levels, the president and the attorney general.

The underlying reality was that the decision to proceed was made on the basis of a complex set of reasons. The government tried hard to pressure Debs and the Socialist Party into reversing their initial position of resistance to the war and instead become enthusiastic proponents of the war effort. When this maneuver failed, the decision was made to target the party's leadership for prosecution. In part, this was because Debs and the Socialist Party were viewed as a threat to the war effort, but it also reflected concerns that socialists were developing a significant base and were challenging the hold of the Democratic Party on the working-class vote.

For Holmes, the situation was straightforward. As judges, one had to put aside one's own political biases in order to determine a case strictly on the basis of the law. Yet Holmes understood that some officials in the administration were initiating prosecutions under the Espionage Act in order to stifle their political opponents. In fact, this was not only true of the Justice Department and the president, but also of most judges in both the federal and state courts. Indeed, Judge David Westenhaver who presided over the *Debs* case was extremely hostile to Debs and to socialism. His bias affected the conduct of the trial and led him to impose a harsh sentence once Debs was found guilty.

Holmes was clear in the *Abrams* case that a critical function of the courts should be to act as a check on the tendency of the administration to use the wartime crisis as a rationale to suppress its radical critics. Nevertheless, he had failed to take these factors into consideration in affirming the verdict in the *Debs* case. Holmes believed that the courts had to grant the government a considerable leeway in deciding which cases it chose to prosecute in order to protect the war effort. Thus, even though he thought the prosecution of Debs was a mistake, Holmes was still willing to uphold Debs's conviction. Yet this argument was based on the assumption that the administration was acting in good faith and that its professed reasons for the decision to prosecute were the real ones. Holmes's verdict in the *Abrams* case raised the significant possibility that this was not true. Logically, he should have taken this into account in deciding the *Debs* case. The *Abrams* decision left Holmes in an even more awkward situation as he attempted to defend his earlier opinion in the *Debs* case.

11

Free Speech as an Absolute Right

The right to dissent is a fundamental right. It does not vary and it is not contingent on the specific circumstances. Contrary to Brandeis, free speech rights are absolute and are not "one of degree."[1]

People have the right to debate public policy issues unfettered by any restrictions. This holds as long as peace prevails within the United States, even when the country is at war. Furthermore, it is the primary duty of the judicial system to protect and defend the guarantees embodied in the Bill of Rights.

These basic principles are in direct contradiction to the pragmatic doctrines espoused by Chafee, Holmes, and Brandeis. Instead of viewing the right to dissent as a conjunctural question that depends on the specific circumstances, the alternative theory is based on the belief that individual rights are absolute and must be maintained intact even in difficult times.

Before fully exploring this alternative theory, two preliminary issues must be resolved. First, the question of whether free speech can be subject to special restrictions during a time of war. The second question asks whether judicial oversight extends to legislation or whether it is limited to a review of the government's decision to prosecute dissenters for allegedly going beyond the limits of the permissible.

WARTIME

Both Chafee's "balancing of conflicting interests" theory and the "clear and present danger" doctrine of Holmes emerged in response to the Wilson administration's relentless repression of dissent during the First World War. Holmes and Brandeis were willing to give the federal government a great deal of leeway in suppressing dissent during wartime.[2] Yet Brandeis also insisted that the "constitutional right of free speech has been declared to be the same in peace and in war." Efforts to resolve these contradictory positions proved to be difficult.[3]

Chafee confronted the same dilemma. He had developed the balance of conflicting interests theory in relation to cases that had arisen during the war. In his initial book on the topic of free speech, he set as a guideline that the government could only ban statements that are "clearly liable to cause direct and dangerous interference with the conduct of the war."[4] Although this is a dictum that is consistent with his overall theory, it is clearly more restrictive than Holmes's doctrine that statements are protected by the First Amendment unless they create a "clear and present danger" that those listening will be convinced to engage in actions that involve serious crimes.

Still, Chafee did not present an argument that would justify a greater restriction of dissenting views during wartime. In his dissent in the *Abrams* case, Holmes held that "only the emergency that makes it immediately dangerous to leave the correction of evil counsels to time warrants making any exception" to the First Amendment's protection of free speech. Brandeis took this argument and further developed it. In his dissent in the landmark *Whitney* case in 1927, Brandeis emphasized the importance of an unfettered discourse as a basis for making the optimal decisions on controversial policy decisions. In this context, "only an emergency can justify repression." His opinion in the *Gilbert* case of 1921 presented a more detailed version of this argument. During wartime, the federal government could repress dissenting opinions that would be legal in time of peace "because the emergency does not permit reliance upon the lower conquest of error by truth."[5]

Underlying the argument advanced by Holmes and Brandeis is the belief that the high stakes involved during wartime make it necessary for the government to suppress those who disagree with its policies. From this perspective, victory in the First World War was not just an issue of life and death, but of national survival. The United States was defending itself against foreign aggression by sending millions of soldiers to Europe to defeat Germany and its allies. A public debate took time and during that interval the war might be lost, with disastrous consequences for the United States.

The argument has a certain superficial logic, but it falls apart upon closer examination. To start, the United States was not confronted with an imminent invasion in April 1917 and, contrary to Chafee, it was not passing "through a period of great danger."[6] In reality, the United States had remained neutral for more than two and a half years of total war, during which time the president repeatedly urged both sides to reach a negotiated settlement. Only when Germany was about to defeat Britain did the United States decide to intervene. Wilson opted to push through a declaration of war not because the United States was in imminent danger, but because he had decided that it was in the strategic interest of this country to see Germany crushed.

The argument that debate needed to be restricted so that a decision could be rapidly made is also unconvincing. Although the First World War lacked popular support from the moment the United States entered the war in April 1917, it became even more unpopular as conscripted soldiers were sent overseas to be killed in the trenches. This despite the government's lavish efforts at propaganda and the silencing of those who dissented. The administration did not suppress its opponents because it needed to quickly respond to an emergency, but because it knew full well that its policies were unpopular and it feared that allowing dissenters to organize would enable them to form a movement that could pressure officials to reverse the existing policy and start negotiating an immediate peace.

Instead of accepting the position advanced by Chafee and Holmes, it would be more insightful to start from the opposite position. Unlimited discussion of public policy becomes even more important during wartime, when a decision by the government can lead to the deaths of millions of people. Chafee conceded this point, holding that the "social interest" in free speech became "especially important" during wartime.[7] Nevertheless, he still believed that the emergency situation created by the war weighed more heavily and thus free speech could be limited in wartime.

The debates that emerged during the Civil War are still relevant today. The Confederate rebellion nearly succeeded in dividing the nation. Northern states were invaded by Confederate troops and covert agents engaged in acts of sabotage. Furthermore, a bitter guerilla war lasted for several years in Missouri and, to a lesser extent, in other border states. These were real threats, not just greatly exaggerated fears.

Nevertheless, Justice David Davis's opinion in the *Milligan* case upheld the validity of the Constitution's protection of individual rights even during a time of turmoil. Although the specific issue addressed by Davis focused on the creation of military commissions to try civilians in an area where peace prevailed, Davis deliberately went further than the immediate case at issue. Thus, the Constitution of the United States was "a law for rulers and people equally in war and peace" and "under all circumstances." Furthermore, "no doctrine involving more pernicious consequences was ever invented" than that holding that any of the Constitution's "provisions can be suspended during any of the great exigencies of government." Davis understood that "troublous times would arise" when rulers would "seek by sharp and decisive measures to accomplish ends deemed just and proper." As a result, "principles of constitutional liberty would be in peril" with the risk of sliding into "anarchy or despotism."

Davis's point was well taken. Those who control the government frequently believe that their policies are the only correct ones and that it is in the paramount national interest that these policies be speedily implemented. Those who organize in opposition to those policies are viewed as irritating obstacles to be circumvented and, if necessary, suppressed. Yet the very essence of democracy is a robust debate on the critical issues confronting the populace. Indeed, as Davis has suggested, restrictions on free speech, or the erosion of other essential rights, move society toward autocracy and despotism. This argument holds even, if not more so, in "troublous times" such as during a war, whether declared or not.

LEGISLATION AND FREE SPEECH

Another issue has frequently arisen when legislators enact statutes that contradict constitutional provisions guaranteeing fundamental rights. Does the judicial system have the right to nullify such legislation, or does the mandate given to elected officials provide them with the authority to act as they will?

The issue became acute during the first years of the twentieth century, prior to the First World War. Progressives had taken control of several state legislatures and began enacting legislation regulating corporations and guaranteeing workers certain rights. Corporations challenged the validity of these laws and the issue was finally placed before the U.S. Supreme Court in 1905 in the Lochner case.

The New York state legislature had passed a law limiting the hours of employment for those working in bakeries to ten hours a day and sixty hours a week. One of the bakeries refused to abide by the law and the majority of the U. S. Supreme Court agreed, holding that the statute violated the Fourteenth Amendment and was therefore unconstitutional. The opinion by Justice Rufus Peckham, a confidant of J. P. Morgan, argued that the right to sign a business contract was a "part of the liberty of the individual protected by the Fourteenth Amendment," in particular the clause that held that no state could enact a law that would "deprive any person of life, liberty or property without due process of law."[8]

Peckham conceded that the state had the right to regulate the activities of businesses through its duty to ensure public safety. Laws that constituted "a fair, reasonable and appropriate exercise of the police power of the State" would be found to be constitutional. Still, in this case, he ruled, the New York statute included "no reference whatever to the question of health" and was thus invalid.[9]

Peckham's ruling, which prevailed for three decades, placed the burden of proof on the state legislature to demonstrate that it was imposing a regulation on a business that was "necessary" to ensure the health of its employees or customers. His opinion seems now to be a far-fetched and strained interpretation of the due process clause. It is doubtful that even the conservatives on the court today would advance the same argument. Nevertheless, at the time the debate around this issue was bitter and lengthy.

In one of his most famous dissents, Holmes rejected the majority opinion. He began by stating that he reserved judgment on the economic theory underlying the New York statute, but that in any case it was not his role as a judge to interfere "with the right of a majority to embody their opinions in law." Courts should not nullify a state law except when it "would infringe fundamental principles." Holmes saw the issue of maximum hours as a debatable one, with valid arguments on both sides. He therefore concluded that a "sweeping condemnation" could not "be passed upon the statute before us."[10]

The problem with this argument was that Peckham and those who agreed with his position saw the freedom of corporations to establish the wages and conditions of work for their employees without interference from the state as a fundamental principle to be overridden only when it could be firmly established that state regulation was essential for the public safety. Holmes rejected this position. In his view, "state constitutions and state laws may regulate life in many ways" that judges "might think injudicious" and that "interfere with the liberty to contract." Nevertheless, the U.S. Constitution was "not intended to embody a particular economic theory" including that "of laissez-faire."[11]

Holmes's opinion became a cornerstone of progressive thought. Frankfurter invited Holmes to dine at the House of Truth because of this opinion. Holmes might have doubted the efficacy of the reform agenda, but he stood with the progressives in rejecting the idea that the courts could overturn the result of an election.

Still, this left the broader issue of whether the courts could rule as unconstitutional a statute that violated the Bill of Rights on the basis that such acts would "infringe fundamental principles." Holmes was still wary of nullifying legislation that came from a state legislature, or Congress, and that could therefore be viewed as the will of the majority. This led to a quandary after the United States entered the war in April 1917.

When state governments began passing legislation suppressing those who opposed the war and court cases began moving through the judicial system, progressives felt unsure of their response. They had vehemently rejected the concept that federal courts should overturn statutes that furthered the reform agenda. One argument had been that an unelected official such as a federal judge should not be given the power to overturn the mandate of the majority held by those who had been elected. It was difficult to then argue that federal courts had the obligation to review state laws to ensure that they did not violate the constitutional provisions protecting civil liberties.

Holmes continued to uphold this position even in the years following the First World War. It was Brandeis who first overturned the previous policy as set by the Supreme Court. In *Gilbert v. Minnesota*, a case decided in 1921, but which arose out of an incident that occurred during the war, Brandeis issued a dissent that held that the right to "speak freely" on policy issues, such as the country's war policies, was a fundamental right that could not be curtailed by the states. In passing, Brandeis observed that the "liberty guaranteed by the Fourteenth Amendment" did not only refer to property issues but also encompassed the freedoms codified in the Bill of Rights.[12]

Chafee had not addressed this issue in his 1920 book. Still, Brandeis's decision in the *Gilbert* case was significantly influenced by Chafee's perspective on civil liberties. Before being appointed to the Supreme Court, Brandeis had been closely linked to *The New Republic*, even contributing articles to the journal. Almost certainly, he would have closely read Chafee's initial piece in *The New Republic* when it was published in November 1918. Furthermore, in one of his first opinions on these issues, in *Schaefer v. United States* in 1920, Brandeis cited Chafee's article in the *Harvard Law Review* in support of his rejection of the "natural and reasonable consequences" doctrine. Brandeis went further by incorrectly attributing the "clear and present danger" doctrine to Chafee.[13] Yet, in essence, Brandeis was correct. Chafee's article in *The New Republic* had provided the theoretical foundation for Holmes's decision in the *Schenck* case.

It is therefore not surprising that Chafee had sent proofs of his first book prior to publication to Brandeis, who "clearly had studied them closely" before writing his dissent in the *Gilbert* case.[14] This was an interactive relationship, with Chafee influencing the decisions of Brandeis and Holmes and, in turn, being influenced by them.

Holmes did not support Brandeis's opinion in the *Gilbert* case, having decided that Brandeis had gone "too far."[15] Brandeis's opinion thus stood as a lone dissent and yet within a few years his point on the Fourteenth Amendment had come to be accepted as the correct interpretation by the justices of the Supreme Court, including Holmes.[16]

When it came to statutes approved by Congress, there was no question that the courts could review acts that appeared to contradict the Bill of Rights. Nevertheless, both Holmes and Brandeis were reluctant to intervene. Holmes's landmark opinions establishing the "clear and present danger" doctrine avoided any discussion of the constitutionality of the Espionage Act or the amendments to it that constituted the Sedition Act. Privately, Holmes made it clear that he was prepared to give Congress a great deal of leeway in dealing with dissent during the wartime emergency.

Still, Chafee had implicitly raised this set of issues in his initial article in *The New Republic*, albeit only with regard to federal legislation. The focus of that article had been a condemnation of the Sedition Act of May 1918 as an unwarranted infringement of the First Amendment, since it restricted statements that did not constitute a "direct and dangerous" threat to the war effort. Although Chafee restricted himself to a call to Congress to repeal this legislation, there was also an implication that the courts needed to review prosecutions based on alleged violations of the Sedition Act.

Chafee also dealt with the constitutionality of the Espionage Act, but he failed to address the underlying questions. In his *Harvard Law Review* article, he argued that the Espionage Act "seems on its face constitutional," but "it may have been construed so extremely as to violate the First Amendment." This was his assessment of a bill that provided jail sentences of up to twenty years for those found guilty of "obstructing" the draft.[17]

A more forthright approach to this issue would hold that the foremost responsibility of the judicial system is the guarantee of fundamental human rights. One of these is the right to be warned by the government as to which specific acts are deemed to be illegal and subject to prosecution. The Espionage Act was deliberately written in nebulous language, thus allowing the government to arbitrarily imprison those it viewed as threats. Debs could be prosecuted and jailed for obstructing the draft after delivering a speech in which conscription was not even mentioned.

Chafee was dodging the real problem. Charles Warren had written the Espionage Act with the Defence of the Realm Regulations in mind. The UK government had drawn up these regulations with the aim of suppressing any dissent from the government's war policies. Warren knew this and, in crafting the Espionage Act, he deliberately followed this model for the same reason.

THE BRITISH VERSUS U.S. EXPERIENCE

The legal systems of the United Kingdom and the United States are based on fundamentally different foundations. In the UK, Parliament has the ultimate authority to determine any matter of public policy, including the limits of dissent. Although there are key legal landmarks setting guidelines, such as the Magna Carta, Parliament can override these guidelines at its own discretion.

The U.S. legal system starts with the Constitution. In terms of civil liberties, the Bill of Rights establishes the essential framework. Thus, in theory, Congress and the president are bound by the First Amendment guarantee of free speech and the judicial system is tasked with ensuring that neither statutes nor executive actions infringe upon this basic right.

In spite of this, Warren saw no problem in relying on the DORA regulations as a model for the Espionage Act because he was convinced that the Bill of Rights was not in effect during wartime. Furthermore, with Congress giving the president vast powers, the judicial system failed to establish a meaningful check on the administration's campaign to suppress dissent.

In general, the record of the UK and U.S. governments in terms of civil liberties during the First World War was remarkably similar. In both countries, dissent was suppressed and basic rights were trampled upon. This is not to say that there were no differences. British courts gave the government a virtual carte blanche to crush any opposition to the war. In the United States, courts maintained a nominal oversight over government actions, but failed to act as an effective restraint. In addition, the UK ceded to the military a vast authority to quell dissent. In contrast, Woodrow Wilson was wary of delegating too much authority to military commanders. Constitutional guidelines and previous court rulings also acted as a check to military power.

Nevertheless, in the end a written constitution enshrining basic rights proved to be of minimal value in guaranteeing fundamental civil liberties.

Free Speech as an Absolute Right

Constitutional rights are fundamental and should not be restricted during wartime. Furthermore, neither Congress nor state legislatures have the authority to override the Bill of Rights. It is a prime responsibility of the judiciary to ensure that civil liberties are guaranteed. This then leaves the essential issue as to the basic principles underlying freedom of speech.

The permissible limits of free speech do not vary with the specific circumstances in which the statements are made, but rather are constant since free speech is an absolute right. As set out in the majority opinion in the Milligan case, only the threat of an imminent invasion or the existence of a violent rebellion that renders the civil authorities powerless can create a situation in which the right to dissent can be restricted by the government's actions. Free speech is one of several basic human rights that are not subject to restriction except in the most extreme circumstances. Furthermore, the most important duty of the judicial system is to uphold these fundamental rights and to ensure that the government does not infringe upon them. Unfortunately, the judicial system has failed to meet this challenge at critical moments.

In determining the limits to free speech, the starting point has to begin with a clear differentiation between the formulation of an idea and the direct and explicit incitement of violence. A theory of free speech must start with the belief that it is essential that a free and unfettered discussion of controversial issues take place. The most effective way to counter a reprehensible idea is by presenting a convincing alternative. For this to occur, every idea, no matter how repugnant, is permitted and none are banned.

Thomas Jefferson formulated a similar idea and it provided the underpinning for the First Amendment. In his preamble to a bill establishing religious freedom in Virginia, written in 1777, Jefferson provided a broad defense of free speech. Truth "is the sufficient antagonist to error." Indeed, "Truth is great and will prevail if left to herself." Erroneous ideas will cease "to be dangerous when it is permitted freely to contradict them."[18]

Even the most reprehensible and divisive ideas are still protected by the First Amendment. Holocaust denial is a stark example of such an issue. Anti-Semitism is an ideology that has the potential to be enormously dangerous. Furthermore, those who deny the Nazi extermination of millions of Jews are implicitly expressing an intense hatred of Jewish people. Nevertheless, Holocaust denial is an idea that needs to be countered with other ideas and with evidence as to what actually occurred during the Nazi regime. In several European countries, denying the enormity of the Holocaust has been made a crime and a few individuals have actually been prosecuted under these laws. Yet right-wing, anti-Semitic parties continue to gain strength throughout much of Europe. Criminalizing Holocaust denial is bound to be ineffective because it fails to deal with the underlying problems that fuel xenophobia and anti-Semitism. Furthermore, banning any idea erodes the foundation of a free and open society.

The range of ideas protected by the First Amendment encompasses those that suggest that violence might be necessary some time in the indefinite future in the course of an effort to correct a perceived social evil or to introduce a desired social change. Abolitionists in the first half of the nineteenth century often suggested that only a violent confrontation could end slavery in the southern states. They proved to be correct. In any case, they were presenting one view on a controversial issue of public policy and thus were engaged in protected speech.

This question became a critical issue during the decade following the Second World War, when Communists were prosecuted for holding that a violent revolution might be necessary in order to bring about a socialist society. Once again, these opinions were general points about a situation that might arise sometime in the indefinite future. Communists were advancing a set of ideas, not presenting a direct incitement to violence. The danger of prosecuting those who presented themselves as revolutionaries became clear when Senator Joseph McCarthy and his ilk used the same argument to harass anyone on the Left.

The need for an open, unrestricted discussion of ideas and perspectives does not end when the country is at war. Indeed, it becomes even more essential when the debate involves a critical issue of public policy such as the course of a war. This is a point that Chafee conceded. The "social interest" in free speech is "especially important" in wartime.[19]

Unfortunately, Chafee was prepared to override this important point in order to safeguard "national security." It is far too easy for those in power to decide that the national interest requires that their policies be implemented. Repression of those opposed to the government's policies can then be justified as necessary for the common good. The only way to counteract such autocratic tendencies is to insist that all ideas be heard.

Derogatory Epithets

Often, those who argue for the suppression of certain perspectives point to the inflammatory language in which these statements are phrased. While conceding that any opinion, no matter how unpopular, should be permitted in the public discourse, those holding this position believe that the use of derogatory epithets means that the speaker is appealing to emotion rather than to reason. The argument goes that this type of speech is not protected by the First Amendment since it does not add to a reasoned debate on a controversial issue.

This rationale for restricting free speech has dangerous implications. Speakers and writers often use code words as a way of making their argument more lively and interesting, even though some individuals may find those words to be offensive. Furthermore, phrases that might be seen as offensive may also serve as concise descriptions of reality. A pithy phrase may cogently sum up an entire argument, thus making for a more pointed statement.

When the Justice Department considered the question of prosecuting Eugene Debs for the Canton speech, this point became a key factor in the decision to proceed. Debs was charged with obstructing the draft and yet he made no mention of conscription in the course of a lengthy speech. Still, he did refer in passing to army soldiers as "cannon fodder." Furthermore, in his speech to the jury following the Canton speech, Debs reiterated that he "meant exactly what" he had said during his speech.[20]

There can be no doubt that some soldiers found this reference offensive. In any case, the use of this phrase was presented by the government as proof that Debs had violated the Espionage Act by willfully seeking to obstruct the draft.

In making this reference, Debs was furthering a coherent argument. Soldiers were being used as cannon fodder in the war because the United States was not actually fighting for democracy, as Woodrow Wilson claimed, but out of self-interest. The United States was fighting to protect its strategic and economic interests. One can disagree with Debs's analysis, but there can be no doubt that it represented one point of view on a matter of public interest. As such, Debs's speech, including the reference to "cannon fodder," was protected speech under the First Amendment.

Epithets and derogatory comments are inflammatory and divisive, but they are embedded within statements that advance perspectives on controversial issues. They need to be rebutted by other ideas and not banned from free speech venues. Racism, sexism, homophobia, and anti-Semitism are abhorrent and must be opposed, but driving their expression underground will not help to resolve the underlying problems.

Inciting Violence

The only statements that go beyond the boundaries of the legally permissible are those containing a direct, immediate, specific and explicit incitement to violence. All too often, this proposition has been broadened to include any statements that encourage others to disobey the law. Sometimes, statements that merely state a sharp disagreement with government policy have been subject to prosecution. Violent acts have frequently been conflated with nonviolent protest and acts of civil disobedience.

In the landmark case *Whitney v. California,* decided in 1927, Brandeis argued that free speech can only be restricted when "immediate serious violence was to be expected or was advocated." In his 1920 book on free speech, Chafee was even more restrictive. State action was only justified "to head off violence when that is sure to follow the utterances before there is a chance for counter-argument."[21]

Yet the proponents of the clear and present danger doctrine have also presented arguments that blur the difference between calls for nonviolent protest and violent acts against the state. In his opinion in the *Whitney* case, Brandeis also held that free speech could be restricted when this is "required in order to protect the State from destruction or serious injury, political, economic or moral." This is a very nebulous standard. Holmes made a similar point, though more clearly, in his correspondence. In a time of war, it was not "unreasonable" for the government to make illegal statements that create "obstacles intentionally put in the way of raising troops—by persuasion any more than force."[22]

Voicing one's objections to government policy, even in wartime, should not be the basis for being sent to jail. Helping to organize acts of nonviolent civil disobedience is very different from calling for mob violence or assassinations. Those who commit murders or assaults that lead to serious injuries are guilty of felonies and will serve lengthy prison sentences if convicted. Those who participate in a sit-in or occupation commit misdemeanors and may have to spend a few days in jail. Inciting others to engage in violent acts is a serious crime. Encouraging others to join in acts of civil disobedience is an American tradition and should not be made illegal. If it were a serious crime to incite others to nonviolently break the law, Martin Luther King Jr. would have spent much of his time in jail.

The only category of statements that are not covered by the fundamental right of free speech are those that encourage acts of violence against specific individuals and are intended as exhortations to immediate action. In determining which of the statements within this category should be made illegal, the guidelines implicit in the clear and present danger doctrine become relevant. Was the individual making the statement well known? Did she or he have access to the media so that it would be widely distributed to the public? Was the statement likely to reach those who might be persuaded to commit acts of violence? Is the overall context one of turmoil where individuals are more likely to be incited into acts of violence?

The specific circumstances surrounding a statement that directly and immediately incites violence need to be taken into account when determining whether it has remained within the boundaries of the permissible. Nevertheless, such statements constitute a very small segment of those made during debates on controversial issues of public policy. The overwhelming majority of opinions come under the heading of protected free speech. Needless to say, virtually everyone charged with violating the Espionage Act during the First World War would never have been convicted if these guidelines had been in effect. Unfortunately, the great majority were found guilty and some of them served lengthy sentences in prison. Indeed, the statements made by Debs and Schenck did not come close to the limits of permissible speech.

Even for those statements that do go beyond the bounds of the permissible, it is important that any prosecutions be limited to the individuals who are directly responsible for those statements. This issue became critically important during the government's campaign against the Industrial Workers of the World and, later, the Communist Party. Targeting someone for being a member of an organization whose leaders allegedly incited violence runs contrary to the fundamental principles of criminal law. The whole point of a prosecution is to incarcerate those directly responsible for acts of violence so that further violence can be forestalled. Blanket sweeps based on organizational membership necessarily result in sending individuals to jail who had nothing to do with any violent acts and, indeed, may be opposed to them. Joining an organization does not mean that one agrees with every statement made by one of its leaders.

In fact, the government only initiates this scattershot approach when it seeks to suppress a left-wing organization. In the past, the leadership of several trade union locals affiliated with the American Federation of Labor have undertaken systematic efforts to intimidate employers through bombs and other acts of violence. Although the executive boards of these locals were conspiring to commit serious acts of violence, no one suggested that merely being a member of such a local was a sufficient basis to accuse them of a crime.

Ironically, it was not a case directed at a left-wing organization such as those filed against the IWW or the CP that led the Supreme Court to eventually move beyond the clear and present danger doctrine in order to establish a far more libertarian guideline. It was only when the Ku Klux Klan became a target of prosecution that the Supreme Court stepped in.

The Demise of the "Clear and Present Danger" Doctrine

Brandenburg v. Ohio began when a leader of the Ohio Ku Klux Klan was arrested for violating that state's criminal syndicalism law. The law had been enacted in 1919 and it had been specifically aimed at the Industrial Workers of the World. A key provision made it illegal to be a member of an organization "formed to teach or advocate" the need for "sabotage, violence or unlawful methods of terrorism as a means of accomplishing industrial or political reform."[23]

Criminal syndicalism laws had been legislated in twenty-three states during the First World War and its immediate aftermath.[24] Although IWW members had been the first to be prosecuted under its terms, in later years members of the Communist Party were also jailed for violating its provisions. Fifty years after its enactment, the U.S. Supreme Court finally ruled that these laws were unconstitutional in a case with a Ku Klux Klan leader as the defendant.

In 1969, the Supreme Court issued a brief *per curiam* decision that gained the unanimous support of the nine justices. In this ruling, the court established as a "principle that the constitutional guarantees of free speech and free press do not permit the State to forbid or proscribe advocacy of the use of force" unless "such advocacy is directed to inciting or producing imminent lawless action and is likely to incite or produce such action."[25]

Although the ruling did not specifically reject the clear and present danger doctrine as a guideline in free speech cases, it did so by implication. The court nullified the criminal syndicalism laws as unconstitutional and it specifically reversed the court's previous ruling made in 1927 in the *Whitney* case. In that case, a member of the Communist Labor Party (CLP), a predecessor of the Communist Party, was convicted of violating the act because the CLP had established a tenuous tie to the Industrial Workers of the World. In a concurring opinion upholding Whitney's conviction, Brandeis argued that the California legislature had been justified in passing a law banning criminal syndicalism because of the threat posed by the IWW. Thus, he argued, the law was constitutional since the union posed a clear and present danger to the peace and order of California.

The Supreme Court's ruling in the *Brandenburg* case rejected the decision in the *Whitney* case and, by implication, Brandeis's concurring opinion. In nullifying criminal syndicalism laws, the Court established a new standard for free speech cases. Although the justices did not start from the belief that free speech is an absolute right, their guideline came close to the argument presented above. The *Brandenburg* ruling did not resolve all of the relevant issues but it represented a major step forward.

One issue that was not directly addressed focused on the question of membership in a targeted organization. If the leader of such an organization issues statements that incite others to immediately engage in violent acts, could members of that organization be prosecuted on that basis. This possibility seems unlikely given the *Brandenburg* ruling. Nevertheless, the criminal syndicalism laws made it illegal to merely be a member of certain organizations, so the Court could have taken the opportunity to clarify this issue.

Another issue the court failed to address involved free speech rights in a time of a declared war. Still, Justice William Douglas dealt with the issue in a concurring opinion. Since Douglas had been arguing for some time for a broader limit for permissible speech, he welcomed the *Brandenburg* ruling. His concurring opinion expanded on the Court's brief ruling by examining several of the key free speech cases.

In examining the cases that arose out of the First World War, Douglas incorrectly described the *Schenck* case. Contrary to Douglas, Charles Schenck and the Philadelphia local of the Socialist Party had not "urged resistance to the draft." Holmes had first formulated the clear and present danger doctrine in justifying his support for a guilty verdict in the case. Although Douglas endorsed the *Brandenburg* guideline as a general rule, his views on the limits of permissible free speech in wartime were less than clear. Although he was "certain" that there was "no place" for the clear and present danger doctrine in times of peace, he was uncertain otherwise. Indeed, the issue was "debatable." There was some "doubt" as to whether Holmes's guideline was "congenial to the First Amendment in times of a declared war."[26]

The specific issue in question has become moot as wars are now fought with drones and bombs dropped from airplanes rather than with the huge armies that characterized the First World War. The *Brandenburg* ruling was delivered during the Vietnam War and yet Douglas had no doubt that the clear and present danger doctrine did not apply to free speech cases that developed out of the turmoil of the 1960s. Nevertheless, it is important to fully maintain the right to dissent while upholding Davis's ruling in the Milligan case. Even after a war has been officially declared, free speech rights remain intact as long as the courts remain open and peaceful conditions prevail in the United States.

In the last fifty years since the *Brandenburg* ruling, few individuals have been prosecuted for an expression of opinion, even the most controversial. The First Amendment has been upheld and debate on public policy issues has been unfettered. Still, fundamental rights guaranteed by the Bill of Rights continue to be under attack. Since the attack on the Twin Towers in 2001, the federal government has implemented a series of initiatives that have undercut basic rights. These moves have been frequently rationalized on the basis of Chafee's balance of conflicting interests doctrine. The legacy of the legal theories that arose in the context of the First World War continue to impact government actions to this day.

———— 12 ————

Conclusion

We live in perilous times. Economic insecurity has become the norm. The gap between the rich and the poor has widened, while the quality of social services continues to decline. As a result, there is a growing polarization in political perspectives. Mainstream centrist politics have lost their popular appeal as an increasing number of people search for alternatives at both ends of the political spectrum. This sharpening divide can be seen at the electoral level, but it also manifests itself in street actions as angry crowds clash in brawls.

In this context, there is a widespread call from across the political spectrum urging the government to suppress those seen as a threat. Civil liberties are in danger of being sacrificed in the name of national security and law and order. Now is a good time to analyze the lessons of an earlier period when civil liberties were also under attack.

THE SUPPRESSION OF DISSENT DURING THE FIRST WORLD WAR

The First World War was highly unpopular. Throughout the western states, and in major urban centers such as New York City and Milwaukee as well, the U.S. decision to enter the war and then to institute conscription was vehemently opposed by a substantial majority.

Furthermore, the years leading up to the First World War had seen a significant growth in radical opinion and in the membership of left-wing organizations. Both the Socialist Party and the Industrial Workers of the World were opposed to the war, and to the draft, and both had the potential to become the focal point for an effective campaign of resistance. The Left was in the forefront of those calling for free speech and the unfettered debate of controversial issues.

President Woodrow Wilson was intent on continuing the war until Germany agreed to an unconditional surrender. It soon became clear that popular opinion wanted to see a rapid end to the war. Wilson was therefore determined to crush those who spoke out against the war. In this context, the federal government had no hesitation in blatantly disregarding the fundamental liberties guaranteed by the Bill of Rights.

In terms of open acts of repression, the Wilson administration utilized a wide variety of methods to divide and demoralize the antiwar opposition. Many of these methods involved blatant violations of fundamental rights, while others used more subtle methods of control. The federal government was intent on suppressing any organized opposition to the First World War and, unfortunately, it was all too successful in reaching this goal.

Woodrow Wilson authorized the use of troops to break the IWW's strike of timber workers. Hundreds were arbitrarily detained by the military for weeks in makeshift bullpens, where they were harshly treated. These detentions flagrantly violated fundamental constitutional rights. The mass trials of IWW activists for allegedly violating the Espionage Act were an open effort to use the courts to silence dissent. Socialist Party members were jailed for distributing leaflets criticizing the war. The Justice Department's Bureau of Intelligence initiated repeated raids on the offices of a wide array organizations from the IWW to the Socialist Party and the National Civil Liberties Bureau. These raids were usually made on the basis of warrants that did not specify the focus of the search and thus failed to meet the standards set by the Fourth Amendment. The post office sought to hamper the left-wing press by withdrawing the second-class mailing privileges of socialist magazines and newspapers.

Unfortunately, the courts failed to counter the government's autocratic actions. All too often, judges accepted the argument that basic rights had to be sacrificed to national security in a time of war. Even Justices Holmes and Brandeis were willing to grant the administration a great deal of leeway in setting the limits of permissible speech.

In addition to these overt repressive actions, government agencies engaged in clandestine operations in a coordinated campaign of repression. Letters sent by the IWW to solicit funds for its legal defense were intercepted. The U.S. Army's Military Intelligence Division tapped telephones without the authority of a warrant. Roger Baldwin of the National Civil Liberties Bureau, the direct forerunner of the American Civil Liberties Bureau, was a target of one of these taps. Baldwin's willingness to cooperate with the Harding administration in breaking down the cohesive resistance of the IWW prisoners needs to be more closely examined in the light of the MID's interception of his phone calls. The government also sponsored a clandestine effort to pressure the Socialist Party and Debs into supporting the war effort.

These covert operations were generally illegal and in direct violation of the guarantees embedded in the Bill of Rights. Needless to say, today surveillance has become far more pervasive. Information covertly obtained can be used to coerce individuals into cooperating with the intelligence agencies. It can also be used to divide and demoralize dissident organizations.

The lessons of the First World War era are clear. The defense of civil liberties must be an urgent priority for the Left.

Defending Free Speech

When Eugene Debs told the jury during his trial in September 1918 that his speech in Canton, Ohio, was protected by the First Amendment, he was defending the proposition that free speech was a basic right that could not be curtailed during wartime. Yet he was also presenting a broader argument. Debs was confident that his views would gain a wide hearing within the working class. The government was suppressing dissent because it feared that the expression of critical opinions would lead to a stronger and better organized opposition. The contemporary Left needs to regain that same sense of confidence. All too often, leftists appear to lack confidence in the popular appeal of their ideas. Instead, there is a call to suppress the views of those on the radical Right. Sometimes this leads to demands for government action or the institution of restrictive codes of behavior. This trend has become particularly evident on campus where some students have been demanding the exclusion of speakers who deliver talks that contain racist, sexist, or homophobic messages or derisory epithets.

The whole concept underlying free speech is that there must be times and places where an unfettered discussion of controversial issues can take place. Within this context, it makes no sense to argue that those presenting reprehensible ideas should not be given a platform. Free speech means providing everyone with a platform for an open debate.

Ideas can have a powerful impact. Those on the Left who study anarchist and socialist theory are well aware that ideas do matter. Nevertheless, the way to counter ideas that are hateful and divisive is to counter them with other, positive ideas. This is not a new concept. Thomas Jefferson was defending the need for religious freedom by advancing the same argument. It remains as true now as it was then.

The weakness of the Left in the United States will not be overcome by suppressing our most vociferous opponents. This only permits those on the far rightwing to appear as martyrs who are valiantly defending the free exchange of ideas. The Left has to develop a program and strategy that can appeal to the working class in a postindustrial society. Radicals needs to come forward with positive ideas for profound change, rather than being stuck in a defensive mode that is bound to go nowhere.

Defending the Free Speech Platform

One argument that is often advanced by those arguing the no platform position questions why those who have no regard for democratic norms should be able to take advantage of the right to dissent to present views that, if persuasive, would lead to an autocratic society where individual rights were abolished. A similar point had been previously advanced by government officials eager to suppress critics on the Left. During the McCarthy period in the 1950s, those promoting the Red Scare made exactly the same argument, pointing out, correctly, that the Communist Party acted as apologists for a totalitarian country where democratic rights had been eliminated.

Indeed, a similar point was made even earlier in a case arising out of the First World War. Justice Joseph McKenna, writing for the majority of the U.S. Supreme Court in a case that involved the prosecution of editors of a German language newspaper, argued that it was a "curious spectacle" when the Constitution was "invoked to justify the activities of anarchy or the enemies of the United States." This, he held, was "a strange perversion of its precepts."[1]

McKenna was wrong. Picking and choosing those favored with basic rights is bound to undercut the entire principle. Free speech has to be guaranteed for all ideas, even those presented by individuals who are intent on destroying an open society.

Building for the Future

Part of building a movement for fundamental change is the creation of organizational structures that prefigure a future society. This will require building organizations in which the group's policies are determined through a vigorous debate that is not manipulated by a few who hold leading positions. A prefigurative politics needs to expand beyond the democratic norms of the existing society.

An organization presenting a prefigurative perspective will need to construct a program that posits demands that look forward to a future society. Ensuring a genuine democracy must be an essential aspect of such a program. A defense of free speech and the right to dissent need to be integral to our vision of a future society.

It is always easier to defend free speech when one is a dissident and marginalized minority. Our insistence that we are working toward a fundamental transformation of society is bound to sound hollow if we support restrictions on the free speech rights of belligerent right-wing zealots and the fascist fringe.

The right to dissent will not be given to us. We cannot simply refer to the Bill of Rights or rely on the judiciary to uphold those rights. We need to be on the streets demanding our right to protest and dissent. We can expect that as the current system continues to unravel, opposition at both ends of the spectrum will grow and the government will ratchet up the level of repression. The history of civil liberties during the First World War era demonstrates this proposition. We can learn from this history to prepare for the future.

CHRONOLOGY

April 12, 1861: Troops loyal to the South Carolina state government fire on Fort Sumter, near Charleston, thus beginning the U.S. Civil War. Eleven Southern states secede and form the Confederate States. President Abraham Lincoln mobilizes an army to crush the rebellion.

April 9, 1865: General Robert Lee surrenders the Army of Northern Virginia. His surrender marks the end of the Civil War.

December 1866: The Supreme Court issues the *Milligan* decision holding that civilians could not be tried in military tribunals in places where civilian courts were still functioning.

January 14–16, 1893: The founding conference of the Independent Labour Party is held in Bradford, England. The ILP becomes the most moderate tendency within British socialism. Instrumental in the founding of the British Labour Party.

August 4, 1914: The United Kingdom declares war on Germany.

August 10, 1914: The Union of Democratic Control is formed. Pushes for an end to secret diplomacy and a conclusion to the war that is based on an equitable peace treaty.

May 25, 1915: A coalition government is formed in Britain. The Liberals remain the majority within the cabinet, but Conservatives hold important positions as well. Herbert Asquith of the Liberal Party continues to serve as prime minister.

April 1916: The American Union Against Militarism is formed by prominent progressives to oppose the calls for a rapid buildup of the U.S. military as a first step toward entering the First World War.

December 1916: The coalition government dominated by the Liberal Party and led by Herbert Asquith is toppled and replaced by a five-member War Cabinet, with David Lloyd George, a Liberal, as prime minister, three leading Conservative Party members, and one member of the Labour Party. The War Cabinet makes most of the important decisions for the rest of the war. Dissolved in October 1919.

March 15, 1917: Tsar Nicholas II abdicates as mass demonstrations sweep through Russia. Power is shared by the Petrograd soviet and a provisional and more moderate government.

March 1917: Roger Baldwin joins the staff of the American Union Against Militarism.

April 6, 1917: Congress declares war on Germany. The United States enters the First World War.

April 7, 1917: An emergency convention of the Socialist Party convenes in St. Louis. After lengthy discussions, it overwhelmingly approves a resolution calling for militant resistance to the war effort. Eugene Debs is not present, but he enthusiastically supports the majority resolution.

April 12, 1917: Timber workers strike in camps along the Fortine River in northwestern Montana. The strike rapidly spreads throughout the Pacific Northwest. Organized by the IWW's Lumber Workers' Industrial Union (LWIU).

June 5, 1917: Registration day. Millions of men aged between twenty-one and thirty-nine are required to register for the draft.

June 15, 1917: Congress passes the Espionage Act, and the president signs the bill. One provision holds that those obstructing the war effort or the draft can be sentenced to a prison term of up to twenty years. Hundreds of dissidents are jailed under this provision.

June 24, 1917: A district judge in Montana, Judge T. A. Thompson, issues a writ of habeas corpus freeing two IWW organizers, Joseph Ratti and Fred Hegge, from military detention. Hegge had been held by the military without charges for fifty-eight days.

July 13, 1917: The Civil Liberties Bureau of the American Union Against Militarism is established.

August 19, 1917: James Rowan, the secretary of the LWIU, and twenty-six other IWW members and sympathizers are indefinitely detained by the military without charges on the eve of a general strike called by the union for the Pacific Northwest.

September 1, 1917: The founding conference of the People's Council of America for Democracy and the Terms of Peace, scheduled to meet in Minneapolis, Minnesota, is banned by order of Governor Joseph Burnquist.

October 1, 1917: The National Civil Liberties Bureau is founded as an independent organization separate from the American Union Against Militarism. Roger Baldwin is named its executive director.

November 7, 1917: Provisional government of Russia toppled by Bolsheviks. A new government led by Lenin committed to an immediate peace takes power.

November 23, 1917: The official newspapers of the Soviet Union, *Izvestia* and *Pravda*, publish the secret treaties signed by Czarist Russia and its allies, primarily the United Kingdom and France. The *Manchester Guardian* prints the treaties in full on November 26, 1917.

December 1917: The Soviet Union invades Ukraine. Soviet troops meet little resistance from the forces of the Rada that had gained control of the Ukraine after the collapse of the czarist regime.

January 8, 1918: President Wilson speaks to Congress about U.S. war aims, providing his view of the 14 Points that were essential to a peace treaty.

February 9, 1918: With peace talks with the Soviet Union stymied, the German government signs an agreement with the Ukrainian Rada. German troops meet little resistance from Soviet troops occupying Ukraine, and by the end of April German troops have occupied most of Ukraine.

February 18, 1918: German troops attack across the Eastern Front as peace talks with the Soviet Union stall.

March 3, 1918: Soviet Russia and Imperial Germany sign the Brest-Litovsk Treaty, a separate peace by which Russia cedes territory to Germany.

March 9, 1918: Victor Berger, Adolph Germer, and three other leading members of the Socialist Party are indicted by a Chicago grand jury and charged with violating the Espionage Act.

March 19, 1918: Irvine Lenroot wins hotly contested Republican primary for the U.S. Senate seat from Minnesota vacated by the accidental death of Paul Husting.

April 2, 1918: Lenroot elected to the U.S. Senate after a bitterly contested election, defeating Victor Berger, the Socialist Party candidate, and John Davies, the Democrat.

April 1918: German forces join White Army units in attacks against the Soviet Union's occupation of Finland. By the end of the month, German troops are within a few miles of Petrograd.

May 13, 1918: The German government decides that further attacks will lead to the collapse of the Bolshevik government. Permanent truce between German and Russian forces. Russia definitively ceases to be a combatant in the First World War.

June 6, 1918: Eugene Victor Debs speaks in Canton, Ohio, to a public rally marking the end of the state convention of the Ohio Socialist Party.

Debs condemns the war and denounces the government's violation of fundamental civil liberties.

June 29, 1918: Debs indicted by a federal grand jury for violating the Espionage Act during his Canton speech.

August 11, 1918: Debs speaks to a national meeting of state secretaries of the Socialist Party urging them not to dilute the antiwar message of the party. The state secretaries reaffirm the SP's opposition to the war.

August 31, 1918: The New York City office of the National Civil Liberties Bureau is raided by federal agents.

September 1918: Herbert Croly asks Zechariah Chafee Jr. to write an article for the *New Republic* on civil liberties. The piece appears in the November 1918 issue, presenting the fundamental tenets of the "balance of conflicting interests" legal doctrine.

September 9, 1918: Trial of Eugene Debs begins in the federal district court in Cleveland, Ohio. Convicted on September 13 and sentenced to a ten-year term in prison the following day.

November 11, 1918: The First World War ends as the German imperial government collapses and the new government agrees to an unconditional surrender.

March 4, 1919: Attorney General Thomas Gregory resigns and is replaced on the following day by Alexander Mitchell Palmer.

March 3, 1919: Charles Schenck of the Philadelphia Socialist Party has his conviction for violating the Espionage Act affirmed by the Supreme Court in a unanimous decision as Oliver Wendell Holmes Jr. enunciates the "clear and present danger" doctrine. A week later, the U.S. Supreme Court upholds Debs's conviction in a unanimous opinion written by Holmes.

April 1919: Charles Warren testifies in a secret session before the Senate Military Affairs Committee in support of a bill to extend the scope of military tribunals to civilians. Dissidents would also be charged with being spies and thus subject to the death penalty. He is removed as an assistant attorney general shortly afterwards.

April 13, 1919: Debs begins to serve his sentence at the West Virginia State Penitentiary in Moundsville.

June 1919: Chafee's article further elaborating his legal theory appears in the *Harvard Law Review*. The article contains a criticism of Holmes's rulings in the *Debs* and *Schenck* cases.

June 14, 1919: Debs is transferred from Moundsville to the Atlanta Federal Penitentiary.

October 2, 1919: Woodrow Wilson suffers a massive stroke from which he never fully recovers. He is totally incapacitated for months.

November 10, 1919: In the *Abrams* case, Holmes files a dissent, with the agreement of Louis Brandeis, for the first time citing the "clear and present danger" doctrine as a basis for overturning a conviction under the Espionage Act.

January, 19, 1920: The National Civil Liberties Bureau is renamed the American Civil Liberties Union. Baldwin remains executive director.

March 19, 1920: Congress definitively defeats the Versailles Treaty ending the First World War.

March 4, 1921: Warren Harding inaugurated as president.

March 24, 1921: Eugene Debs has a three-hour meeting with Attorney General Harry Daugherty and then returns to Atlanta Federal Penitentiary on his own to serve the rest of his sentence.

November 15, 1921: A peace treaty between the United States and Germany goes into effect, thus providing the official end to the First World War.

December 25, 1921: Harding issues an unconditional commutation releasing Debs from prison. A few of the IWW prisoners who have recanted are also released.

September 1922: Roger Baldwin visits Leavenworth Federal Penitentiary to convince IWW prisoners to accept a plan by which some of them would become eligible for a conditional commutation of their sentences. Most of the prisoners refuse to accept the plan. Those few who do are released from prison over the next months.

August 2, 1923: Warren Harding dies and Calvin Coolidge, as vice president, becomes president.

December 15, 1923: Coolidge grants an unconditional commutation and the last of the IWW prisoners are finally released from jail.

Notes

The following abbreviations are being used: National Archives, CP=National Archives, College Park, Maryland; National Archives, DC=National Archives, Washington, D. C.

2. The British Experience in Suppressing Dissent

In this chapter, the first cite of the National Archives is listed as National Archives, London, England. For all the other cites of these archives in this chapter, the cite is listed as National Archives, London.

1. In July 1911, the German government sent two small warships to the Atlantic Ocean coast of Morocco. This act threatened French control over Morocco, but it also was seen as part of a broader campaign by the German government to assert its position as a colonial power in Africa. War was averted when a deal was negotiated by which the German government conceded the authority of the French government over Morocco, but was rewarded with a new colony in central Africa. Margaret MacMillan, *The War That Ended Peace* (London: Profile Books, 2013), 411–13, 427.

2. David Hooper, *The Official Secrets Act: The Use and Abuse of the Act* (London: Secker and Warburg, 1987), 31.

3. K. D. Ewing and C. A. Gearty, *The Struggle for Civil Liberties: Political Freedom and the Rule of Law in Britain, 1914–1945* (Oxford: Oxford University Press, 2000), 41; Hooper, *The Official Secrets Act*, 31.

4. Ewing and Gearty, *Struggle for Civil Liberties*, 41.

5. The Defence of the Realm Act, August 8, 1914, *Acts of Parliament*, 1914, chap. 29; Reginald McKenna, August 7, 1914, *House of Commons Debates*, Fifth Series, vol. 65, col. 2192.

6. *House of Lords Debates*, August 8, 1914, Fifth Series, vol. 17, col. 477; *House of Commons Debates*, 5th Series, vol. 65, col. 2212.

7. The Defence of the Realm Act (Amended), August 28, 1914, *Acts of Parliament*, 1914, chap. 63.

8. The Defence of the Realm Act (Amended), August 28, 1914, *Acts of Parliament*, 1914, chap. 63.

9. Charles Trevelyan, August 26, 1914, *House of Commons Debates*, Fifth Series, vol. 69, col. 88.

10. Reginald McKenna, August 26, 1914, *House of Commons Debates*, Fifth Series, vol. 69, col. 89.

11. Wentworth Beaumont (Lord Allendale), August 27, 1914, *House of Lords Debates*, Fifth Series, vol. 17, col. 541.

12. The Defence of the Realm Act (Consolidated), November 27, 1914, *Acts of Parliament*, 1914, chap. 8.

13. Robert Cecil, November 16, 1914, *House of Commons Debates*, Fifth Series, vol. 68, col. 910.

14. Cecil held the post of parliamentary under secretary of state with Edward Grey of the Liberal Party serving as secretary of state for foreign affairs.

15. Richard Haldane, November 27, 1914, *House of Lords Debates*, Fifth Series, vol. 18, col. 205.

16. John Simon, February 24, 1915, *House of Commons Debates*, Fifth Series, vol. 68, col. 290.

17. The Defence of the Realm Act (Amended), March 16, 1915, *Acts of Parliament*, 1915, chap. 34; Ewing and Gearty, *The Struggle for Civil Liberties*, 50.

18. Charles Cook, ed., *Defence of the Realm Manual*, 6th ed. (London: HMSO, 1918), 91, 186.

    November 28, 1914. Later, many of these regulations were modified and additional sections were added. The additions did not act as amendments to the original regulation, so the entire version of the original regulation remained in force. Thus a specific issue could be addressed in two distinct ways, with the government having the option to choose which one to implement.

    In a few cases, new regulations were issued on a topic that had not been covered previously. Sometimes the new regulation was given a number that had already been taken. This probably occurred because the compilers sought to place regulations concerning a general topic in the same sequence within the regulations. As a result, a regulation previously issued would have to be moved in the order. Thus, the numbering of the regulations was not entirely in chronological order.

19. Cook, ed., *Manual*, 105.

20. Nan Milton, *John Maclean* (London: Pluto Press, 1973), 121.

21. Frederick Maurice to Herbert Samuel, [June 1917], SAM/A/60, Herbert Samuel Papers, Parliamentary Archives, London.

22. Trevor Wilson and Robin Prior, "Sir Frederick Barton Maurice (1871–1951)," *Oxford Dictionary of National Biography* (Oxford, England: Oxford University Press, 2004).

23. Thomas Pakenham, *The Boer War* (London: Weidenfeld and Nicolson, 1979), 486.

24. Cook, ed., *Manual*, 173.

25. Cook, ed., *Manual*, 126.

26. Cook, ed., *Manual*, 184.
27. Christopher Matthews, Memorandum [July 1915], HO45/10786/ 297549, National Archives, London, England; Cook, ed., *Manual*, 184.
28. Milton, *John Maclean*, 116.
29. Cook, ed., *Manual*, 91.
30. Cook, ed., *Manual*, 196–97.
31. Cook, ed., *Manual*, 198–99.
32. Eric Holt-Wilson to Edward Atkinson, October 19, 1934, with enclosure "Certain Offense Against the Defence of the Realm Regulations, 1914– 1919," in MI5, "The Game Book" [1934], KV 4/114, National Archive, London.
33. Cook, ed., *Manual*, 106.
34. George Cave, October 22, 1917, *House of Commons Debates*, Fifth Series, vol. 98, col. 483; George Cave, October 25, 1917, *House of Commons Debates*, Fifth Series, vol. 98, col. 1022.
35. Alfred William Brian Simpson, *In the Highest Degree Odious: Detention Without Trial in Wartime Britain* (Oxford, England: Clarendon Press, 1992), 15–19.
36. MI5, "The Game Book," [1934], KV 4/114, National Archives, London; Simpson, *In the Highest Degree*, 15; Herbert Samuel, February 17, 1916, *House of Commons Debates*, Fifth Series, vol. 80, col. 220.
37. William Knox, ed., *Scottish Labour Leaders, 1918–39: A Biographical Dictionary* (Edinburgh: Mainstream Publishing, 1984), 224–27; Harry McShane and Joan Smith, *No Mean Fighter* (London: Pluto Press, 1978), 78–80.
38. MI5, "The Game Book," vol. 2, KV 4/113, National Archives, London.
39. Vernon Kell, Lecture Notes, "Control of Civil Populations in War," 1930, Microfilm, Reel 1, Papers of Vernon Kell, Imperial War Museum, London.
40. Maclean was arrested in October 1915 for giving an antiwar speech. He was accused of obstructing the draft and sentenced to five days in jail. He was arrested for another speech in February 1916. This time he was accused of hindering the production of war materiel and sentenced to three years in prison. He was released to enormous popular acclaim in June 1917. Undaunted, Maclean continued to condemn the war and was arrested for the third time in April 1918. This time he was tried for sedition and received a five-year jail sentence. He was released from prison in early December 1918, a few weeks after the war had ended. Milton, *Maclean*, 99, 117, 140, 164, 175, 180.
41. Joseph Clayton, *The Rise and Decline of Socialism in Great Britain, 1884–1924* (London: Faber and Gwyer, 1926), 165.
42. David Marquand, *Ramsay MacDonald* (London: Jonathan Cape, 1977), 32.

43. Robert Edward Dowse, *Left in the Centre: The Independent Labour Party, 1893–1940* (Evanston, IL: Northwestern University Press, 1966), 25.

44. Helena Maria Lucy Swanwick, *Builders of Peace: Being the Ten Years' History of the Union of Democratic Control* (London: Swarthmore Press, 1924), 31.

45. Marvin Swartz, *The Union of Democratic Control in British Politics During the First World War* (Oxford: Clarendon Press, 1971),13.

46. Peter Cain, "Introduction," to Edmund Dene Morel, *Africa and the Peace of Europe* (London: Routledge, 1998), 4.

47. Swanwick, *Builders*, 31–33.

48. Robert Duncan, *Objectors and Resisters: Opposition to Conscription and War in Scotland, 1914–18* (Glasgow: Common Print, 2015), 34–35.

49. Thomas C. Kennedy, *The Hounds of Conscience: A History of the No-Conscription Fellowship, 1914–1919* (Fayetteville: University of Arkansas Press, 1981), 65–66.

50. *Labour Leader*, February 11, 1915.

51. Charles Matthews, Memorandum, January 1, 1917, HO 45/2786/297549, National Archives, London.

52. *Labour Leader*, August 26, 1915; *Labour Leader*, August 19, 1915.

53. R. J. Q. Adams and Philip Poirier, *The Conscription Controversy in Great Britain, 1900–18* (London: Macmillan, 1987), 143.

54. *Labour Leader*, January 20, 1916.

55. Archibald Fenner Brockway, *Inside the Left* (London: George Allen and Unwin, 1942), 77.

56. Victor Ferguson, Memorandum, October 14, 1916, KV 2/1917, National Archives, London; Victor Ferguson, Memorandum, December 31, 1916, KV 2/1917, National Archives, London. The next paragraph is from the same source.

57. Ferguson, Memorandum, December 31, 1916, KV 2/1917, National Archives, London.

58. E. Blackwell to Hardinge, December 7, 1916, HO 45/2786/297549, National Archives, London.

59. Ferguson, Memorandum, December 31, 1916, KV 2/1917, National Archives, London.

60. Hooper, *The Official Secrets Act*, 31.

61. Edward Tyas Cook, *The Press in Wartime* (London: Macmillan, 1920), 39.

62. Hooper, *The Official Secrets Act*, 223.

63. Cook, *The Press in Wartime*, 59.

64. Cook, *The Press*, 58.

65. Cook, *The Press*, 58.

66. Cook, *The Press*, 46-47.
67. Cook, *The Press*, 38.
68. Cook, *The Press*, 41.
69. Swartz, *The Union of Democratic Control*,
70. Swanwick, *Builders of Peace*, 92.
71. *Daily Express*, November 26, 1915.
72. Swanwick, *Builders of Peace*, 95.
73. *Daily Express*, November 30, 1915; Swanwick, *Builders of Peace*, 96.
74. Charles Trevelyan to John Simon, November 26, 1915, HO45/10817/3/6469, National Archives, London.
75. Phillip Snowden to Herbert Samuel, May 18, 1916, HO45/10817/3/6469, National Archives, London.
76. Herbert Samuel to Phillip Snowden. [May 1916]. HO45/10817/3/6469, National Archives, London.
77. Leaflet, Announcement of Cory Hall Conference, [1917], File KV 2/663, National Archives, London.
78. Brock Millman, "The Battle of Cory Hall, November 1916," *Canadian Journal of History* 35 (April 2000): 73-74.
79. A. B., Memorandum, October 27, 1916, KV 2/664, National Archives, London.
80. Millman, "The Battle of Cory Hall," *Canadian Journal of History* 72.
81. Cook, ed., *Manual*, 91; George Chrystal to Vernon Kell, November 6, 1916, KV 2/663, National Archives, London. Chrystal served as the principal assistant to Troup. Unfortunately, Kell's original letter requesting the Home Office to prohibit the NCCL conference from happening does not seem to have survived.
82. National Council for Civil Liberties, *British Freedom, 1914-1917* (London: Headley Brothers, 1917) 33.
83. Millman, "The Battle of Cory Hall," 72.
84. Millman, "The Battle of Cory Hall," 76-77.
85. National Council for Civil Liberties, *British Freedom*, 33.
86. Edward Carson, November 13, 1917, *House of Common Debates*, Fifth Series, vol. 99, cols. 312, 316.
87. Parliament approved a measure giving executive authority to the War Cabinet. Although the membership of the War Cabinet changed over time, it was usually composed of five members, three representing the Conservative Party, one representing the Labour Party, and Lloyd George as a Liberal and prime minister.
88. Newton Wallop (Lord Portsmouth), November 17, 1915, *House of Lords Debates*, Fifth Series, vol. 20, cols. 393-94.
89. Robert Milnes (Earl of Crewe), November 17, 1915, *House of Lords Debates*, Fifth Series, vol. 20, cols. 398-99. Milnes was a close ally of

Asquith and therefore refused to support the War Cabinet. Nevertheless, he and Asquith avoided any sustained opposition to the War Cabinet's policies.

90. David Monger, *Patriotism and Propaganda in First World War Britain* (Liverpool: Liverpool University Press, 2012), 135–36. In October 1917, the NWAC received £113,000 from the UK Treasury to fund its efforts for six months (38).

91. George Cave, Memorandum, "Pacifist Propaganda," November 1, 1917, CAB 24/4/23, National Archives, London. The next paragraph is derived from the same source.

92. Cave, Memorandum, "Pacifist Propaganda," November 1, 1917, CAB 24/4/23, National Archives, London.

93. Minutes of the War Cabinet, Meeting 274, November 15, 1917, CAB 23/4/68, National Archives, London.

94. Cave, Memorandum, "Pacifist Propaganda," November 1, 1917, National Archive,s London.

95. George Cave, November 22, 1917, *House of Common Debates*, Fifth Series, vol. 99, col. 1352.

96. Herbert Samuel to George Cave, November 27, 1917, CAB 24/34/20, National Archives, London.

97. Cook, ed., *Manual*, 128. The revised version of Regulation 27C was issued on December 21, 1917.

98. Swartz, *The Union of Democratic Control*, 47–49; *Sheffield Evening Telegraph*, August 30, 1918. Hardyman was twenty-three when he died.

99. Swanwick, *Builders of Peace*, 106.

100. Swanwick, *Builders of Peace*, 31.

101. Swanwick, *Builders of Peace*, 178.

102. *House of Commons Debates*, October 31, 1917, vol. 98, col. 1586.

103. Charles Cook, ed., *Defence of the Realm Manual*, 6th ed. (London: HMSO, 1918), 122, 124.

104. Swartz, *Union of Democratic Control*, 123.

105. *The Persecution of E. D. Morel* (Glasgow: Reformer's Bookstall, 1918), 7; Donald Mitchell, *The Politics of Dissent: A Biography of E. D. Morel* (Bristol, UK: Silverwood Books, 2014), 133–34.

106. Mitchell, *The Politics of Dissent*, 134.

107. Mitchell, *The Politics of Dissent*, 136.

108. Mitchell, *The Politics of Dissent*, 138.

109. Swartz, *Union*, 52.

110. Mitchell, *The Politics of Dissent*, 141, 149.

111. The minutes of the War Cabinet do not include a specific resolution creating the X Committee and giving it the authority to take action. Still, the members of the War Cabinet knew of the X Committee and

tacitly accepted its authority. Furthermore, some meetings of the War Cabinet were so sensitive that minutes were handwritten and only a few copies were made. It is quite possible, even likely, that the public record still does not include the entirety of the War Cabinet meetings, including a discussion of the X Committee.

112. John Barnes and David Nicholson, *The Leo Amery Diaries* (London: Hutchinson, 1980), 1:220.

113. Marc Brodie, "Pringle, William Mather Rutherford," *Oxford National Biography* (Oxford: Oxford University Press, 2004), 408–9.

114. William Pringle, June 18, 1918, *House of Commons Debates,* Fifth Series, vol. 68, col. 249; Richard Holt, June 18, 1918, *House of Commons Debates,* Fifth Series, vol. 68, cols. 290, 292.

115. Minutes of the X Committee, June 19, 1918, File 1/3/34, Papers of Leopold Amery, Churchill Archives, Cambridge University.

116. Minutes of the War Cabinet, November 15, 1917, CAB 23/4/68, National Archives, London.

117. A. J. A Morris, *Reporting the First World War: Charles Repington, the Times, and the Great War* (Cambridge: Cambridge University Press, 2015), 4, 14–15.

118. Peter Rowland, *Lloyd George* (London: Barrie and Jenkins, 1975), 433.

119. Rowland, *Lloyd George,* 434.

120. A. M. Gollin, *Proconsul in Politics* (London: Anthony Blond, 1964), 274–75; Morris, *Repington,* 274–75.

121. Minutes of the X Committee, May 16, 1918, File 1/3/34, Churchill Archives, Cambridge University.

3. Stifling the National Civil Liberties Union

In this and succeeding chapters, when the United States Archives located in Maryland are first cited, the citation will be National Archives, College Park, Maryland. Thereafter, material from this archive will be cited as National Archives, CP. For the United States Archives located in Washington D.C., the first cite will read National Archives, Washington, D. C. Thereafter, material from this archive will be cited as National Archives, DC.

1. Report, September 29, 1914, Microfilm, Reel 103, Lillian Wald Papers, New York Public Library [1983].

2. Memorandum, "Committee on America's Future" [n.d.], Reel 103, Lillian Wald Papers.

3. Memorandum, "Committee on America's Future" [n.d.], Reel 103, Lillian Wald Papers.

4. Memorandum, "Committee on America's Future" [n.d.], Reel 103, Lillian Wald Papers.

5. Report, January 12, 1915, Microfilm, Reel 102, Lillian Wald Papers.

6.   Arthur Stanley Link, ed., *Wilson: Confusions and Crises, 1915-1916* (Princeton: Princeton University Press, 1964), 15, 34–35, 44.

7.   Lillian Wald to L. Hollingsworth Wood, January 25, 1916, Microfilm, Reel 103, Lillian Wald Papers; Crystal Eastman, Memorandum, "Past Programs of the American Union Against Militarism," [September 1917], Lillian Wald Papers, Special Collections, in Microfilm, Reel 1, Lillian Wald Papers, New York Public Library,.

8.   Blanche Wiesen Cook, "Introduction," in *Crystal Eastman on Women and Revolution* (New York: Oxford University Press, 1978), 18.

9.   Baldwin had been offered a job with the American Committee to Limit Armaments in January 1915 and refused it. At this point, the organizational efforts to counter the slide into war were at their earliest stages. There was no structure and few resources. Crystal Eastman took the position of unpaid secretary and was instrumental in creating a functioning, financially solvent organization. Samuel Walker, *In Defense of American Liberties: A History of the ACLU* (Carbondale: Southern Illinois University Press, 1999), 36.

10. Cook, "Introduction," *Eastman*, 28.

11. Robert C. Cottrell, *Roger Nash Baldwin* (New York: Columbia University Press, 2000), 1–36.

12. American Union Against Militarism, "Wartime Program," May 1, 1917, Papers of the American Union Against Militarism, Swarthmore Peace Collections, Swarthmore, Pennsylvania, in Microfilm, Reel 1, *Papers of the American Union Against Militarism* (Wilmington, DE: Scholarly Resources, [2001]).

13. Roger Baldwin to Conference Committee on the Conscription Act, May 2, 1917, Microfilm, Reel 1, Lillian Wald Papers.

14. Crystal Eastman, Memorandum, October 1, 1917, Microfilm, Reel 2, *Papers of the American Union Against Militarism.*

15. Levi Hollingsworth Wood, "Response to the U.S. Attorney" [November 1918], vol. 108, Papers of the American Civil Liberties Union, Princeton University, Princeton, New Jersey in Microfilm, Reel 14, *American Civil Liberties Union Records* (Glen Rock, NJ: Microfilming Corporation of America, 1976).

16. Roger Baldwin, Scott Nearing, Norman Thomas, Oswald Villard, Lillian Wald, et al., "Statement," May 23, 1917, Microfilm, Reel 102, Lillian Wald Papers.

17. In general, Wilson avoided any discussion of the war during his 1916 campaign speeches. Still, there were exceptions. In a speech given at his New Jersey country home, the president observed that electing the Republican candidate, Charles Evans Hughes, would mean that U.S. foreign policy would be "radically changed." Furthermore,

"There is only one choice as against peace and that is war." Woodrow Wilson, Speech, September 30, 1916, in Arthur Link, ed., *The Papers of Woodrow Wilson* (Princeton: Princeton University Press, 1983), 38:306. In a later speech, Wilson proposed the formation of a "society of nations," looking ahead to the creation of the League of Nations and the United Nations. He also held that the First World War had come out of "a complex web of intrigue and spying." October 26, 1916, Link, ed., *The Papers of Woodrow Wilson,* 38:531. Finally, in the days leading up to the election, Wilson warned that Republican attacks on his policy of neutrality could "bring the country at any moment into the world conflict" that was "devastating Europe." November 4, 1916, Link, ed., *The Papers of Woodrow Wilson,* 38:613.

   The Democratic Party's presidential campaign committee was even clearer. It dispatched speakers around the country to boast: "He kept us out of war." (Arthur Link, *Wilson Campaigns for Progressivism and Peace (1916-1917)* (Princeton: Princeton University Press, 1967), 109.

18. Oswald Garrison Villard, Memorandum of Conversation with Enoch Crowder, May 24, 1917, Microfilm, Reel 1, *Papers of the American Union Against Militarism.*

19. Lillian Wald to the AUAM Executive Committee, June 5, 1917, Microfilm, Reel, Papers of Lillian Wald.

20. Crystal Eastman to Emily G. Balch, June 14, 1917, Papers of the American Union Against Militarism, Swarthmore Peace Collections, Swarthmore, Pennsylvania, reprinted in Blanche Wiesen Cook, ed., *Crystal Eastman on Women and Revolution* (New York: Oxford University Press), 257. Eastman is directly quoting from Kellogg's letter to her.

21. Crystal Eastman to Lillian Wald, June 14, 1917, Microfilm, Reel 2, *Papers of the American Union Against Militarism.*

22. Eastman to Balch, June 14, 1917, *Papers of the American Union Against Militarism,* reprinted in Cook, ed., *Crystal Eastman on Women and Revolution,* 257.

23. Crystal Eastman to Thomas Horner, June 20, 1917, enclosed in Agent Wright, Report, July 3, 1917. File 10101–10, Entry 65; Military Intelligence Division, Correspondence, 1917–41, Record Group 165, National Archives, College Park, Maryland..

24. Robert C. Cottrell, *Roger Nash Baldwin* (New York: Columbia University Press, 2000), 57.

25. *New York Tribune,* August 16, 1917.

26. *New York Tribune,* August 6, 1917.

27. Crystal Eastman, Letter to the Editor of the *New York Tribune,* August 28, 1917.

28. Lillian Wald to Crystal Eastman, August 27, 1917, Microfilm, Reel 102, Papers of Lillian Wald.

29. Frank L. Grubbs, *The Struggle for Labor Loyalty: Gompers, the A.F. of L. and the Pacifists, 1917–1920* (Durham, NC: Duke University Press, 1968), 60–64.

30. Report, T. Sanders, September 13, 1917. File 10101-10, Correspondence of the Military Intelligence Division, Record Group 165, National Archives, CP; Report, J. F. Kropidlowski, September 13, 1917. File 10101-10, Correspondence of the Military Intelligence Division, Record Group 165, National Archives, CP.

31. Report, T. Sanders, September 13, 1917. File 10101-10, Correspondence of the Military Intelligence Division, Record Group 165, National Archives; Report, J. F. Kropidlowski, September 13, 1917, File 10101–10, Correspondence of the Military Intelligence Division, Record Group 165, National Archives, CP.

32. Crystal Eastman, "A Proposed Announcement to the Press" [September 1917], Microfilm, Reel 1, Papers of Lillian Wald.

33. Report, T. Sanders, September 24, 1917, File 10101-10, Correspondence of the Military Intelligence Division, Record Group 165, National Archives, CP; Report, J. F. Kropidlowski, September 24, 1917, File 10101–10, Correspondence of the Military Intelligence Division, Record Group 165, National Archives, CP.

34. Report, T. Sanders, September 24, 1917, File 10101–10; Report, J. F. Kropidlowski, September 24, 1917, File 10101-10; Roger Baldwin, Circular Letter, November 1, Microfilm, Reel 1, Lillian Wald Papers.

35. Roger Baldwin, Memorandum, October 1, 1917, File 10902–13, Correspondence of the Military Intelligence Division, Record Group 165, National Archives, CP.

36. Minutes of the Civil Liberties Bureau Directing Committee, October 1, 1917, File 10902-13, Correspondence of the Military Intelligence Division, Record Group 165, National Archives, CP.

37. Walter Nelles, *A Liberal in Wartime: The Education of Albert DeSilver* (New York: W. W. Norton, 1940), 121; *The New York Times*, April 1, 1937. After he left the ACLU, Nelles became an authority in court injunctions used to break up strikes.

38. Jack Whiteclay Chambers II, *To Raise an Army: The Draft Comes to Modern America* (New York: Macmillan, 1981), 211.

39. Chambers, *To Raise an Army*, 213.

40. Chambers, *To Raise an Army*, 216.

41. Howard W. Moore, *Plowing My Own Furrow* (Syracuse, NY: Syracuse University Press, 1985), 100-3.

42. Horace Cornelius Peterson and Gilbert Courtland Fite, *Opponents of*

War, 1917–1918 (Madison, WI: University of Wisconsin Press, 1957), 126.

43. Newton Baker to Woodrow Wilson, September 19, 1917, in Link, ed., *The Papers of Woodrow Wilson* (Princeton: Princeton University Press, 1984), 44:221; Woodrow Wilson to Newton Baker, October 2, 1917, *Papers of Woodrow Wilson*, 44:293; Diary of Josephus Daniels, October 12, 1917, *Papers of Woodrow Wilson*, 44:370.

44. Moore, *Plowing My Own Furrow*, 108.

45. *Webster's American Military Biographies* (Springfield, MA: G. C. Merriam's, 1978), 407–8.

46. Herman Hagedorn, *Leonard Wood* (New York: Harper and Brothers, 1931), 2:247, 311; Chambers, *To Raise an Army*, 215.

47. Daniel R. Beaver, *Newton D. Baker and the American War Effort, 1917–1919* (Lincoln, NE: University of Nebraska Press, 1966), 233; Moore, *Plowing My Own Furrow*, 127–28;

48. Donald Eberle, "The Plain Mennonite Face of the World War One Conscientious Objector," *Journal of Amish and Plain Anabaptist Studies* 3 (2015): 193.

49. Eberle, "The Plain Mennonite Face," 3:193–94.

50. Eberle, "The Plain Mennonite Face," 3:195–96.

51. Duane C. S. Stoltzfus, *Pacifists in Chains: The Persecution of the Hutterites During the Great War* (Baltimore: Johns Hopkins Press, 2013), 92.

52. Stoltzfus, *Pacifists in Chains*, 5, 92.

53. Stoltzfus, *Pacifists in Chains*, 92.

54. Stoltzfus, *Pacifists in Chains*, 121, 127.

55. Stoltzfus, *Pacifists in Chains*, 157–59, 173–74.

56. Newton Baker to Woodrow Wilson, July 22, 1918, Link, ed., *The Papers of Woodrow Wilson* (Princeton, NJ: Princeton University Press, 1985), 49:56.

57. Woodrow Wilson to Newton Baker, September 13, 1918, Link, ed., *The Papers of Woodrow Wilson* (Princeton, NJ: Princeton University Press, 1986), 54:542. Wilson enclosed a letter from Hays Hochbaum to the president, September 8, 1918.

58. Moore, *Plowing My Own Furrow*, 106; Chambers, *To Raise an Army*, 344; Eberle, "The Plain Mennonite Face," 3:197–98.

59. Peterson and Fite, *Opponents of War*, 137.

60. Keppel had been the dean of Columbia College, the undergraduate college of Columbia University. He joined the government as civilian assistant to Secretary of War Newton Baker. He then became the Third Assistant Secretary of War, a post especially created for him.

61. Roger Baldwin, Memorandum to the Directing Committee of the Civil Liberties Bureau, [October 1917], File 10902-13, Correspondence of the

Military Intelligence Division, Record Group 165, National Archives, CP. The following paragraphs are drawn from the same source.

62. Roger Baldwin, Bulletin, November 1, 1917, Microfilm, Reel 1, Lillian Wald Papers.

63. Roger Baldwin, Memorandum to the Members of the American Union Against Militarism, November 1, 1917, Box 1, Microfilm, Reel 1, Lillian Wald Papers.

64. Levi Hollingsworth Wood to John Knox, April 3, 1918, vol. 108, Papers of the American Civil Liberties Union, Princeton University, Microfilm, Reel 14. Knox held the post of Assistant U.S. Attorney for the judicial district covering Manhattan. He was also an expert on prosecuting cases brought under the Espionage Act.

65. Eric Thomas Chester, *The Wobblies in Their Heyday* (Santa Barbara, CA: Praeger, 2014), 160–87.

66. Woodrow Wilson, Speech to Congress, January 8, 1918, Link, ed., *The Papers of Woodrow Wilson* (Princeton, NJ: Princeton University Press, 1984), 45:536–38.

67. Roger Baldwin, Memorandum, January 24, 1918, enclosed in Edward House to Woodrow Wilson, February 18, 1918, Link, ed., *The Papers of Woodrow Wilson* (Princeton, NJ: Princeton University Press, 1984), 46:481.

68. Bruce W. Bidwell, *History of the Military Intelligence Division, Department of the Army General Staff, 1775–1941* (Frederick, MD: University Publications of America, 1986), 127; Norman Thwaites to William Wiseman, November 22, 1918. Series 1, Box 3, William Wiseman Papers, Manuscripts and Special Collections, Yale University.

69. Ralph Van Deman to Intelligence Officers, February 6, 1918. File 10589–12. Correspondence of the Military Intelligence Division, Record Group 165, National Archives, CP.

70. Charles Lloyd, Memorandum, "Subject: Roger N. Baldwin," March 6, 1918, File 10434–8, Correspondence of the Military Intelligence Division, Record Group 165, National Archives, CP; Nicholas Biddle to Ralph Van Deman, April 16, 1918. File 10902–13, Correspondence of the Military Intelligence Division, Record Group 165, National Archives, CP.

71. Nicholas Biddle to Ralph Van Deman, April 16, 1918, File 10902–13, Correspondence of the Military Intelligence Division, Record Group 165, National Archives, CP.

72. Charles Lloyd, Report, March 6, 1918. File 10902–13, Correspondence of the Military Intelligence Division, Record Group 165, National Archives, CP.

73. The Fourth Amendment prohibits "unreasonable searches and seizures," that is, those undertaken without a warrant. A magistrate can

only issue a search warrant when there is "probable cause" that a person has committed a serious crime. The warrant has to specify "the place to be searched and the person or things to be seized."

74. Roger Baldwin and Alan Westin, "Recollections of a Life in Civil Liberties–I," *Civil Liberties Review* 2 (Spring 1975): 62. Baldwin brought with him John Codman, a supporter of the war effort.

75. Roger Baldwin to Nicholas Biddle, March 8, 1918. File 10589–12, Correspondence of the Military Intelligence Division, Record Group 165, National Archives, CP; Ralph Van Deman to Nicholas Biddle, March 7, 1918, File 10589–12, Correspondence of the Military Intelligence Division, Record Group 165, National Archives, CP.

76. Ralph Van Deman to Frederick Keppel, March 9, 1918. File 10589–12. Correspondence of the Military Intelligence Division, Record Group 165, National Archives, CP.

77. Blanche Wiesen Cook, "Introduction," *Crystal Eastman*, 14.

78. Nicholas Biddle to Ralph Van Deman, March 18, 1918, File 10110–709, Correspondence of the Military Intelligence Division, Record Group 165, National Archives, CP.

79. Roger Baldwin to Harold Rotzel, March 13, 1918, File 10902–13, Correspondence of the Military Intelligence Division, Record Group 165, National Archives, CP.

80. Roger Baldwin to Nicholas Biddle, March 30, 1918, File 10902–13, Correspondence of the Military Intelligence Division, Record Group 165, National Archives, CP.

81. Ralph Van Deman to Frederick Keppel, May 15, 1918 File 10902–13, Correspondence of the Military Intelligence Division, Record Group 165, National Archives, CP. Van Deman's letter quotes extensively from a letter by Baldwin to Keppel. Although no date is given, it is clear from the context that it was written before April 18, 1918.

82. Roger Baldwin to Frederick Keppel, April 23, 1918, File 10902–13, Correspondence of the Military Intelligence Division, Record Group 165, National Archives, CP.

83. Alfred Bettman to Alexander Bruce Bielaski, April 22, 1918, File 10902–13, Correspondence of the Military Intelligence Division, Record Group 165, National Archives, CP. The next paragraphs come from the same source.

84. Albert DeSilver to John Codman, January 25, 1919, Microfilm, Reel 14, American Civil Liberties Union Records, Seeley G. Mudd Manuscript Library, Princeton University.

85. Archibald Stevenson to Nicholas Biddle, November 20, 1918, File 10902–13, Correspondence of the Military Intelligence Division, Record Group 165, National Archives, CP.

86. Roger Baldwin to Woodrow Wilson, February 27, 1918, in Link, ed., *Papers of Woodrow Wilson*, 46:481.

87. National Civil Liberties Bureau, Memorandum [February 1918], in Link, ed., *Papers of Woodrow Wilson*, 46:481.

88. DeSilver to Codman, January 25, 1919, Reel 14, American Civil Liberties Union Records.

89. Roger Baldwin, "Reminiscences," Oral History, Rare Book and Manuscript Library, Columbia University, New York, vol. 1, Part 2, 287; Peggy Lamson, *Roger Baldwin, Founder of the American Civil Liberties Union: A Portrait* (Boston: Houghton Mifflin, 1976), 80.

90. DeSilver to Codman, January 25, 1919, Reel 14, American Civil Liberties Union Records.

91. National Civil Liberties Bureau, *The Truth about the I.W.W.* (New York: 1918), 3.

92. NCLB, *The Truth about the I.W.W.*, 16. The quote is from Carleton Parker taken from an article he had written for *Atlantic Monthly*.

93. NCLB, *The Truth about the I.W.W.*, 35.

94. William Lamar to the Chicago Postmaster, April 17, 1918, File OG 124597, Records of the Bureau of Intelligence, Record Group 65, National Archives, CP; National Civil Liberties Bureau, Memorandum, "Interference by Federal Agents" [October 1918], vol. 86, ACLU Papers, Princeton University, Microfilm, Reel 11, ACLU Records; Hinton Clabaugh to A. Bruce Bielaski, May 19, 1918, File OG 124597, Records of the Bureau of Intelligence.

95. Ralph Van Deman to Frederick Keppel, May 15, 1918, File 10902-13, Correspondence of the Military Intelligence Division, Record Group 165, National Archives, CP.

96. Frederick Keppel to Roger Baldwin, May 19, 1918, File 10902-13, Correspondence of the Military Intelligence Division, Record Group 165, National Archives, CP.

97. Marlborough Churchill to William Lamar, June 3, 1918, File 10902-13, Correspondence of the Military Intelligence Division, Record Group 165, National Archives, CP.

98. Marlborough Churchill to Bryant Venable, June 17, 1918, File 10101-10, Correspondence of the Military Intelligence Division, Record Group 165, National Archives, CP. Venable held the post of assistant to the president of Whitaker Paper Company.

99. Roger Baldwin, Memorandum, "The Fight for Civil Liberty During the War" [January 1920], vol. 108, ACLU Papers, Princeton University, Microfilm, Reel 14.

100. Nelles, *Liberal in Wartime,* 117.

101. Advertisement, *The New Republic* 15 (June 22, 1918): 242. The next

NOTES TO PAGES 113-118

paragraph is from the same source. The Chicago trial lasted nearly five months and depleted the resources of the IWW. Ninety-three IWW leaders and activists were convicted of violating the Espionage Act and sentenced to prison terms ranging from five to twenty years.

102. National Civil Liberties Bureau, Memorandum, "Interference by Federal Agents" [October 1918], vol. 86, ACLU Papers, Princeton University, Microfilm, Reel 11, in Link, ed., *Papers of Woodrow Wilson*, 46:481; Nelles, *Liberal in Wartime*, 140.

103. A. M. White to Captain Uterhart, Memorandum, "Subject: Roger Baldwin," June 26, 1918, File 10110-235, Correspondence of the Military Intelligence Division, Record Group 165, National Archives, CP.

104. Nicholas Biddle to Marlborough Churchill, August 31, 1918, File 10902-13, Correspondence of the Military Intelligence Division, Record Group 165, National Archives.

105. Lamson, *Baldwin*, 84.

106. Nelles, *Liberal in Wartime*, 147-48; Lamson, *Baldwin*, 84.

107. Levi Hollingsworth Wood, Circular Letter, September 17, 1918, vol. 108, ACLU Papers, Princeton University, Microfilm, Reel 14; Nelles, *Liberal in Wartime*, 151; Vincent Rothwell and Ray Berman, Memorandum of Conversation [September 1918], vol. 108, ACLU Papers, Princeton University, Microfilm, Reel 14.

108. Roger Baldwin to Frederick Keppel, September 16, 1918, File 10902-13, Correspondence of the Military Intelligence Division, Record Group 165, National Archives, CP.

109. Roger Nash Baldwin, "Reminiscences," Oral History, Rare Book and Manuscript Library, Columbia University, New York, 1954, vol. 1, 71.

110. Baldwin to Keppel, September 16, 1918, File 10902-13, Correspondence of the Military Intelligence Division, National Archives.

111. Frederick Keppel to Roger Baldwin [September 1918], File 10902-13, Correspondence of the Military Intelligence Division, Record Group 165, National Archives, CP.

112. Baldwin, "Reminiscences," Oral History, 1: 71.

113. Lamson, *Baldwin*, 84.

114. Clifton Hood, *In Pursuit of Privilege: A History of New York City's Upper Class and the Making of a Metropolis* (New York: Columbia University Press, 2016), 202.

115. Brewer Corcoran to Rupert Hughes, October 14, 1918, Box 1, Papers of Rupert Hughes, Records of the Military Intelligence Division, Record Group 165, National Archives, CP; Brewer Corcoran to Rupert Hughes, November 12, 1918, Box 1, Papers of Rupert Hughes, Records of the Military Intelligence Division, Record Group 165, National Archives,

CP. Hughes was the director of MI10, the division of the MID that handled censorship matters.

116. Corcoran to Hughes, October 14, 1918, Box 1, Papers of Rupert Hughes, Records of the Military Intelligence Division, Record Group 165, National Archives, CP; Corcoran to Hughes, November 12, 1918, Box 1, Papers of Rupert Hughes, Records of the Military Intelligence Division, Record Group 165, National Archives, CP.

117. Marlborough Churchill to Nicholas Biddle, October 17, 1918, File 10902-13, Correspondence of the Military Intelligence Division, Record Group 165, National Archives, CP.

118. Roger Baldwin, *Civil Liberties Review* (1975): 2; Levi Hollingsworth Wood to John Lord O'Brian, September 1, 1918, vol. 108, ACLU Papers, Princeton University, Microfilm, Reel 14; Donald Johnson, *The Challenge to American Freedom: World War I and the Rise of the American Civil Liberties Union* (Lexington: University of Kentucky Press, 1963), 46.

119. Johnson, *The Challenge to American Freedom*, 44–45; Cottrell, *Baldwin*, 86.

120. "Profiles: Mr. Chairman," *The New Yorker*, March 11, 1933, 21–24.

121. Nicholas Biddle to Marlborough Churchill, October 11, 1918, File 10902-13, Correspondence of the Military Intelligence Division, Record Group 165, National Archives, CP.

122. Marlborough Churchill to Nicholas Biddle, October 17, 1918, File 10902-13 Correspondence of the Military Intelligence Division, Record Group 165, National Archives, CP.

123. Churchill to Biddle, October 17, 1918, File 10902-13, Correspondence of the Military Intelligence Division, Record Group 165, National Archives, CP.

124. Churchill to Biddle, October 17, 1918, File 10902-13, Correspondence of the Military Intelligence Division, National Archives, CP.

125. Cottrell, *Baldwin*, 104.

126. Thomas Gregory to Woodrow Wilson, November 9, 1918, Case 4898, Series 4, Papers of Woodrow Wilson, Library of Congress, Microfilm, Reel 375.

127. Cottrell, *Baldwin*, 369. Cottrell presents an array of material on the issue of Baldwin's homosexuality. Although he concludes that Baldwin "perhaps" engaged in homosexual relationships, the evidence that he did so is convincing.

128. George Foster Peabody to Joseph Tumulty, November 26, 1918, Case 4898, Series 4, Papers of Woodrow Wilson, Library of Congress, Microfilm, Reel 375; George Foster Peabody to Joseph Tumulty, December 16, 1918, Case 4898, Series 4, Papers of Woodrow Wilson, Microfilm, Reel 375.

129. Johnson, *Challenge*, 46–47, 145; Cottrell, *Baldwin*, 122.
130. Roger Baldwin, Norman Thomas, Levi Hollingsworth Wood to Lillian Wald, January 19, 1920, Microfilm, Reel 10, Lillian Wald Papers; Johnson, *Challenge*, 146–47.
131. Baldwin, Thomas, Wood to Wald, Reel 10, Lillian Wald Papers.
132. Cottrell, *Baldwin*, 122.
133. NCLB, *The Truth about the I.W.W.*
134. NCLB, *The Truth about the I.W.W.*
135. "Open Letter of the 78 IWW Prisoners," reprinted in NCLB, *The Truth about the I.W.W.*
136. E. F. Doree, *A Wobbly Life* (Detroit: Wayne State University, 2004), 117–18, 170.
137. *An Open Letter to the President from 52 Members of the I.W.W. Now in Leavenworth Penitentiary* (Chicago: General Defense Committee, [1922]), 15.
138. Summary Memorandum of Conversation, July 19, 1922, Microfilm, Reel 178, Papers of Warren Harding (Columbus: Manuscripts Dept., Ohio Historical Society, 1969).
139. Memorandum, Roger Baldwin, Reverend Ralph Gowan, Harold Pollack, August 8, 1922, Reel 178, Microfilm, Papers of Warren Harding.
140. The evidence for the government's claim that the California Wobblies had actually engaged in arson was flimsy. This issue is discussed in detail in Eric Thomas Chester, *The Wobblies in Their Heyday: The Rise and Destruction of the Industrial Workers of the World During the World War I Era* (Santa Barbara, CA: Praeger, 2014), 196–201.
141. Baldwin, Gowan, and Pollack, August 8, 1922, in Reel 178, Microfilm, Papers of Warren Harding.
142. James Finch to Roger Baldwin, August 28, 1922, Box 2, Records of the Pardon Attorney, Record Group 204, National Archives, CP.
143. On his visit to Leavenworth, Baldwin was accompanied by Robertson Trowbridge, a member of the Union League Club, a private club in midtown Manhattan for wealthy businessmen. Its members had actively participated in the wartime effort to crush dissent. Thus, it would seem that the authorities did not entirely trust Baldwin. Nevertheless, Baldwin could have carried messages to the IWW prisoners, and he could have helped in sending messages out of the penitentiary, despite Trowbridge's presence at the confidential interviews. Baldwin did neither. Baldwin, "Reminiscences," Oral History, vol. 1, Part 2, 294.
144. Baldwin, "Reminiscences," Oral History, vol. 1, Part 2, 294.
145. Baldwin, "Reminiscences," Oral History, vol. 1, Part 2, 293. The government did not entirely trust Baldwin. He was therefore

accompanied on his trip to Leavenworth by Robertson Trowbridge, a member of the Union League Club who would not have been sympathetic to the Wobblies. Still, Baldwin was given a unique opportunity to meet with the IWW prisoners. Indeed, he believed that he had been given a "free hand" to talk with them. There is no evidence that he helped the IWW prisoners to get messages out of Leavenworth. Instead, he spent his time trying to persuade them to submit pleas for a commutation of their sentences in accordance with the procedure he had negotiated with Finch and the Department of Justice.

146. Memorandum, "Summary List of Pardons," [1923], Box 3, Political Prisoner Case Files, Record Group 204, Records of the Pardon Attorney, National Archives, College Park, MD.

147. Baldwin, "Reminiscences," Oral History, vol. 1, Part 2, 293–94.

148. Chester, *Wobblies in Their Heyday*, 219–22.

149. Baldwin, "Reminiscences," Oral History, vol. 1, Part 2, 294; Baldwin, "Reminiscences," Oral History, vol. 1, Part 1, 68.

4. Quashing the Socialist Party and Targeting Eugene Victor Debs

1.   Statement of the Socialist Party's National Executive Committee, December 31, 1914, in William English Walling, ed., *The Socialists and the War* (New York: Henry Holt, 1915), 467.

2.   Statement of the Socialist Party's National Executive Committee, 468–69.

3.   Eugene V. Debs to Upton Sinclair, January 12, 1918, Microfilm, Reel 2, Papers of Eugene V. Debs (Sanford, NC: Microfilming Corporation of America, 1982).

4.   Arthur S. Link, *Wilson: Confusions and Crises, 1915–1916* (Princeton: Princeton University Press, 1964), 15.

5.   Sally M. Miller, *Victor Berger and the Promise of Constructive Socialism, 1910–1920* (Westport, CT: Greenwood Press, 1973), 126.

6.   David A. Shannon, *The Socialist Party: A History* (New York: Macmillan, 1955), 89.

7.   Eugene V. Debs to *New York Sun*, telegram, November 29, 1915, Microfilm, Reel 2, Papers of Eugene V. Debs.

8.   *New York Times*, March 8, 1917; Ray Ginger, *Bending Cross* (New Brunswick, NJ: Rutgers University Press, 1949), 339.

9.   "The Socialist Party and the War," in Alexander Trachtenberg, ed., *The American Labor Year Book, 1917–18* (New York: Rand School of Social Sciences, 1918), 50.

10. Ernest Freeberg, *Democracy's Prisoner: Eugene V. Debs, The Great War and the Right to Dissent* (Cambridge, MA: Harvard University Press, 2008), 61–62.

11. Eugene V. Debs to Adolph Germer, April 11, 1917, Microfilm, Reel 2, Papers of Eugene V. Debs.

12. Eugene V. Debs, "The Emergency Convention," *Social Revolution* (May 1917). The St. Louis resolution was approved in a membership referendum by a vote of 21,600 to 2,700, an overwhelming majority of 89 percent.

13. Eugene V. Debs to Louis Kopelin, December 14, 1917, Microfilm, Reel 2, Papers of Eugene V. Debs. Debs's prediction proved to be correct. The *Appeal to Reason* lost most of its readers due to its pro-war policies, and ceased publication in 1922.

14. Eugene V. Debs, *Debs White Book* (Girard, KS: Appeal to Reason, [1919]).

15. Morris Hillquit, *Loose Leaves from a Busy Life* (New York: Macmillan, 1934), 185.

16. *New York Times*, November 2, 1917.

17. Morris Hillquit, speech transcript, October 5, 1917, Box 52, John Purroy Mitchel Papers, Manuscript Room, Library of Congress. Mitchel was worried that Hillquit would be elected mayor, so he paid a stenographer to record Hillquit's speeches.

18. *New York Times*, October 23, 1917.

19. Woodrow Wilson to Thomas Gregory, October 29, 1917, Series 4, Case 4244, Microfilm, Reel 364, Woodrow Wilson Papers, Princeton University.

20. Thomas Gregory to Woodrow Wilson, November 3, 1917, in Arthur S. Link, ed., *Papers of Woodrow Wilson* (Princeton: Princeton University Press, 1983), 44:504.

21. Hillquit, *Loose Leaves*, 206.

22. James Hamilton Lewis to Woodrow Wilson, December 13, 1917, in Link, ed., *Papers of Woodrow Wilson* (Princeton: Princeton University Press, 1984), 45:319. Lewis did not name Stedman as the person who had initiated this proposal. Instead, Lewis mentioned that this individual was an attorney and that Lewis had worked with him as joint counsel on a case. Both Lewis and Stedman were well-known attorneys in the Chicago area. A founding member of the Socialist Party of America, Stedman had served one term in the Illinois state legislature. He would be nominated as Debs's vice presidential candidate in 1920.

23. Lewis to Wilson, December 13, 1917, in Link ed., *Papers of Woodrow Wilson*, 45:319.

24. Woodrow Wilson to Joseph Tumulty, December 18, 1917, in Link ed., *Papers of Woodrow Wilson*, 45:318.

25. An English translation of the secret treaties first appeared in the *Manchester Guardian* in a series of articles starting in December 1917.

The Union of Democratic Control then published a pamphlet that collected the treaties and provided a brief background. F. Seymour Cocks, *The Secret Treaties* (London: Union of Democratic Control 1918).

26. Woodrow Wilson, speech, December 4, 1917, in Link ed., *Papers of Woodrow Wilson* 45:191, 195–96.

27. Woodrow Wilson, "A Joint Address to Congress," January 8, 1918, in Link ed., *Papers of Woodrow Wilson*, 45:534–38. The next paragraphs are based on the same source.

28. George Frost Kennan, *Soviet-American Relations, 1917–1920, Russia Leaves the War* (Princeton: Princeton University Press, 1956), 370–71.

29. *New York Times*, March 3, 1918.

30. Adolph Germer to Morris Hillquit, March 14, 1918, Microfilm, Reel 2, Morris Hillquit Papers, 1886–1940 (Madison: State Historical Society of Wisconsin, 1969).

31. For a report on Bohn's activities in Switzerland see Frank Bohn to George Creel, June 25, 1918, Box 7, Foreign Section, Records of the Committee on Public Information, Record Group 63, National Archives, College Park, Maryland.

32. Elliott Shore, *Talkin' Socialism: J. A. Wayland and the Role of the Press in American Radicalism, 1890–1912* (Lawrence: University Press of Kansas, 1988), 124–26, 162.

33. Allen Ricker to Albert Burleson, November 8, 1917, Case #47503, Box 21, Entry 40, Records Relating to the Espionage Act Case Files, Records of the Post Office, Office of the Solicitor, Record Group 28, National Archives, Washington, D.C.; Allen Ricker to George Creel, May 1, 1917, Box 20, Entry 1, General Correspondence of George Creel, Records of the Committee on Public Information, Record Group 63, National Archives, CP.

34. Allen Ricker to Woodrow Wilson, March 5, 1918, Box 20, Correspondence of George Creel, Records of the Committee on Public Information, National Archives, CP.

35. Allen Ricker to George Creel, December 4, 1917, Box 20, Correspondence of George Creel, Records of the Committee on Public Information, National Archives, CP.

36. George Creel to Allen Ricker, December 7, 1917, Box 20, Correspondence of George Creel, Records of the Committee on Public Information, National Archives, CP.

37. Frank Harris, "The Idiot," *Pearson's* 38 (January 1918): 290; Frank Harris, "Conscientious Objectors," *Pearson's* 38 (January 1918): 304.

38. *New York Times*, December 19, 1917; Frank Harris, "Warned," *Pearson's* 38 (February 1918):338

39. William Lamar to Thomas Patten, February 15, 1918, Case #47503, Records Relating to the Espionage Act Case Files, Records of the Post Office, Office of the Solicitor, Record Group 28, National Archives, DC; William Lamar to Dockery, February 16, Case #47503, Records Relating to the Espionage Act Case Files, Records of the Post Office, Office of the Solicitor, Record Group 28, National Archives, DC.

40. Albert Burleson to Edward House, February 23, 1918, Series 1, Box 22, Edward House Papers, Special Collections, Yale University.

41. *New York Times*, March 21, 1918.

42. *New York Globe*, May 24, 1918. This can be found in Series 4, Case 298. Woodrow Wilson Papers, Library of Congress.

43. Allen Ricker to Edward House, April 20, 1918, Series 1, Box 94, Edward House Papers, Special Collections, Yale University; Edward House, Diary, April 24, 1918, Edward House Papers, Special Collections, Yale University.

44. Allen Ricker to Edward House, April 25, 1918, in Link, ed., *Papers of Woodrow Wilson* (Princeton: Princeton University Press, 1984), 47:437–9. The quotes in the following three paragraphs are from the same source.

45. Scott Nearing to Allen Ricker, April 30, 1918, Series 1, Box 94, Edward House Papers, Yale University.

46. Carl Thompson to Allen Ricker, April 17, 1917, Case #47503, Records Relating to the Espionage Act Case Files, Records of the Post Office, Office of the Solicitor, Record Group 28, National Archives, DC; *New Appeal*, May 18, 1918. The *Appeal to Reason* changed its name to the *New Appeal* in 1918. It fervently supported the war beginning in December 1917.

47. Allen Ricker to Carl Thompson, May 10, 1918, Series 1, Box 94, Edward House Papers, Special Collections, Yale University.

48. Frank L. Grubbs, *The Struggle for Labor Loyalty: Gompers, the A.F. of L. and the Pacifists, 1917–1920* (Durham, NC: Duke University Press, 1968), 44–45. The National Security and Defense Fund was unvouchered. The president did not have to provide Congress with an explanation for expenditures made from the fund. Thus, Woodrow Wilson had sole and total control over the National Security and Defense Fund.

49. Allen Ricker to Carl Thompson, May 10, 1918, Series 1, Box 94, Edward House Papers, Yale University.

50. Allen Ricker to Edward House, May 14, 1918. Series I, Box 94. Edward House Papers, Special Collections, Yale University; Edward House, May 16, 1917. Diary, Edward House Papers, Special Collections, Yale University.

51. Allen Ricker to Woodrow Wilson, May 15, 1918, Series 4, Case 298, Woodrow Wilson Papers, Library of Congress, in Microfilm, Reel 253; Allen Ricker to Woodrow Wilson, June 27, 1918, Box 94, Edward House Papers, Special Collections, Yale University.

52. Allen Ricker to Woodrow Wilson, May 15, 1918, Series 4, Case 298, Microfilm Reel 253, Woodrow Wilson Papers.

53. Germer to the National Executive Committee, May 6, 1918, Microfilm, Reel 54, Victor Berger Papers (Wilmington, DE: Scholarly Resources, 1994).

54. Adolph Germer to Eugene Debs, April 18, 1918, Microfilm, Reel 2, Papers of Eugene V. Debs

55. Allen Ricker to Edward House, April 30, 1918, Series I, Box 94, Edward House Papers, Special Collections, Yale University, reprinted in Link, ed., Papers of Woodrow Wilson, 47:471–72.

56. Woodrow Wilson to Albert Burleson, May 4, 1918, Papers of Woodrow Wilson, 47:516.

57. Sally M. Miller, Victor Berger and the Promise of Constructive Socialism, 1910–1920 (Westport, CT: Greenwood Press, 1973), 205; Eugene Debs, "Indicted, Unashamed and Unafraid," Eye–Opener, March 16, 1918, Microfilm, Reel 8, Papers of Eugene V. Debs. The Eye–Opener served as the official newsletter of the Socialist Party.

58. Adam Ulam, Expansion and Coexistence (London: Secker and Warburg, 1968), 59, 66–68. The Rada served as the de facto parliament for the Ukraine in the wake of the collapse of the tsarist empire in March 1917. It was dominated by the Ukraine Social Democratic Party and the Ukraine Socialist Revolutionaries.

The alliance between the Rada and Germany was short-lived. The German government sponsored a coup on April 29, 1918. The Rada was replaced by a more compliant regime headed by General Skoropadski.

59. Ulam, Expansion and Coexistence, 71; Kennan, Soviet-American Relations, 1917–1920, 370–71.

60. Taras Hunczak, "The Ukraine Under Hetman Pavlo Skoropadski," 61–81. In Taras Hunczak, ed., The Ukraine, 1917–1921: A Study in Revolution (Cambridge, MA: Harvard University Press, 1977), 61.

61. Michael Kettle, The Road to Intervention, March–November 1918 (New York: Routledge, 1988), 81–84.

62. Carl Thompson to Eugene V. Debs, April 12, 1918, Microfilm, Reel 2, Papers of Eugene V. Debs .

63. Eugene V. Debs to Adolph Germer, April 8, 1918, Microfilm, Reel 2, Papers of Eugene V. Debs.

64. "Memorandum of the Inter-Allied Labour and Socialist Conference," The New Republic (March 28, 1918), 14: Section 2: 3. The New Republic

printed the text of the entire resolution as an appendix to its regular issue of March 28, 1918.

65. "Memorandum," *The New Republic* (March 28, 1918), 5.

66. David G. Kirby, *War, Peace and Revolution: International Socialism at the Crossroads* (Aldershot,UK: Gower, 1986), 224–25.

67. Eugene V. Debs to Adolph Germer, April 8, 1918, Microfilm, Reel 2, Papers of Eugene V. Debs.

68. Eugene V. Debs, "The Socialist Party and the War," *Social Builder*, May 1918. The *National Rip-Saw* was one of the most widely read journals linked to the Socialist Party in the prewar period. It was renamed *Social Revolution* in March 1917 and came under intense pressure from the federal government due to its opposition to the war. The May 1918 issue was renamed *Social Builder*, but it then ceased publication. Debs often wrote for it starting in 1914.
The next paragraph is drawn from the same source.

69. Z. A. B. Zeman, *Germany and the Revolution in Russia, 1915–1918, Documents from the Archives of the German Foreign Ministry* (London: Oxford University Press, 1958), 124–25; Kettle, *The Road to Intervention*, 318.

70. Allen Ricker to William Lamar, May 17, 1918, Case #47503, Records Relating to the Espionage Act Case Files, Records of the Post Office, Office of the Solicitor, Record Group 28, National Archives, DC; Allen Ricker to Woodrow Wilson, June 27, 1918, Box 94, Edward House Papers, Special Collections, Yale University.

71. Eugene V. Debs to Stephen Reynolds, May 25, 1918, Microfilm, Reel 2, Papers of Eugene V. Debs.

72. *Terre Haute Tribune*, February 10, 1918, Microfilm, Reel 8, Papers of Eugene V. Debs.

73. Eugene Debs, Editorial, February 1918, *Social Revolution*.

74. *Marion Leader-Tribune*, June 11, 1918, Microfilm, Reel 8, Papers of Eugene V. Debs.

75. *Indianapolis News*, June 18, 1918, File 10101–46, Correspondence of the Military Intelligence Department, Record Group 165, National Archives, CP. The fact that this clipping can be found in the papers of the Military Intelligence Division is indicative of the MID's covert responsibility for this and other deliberately misleading newspaper articles.

76. Eugene V. Debs, "Public Statement" [June 4, 1918], Microfilm, Reel 2, Papers of Eugene V. Debs. The statement was printed in the *Miami Valley Socialist*, June 14, 1918, and the *Ohio Socialist*, July 2, 1918. The next paragraphs draw from the same source.

77. "Majority Report," in Alexander Trachtenberg, ed., *The American Socialists and the War* (New York: Rand School, 1917), 43.

78. Freeberg, *Democracy's Prisoner,* 67.

79. *Canton Repository,* June 16, 1918.

80. *Canton Repository,* June 16, 1918.

81. Clyde R. Miller, "The Man I Sent to Prison," *The Progressive* (October 1963), 34; Ginger, *Bending Cross,* 355.

82. Eugene V. Debs, *Debs White Book* (Girard, KS: Appeal to Reason, [1919]).

83. *Canton Repository,* June 17, 1918. Clyde Miller testified that 1,200 to 1,500 were in the audience at Nimisila Park. (Clyde Miller, Transcript of Record, *United States v. Eugene V. Debs,* 1918.) U.S. Attorney Edwin Wertz reported that the crowd numbered more than three thousand. Edwin Wertz to Thomas Gregory, June 17, 1918, File 77175, Record Group 60, Department of Justice Records, National Archives, CP.

84. Edwin Wertz, the U. S. attorney for the northern district of Ohio, stated soon after the speech that he believed that the Canton police should have blocked the rally from being held. *Canton Repository,* June 17, 1918.

85. Ginger, *Bending Cross,* 357; *The Heritage of Debs: The Fight Against War* (Chicago: 1935), 12.

86. Eugene V. Debs, *Debs White Book* (Girard, KS: Appeal to Reason, [1919]). The quotes from this and the next paragraph are from Debs's speech at Canton as presented in the *Debs White Book.*

87. "The Canton Speech," in Jean Y. Tussey, ed., *Eugene V. Debs Speaks* (New York: Pathfinder Press, 1970), 267.

88. Edwin Wertz to Thomas Gregory, June 17, 1918, File 77175, Record Group 60, Department of Justice Records, National Archives, CP.

89. Ginger, *Bending Cross,* 353; Eugene V. Debs, interview with David Karsner, [August 1921], Box 1, David Karsner Papers, Special Collections, New York Public Library.

90. Theodore Debs to Allen Cook, July 6, 1908, Microfilm, Reel 2, Papers of Eugene V. Debs.

91. David C. Westenhaver to Thomas Gregory, March 21, 1919, File 77175-274, Straight Decimal File, Records of the Department of Justice, Record Group 60, National Archives, CP.

92. Edwin Wertz to Thomas Gregory, June 17, 1918, File 77175, Record Group 60, Department of Justice Records, National Archives, CP.

93. John Lord O'Brian to Edwin Wertz, June 20, 1918, File 77175, Record Group 60, Department of Justice Records, National Archives, CP.

94. John Lord O'Brian to Edwin Wertz, June 20, 1918, File 77175, Record Group 60, Department of Justice Records, National Archives, CP.

95. John Lord O'Brian to Edwin Wertz, June 20, 1918, File 77175, Record Group 60, Department of Justice Records, National Archives, CP.

96. John Lord O'Brian to John Burt, December 21, 1956, Box 1, John Lord O'Brian Papers, University of Buffalo.

97. Alfred Bettman, Memorandum, "Eugene V. Debs," February 10, 1919, File 77175A, Record Group 60, Department of Justice Records, National Archives, CP.

98. Edwin Wertz to Thomas Gregory, June 17, 1918, File 77175. Record Group 60, Department of Justice Records, National Archives, CP.

99. Clyde Miller, Review of Irving Stone's *Adversary in the House, Woman's Magazine*, September 28, 1947.

100. *Cleveland Press*, September 9, 1918; *Canton Repository*, July 1, 1918.

101. Job Harriman to Morris Hillquit, May 14, 1918, Microfilm, Reel 2, Papers of Morris Hillquit (Madison, WI: State Historical Society of Wisconsin, 1969.)

102. Morris Hillquit to Job Harriman, June 28, 1918, Microfilm, Reel 2, Hillquit Papers.

103. In passing this constitutional amendment, the emergency convention had been heavily influenced by the Socialist Party's left wing, which considered the state secretaries as being closer to the rank and file than the moderate leadership and thus more likely to actually implement a militant, antiwar resolution.

104. Eugene V. Debs, "Remarks," Minutes of the Conference of State Secretaries, Microfilm, Reel 7, Papers of Eugene V. Debs.

105. Ginger, *Bending Cross*, 364.

106. *Cleveland Press*, September 9, 1918.

107. Charles E. Clarke, *The Debs Case* (Los Angeles: Better America Federation of California, [1919]). Debs addressed the jury on September 11, 1918, and his speech lasted an hour and a half.

108. Eugene V. Debs, *Debs White Book* (Girard, KS: Appeal to Reason, 1919).

109. David Westenhaver, Charge to the Jury, *United States v. Eugene V. Debs*, Transcript of the Court Proceeding, 269–70, Microfilm, Reel 13, *American Civil Liberties Union Records* (Glen Rock, NJ: Microfilming Corporation of America, 1976).

110. Edwin Wertz, Address to the Jury, 20, Microfilm, Reel 13, American Civil Liberties Union Records; David Westenhaver, Charge to the Jury, 264, Microfilm, Reel 13, American Civil Liberties Union Records.

111. *Canton Repository*, September 14, 1918.

112. Adolph Germer to Morris Hillquit, October 23, 1918, Microfilm, Reel 2, Papers of Morris Hillquit.

113. Eugene Debs to Morris Hillquit, October 14, 1918, in J. Robert Constantine, *Letters of Eugene V. Debs* (Urbana: University of Illinois Press, 1990), 2:456.

114. William J. Burns to Joseph Tumulty, September 21, 1918, File 77175A, Straight Decimal Files, Records of the Department of Justice, Record Group 60, National Archives, CP.

115. Alfred Bettman to John Lord O'Brian, September 25, 1918, File 77175A, Records of the Department of Justice, Straight Decimal Files, Record Group 60, National Archives, CP.

116. Eugene Debs to Theodore Debs [October 1920], Constantine, *Letters of Eugene V. Debs,* 3:252.

117. Alexander Trachtenberg, ed., *The Heritage of Gene Debs* (New York: International Publishers, 1928), 56–57.

5. The Struggle to Free Eugene Victor Debs

1. David Westenhaver to A. Mitchell Palmer, March 21, 1919, File 77175-274, Straight Decimal Files, Records of the Department of Justice, Record Group 60, National Archives, College Park, Maryland. Thomas Gregory had resigned from his post as attorney general effective March 4, 1919. Palmer took over, initially as a recess appointment, the following day.

2. Alfred Bettman, Memorandum, March 25, 1914, File 77175-274, Straight Decimal Files, Records of the Department of Justice, Record Group 60, National Archives, CP.

3. *New York Times,* August 11, 1917.

4. Joseph Tumulty to Woodrow Wilson, March 24, 1919, in Arthur Link, ed., *Papers of Woodrow Wilson* (Princeton: Princeton University Press, 1987), 56:245.

5. Woodrow Wilson to Joseph Tumulty, March 26, 1919, *Papers of Woodrow Wilson,* 56:310.

6. Eugene Victor Debs, Statement, March 10, 1919, reprinted in Alexander Trachtenberg, ed., *The Heritage of Gene Debs* (New York: International Publishers, 1928), 56–57; Joseph Tumulty to Woodrow Wilson, April 4, 1919, *Papers of Woodrow Wilson,* 56:618.

7. Ernest Freeberg, *Democracy's Prisoner: Eugene V. Debs, The Great War and the Right to Dissent* (Cambridge, MA: Harvard University Press, 2008), 141–44.

8. David Karsner, *Debs: His Authorized Life and Letters from Woodstock Prison to Atlanta* (New York: Boni and Liveright, 1919), 68.

9. Freeberg, *Democracy's Prisoner,* 149–53.

10. Freeberg, *Democracy's Prisoner,* 149–51.

11. Freeberg, *Democracy's Prisoner,* 154, 172.

12. *Miami Valley Socialist,* September 26, 1919.

13. Eugene V. Debs, *Walls and Bars* (Chicago: Charles Kerr, 1927), 65, 72; Frederick Zerbst to A. Mitchell Palmer, August 13, 1919, Series 4, Case

#4963, Microfilm, Reel 376, *Woodrow Wilson Papers* (Washington, DC: Library of Congress, 1973).

14. Debs, *Walls and Bars*, 78; *Miami Valley Socialist*, September 26, 1919; Ray Ginger, *Bending Cross* (New Brunswick, NJ: Rutgers University Press, 1949), 392.

15. Debs, *Walls and Bars*, 79.

16. Markku Ruotsila, *John Spargo and American Socialism* (New York: Palgrave Macmillan, 2006), 84–85.

17. *New York Times*, June 2, 1917. The quote is from Spargo's statement of resignation from the Socialist Party, which the *Times* published in its entirety.

18. John Spargo to Harry Daugherty, March 29, 1921, John Spargo Papers, Correspondence Series, University of Vermont Special Collections, Burlington, VT. The next paragraph is derived from the same source.

19. *New York Times*, June 2, 1917; John Spargo to Woodrow Wilson, July 22, 1920 in Link, ed., *Papers of Woodrow Wilson* (Princeton: Princeton University Press, 1991), 65:541.

20. Clarence Darrow, *The Story of My Life* (New York: Charles Scribner's Sons, 1932), 61. In addition to defending Debs during the strike of railroad workers, Darrow had successfully defended Bill Haywood and two other leaders of the Western Federation of Miners for allegedly assassinating an ex-governor of Idaho. He had also led the unsuccessful defense of the McNamara brothers in the *Los Angeles Times* bombing case. Darrow would go on to represent John Thomas Scopes in the celebrated trial concerning the teaching of evolution.

21. *New York Times*, July 22, 1918; *New York Times*, September 16, 1917.

22. Darrow, *The Story of My Life*, 68–69; Clarence Darrow to Eugene Debs, July 20, 1918, J. Robert Constantine, ed., *Letters of Eugene V. Debs* (Urbana: University of Illinois Press, 1990), 2:434.

23. Clarence Darrow to A. Mitchell Palmer, September 27, 1919, File 77175–430, Records of the Department of Justice, Record Group 60, National Archives, CP.

24. Josephus Daniels, *The Wilson Years* (Chapel Hill: University of North Carolina Press, 1946), 3:365.

25. Clarence Darrow to Woodrow Wilson, July 29, 1919, in Link, ed., *Papers of Woodrow Wilson* (Princeton: Princeton University Press, 1990), 62:59.

26. Clarence Darrow to A. Mitchell Palmer, September 27, 1919, File 77175–430, Records of the Department of Justice, Record Group 60, National Archives, CP.

27. A. Mitchell Palmer to Woodrow Wilson, July 30, 1919, Series 4, Case #4896, Woodrow Wilson Papers, Library of Congress, in *Woodrow*

Wilson Papers, Microfilm, Reel 375; Woodrow Wilson to A. Mitchell Palmer, August 1, 1919, Series 4, Case #4896, Woodrow Wilson Papers, Library of Congress, in Microfilm, Reel 375.

28. John Hanna, Memorandum, Pardon Review, September 5, 1919, File 197009-1, Straight Decimal Files, Records of the Department of Justice, Record Group 60, National Archives, CP.

29. National League for the Release of Political Prisoners, Circular [June 1919], Microfilm, Reel 9, Socialist Party of America Papers, 1897-1963 (Glen Rock, NJ: Microfilming Corporation of America, 1975).

30. Circular [June 1919], Microfilm, Reel 9, Socialist Party of America Papers.

31. Blatch, Harriot Stanton. *Challenging Years* (New York: G. P. Putnam's Sons, 1940).

32. *New York Times*, September 10, 1917.

33. *New York Times,* November 16, 1918.

34. Lucy Fox Robins, *Tomorrow Is Beautiful* (New York: Macmillan, 1948), 16.

35. Richard H. Frost, *The Mooney Case* (Stanford, CA: Stanford University Press, 1968), 11-17.

36. *New York Times*, March 8, 1917.

37. Frost, *The Mooney Case*, 284-85.

38. Frost, *The Mooney Case*, 285; Robert Lansing to Woodrow Wilson, May 10, 1917, in Link, ed., *Papers of Woodrow Wilson* (Princeton: Princeton University Press, 1983), 42:272.

39. Woodrow Wilson to William Dennison Stephens, May 11, 1917, in Link, ed., *Papers of Woodrow Wilson*, 42:271; Frost, *The Mooney Case,* 286.

40. Melvyn Dubofsky, *The State and Labor in Modern America* (Chapel Hill, N.C.: University of North Carolina Press, 1994).

41. "President's Mediation Commission Report," in Link, ed., *Papers of Woodrow Wilson*, 42:73-74.

42. Joseph Tumulty to Woodrow Wilson, January 23, 1918, in Link, ed., *Papers of Woodrow Wilson* (Princeton: Princeton University Press, 1984), 46:84; Woodrow Wilson to Joseph Tumulty, January 23, 1918, in Link, ed., *Papers of Woodrow Wilson*, 46:84; Memorandum, White House Staff, January 23, 1918, January 23, 1918, in Link, ed., *Papers of Woodrow Wilson*, 46:84. Ray Stannard Baker, who had close ties to the Wilson administration, attributes this memorandum to Tumulty, who wrote it after consulting with Secretary of Labor Wilson. Ray Stannard Baker, *Woodrow Wilson: Life and Letters* (Garden City, NY: Doubleday, Page and Co.), 7:491.

43. Woodrow Wilson to William Dennison Stephens, January 22, 1918, in Link, ed., *Papers of Woodrow Wilson*, 46:74.

44. *New York Times*, April 23, 1918; A. Bruce Bielaski to John A. Moffett, April 23, 1918, File 16/510, Box 51, General Records of the Department of Labor, 1907–1942, Record Group 174, National Archives, CP. This is a memorandum from the chief of the Bureau of Intelligence to the head of the Labor Department's small intelligence unit warning of the coming one-day strike in support of Mooney.

45. Samuel Gompers to William B. Wilson, March 25, 1918, File 16/510, Box 51, General Records of the Department of Labor, 1907–1942, Record Group 174, National Archives, CP.

46. Gompers to Wilson, March 25, 1918, File 16/510, Box 51, Record Group 174.

47. William Wilson to Samuel Gompers, April 5, 1918, File 16/510, Box 51, General Records of the Department of Labor, 1907–1942, Record Group 174; Woodrow Wilson to William Dennison Stephens, March 27, 1918, in Link, ed., *Papers of Woodrow Wilson* (Princeton: Princeton University Press, 1984), 47:160; William Dennison Stephens to Woodrow Wilson, March 30, 1918, in Link, ed., *Papers of Woodrow Wilson*, 47:160; *New York Times*, April 23, 1918

48. *New York Times*, March 30, 1918.

49. *New York Times*, April 23, 1918. The *Times* printed the entire statement. The next paragraph comes from the same source.

50. Joseph Tumulty to Woodrow Wilson, April 1918, in Link, ed., *Papers of Woodrow Wilson*, 47: 397. Wilson wrote his agreement on this note.

51. *New York Times*, April 24, 1918.

52. *New York Times*, April 29, 1918.

53. Robins, *Tomorrow,* 127.

54. *New York Times*, May 29, 1918; *New York Times*, July 18, 1918.

55. Woodrow Wilson to Samuel Gompers, June 24, 1918, in Link, ed., *Papers of Woodrow Wilson* (Princeton: Princeton University Press, 1985), 48: 404.

56. *New York Times*, June 20, 1918.

57. Woodrow Wilson to Samuel Gompers, June 24, 1918, Box 1, Record Group 1–13, American Federation of Labor Papers, Office of the President, Samuel Gompers Copybooks, Hornbake Library, University of Maryland, College Park, MD.

58. *New York Times*, November 29, 1918.

59. *New York Times*, November 29, 1918; Thomas Mooney to Woodrow Wilson, December 1, 1918, in Link, ed., *Papers of Woodrow Wilson* (Princeton: Princeton University Press, 1986), 53:273.

60. Robins, *War Shadows,* 16.

61. Robins, *Tomorrow,* 130.

62. *Report of Proceedings of the Thirty-Ninth Annual Convention of the*

American Federation of Labor (Washington, DC: Law Reporter Printing, 1920), 392.

63. Robins, *Tomorrow*, 24.

64. *Proceedings of the Thirty-Ninth Annual Convention of the American Federation of* Labor, 392; Lucy Fox Robins, *War Shadows* (New York: Central Labor Bodies Conference for the Release of Political Prisoners, 1922), 29.

65. *Proceedings of the Thirty-Ninth Annual Convention of the American Federation of Labor*, 394.

66. *Proceedings of the Thirty-Ninth Annual Convention of the American Federation of Labor*, 394.

67. Dr. Bert E. Park, "Woodrow Wilson's Stroke," in Link, ed., *Papers of Woodrow Wilson* (Princeton: Princeton University Press, 1990), 63:639–41.

68. Kendrick A. Clements, *The Presidency of Woodrow Wilson* (Lawrence: University Press of Kansas, 1992), 198–99.

69. Josephus Daniels, Diary, August 10, 1920, in Link, ed., *Papers of Woodrow Wilson* (Princeton, NJ: Princeton University Press, 1992), 66:25.

70. Robins, *War Shadows*, 47.

71. Robins, *War Shadows*, 47.

72. Robins, *War Shadows*, 88; *New York Times*, February 27, 1920; *New York Times*, November 25, 1920.

73. Lucy Robins to William Green, March 5, 1920, reprinted in Robins, *War Shadows*, 59; *Report of Proceedings of the Forty-Second Annual Convention of the American Federation of Labor* (Washington, DC: Law Reporter Printing, 1922), 137. Green later became the president of the AFL in December 1924 after Gompers died.

74. Eugene Victor Debs to Lucy Robins, July 16, 1920, Constantine, ed., *Letters of Debs*, 3:110; *Socialist World*, August 1920.

75. *New York Times*, March 21, 1920.

76. Robins, *War Shadows*, 117.

77. *Washington Times*, April 14, 1920; *New York Tribune*, April 14, 1920.

78. *Report of Proceedings of the Fortieth Annual Convention of the American Federation of Labor* (Washington, DC: Law Reporter Printing, 1920), 269.

79. *Proceedings of the Fortieth Annual Convention of the American Federation of Labor*, 366.

80. *Proceedings of the Fortieth Annual Convention of the American Federation of Labor*, 269.

81. Mabel Dunlap Curry to Lucy Robins, July 5, 1920, Microfilm, Reel 3, Papers of Eugene Debs, 1834–1945 (Sanford, NC: Microfilming Corporation of America, 1982).

Curry worked in the Terre Haute, Indiana, office with Theodore Debs while his brother was in prison. Theodore sometimes suffered from "eye strain," probably mental and physical exhaustion, and Curry then acted in place of him in answering letters sent to the office, including the one from Robins.

82.	A. Mitchell Palmer to Joseph Tumulty, September 16, 1920, Link, ed., *Papers of Woodrow Wilson*, 66:120.

83.	Samuel Gompers to Woodrow Wilson, October 15, 1920, Link, ed., *Papers of Woodrow Wilson*, 66:231. Wilson read the letter but did not respond to it.

84.	*New York Call*, October 8, 1920.

85.	Lucy Robins to Eugene Victor Debs, October 19, 1920, Constantine, ed., *Letters of Debs*, 3:137. The quotes from the next paragraph come from the same source.

86.	Eugene Victor Debs to Lucy Robins, October 27, 1920, Constantine, ed., *Letters of Debs*, 3:143. The quotes from the next paragraph come from the same source.

87.	Samuel Gompers to Woodrow Wilson, December 1920, Link, ed., *Papers of Woodrow Wilson*, 66:515.

88.	*Christian Science Monitor*, September 21, 1920.

89.	Theodore Debs to Eugene Debs, October 20, 1920, Constantine, ed., *Letters of Debs*, 3:139; Eugene Debs to Mabel Curry [October 1920], Constantine, ed., *Letters of Debs*, 3:139.

90.	A. Mitchell Palmer, Memorandum, Link, ed., *Papers of Woodrow Wilson* (Princeton: Princeton University Press, 1992), 67:101–2. The next paragraph is derived from the same source. Palmer also summarized a letter from U.S. Attorney Edwin Wertz that again denounced Debs as a traitor and argued that he should remain in prison.

91.	Ginger, *Bending Cross*, 405; Joseph Patrick Tumulty, *Woodrow Wilson as I Knew Him* (Garden City, NY: Garden City Publishing, 1925), 505.

92.	*American Monthly*, March 1921.

93.	Theodore Debs to Hattie Norris, March 3, 1921, Constantine, ed., *Letters of Debs*, 3:190; *New York Times*, March 2, 1921.

94.	Eugene Debs to [Mabel Dunlap Curry], December 6, 1921, Constantine, ed., *Letters of Debs* 3:273.

95.	Ida Minerva Tarbell, Memorandum of Conversation, May 5, 1922, Link, ed., *Papers of Woodrow Wilson* (Princeton: Princeton University Press, 1993), 68:48.

96.	*New York Times*, March 18, 1921.

97.	Genevieve Bennett Clark to Theodore Debs, March 24, 1921, Constantine, ed., *Letters of Debs* 3:196.

98.	*Chicago Tribune*, March 19, 1921.

99. Ginger, *Bending Cross*, 408; Mark Sullivan, *Our Times, The United States, 1900-1925* (New York: Charles Scribner's Sons, 1935), 6:231.

100. *New York Times*, March 26, 1921.

101. *New York Times*, March 26, 1921; Harry M. Daugherty, and Thomas Dixon, *The Inside Story of the Harding Tragedy* (New York: Churchill, 1932), 118.

102. Theodore Debs to Roger Baldwin, January 20, 1922, Microfilm, Reel 4, Papers of Eugene Debs.

103. Eugene Debs to Otto Branstetter, March 28, 1921, Constantine, ed., *Letters of Debs*, 3:198.

104. *New York Times*, March 30, 1921.

105. Otto Branstetter to Eugene Debs, April 4, 1921, Constantine, ed., *Letters of Debs*, 3: 203-4. The next paragraph is from the same source.

106. Theodore Debs to Otto Branstetter, April 9, 1921, Constantine, ed., *Letters of Debs*, 3:210-11.

107. *New York Times*, April 13, 1921.

108. *New York Times*, March 26, 1921.

109. Theodore Debs to Warren Harding, April 9, 1921, Constantine, ed., *Letters of Debs*, 3:246.

110. *American Federationist* (Marc, 1921), 28:240. The convention was scheduled to meet on September 12, 1921.

111. Robins, *War Shadows*, 351-52.

112. Samuel Gompers, *Seventy Years of Life and Labor: An Autobiography* (New York: E. P. Dutton, 1925), 1:416.

113. Karsner, *Debs*, 60; *New York Times*, September 17, 1921.

114. Samuel Gompers to Harry Lang, October 13, 1921, in Peter J. Albert and Grace Palladino, eds., *The Samuel Gompers Papers* (Urbana: University of Illinois Press, 2008), 11:532.

115. Theodore Debs to Albert Todd, November 14, 1921, Microfilm, Reel 4, Papers of Eugene Debs.

116. Eugene Victor Debs to Theodore Debs [November 21, 1921], Constantine, ed., *Letters of Debs* 3:271. *Washington Herald*, November 15, 1921; *Washington Herald*, November 16, 1921.

117. *New York Times*, November 19, 1921.

118. *New York Times*, November 16, 1921.

119. The granting of pardons has been an important presidential power since George Washington. Andrew Johnson began the tradition of a Christmas list of pardons by issuing a pardon for every person convicted of treason for aiding the Confederacy on Christmas Day, December 25, 1868.

120. *New York Times*, November 23, 1921.

121. *New York Times*, November 23, 1921.

122. Lincoln Steffens to Will Hays, November 1, 1921, in Ella Winter and Granville Hicks, eds., *The Letters of Lincoln Steffens* (New York: Harcourt, Brace, 1938), 2:1042.

123. Lincoln Steffens to Allen Suggett, December 5, 1921, in Winter and Hicks, eds., *Letters*, 2:577.

124. Lincoln Steffens to Allen Suggett, December 16, 1921, in Winter and Hicks, eds., *Letters*, 2:580.

125. Harry Daugherty to Warren Harding, December 17, 1923, File 111, Executive Office Files, Warren Harding Papers, Ohio Historical Society, Columbus, Ohio, Microfilm, Reel 178.

126. Lincoln Steffens to Allen and Laura Suggett, December 20, 1921, in Winter and Hicks, eds., *Letters*, 2:581.

127. *New York Times*, December 21, 1921.

128. Eugene Debs to Theodore Debs, December 19, 1921, Constantine, ed., *Letters of Debs,* 3:276.

129. Eugene Debs to Kate Debs, December 25, 1921, Microfilm, Reel 4, Papers of Eugene Debs.

130. *Indianapolis Star,* December 26, 1921.

131. *New York Times*, December 26, 1921.

132. *Terre Haute Post*, December 26, 1921; *Washington Times*, December 26, 1921.

133. *New York Times*, December 27, 1921; *Indianapolis Star,* December 27, 1921. Debs's description of Harding, a smooth politician but hardly a refined gentleman, may have been intended as irony.

    Ginger (*Bending Cross*, 415) quotes Debs as describing Harding as "a kind gentleman" who "possesses humane impulses." Neither the reporter from the *New York Times* nor the *Indianapolis Star* noted any such statement from Debs. Ginger does not provide a citation for his doubtful quotes.

134. *New York Times*, December 27, 1921.

135. Theodore Debs to Roger Baldwin, January 20, 1922, Microfilm, Reel 4, Papers of Eugene Debs.

136. The *New York Times*, December 29, 1921.

137. Nick Salvatore, *Eugene V. Debs: Citizen and Socialist* (Urbana: University of Illinois Press, 1982), 331.

138. Debs to Baldwin, January 20, 1922, Microfilm, Reel 4, Papers of Eugene Debs.

139. *New York Times*, July 18, 1922.

140. *New York Times*, November 27, 1922.

141. Salvatore, *Debs*, 339.

142. Salvatore, *Debs*, 341.

6. Traitors, Spies, and Military Tribunals

1. William Wiseman to Mansfield Cumming, February 7, 1917, Box 4, Wiseman Papers, Yale University. Cumming was the first head of MI6, the original "C" of James Bond fame.

    Wiseman's report cannot be located in his own papers at Yale, or the British National Archives in Kew Gardens or the U.S. National Archives at College Park, Maryland. It would make interesting reading.

2. Wiseman to Cumming, February 7, 1917, Box 4, Wiseman Papers.

3. Charles Warren to Rufus Isaacs (Lord Reading), October 12, 1917, Reading Papers, British Library, London. Warren also pointed to two other items that he drafted in this context. These were the Trading with the Enemy Act and a presidential proclamation allowing for the detention of enemy aliens.

4. Charles Cook, ed., *Defence of the Realm Manual*, 6th ed. (London: HMSO, 1918), 126.

5. Albert Burleson to Woodrow Wilson, October 16, 1917, in Arthur S. Link, ed., *Papers of Woodrow Wilson* (Princeton: Princeton University Press, 1983), 44:390.

6. William Blackstone, *Commentaries on the Laws of England* (Oxford: Clarendon Press, 1765), 4: 82.

7. William Searle Holdsworth, *A History of English Law* (London: Methuen, [1925]), 8:307.

8. John Marshall, Opinion Sitting in the U.S. Circuit Court for Virginia, August 31, 1807, *U.S. v. Burr*, 25 Fed Cases 159–80.

9. Charles Warren to Thomas Gregory, August 6, 1917, File 190470. Straight Numerical Series, Papers of the Department of Justice, Record Group 60, National Archives, CP. .

10. Eric Thomas Chester, *The Wobblies in Their Heyday* (Santa Barbara, CA: Praeger, 2014), 161–62.

11. Warren, "What Is Giving Aid and Comfort to the Enemy," *Yale Law Journal* 27 (January 1918): 337.

12. Blackstone, *Commentaries*, 4: 151.

13. Indictment, Transcript of Record, *United States v. Debs*, 1918, Law Library, Library of Congress, 2.

14. Chief Justice Lord Reading in *Rex v. Casement* (1916), cited in Charles Warren, "What Is Giving Aid and Comfort to the Enemy," *Yale Law Journal* 27 (January 1918):3.

15. Jonathan Peter Spiro, *Defending the Master Race: Conservation, Eugenics, and the Legacy of Madison Grant* (Burlington: University of Vermont Press, 2009), 142–44, 162.

16. Charles Stewart Davison, "The Law of Treason," *New York Tribune*, August 17, 1917.

17. Charles Warren, "What Is Giving Aid and Comfort to the Enemy," *Yale Law Journal* 27 (January 1918): 341.

18. Thomas Gregory to Senator Morris Sheppard, February 25, 1918. File 9-19 (General), Classified Subject Files. Justice Department Records, Record Group 60, National Archives, CP.

19. Dozens of IWW leaders were tried and convicted of violating the Espionage Act in a mass trial held in Chicago in 1918. One set of charges was based on alleged acts of sabotage. In October 1920, the U.S. Circuit Court of Appeals reversed the convictions on these charges on the basis that the alleged acts of sabotage had occurred prior to the passage of the Espionage Act in June 1917. Chester, *Wobblies in Their Heyday*, 212.

20. Chester, *Wobblies in Their Heyday*, 146–49.

21. Gregory to Sheppard, February 25, 1918, File 9-19 (General), Classified Subject Files, Record Group 60, National Archives, CP.

22. Hans L. Trefusse, *Ben Butler: The South Called Him BEAST!* (New York: Twayne, 1957), 105, 114; D. H. Dilbeck, *A More Civil War: How the Union Waged a Just War* (Chapel Hill: University of North Carolina, Press, 2016), 41.

23. Charles Warren to George Chamberlain, April 12, 1918, Box 1, Charles Warren Papers, Library of Congress; Charles Warren to Warren Gard, April 22, 1918, Box 1, Warren Papers, Library of Congress. Gard was a Democrat and an influential member of the House Judiciary Committee.

24. Warren to Gard, April 22, 1918, Box 1, Warren Papers, Library of Congress.

25. 64th Congress, 1st Session, Report #130, December 11, 1918, 6, 10.

26. Zechariah Chafee, ed., *Fundamental Human Rights* (Cambridge, MA: Harvard University Press, 1951), 2: 328.

27. Proctor had worked as an assistant U.S. attorney for the District of Columbia from 1905 to 1913. becoming the chief assistant attorney in 1909. He then went into private practice and remained so through the First World War. He later became a federal district judge until he was confirmed as a member of the Circuit Court of Appeals for DC.

28. Samuel Klaus, ed., *The Milligan Case* (London: Routledge and Sons, 1929), 68–70; Kenneth Stampp, *Indiana Politics During the Civil War* (Indianapolis: Indiana Historical Bureau, 1949), 206–8.

29. Frank Ludwig Klement, "The Indianapolis Treason Trials and Ex Parte Milligan," in Michael R. Belknap, ed., *American Political Trials* (Westport, CT: Greenwood Press, 1981), 104.

30. Klement, "The Indianapolis Treason Trials," 107–8.

31. Klement, "The Indianapolis Treason Trials," 107–9.

32. Klement, "The Indianapolis Treason Trials," 107–9; Klaus, *The Milligan Case*, 30.

33. Abraham Lincoln, Proclamation, September 15, 1862, in Roy B Basler, ed., *The Collected Works of Abraham Lincoln* (New Brunswick, NJ: Rutgers University Press, 1953), 5:451; Lincoln, Message to Congress, July 4, 1861, in Basler, ed., *Collected Works*, 4:430.

34. In the March 3, 1863, statute authorizing the president to declare martial law in any part of the country, another section limited its application. The president was ordered to submit lists to federal district courts with the names of those being detained in that jurisdiction. If a grand jury sitting in that district did not indict the person detained, a federal judge in that district had the authority to release the person, once they signed a loyalty oath. Indiana had convened a grand jury but the grand jury had not indicted Milligan. Thus, the government had no right to continue to hold Milligan once the term of the grand jury had ended. Lincoln ignored this section of the statute. *Congressional Globe*, 37th Congress, 3rd Session, 755.

35. Ex Parte *Milligan*, 71 U.S. 2, 1866.

36. Ex Parte *Milligan*, 71 U.S. 2.

37. Ex Parte *Milligan*, 71 U.S. 2.

38. James Proctor, Memorandum to the Attorney General, April 14, 1917, File 190470 Box 2823 Department of Justice Records, Straight Numerical Series, Record Group 60, National Archives, CP.

39. *New York Times*, April 17, 1918.

40. Woodrow Wilson to Robert Latham Owen, February 1, 1918, in Link, ed., *Papers of Woodrow Wilson* (Princeton: Princeton University Press, 1984), 46:206. Owen's original letter is not in the Wilson Papers.

41. Wilson to Owen, February 1, 1918, in Link, ed., *Papers of Woodrow Wilson*, 46:206. Owen also proposed that "enemy aliens," that is, recent immigrants from either Germany or the Austrian-Hungarian Empire, be prosecuted by military tribunals if charged with treason. The president was unsure of his position on this issue and referred it to Gregory. Nothing more was heard of the matter, as the Department of Justice asserted its authority to prosecute civilians, even aliens, on criminal charges.

42. *New York Times*, April 17, 1918. The wording of Chamberlain's proposed legislation can also be found in Senate Committee on Military Affairs, Hearing, "Extending Jurisdiction of Military Tribunals," April 17, 1918, 65th Congress, 2nd Session.

43. Pub. L. 65-24.

44. Fisher, Louis. *Military Tribunals: Historical Patterns and Lessons* (Washington, D.C.: Congressional Research Service, 2004), 1–5.

45. Warren, "Spies and the Power of Congress," *American Law Review* 53 (March 1919): 206–7.

46. *Congressional Globe*, 37th Congress, 3rd Session, 755.

47. Abraham Lincoln, September 1863, Basler, ed., *Collected Works*, 6:451.

48. Thomas Allen, *Intelligence in the American Civil War* (New York: Nova Science, 2010), 67–71.

49. Abraham Lincoln, Memorandum, October 25, 1861, Roy B. Basler, ed., *The Collected Works of Abraham Lincoln* (New Brunswick, NJ: Rutgers University Press, 1953), 5:475.

50. The most renowned civilian Confederate spy was Rose O'Neal Greenbow. Operating within Washington, D.C., which had been placed under martial law, she was initially detained under house arrest. This was followed by five months in the local jail. While in prison, Greenbow was the subject of an administrative hearing. At no point was she a defendant in a trial, civilian or military. Greenbow was finally deported to the Confederacy. Edwin Fishel, *The Secret War for the Union: The Untold Story of Military Intelliegence in the Civil War* (Boston: Houghton Mifflin, 1996), 66–67.

51. Charles Warren, "Spies and the Power of Congress to Subject Certain Classes of Civilians to Trial by Military Tribunal," *American Law Review* 53 (March 1919): 201.

52. Loren Lee Cary, "The Wisconsin Loyalty Legion," *Wisconsin Magazine of History*, 53: 38.

53. In September 1917, a month after the meeting between Warren and Husting, the *Leader* lost its second-class mailing privilege, thus effectively excluding it from being circulated through the postal mail. The *Leader* still continued to publish, relying on its large subscriber base in the Milwaukee area. Sally M. Miller, *Victor Berger and the Promise of Constructive Socialism, 1910–1920* (Westport, CT: Greenwood Press, [1973]), 198.)

54. Sally Miller, *Victor Berger and the Promise of Constructive Socialism*, 180.

55. Wheeler Bloodgood, Testimony, April 17, 1918, Senate Committee on Military Affairs, Hearing, "Extending Jurisdiction of Military Tribunals," 65th Congress, 2nd Session.

56. Bloodgood, Testimony, April 17, 1918.

57. John Lord O'Brian, Oral History, Columbia University, 229–30, 234. Warren wrote the Trading with the Enemy Act as well as the Espionage Act.

58. Bloodgood, Testimony, April 17, 1918, "Extending Jurisdiction of Military Tribunals."

59. *New York Call*, March 2, 1918. The special election for Wisconsin's U.S.

Senate seat held in April 1918 was a three-way contest, with Irvine Lenroot, the Republican candidate, winning a plurality of votes. Berger received more than 25 percent of the vote, a very respectable result. He would go on to be elected to the U.S. House of Representatives from Wisconsin in the November 1918 election. Herbert F. Margulies, *Senator Lenroot of Wisconsin: A Political Biography, 1900-1929* (Columbia: University of Missouri Press, 1977), 247.

60. The five Socialist Party leaders were convicted of violating the Espionage Act in February 1919 and Berger received a twenty-year sentence. Ultimately, in January 1921 the U.S. Supreme Court overturned the convictions on the basis of the blatant bias evidenced by Judge Kenesaw Landis during the trial. Miller, *Victor Berger,* 189, 205, 212-13.

61. Bloodgood, Testimony, April 17, 1918, "Extending Jurisdiction of Military Tribunals."

62. Charles Warren to George Chamberlain, April 12, 1918, Box 1, Charles Warren Papers, Manuscripts, Library of Congress.

63. *Congressional Record,* 65th Congress, 2nd Session, April 5, 1918, 4645-46.

64. *Congressional Record,* 65th Congress, 2nd Session, April 5, 1918, 4646, 4648.

65. E. A. Schwartz, "The Lynching of Robert Prager, the United Mine Workers and the Problems of Patriotism in 1918," *Journal of the Illinois Historical Society* 95 (Winter 2000): 414-37.

66. *New York Times,* April 17, 1918.

67. *New York Times,* April 17, 1918.

68. *New York Times,* April 17, 1918.

69. Ralph Van Deman, Testimony, April 19, 1918, Senate Committee on Military Affairs, Hearing, "Extending Jurisdiction of Military Tribunals," 65th Congress, 2nd Session.

70. Alfred Bettman to John Lord O'Brian, Memorandum. July 11, 1918, File 186701-39, Straight Numerical Series, Department of Justice Records, Record Group 60, National Archives, CP. Bettman had looked at the MID files for Pittsburgh, but it is clear that his dismissal of the MID as an effective intelligence agency went beyond Pittsburgh. Bettman was so disdainful of the MID that he questioned "what value" there was "to the Government in using the time and energy of these investigators" for "the accumulation of this sort of matter."

71. *New York Times,* April 23, 1918; Roy Talbert Jr., *Negative Intelligence: The Army and the American Left, 1917-1941* (Jackson: University Press of Mississippi, 1991), 27. Warren testified in a closed session before the Senate Military Affairs Committee during the hearings on the Chamberlain bill. He was forced to resign shortly afterward.

72. Thomas Gregory to William Gordon, in *New York Times*, April 23, 1918. The article gives the letter in full, but does not supply its date. It was written sometime between April 19 and April 22, 1918.

73. Woodrow Wilson to Lee S. Overman, April 20, 1918, in *New York Times*, April 23, 1918.

7. The IWW and the Suspension of the Writ of Habeas Corpus

1. Abraham Lincoln to Winfield Scott, April 27, 1861, Roy B. Basler, ed., *The Collected Works of Abraham Lincoln* (New Brunswick, NJ: Rutgers University Press, 1953), 4:347; Lincoln to Scott, July 2, 1861, Basler. ed., *Lincoln*, 4: 419.

2. Dean Sprague, *Freedom Under Lincoln* (Cambridge, MA: Houghton Mifflin, 1965), 211–12. George Kane, the chief of police in Baltimore and a Confederate sympathizer, was detained from June 1861 until November 1862.

3. Louis Fisher, *Military Tribunals: Historical Patterns and Lessons* (Washington, D.C.: Congressional Research Service, 2004); Mark Neely, *Fate of Liberty: Abraham Lincoln and Civil Liberties* (New York: Oxford University Press, 1991), 34.

4. Lincoln, Proclamation, September 24, 1862, Basler, ed., *The Collected Works of Abraham Lincoln*, 4:437.

5. Gregory P. Downs, *After Appomattox: Military Occupation and the Ends of War* (Cambridge, MA: Harvard University Press, 2015), 172, 181.

6. Downs, *After Appomattox*, 184–85.

7. Willard L. King, *Lincoln's Manager: David Davis* (Cambridge, MA: Harvard University Press, 1960), 263.

8. Richard Aarstad, "Montana's Other Strike: The 1917 IWW Timber Strike in the Kootenai Valley," PhD diss. (University of Montana, 2000), 41; John Earl Haynes, "Revolt of the 'Timber Beasts': IWW Lumber Strike in Minnesota," *Minnesota History* 42 (Spring 1971): 166.

9. Robert L. Tyler, *Rebels of the Woods: The I. W. W. in the Pacific Northwest* (Eugene: University of Oregon Books, 1967), 89–91; Vernon H. Jensen, *Lumber and Labor* (New York: Farrar, Rinehart, 1945), 106–7.

10. Tyler, *Rebels*, 90; Haynes, "Revolt," 168–69; Benjamin G. Rader, "The Montana Lumber Strike of 1917," *Pacific Historical Review* 36 (May 1967): 189–207; Andrew Mason Prouty, *More Deadly Than War* (New York: Garland, 1985), 159.

11. Eric Thomas Chester, *The Wobblies in Their Heyday* (Santa Barbara, CA: Praeger, 2014), 122.

12. Aarstad, "Montana's Other Strike," 41.

13. James Rowan, Testimony, 25244, transcript of the IWW Chicago Conspiracy Trial. File 10110–120, Box 2745, Entry 65, Correspondence

of the Military Intelligence Division, Record Group 165, National Archives, College Park, MD.

14. *Industrial Worker*, July 7, 1917; *Industrial Worker*, July 14, 1917.

15. "Demands of the Lumber Workers," March 1917, in Eric Thomas Chester, *Yours for Industrial Freedom* (Amherst, MA: Levellers Press, 2017), 108–9; *Solidarity*, April 28, 1917; Rader, "Montana Lumber Strike," 193–94; Haynes, "Revolt," 169.

16. *Solidarity*, April 28, 1917.

17. Rowan, Testimony, Transcript of the IWW Chicago Conspiracy Trial.

18. "Demands," in Chester, *Yours for Industrial Freedom*, 108–9.

19. Jensen, *Lumber and Labor*, 101; Rader, "Montana Lumber Strike," 191.

20. *Solidarity*, April 28, 1917.

21. Aarstad, "Montana's Other Strike," 68; *Solidarity*, April 28, 1917.

22. Aarstad, "Montana's Other Strike," 73; Thomas Walsh to Samuel Stewart, April 17, 1917, Box 1, 191, Walsh Papers, Library of Congress; Thomas Walsh to Samuel Stewart, April 19, 1917, Box 1, 191, Walsh Papers; Abraham Glasser, Report, [1938], Record Group 60, Department of Justice Records, National Archives, College Park, MD; Don Sheridan, Testimony, 25150, transcript of the IWW Chicago Conspiracy Trial, Box 2744, File 10110–120, Record Group 165, Correspondence of the Military Intelligence Division, National Archives, CP; Chester, *Wobblies*, 143–44.

Walsh was an influential senator, so Governor Stewart went through him to quickly reach Baker and the president. In the April 17, 1917, letter, Walsh is paraphrasing an earlier letter from Stewart that is not in Walsh's files.

Although most of the military units included in the Central Department were in the Midwest, Fort Missoula, Montana, was also in its jurisdiction. Fort Missoula was the closest army post to the Fortine River where the first strikes of the lumberjacks were taking place. Later, as the strike spread into Idaho and Washington, troops were sent to strike zones from military bases under control of the Western Command in San Francisco.

23. Samuel Stewart to Thomas Walsh, April 21, 1917, Box 1, 191, Walsh Papers.

24. Jack Metcalfe, Testimony, Transcript of the Chicago Conspiracy Trial, 12960, File 10110–120. Entry 65.

25. *Industrial Worker*, July 14, 1917.

26. *Solidarity*, June 30, 1917.

27. *Industrial Worker*, June 2, 1917.

28. T. H. MacDonald to Thomas Gregory, August 21, 1917, Box 1, 191. Walsh Papers.

29. Wade R. Parks to Thomas Gregory, August 29, 1917, File 186701–27, Records of the Justice Department, Record Group 60, National Archives, CP. The next paragraph relies on the same source. The underlined words in the next paragraph were underlined in the original report.

30. *Daily Missoulian,* April 26, 1917.

31. *Industrial Worker,* June 23, 1917; *Fallon County Times,* May 10, 1917.

32. *Fallon County Times,* May 10, 1917; *Industrial Worker,* June 23, 1917.

33. *Fallon County Times,* May 10, 1917.

34. *Solidarity,* May 19, 1917.

35. Chester, ed., *Yours for Industrial Freedom,* 241n5.

36. Don Sheridan to Joseph Ratti, April 23, 1917, in Chester, *Yours for Industrial Freedom,* 164.

37. *Solidarity,* June 16, 1917.

38. *Industrial Worker,* June 23, 1917.

39. Rowan, Testimony, 25307, Transcript of the IWW Chicago Conspiracy Trial, File 10110–120, Correspondence of the Military Intelligence Division, National Archives, CP; *Solidarity,* July 7, 1917. The cited issue of *Solidarity* includes a strike bulletin from Rowan in which he mentions that Hegge had just been released after being held for fifty-eight days by the military.

40. Hugh T. Lovin, "Moses Alexander and the Idaho Lumber Strike of 1917: The Wartime Ordeal of a Progressive," *Pacific Northwest Quarterly* 66 (July 1975): 116.

41. *Solidarity,* May 16, 1917.

42. Lovin, "Moses Alexander and the Idaho Lumber Strike of 1917," 120, 122.

43. Rowan, Testimony, 25292, Transcript of the IWW Chicago Conspiracy Trial, File 10110–120, Box 2745; Hugh T. Lovin, "Moses Alexander and the Idaho Lumber Strike of 1917," 116.

44. *Solidarity,* August 11, 1917; *Tacoma Times,* July 19, 1917; Clay Allen to Thomas Gregory, July 30, 1917, File 186701–49, Straight Numerical Series, Record Group 60, Department of Justice Records, National Archives, CP.

45. Rowan, Testimony, 25385, 25387. Some of the strike bulletins were printed in *Solidarity.*

46. *Seattle Star,* July 10, 1917. March was not a conservative craft unionist of the Gompers persuasion. On the contrary, he supported the formation of industrial unions as well as progressive candidates standing for office in Washington.

47. Francis Garrecht to Thomas Gregory, July 14, 1917, File 186701–49, Straight Numerical Series, Record Group 60, Department of Justice

Records, National Archives, CP. The next paragraph is derived from the same source.

48. *Tacoma Times*, July 7, 1917. The next paragraph is derived from the same source. For a discussion of the question of German funding of the IWW, see Chester, *Wobblies In Their Heyday*, 146–49.

49. *Lynden Tribune*, July 26, 1917.

50. *Tacoma Times*, July 20, 1917; *Solidarity*, August 23, 1917. The Ellensburg detainee was only identified as "FW Hayes."

51. *Solidarity*, July 28, 1917; *Solidarity*, August 23, 1917; Rowan, Testimony, 25283.
    North Yakima was renamed Yakima in 1918.

52. George Vanderveer to Ernest Lister, August 14, 1917, Transcript of the IWW Chicago Conspiracy Trial; *Seattle Times*, August 17, 1917. The last group of strikers to be freed in North Yakima were released on September 8, 1917. *Industrial Worker*, September 15, 1917.

53. Rowan, Testimony, 25429, Transcript of the IWW Chicago Conspiracy Trial.

54. Rowan, Testimony, 25395, Transcript of the IWW Chicago Conspiracy Trial; *Seattle Times*, August 15, 1917; *New York Times*, August 16, 1917.

55. Chester, *Wobblies in Their Heyday*, 144, 153.

56. *New York Times*, August 17, 1917.

57. *Spokane Daily Chronicle*, August 21, 1917; *Spokane Spokesman-Review*, August 20, 1917.

58. *New York Times*, August 20, 1917.

59. Newton Baker to Woodrow Wilson, October 9, 1917, in Arthur Link, ed., *The Papers of Woodrow Wilson* (Princeton: Princeton University Press, 1983), 44:344. This letter includes the cable from Nowaka to Wilson from August 21, 1917.

60. *Spokane Daily Chronicle*, August 21, 1917.

61. *Spokane Spokesman-Review*, August 20, 1917.

62. *Spokane Daily Chronicle*, August 21, 1917.

63. Baker to Wilson, October 9, 1917, in Link, ed., *Papers of Woodrow Wilson*, 44:344.

64. Henry Middleton White and Edgar Callender Snyder, August 21, 1917, in Link, ed., *Papers of Woodrow Wilson*, 44:50. White had been an attorney based in Bellingham, Washington, and Snyder had been a journalist with the *Omaha Bee*.

65. Tyler, *Rebels*, 134.

66. Chester, *Wobblies in Their Heyday*, 223.

67. *Spokane Daily Chronicle*, August 22, 1917; *New York Times*, August 22, 1917.

68. Jensen, *Lumber and Labor*, 128.

69. Jensen, *Lumber and Labor,* 129.

70. Tyler, *Rebels,* 102–6.

71. Tyler, *Rebels,* 114.

72. Jensen, *Lumber and Labor,* 143; Tyler, *Rebels,* 202–3; Chester, *Heyday,* 223–24.

73. Aarstad, "Montana's Other Strike," 134.

74. Lt. Col. C. V. Thomas, Jr., Report enclosed with Baker to Wilson, October 9, 1917, in Link, ed., *Papers of Woodrow Wilson,* 44:345.

75. ᴶᵃᵐᵉˢ Proctor, Memorandum to the Attorney General, April 14, 1917, File 190470, Box 2823, Straight Numerical Series, Department of Justice Records, Record Group 60, National Archives, CP.

76. Proctor, Memorandum, April 1917, File 190470, Record Group 60, National Archives, CP.

77. Memorandum, "Proposed Federal Program," Box 1, Simon Lubin Papers, Bancroft Library, University of California, Berkeley, cited in Chester, *Wobblies in Their Heyday,* p. 153; Simon Lubin to Woodrow Wilson, March 29, 1918, in Link, ed., *Papers of Woodrow Wilson,* 47: 197.

78. Chester, *Wobblies in Their Heyday,* 156.

79. Greg Hall, *Harvest Wobblies: The Industrial Workers of the World and Agricultural Laborers in the American West* (Corvallis: Oregon State University Press, 2001), 129–30.

8. Herbert Croly, *The New Republic,* and the "Clear and Present Danger" Doctrine

1.   David W. Levy, *Herbert Croly of The New Republic: The Life and Thought of an American Progressive* (Princeton: Princeton University Press, 1985), 13, 42; Charles Forcey, *The Crossroads of Liberalism: Croly, Weyl, Lippmann and the Progressive Era, 1900–1925* (New York: Oxford University Press, 1961), 13–18.

2.   Levy, *Croly,* 84; Forcey, *The Crossroads of Liberalism,* 22.

3.   Forcey, *The Crossroads of Liberalism,* 124–25.

4.   Herbert David Croly, *The Promise of American Life* (New York: Macmillan, 1909), 115.

5.   Croly, *Promise,* 255, 259.

6.   Croly, *Promise,* 93–94.

7.   Levy, *Croly,* 79; Gerald Gunther, *Learned Hand: The Man and the Judge* (New York: Alfred A. Knopf, 1994), 208–10.

8.   Gunther, *Hand,* 188; David G. Dalin, *Jewish Justices of the Supreme Court: From Brandeis to Kagan* (Waltham, MA: Brandeis University Press, 2017), 120.

9.   Valentine served as the head of the Bureau of Indian Affairs in the Taft administration.

10. Gunther, *Hand*, 620; Forcey, *The Crossroads of Liberalism*, 182; Dalin, *Eight Jewish Justices*, 121.

11. Ronald Steel, *Walter Lippmann and the American Century* (Boston: Little, Brown, 1980), 13, 26, 41–42.

12. Steel, *Lippmann*, 46.

13. Brad Snyder, *The House of Truth: A Washington Political Salon and the Foundations of American Liberalism* (New York: Oxford University Press, 2017), 87–89.

14. Allon Gael, *Brandeis of Boston* (Cambridge, MA: Harvard University Press), 142–43.

15. Snyder, *House*, 125; Melvin I. Urofsky and David Levy, eds., *Letters of Louis D. Brandeis* (Albany: State University of New York Press, 1971–78), 4:119, 141.

16. Snyder, *House*, 22.

17. Arthur S. Link, ed., *Wilson: The Road to the White House* (Princeton: Princeton University Press, 1947), 468.

18. Nick Salvatore, *Eugene V. Debs: Citizen and Socialist* (Urbana: University of Illinois Press, 1982), 263–64.

19. Levy, *Croly*, 156; Steel, *Lippman*, 65.

20. *New York Times*, February 25, 1904. William Whitney left 30 percent of his estate to his daughter Dorothy and a 50 percent share to his son, Harry. Harry Whitney's inheritance was estimated at twelve million dollars, so Dorothy Straight's share of the Whitney fortune came to seven million dollars.

21. Herbert David Croly, *Willard Straight* (New York: Macmillan, 1924), 410.

22. Levy, *Croly*, 207.

23. Herbert Croly, "The Two Parties in 1916," *The New Republic* 8 (October 14, 1916): 286, 289.

24. Walter Lippmann, "The Case for Wilson," *The New Republic* 8 (October 14, 1916): 264.

25. Levy, *Croly*, 245.

26. Herbert Croly to Edward House, December 29, 1916, in Arthur S. Link, ed., *Papers of Woodrow Wilson* (Princeton: Princeton University Press, 1982), 40:360; Woodrow Wilson, Speech to the Senate, January 22, 1917, in Link, ed., *Papers of Woodrow Wilson*, 40:536; Edward House to Woodrow Wilson, January 22, 1917, in Link, ed., *Papers of Woodrow Wilson*, 40:539.

27. Michael E. Parrish, *Felix Frankfurter and His Times: The Reform Years* (New York: Free Press, 1982), 80.

28. Levy, *Croly*, 246.

29. Walter Lippmann to Woodrow Wilson, April 3, 1917, in Link, ed., *Papers of Woodrow Wilson* 41:538.

30. Lillian Wald, Jane Addams, Benjamin Lindsay, Paul Kellogg, and Herbert Croly, Open Letter, April 16, 1917, in Link, ed., *Papers of Woodrow Wilson*, 42:119.

31. Woodrow Wilson to Lillian Wald, April 28, 1917, in Link, ed., *Papers of Woodrow Wilson*, 42:119. Wilson's letter was printed in the *New York Times* on May 6, 1917.

32. Levy, *Croly*, 251.

33. "Editorial Notes," *The New Republic* 12 (September 15, 1917): 177.

34. "Editorial Notes," *The New Republic* 16 (August 24, 1918): 88.

35. Richard Burket Kielbowicz, *A History of Mail Classification and Its Underlying Policies and Purposes* (Seattle: United States Postal Rate Commission, 1995), 6, 44.

36. *New York Times*, October 15, 1917. On October 8, the *New York Call* was told by the post office to appear for a hearing on the following day. The hearing was postponed until October 15 and the *Call* had its second-class mailing privilege revoked on or about November 13, 1917. Link, ed., *Papers of Woodrow Wilson*, 43:429.

37. Forcey, *The Crossroads of Liberalism*, 20.

38. John Dewey, "Conscription of Thought," *The New Republic* 12 (September 1, 1917): 128.

39. Dewey, "Conscription," *The New Republic* 12 (September 1, 1917): 129–30.

40. John Dewey, "In Explanation of Our Lapse," *The New Republic* 13 (November 3, 1917): 17.

41. Walter Lippmann to Woodrow Wilson, October 8, 1917, in Link, ed., *Papers of Woodrow Wilson* (Princeton: Princeton University Press, 1983), 44:333–34. The next two paragraphs are from the same source.

42. Woodrow Wilson to William Redfield Cox, October 29, 1917, in Link, ed., *Papers of Woodrow Wilson*, 44:464.

43. Herbert Croly to Woodrow Wilson, October 19, 1917, in Link, ed., *Papers of Woodrow Wilson*, 44:408. The next three paragraphs are from the same source.

44. William Hard, "The New York Mayoralty Campaign," *The New Republic* 12 (October 6, 1917): 270.

45. Morris Hillquit, Letter, *The New Republic* 12 (October 13, 1917): 302.

46. Gilbert Roe et al., Letter, "Mr. Hillquit for Mayor," *The New Republic* 12 (October 27, 1917): 356. Among those signing the letter were Gilbert Roe, Senator La Follette's closest confidant and legal advisor. In the fall of 1917, La Follette was an outspoken critic of the administration and its most prominent opponent.

47. Roe et al., 12 *The New Republic* (October 27, 1917): 357.

48. "Editorial Notes," *The New Republic* 13 (November 3, 1917): 3.

49. "Editorial Notes," *The New Republic* 13 (November 3, 1917): 3.

50. Morris Hillquit, *Loose Leaves of a Busy Life* (New York, NY: Macmillan, 1934), 205–6.

51. "Editorial Notes," *The New Republic* 13 (November 10, 1917): 31.

52. Horace Cornelius Peterson and Gilbert Courtland Fite, *Opponents of War, 1917–1918* (Madison: University of Wisconsin Press, 1957), 164–65.

53. "Ending the Socialist Schism," *The New Republic* 15 (May 11, 1918): 34. The following paragraph is taken from the same source.

54. William L. O'Neill, *The Last Romantic: A Life of Max Eastman* (New York: Oxford University Press, 1978), 65, 75. The second trial ended in a hung jury.

55. "Editorial Notes," *The New Republic* 15 (May 4, 1918): 3.

56. "Editorial Notes," *The New Republic* 15 (May 25, 1918): 98.

57. Sedition Act, May 16, 1918, *Congressional Record*, 65th Congress, 2nd Session, 553.

58. "Editorial Notes," *The New Republic* 15 (May 18, 1918): 66.

59. "Editorial Notes," *The New Republic* 15 (May 18, 1918): 66.

60. Isaac Kramnick and Barry Sheerman, *Harold Laski: A Life on the Left* (London: Allen Lane, The Penguin Press, 1993), 86–88.

61. Kramnick and Sheerman, *Laski*, 88–89, 94.

62. Kramnick and Sheerman, *Laski*, 88; Zechariah Chaffe Jr., "Freedom of Speech in Wartime," *Harvard Law Review* 32 (June 1919): 932.

9. Zechariah Chafee Jr. and the "Balancing of Conflicting Interests" Doctrine

1. Edward D. Re, "Biography," in Re, ed., *Freedom's Prophet: Selected Writings of Zechariah Chafee, Jr.* (New York: Oceana, 1981).

    John Lippitt arrived in Providence in 1638, two years after Roger Williams founded the new colony to escape the oppressive theocracy of the Puritans who ruled Boston. Chafee settled in Rhode Island shortly afterward. Christopher Lippitt served as an officer in the Revolutionary Army during the revolt that ended British rule of the American colonies. In 1809 Lippitt built one of the first textile mills in Rhode Island. By the end of the nineteenth century, the Lippitt Woolen Company had grown to become one of the largest producers of cloth in New England and the Lippitts had become extremely wealthy. With this financial backing, the members of the Chafee/Lippitt family became a political dynasty, winning elections for governor and to Congress.

2. Norman Dorsen, "Zechariah Chafee, Jr.," *American National Biography* (New York: Oxford University Press, 1999), 4:618.

3. Re, *Freedom's Prophet*; Donald L. Smith, *Zechariah Chafee, Jr.: Defender of Liberty and Law* (Cambridge, MA: Harvard University Press, 1986), 17, 74.

4.   Zechariah Chafee, Jr., *Thirty-Five Years with Freedom of Speech* (New York: Roger Baldwin Civil Liberties Foundation, 1954), 3.

5.   Sedition Act, May 16, 1918, *Congressional Record*, 65th Congress, 2nd Session, 553; Zechariah Chafee, Jr., "Freedom of Speech," *The New Republic* 17 (November 16, 1918): 69.

6.   Chafee, "Freedom of Speech," 67.

7.   Chafee, "Freedom of Speech," 67-68.

8.   Chafee, "Freedom of Speech," 69.

9.   Zehariah Chafee, Jr., "Freedom of Speech in Wartime," *Harvard Law Review* 32 (June 1919): 937.

10. Chafee, "Freedom of Speech in Wartime," 937.

11. Chafee, "Freedom of Speech in Wartime," 955.

12. Chafee, "Freedom of Speech," *The New Republic,* 68.

13. William Blackstone, *Commentaries on the Laws of England* (Oxford: Clarendon Press, 1765), 4:151.

14. Thomas Jefferson, "A Bill for Establishing Religious Freedom," in Julian P. Boyd, ed., *The Papers of Thomas Jefferson* (Princeton: Princeton University Press, 1950), 6:546; Chafee, "Freedom of Speech in Wartime," 954. Jefferson wrote the proposed legislation guaranteeing religious freedom in 1779, but it was only enacted into law in 1786.

15. Chafee, "Freedom of Speech in Wartime," 960, 967-69.

16. Chafee, "Freedom of Speech in Wartime," 968.

17. Chafee, "Freedom of Speech in Wartime," 972-73.

18. Zechariah Chafee, Jr., *Free Speech in the United States* (Cambridge, MA: Harvard University Press, 1941), xi-xii.

19. Zechariah Chafee, Jr., *Freedom of Speech* (New York: Harcourt, Brace and Howe, 1920), 2. Although the two books overlap in topics covered, they substantially differ in their content and should be treated as two separate and distinct works.

20. Chafee, *Free Speech* (1941), 228.

21. Eric Thomas Chester, *The Wobblies in Their Heyday* (Amherst, MA: Levellers Press, 2016), 162.

22. Chafee, *Freedom of Speech* (1920), 163.

23. Alexander Sidney Lanier, "To the President," *The New Republic* 18 (April 19, 1919): 383-84.

24. American Civil Liberties Union, *The Truth About the IWW Prisoners* (New York: ACLU, 1922), 29.

25. Chafee, *Free Speech* (1941), 133.

26. Chafee, *Freedom of Speech* (1920), 90.

27. Chafee, *Free Speech* (1941), 84.

28. Chafee, *Freedom of Speech* (1920), 88.

29. Chafee, *Freedom of Speech* (1920), 319-20.

30. Sally M. Miller, *Victor Berger and the Promise of Constructive Socialism, 1910–1920* (Westport, CT: Greenwood Press, [1973]), 180.

31. *Milwaukee Journal,* March 16, 1918; *Milwaukee Journal,* March 16, 1918.

32. In September 1918, Berger and four other Socialist Party leaders were tried for allegedly violating the Espionage Act. All five of the defendants were convicted and Berger received a twenty-year jail sentence. The verdict was reversed by the U. S. Supreme Court in January 1921. Miller, *Victor Berger and the Promise of Constructive Socialism,* 189, 205, 213; Chafee, *Freedom of Speech* (1920), 318–19; *New York Times,* February 1, 1921.

33. Chafee, *Free Speech* (1941), 25.

34. Chafee, *Freedom of Speech* (1920), 38.

35. Chafee, *Freedom of Speech* (1920), 8; Chafee, *Free Speech* (1940), 106.

36. Chafee, *Freedom of Speech* (1920), 48.

37. Chafee, *Freedom of Speech* (1920), 41, 106.

38. Chafee, *Freedom of Speech* (1920), 120, 124.

39. Chafee, *Freedom of Speech* (1920), 159.

40. Chafee, *Freedom of Speech* (1920), 117.

41. Chafee, *Freedom of Speech* (1920), 3.

42. Chafee, *Freedom of Speech* (1920), 46.

43. Chester, *Wobblies,* 153–56.

44. Chafee, *Freedom of Speech* (1920), 41.

45. Chafee, *Freedom of Speech* (1920), 169, 88–89.

46. Chafee, *Free Speech* (1941), 36.

47. Chafee, *Freedom of Speech* (1920), 47, 173.

10. The "Clear and Present Danger" Doctrine in Historical Context

1. Oliver Wendell Holmes Jr. to Frederick Pollock, April 5, 1919, in Mark De Wolfe, ed., *Holmes-Pollock Letters: The Correspondence of Mr. Justice Holmes and Sir Frederick Pollock, 1874–1932* (Cambridge, MA: Harvard University Press, 1941), 2:7.

2. The *Schenck* case was heard on January 8, 1919, and the ruling was issued March 3, 1919. The *Debs* case was heard on January 27, 1919, and the ruling was issued on March 10, 1919.

3. *Schenck v. United States,* 249 US 47 (1919).

4. Report, Frank Garbarino, March 14, 1918, File 10101-200. Record Group 165, Correspondence of the Military Intelligence Division, National Archives, College Park, Maryland. Garbarino was in charge of the Bureau of Intelligence's Philadelphia office. During the First World War, the U.S. Army's Military Intelligence Division served as a clearinghouse for intelligence reports.

5. Robert M. La Follette Sr., Speech, April 27, 1917, *Congressional Record*, 65th Congress, 1st Session, 1358. The Senate leadership only permitted La Follette to begin his speech at 11:30 p.m., so virtually no one heard it. The speech lasted more than two hours. Belle Case and Lola La Follette, *Robert M. La Follette* (New York: Macmillan, 1953), 2:733.

6. *Arver v. United States*, 245 US 358 (1918).

7. *Keegan v. United States*, 325 US 493-94 (1945).

8. Oliver Wendell Holmes Jr. to Harold Laski, April 20, 1919, in Howe, ed., *Holmes-Laski Letters*, 1:197.

9. "Editorial Notes," *The New Republic* 16 (September 21, 1918): 210.

10. "Editorial Notes, *The New Republic* 18 (April 19, 1919): 362.

11. Oliver Wendell Holmes Jr. to Herbert Croly, April 20, 1919, in Howe, ed., *Holmes-Laski Letters*, 1:197.

12. Oliver Wendell Holmes Jr. to Lewis Einstein, April 5, 1919, in James Bishop Peabody, ed., *The Holmes-Einstein Letters, Correspondence of Mr. Justice Homes and Lewis Einstein, 1903–1935* (New York: Macmillan, 1964), 184.

13. Ernst Freund, "The Debs Case and Freedom of Speech," *The New Republic* 19 (May 3, 1919): 14.

14. Edwin Wertz, Transcript of the Debs Trial, 1918, *United States v. Eugene V. Debs*, 249, Law Library, Library of Congress.

15. *Schenck v. United States*, 249 US 47.

16. Michael Wendland, "The Calumet Tragedy," *American Heritage* 37 (April 1986): 39-48.

17. Freund, "The Debs Case," *The New Republic*, 19: 14.

18. Alfred Bettman, Memorandum, "Eugene V. Debs," February 10, 1919, File 77175A, Record Group 60, Department of Justice Records, National Archives, CP.

19. *National Civil Liberties Bureau, War-Time Prosecutions and Mob Violence Involving Free Speech, Free Press and Peaceful Assemblage* (New York: National Civil Liberties Bureau, 1919), 21. The case was *Baltzer v. US*, 248 US 593 (1918).

20. Sheldon M. Novick, "The Unrevised Holmes and Freedom of Expression," *Supreme Court Review* (1991), 389.

21. Novick, "The Unrevised Holmes," *Supreme Court Review* (1991), 332-33.

22. Oliver Wendell Holmes Jr. to Harold Laski, June 21, 1920, in Howe, ed., *Holmes-Laski Letters*, 2:45.

23. Oliver Wendell Holmes Jr. to Frederick Pollock, December 17, 1920, in Howe ed., *Holmes-Pollock Letters*, 1:297; Holmes to Pollock, June 21, 1920, in Howe, ed., *Holmes-Pollock Letters*, 2:45.

24. Louis Brandeis to Susan Goldmark, December 7, 1919, in Melvin I.

Urofsky and David Levy, eds., *Letters of Louis D. Brandeis* (Albany: State University of New York Press, 1975), 4:441.

25. *Abrams v. United States,* 250 US 629 (1919). The Abrams case was heard on October 21, 1919, and the ruling, including Holmes's dissent, was issued on November 10, 1919.

26. *Abrams v. United States,* 250 US 630.

27. *Abrams v. United States,* 250 US 630.

28. *Gitlow v. United States,* 268 US 671.

29. Alfred Bettman to John Lord O'Brian, Memorandum, May 9, 1918, File 9-19 (General), Classified Subject Files, Record Group 60, Records of the Department of Justice, National Archives, CP.

That same day, a circular letter under Attorney General Thomas Gregory's name was sent to all U.S. attorneys ordering them to administer the Sedition Act "with considerable discretion." Thomas Gregory, Circular Letter, May 9, 1918, File 9-19 (General), Classified Subject Files, Record Group 60, Records of the Department of Justice, National Archives, CP.

11. Free Speech as an Absolute Right

1. *Schaefer v. United States* 251 US 483 (1920). Brandeis in his opinion in the landmark Whitney case argued that although free speech rights are "fundamental," nevertheless these rights "are not, in their nature, absolute." *Whitney v. United States,* 274 US 373 (1927).

2. Holmes told Chafee during their brief meeting that he was "inclined to allow a very wide latitude to Congressional discretion" during wartime. G. Edward White, *Justice Oliver Wendell Holmes: Law and Inner Self* (New York: Oxford University Press, 1993), 428. Holmes's willingness to uphold Debs's conviction, despite his own personal misgivings, indicates Holmes's willingness to give Justice Department prosecutors a wide latitude as well.

3. *Schaefer v. United States,* 251 US 495.

4. Zechariah Chafee, Jr., *Freedom of Speech* (New York: Harcourt, Brace and Howe, 1920), 38.

5. *Abrams v. United States,* 250 US 630-31; *Whitney v. California* (1927), 274 US 377; *Gilbert v. Minnesota* (1921), 254 US 338.

6. Zechariah Chafee, Jr., "Freedom of Speech in Wartime," *Harvard Law Review* 32 (June 1919) 972.

7. Chafee, *Freedom of Speech,* 36.

8. *Lochner v. New York,* 198 US 53 (1905).

9. *Lochner v. New York,* 56-57.

10. *Lochner v. New York,* 75-76

11. *Lochner v. New York,* 75.
12. *Gilbert v. Minnesota,* 254 US, 337, 343.
13. *Schaefer v. United States* (1920), 251 US 486.
14. Melvin I. Urofsky, *Louis D. Brandeis: A Life* (New York: Pantheon, 2009), 563.
15. Urofsky, *Brandeis,* 563.
16. In the landmark case *Gitlow v. New York,* the majority opinion rendered by Justice Edward Terry Sanford held that "we may and do assume that freedom of speech and of the press" are "among the fundamental rights and 'liberties' protected by the due process clause of the Fourteenth Amendment." 268 US 666.

    In his dissent, Holmes wrote that the "general principle of free speech" must "be taken to be included in the Fourteenth Amendment." 268 US 672.

    Thus Brandeis's lone dissent in the Gilbert case had become the accepted interpretation held by the entire court in five years.
17. Chafee, "Freedom of Speech in Wartime," 960.
18. Thomas Jefferson, "A Bill for Establishing Religious Freedom," in Julian G. Boyd, *The Papers of Thomas Jefferson* (Princeton: Princeton University Press, 1950), 546.
19. Chafee, *Freedom of Speech* (1920), 36
20. Eugene Victor Debs, *Debs White Book* (Girard, KS: Appeal to Reason, [1919]), 55-56.
21. *Whitney v. California* (1927), 274 US 376; Chafee, *Freedom of Speech* (1920), 158.
22. Louis Brandeis, Opinion, *Whitney v. California* (1927), 274 US 373; Oliver Wendell Holmes Jr. to Herbert Croly, May 12, 1919, enclosed in Holmes to Harold Laski, May 13, 1919, in Mark deWolfe Howe, ed., *Holmes-Laski Letters: The Correspondence of Mr. Justice Holmes and Harold J. Laski, 1916-1935* (Cambridge, MA: Harvard University Press, 1953), 1:203-4.

    Holmes wrote the letter to Croly and then decided not to send it. Instead, he enclosed it in a letter written to Laski the following day.
23. *Brandenburg v. Ohio* (1969), per curiam, 395 US 447.
24. Eldridge Foster Dowell, *A History of Criminal Syndicalism Legislation in the United States* (Baltimore: Johns Hopkins University, 1939).
25. *Brandenburg v. Ohio* (1969), per curiam, 395 US 447.
26. William O. Douglas, Concurring opinion, 395 US 447, 449, 452, 454.

12. Conclusion

1. *Schaeffer v. United States,* 251 US 477 (1920).

GLOSSARY

Profiles

Baldwin, Roger Nash (1884–1981): Graduated from Harvard as an undergraduate. Went to St. Louis, Missouri, to teach. Served as the chief probation officer for St. Louis youth court. In 1910, became secretary of the local Civic League. Moved to Washington to join staff of the American Union Against Militarism (AUAM) in March 1917. Named the director of the National Civil Liberties Bureau in October 1917 when it split from the AUAM. Served ten months in jail as a conscientious objector starting in October 1918. Became the executive director of the American Civil Liberties Union (ACLU) in January 1920, when the NCLB was renamed. Retired from the ACLU in 1950.

Bettman, Alfred (1873–1945): Attended Harvard and Harvard Law School. Returned to his hometown of Cincinnati where he practiced law. City solicitor from 1909 to 1911. Appointed deputy director of War Emergency Division in 1917. Primary authority within Justice Department concerning the enforcement of the Espionage Act. Wrote government briefs on key Supreme Court decisions on free speech. After war, focused on the legal implications of city planning and zoning.

Biddle, Nicholas (1879–1923): Graduated from Harvard College in 1900. Supervised the estate of William Astor. Served as deputy police commissioner of New York City supervising intelligence units. During the First World War, he became the head of the New York office of the Army's Military Intelligence Division, rising from major to colonel. Had responsibility for investigating the National Civil Liberties Bureau.

Brandeis, Louis Dembitz (1856–1941): Born and raised in Louisville, Kentucky, by Jewish parents who had come from Prague to the United States after the failure of the 1848 revolution. Went to college in Dresden, Germany. Graduated from Harvard Law in 1877 and entered private practice in 1879. Having gained success, he began representing clients for free who were opposing monopolistic corporations. Mediated a strike of garment workers in 1910 and served on the arbitration board.

Became an ardent Zionist prior to the First World War. Appointed to the U.S. Supreme Court in 1916 and served until 1939.

Cave, George (1856–1928): Graduated from Oxford University. Began practicing law in 1880. Elected to Parliament in 1906 as a Conservative. Served as solicitor general in the Asquith coalition government from 1915 to December 1916. Home Secretary in the Lloyd George government until January 1919. Held the position of Lord Chancellor from October 1922 to January 1924 and then from November 1924 until his death.

Chafee, Zechariah, Jr. (1883–1957): From a wealthy family active in Rhode Island politics. Graduated from Brown University in 1907 and then spent three years in the front office of the family iron foundry. Graduated from Harvard Law School in 1913 and joined its faculty in 1916. Became a full professor in 1919 and retired in 1956. Primary focus of research was constitutional law and free speech.

Daugherty, Harry Micajah (1860–1941): Graduated from University of Michigan Law School. Returned to his hometown of Washington Court, Ohio, near Columbus, where he became a prominent attorney. Active in Ohio Republican politics. Served in state legislature from 1891 to 1895. Became Harding's campaign manager during 1920 presidential election. Appointed as attorney general. Closely tied to corruption during Harding administration. Indicted twice on corruption charges, but both times juries failed to arrive at unanimous verdict. Forced to resign in April 1924 by President Calvin Coolidge. Returned to Columbus, Ohio, to practice law.

Debs, Eugene Victor (1855–1926): Parents were Alsatian immigrants who owned a small store in Terre Haute, Indiana. Left school after ninth grade. Briefly worked as a locomotive fireman. In 1875, started working as an official of the Brotherhood of Locomotive Firemen. Became its secretary-treasurer in 1880. Resigned in 1893 to become chief organizer of the American Railway Union. Served a six-month jail sentence for violating an injunction aimed at ending strike of railroad workers. Became a socialist and was the presidential nominee of the Socialist Party for four times from 1900 to 1912. Opposed the First World War. Served two and a half years in prison for obstructing the war effort. While in prison, stood as the Socialist Party's presidential candidate in 1920. Returned to Terre Haute in poor health after leaving jail in December 1921.

Eastman, Crystal (1881–1928): Parents were Congregational ministers. Received an MA degree in sociology from Columbia University and a law degree from New York University. Chief investigator in a study of occupational safety. Active in women's suffrage movement and helped to found the Women's Peace Party in 1914. Became executive secretary of the American Union Against Militarism. Developed strategy for that organization and its offshoot, the National Civil Liberties Bureau. In the spring of 1917 became ill while pregnant and phased out of activity. From 1918 to 1922 co-edited *The Liberator* with her brother Max Eastman. Moved to England and became a freelance journalist.

George, David Lloyd (1863–1945): Born in Manchester, England, but spent most of his childhood in Wales. Became an attorney. In 1891, elected to Parliament as a Liberal. Cabinet minister in 1906 and then chancellor of the Exchequer from 1908 to 1915. Fervent supporter of the war from the start. After briefly serving as minister of munitions and secretary of state for war, became prime minister in December 1916 as part of the War Cabinet, thereby splitting the Liberal Party. Held position of prime minister until October 1922. Returned to the Liberal Party in 1923 but increasingly a marginal figure in British politics.

Gompers, Samuel (1850–1924): Born in London and immigrated with his family to New York City in 1863. Started working as a cigar maker while a teenager. Became an official of the Cigarmakers' Union in 1877. Helped to found the Federation of Organized Trade and Labor Unions in 1881, which became the American Federation of Labor in 1886. He served as president of the AFL from its founding until his death, with the exception of a single year out of office. An ardent supporter of the war effort and an advisor to Woodrow Wilson.

Gregory, Thomas Watt (1861–1933): Practiced law in Austin, Texas, from 1885 to 1913. Delegate to the Democratic National Convention in June 1912, where he led the Texas delegation. He was a close friend of Colonel Edward House, President Wilson's trusted confidante. Served as U.S. attorney general from August 1914 to March 1919. Afterwards, practiced law in Washington, D.C., and Houston, Texas.

Harding, Warren Gamaliel (1865–1923): Born in small town in Ohio. Family moved to Marion, Ohio, where he purchased a failing local newspaper. Became active in Ohio Republican politics. Served in the state legislature from 1900 to 1904 and lieutenant governor from 1904 to 1906. Elected to the U.S. Senate in 1914. Became the Republican presidential nominee after a deadlocked convention. His administration was tainted by pervasive corruption. Died of a heart attack returning from a trip to Alaska.

Hays, William Harrison (1879–1954): Lawyer in a small town in Indiana. Active in Republican Party politics in Indiana. Named chair of the Republic National Committee in June 1918. Harding's choice for postmaster general, a cabinet position. Involved in the Tea Pot Dome scandal. In 1922, became head of the Motion Picture Producers, a committee representing the film industry. Oversaw the creation of the Hays Code in 1930 that acted to censor films. Resigned in 1945.

Holmes, Oliver Wendell, Jr. (1841–1935): Born and raised in Boston. A Boston Brahmin, he had family members who fought in the American Revolution. Went to Harvard College in 1857. Joined Union Army soon after graduating in 1861. Served three years in the army and was wounded three times in Civil War battles. Went to Harvard Law School in 1864. Upon graduating went into private practice. After a brief period as a faculty member at Harvard, was appointed to the Massachusetts State Supreme Court in 1883. Appointed to U. S. Supreme Court in 1902 and served until 1932.

Matthews, Charles (1850–1920): Born in New York City but raised in England. Educated at Eton, an elite private school. Studied law at an attorney's office. Initially an attorney for the treasury. Became a criminal defense lawyer noted for his flamboyant courtroom style. Stood unsuccessfully for Parliament in 1892 for the Liberals. Appointed director of public prosecutions in 1908 and served until his death.

Morel, Edmund Dene (1873–1924): Born in Paris, France. Mother was English and father French. In 1891 began working for a shipping firm that traded with the Belgian Congo. From 1900, started writing articles criticizing Belgian rule. Fired from shipping firm. Wrote articles opposing the drift toward war. Liberal Party candidate for Parliament in 1912. Secretary of the Union of Democratic Control from its inception in the fall of 1914. Served a six-month sentence for violating the DORA regulations in 1917. Elected to Parliament as a Labour Party candidate in 1922. Never recovered his health after his term in prison. Died of heart attack.

O'Brian, John Lord (1874–1973): Graduated from Harvard in 1896. Received a law degree from the University of Buffalo in 1898. Joined one of the leading corporate law firms in 1898. U.S. Attorney for western New York State from 1909 to 1914. In October 1917, he became the head of the newly formed War Emergency Division of the Department of Justice, with overall authority over the entire range of laws suppressing dissent during the First World War. After his resignation in March 1919, he returned to private practice with one of the country's leading corporate law firms.

Ricker, Allen W. (1869–1955): Born in Iowa, he studied to be a minister before opting to become a farmer. Stood as a candidate for Congress as a Populist in 1898. Became a founding member of the Iowa Socialist

Party. Hired in December 1902 as an editorial writer for the *Appeal to Reason*, he clashed with its management. By the start of the First World War, he had become the business manager of *Pearson's*, a populist magazine. Initially opposed to U.S. intervention in the war, he soon switched positions and became an ardent proponent of the war effort. Worked with Edward House in an unsuccessful covert operation to cajole the Socialist Party into endorsing the war.

Robins, Lucy Fox (1884–1962): Born in Kiev, then part of Russia. Moved to United States when nine and family settled in Chicago. Became an anarchist at fifteen. Moved to New York City and was drawn to Emma Goldman's feminist anarchism. Became active in defense committee defending Tom Mooney. When she approached Samuel Gompers for ·support, was convinced of the need to work within the system. In 1919, named secretary of the AFL committee pushing for amnesty of wartime political prisoners. Became unofficial assistant to Gompers. Aligned with Zionism in 1920s. Moved to Los Angeles in 1950s and wrote memoir.

Rowan, James (1878–?): Born in Ireland. Came to the United States in 1898. Worked as a granite cutter in New England. Moved to Pacific Northwest in 1911 and worked as a lumberjack. Joined the IWW in 1912. Elected the secretary of the Lumber Workers' Union #500 at its founding conference in March 1917. Interned by the military in August 1917 and detained for more than a month before being transferred to Chicago as a defendant in the conspiracy trial of IWW leaders. Sentenced to twenty years in jail. One of the last IWW prisoners to be released in December 1923. Instrumental in 1924 split within the IWW. Formed the Emergency Program that ceased to exist in 1930.

Van Deman, Ralph Henry (1865–1923): Graduated from Harvard in 1888 and then went to medical school. After joining army as surgeon became interested in intelligence work. In 1899 went to Philippines and organized counter-intelligence groups. Undertook several assignments, some including mapping, before being assigned to the War College in 1915. Found that military intelligence had been downgraded and was no longer a separate unit. With support of British intelligence, convinced army command to revive Military Intelligence Division (MID). As head of MID, he supervised its rapid growth. In 1918, forced to transfer out of MID to position on intelligence staff of U.S. forces in France after opposing Woodrow Wilson on the role of military tribunals. Upon his return to the United States in 1920, assigned to command positions at army bases and rose to become major general before resigning in 1929. In retirement, compiled dossiers on alleged subversives using contacts made while head of MID.

Warren, Charles (1866–1954): Graduated from Harvard in 1889. Attended classes at Harvard Law School from 1889 to 1892 but did not graduate. Practiced law in Boston from 1897 to 1914. Appointed U.S. assistant attorney general in 1914 directing cases arising from violations of the neutrality laws. From April 1917 to October 1917, Warren had overall responsibility for prosecuting those who opposed the war. Resigned as assistant attorney general in April 1918 after opposing President Wilson on the role of military tribunals. Afterwards, wrote books on the law and legal history and lectured at various universities.

Wilson, Thomas Woodrow (1856–1924): Raised in the South. Graduated from Princeton University in 1879. Received a PhD in political science from Johns Hopkins in 1886. Appointed to the Princeton faculty in 1890. Served as president of Princeton from 1902 to 1910. Governor of New Jersey from 1911 to 1913. Nominated for president by the Democratic National Convention in June 1912. President of the United States from March 1913 to March 1921, winning reelection in 1916. He was disabled by a stroke in October 1919 and was incapacitated for the last months of his term in office. Continued to live in Washington, D.C., after leaving office.

Organizations

Bureau of Investigation: Formed in June 1908 to serve as the intelligence agency for the Department of Justice collecting information on antitrust cases. A small agency until April 1917, when the United States declared war on Germany. Tasked with the primary responsibility for investigating cases arising out of the Espionage Act and other statutes aimed at antiwar dissidents. Grew rapidly during war, opening field offices around the country. Worked closely with the War Emergency Division. Bruce Bielaski served as its chief during this period. Renamed the Federal Bureau of Investigation in July 1935.

Industrial Workers of the World: Founded in 1905 at a Chicago convention. Initiated by the Western Federation of Miners, although the two unions soon became bitter enemies. Committed to direct action and the end of the capitalist market system. Involved in several free speech fights from 1909 to 1913. During the First World War, successfully organized migrant agricultural workers, lumberjacks, and copper miners. In August 1918, ninety-three leading members of the IWW were convicted of violating the Espionage Act and sentenced to long terms in prison. The pressure of the unrelenting repression from the federal government, as well as some state governments, led to demoralization and splits. Survived, but as a small union.

National Civil Liberties Bureau: Created in October 1917 when the Civil Liberties Bureau of the American Union Against Militarism became an independent organization. Roger Baldwin served as executive director. Defended the rights of conscientious objectors as well as those who opposed the war. Upheld the right of IWW leaders to a fair trial. Threatened with prosecution by the Department of Justice but managed to avoid criminal charges by agreeing to a confidential deal. Dissolved and renamed the American Civil Liberties Union in January 1920.

Socialist Party of America: Founded in the summer of 1901 at a conference in Indianapolis. Small at first, it grew rapidly. At its height, in 1912, it had 150,000 members. Nominated Eugene Debs five times as its presidential candidate. Elected mayors, state legislators, and two members of the U.S. House of Representatives. From the start, a deep division between the moderate and radical wings. Opposed the war and became a target of government repression. This and the split of much of the leftwing into the Communist Party led to a sharp decline. Continues to this day, but as a small party.

Union of Democratic Control: Formed in August 1914. Initially pushed for the British government to declare its war aims. Later, demanded a rapid end to the war through a negotiated peace. Printed pamphlets and flyers. Worked closely with the Independent Labour Party. Its secretary, Edmund Morel, was jailed for five months in 1917.

War Emergency Division: Created by Attorney General Thomas Gregory in October 1917. Given overall responsibility for the concerted effort of the Department of Justice to suppress antiwar activists. Advised the Attorney General on relevant policy issues. Determined those aliens from enemy countries who would be detained in camps. Directly supervised the prosecution of most cases involving the Espionage Act. Although IWW cases were handled by another division of the Justice Department, the War Emergency Division established guidelines and overall direction for those cases as well. Headed by John Lord O'Brian, with Alfred Bettman as his chief deputy. Dissolved on May 31, 1919.

BIBLIOGRAPHY

Books and Pamphlets

American Civil Liberties Union. *The Truth about the IWW Prisoners.* New York: ACLU, 1922.

Albert, Peter J., and Grace Palladino. *The Samuel Gompers Papers.* 13 vols. Urbana: University of Illinois Press, 1986–2013.

Allen, Thomas. *Intelligence in the American Civil War.* New York: Nova Science, 2010.

Baker, Ray Stannard. *Woodrow Wilson: Life and Letters.* 8 vols. Garden City, NJ: Doubleday, Page, 1927–39.

Basler, Roy B., ed. *The Collected Works of Abraham Lincoln.* Seven Volumes. New Brunswick, NJ: Rutgers University Press, 1953.

Beaver, Daniel R. *Newton D. Baker and the American War Effort, 1917–1919.* Lincoln: University of Nebraska Press, 1966.

Bidwell, Bruce W. *History of the Military Intelligence Division, Department of the Army General Staff, 1775–1941.* Frederick, MD: University Publications of America, 1986.

Blackstone, William. *Commentaries on the Laws of England.* 4 vols. Oxford: Clarendon, 1765.

Blatch, Harriot Stanton. *Challenging Years.* New York: Putnam, 1940.

Chafee, Jr., Zechariah. *Freedom of Speech.* New York: Harcourt, Brace, and Howe, 1920.

_____. *Free Speech in the United States.* Cambridge, MA: Harvard University Press, 1941.

_____, ed. *Fundamental Human Rights.* 3 vols. Cambridge, MA: Harvard University Press, 1951.

Chambers II, Jack Whiteclay. *To Raise an Army: The Draft Comes to Modern America.* New York: Macmillan, 1981.

Chester, Eric Thomas. *The Wobblies in Their Heyday.* Santa Barbara, CA: Praeger, 2014; Amherst, MA: Levellers, 2016.

Cocks, F. Seymour. *The Secret Treaties.* London: Union of Democratic Control, [1918].

Constantine, J. Robert. *Letters of Eugene V. Debs*. 3 vols. Urbana: University of Illinois Press, 1990.

Cook, Blanche Wiesen, ed. *Crystal Eastman on Women and Revolution*, New York: Oxford University Press, 1978.

Cook, Charles ed., *Defence of the Realm Manual*, 6th ed. London: His Majesty's Stationery Office, 1918.

Cook, Edward Tyas. *The Press in Wartime*. London: Macmillan, 1920.

Cottrell, Robert C. *Roger Nash Baldwin*. New York: Columbia University Press, 2000.

Croly, Herbert David. *The Promise of American Life*. New York: Macmillan, 1909.

_____. *Willard Straight*. New York: Macmillan, 1924.

Dalin, David G. *Jewish Justices of the Supreme Court: From Brandeis to Kagan*. Waltham, MA: Brandeis University Press, 2017.

Daugherty, Harry M. and Thomas Dixon, *The Inside Story of the Harding Tragedy*. New York: Churchill, 1932.

Debs, Eugene Victor. *Debs White Book*. Girard, KS: Appeal to Reason, [1919].

_____. *Walls and Bars*. Chicago: Kerr, 1927.

Dilbeck, D. H. *A More Civil War: How the Union Waged a Just War*. Chapel Hill: University of North Carolina Press, 2016.

Doree, E. F. *A Wobbly Life*. Detroit: Wayne State University, 2004.

Downs, Gregory P. *After Appomattox: Military Occupation and the Ends of War*. Cambridge, MA: Harvard University Press, 2015.

Dowse, Robert Edward. *Left in the Centre: The Independent Labour Party, 1893–1940*. Evanston, IL: Northwestern University Press, 1966.

Ewing, K. D., and C. A. Gearty. *The Struggle for Civil Liberties: Political Freedom and the Rule of Law in Britain, 1914–1945*. Oxford: Oxford University Press, 2000.

Forcey, Charles. *The Crossroads of Liberalism: Croly, Weyl, Lippmann, and the Progressive Era, 1900–1925*. New York: Oxford University Press, 1961.

Freeberg, Ernest. *Democracy's Prisoner: Eugene V. Debs, The Great War and the Right to Dissent*. Cambridge, MA: Harvard University Press, 2008.

Frost, Richard H. *The Mooney Case*. Stanford, CA: Stanford University Press, 1968.

Gilbert, Martin. *Plough My Own Furrow: The Story of Lord Allen*. London: Longmans, 1965.

Ginger, Ray. *Bending Cross*. New Brunswick, NJ: Rutgers University Press, 1949.

Gollin, A. M. *Proconsul in Politics*. London: Bland, 1964.

Gompers, Samuel. *Seventy Years of Life and Labor: An Autobiography*. 2 vols. New York: Dutton, 1925.

Grubbs, Frank L. *The Struggle for Labor Loyalty: Gompers, the A.F. of L. and the Pacifists, 1917–1920*. Durham, NC: Duke University Press, 1968.

Hagedorn, Herman. *Leonard Wood*. 2 vols. New York: Harper, 1931.

Hall, Greg. *Harvest Wobblies: The Industrial Workers of the World and Agricultural Laborers in the American West*. Corvallis: Oregon State University Press, 2001.

Harris, Sally. *Out of Control: British Foreign Policy and the Union of Democratic Control*. Hull: University of Hull Press, 1996.

Hartshorn, Peter. *I Have Seen the Future: A Life of Lincoln Steffens*. Berkeley, CA: Counterpoint, 2011.

Holdsworth, William Searle. *A History of English Law*. 16 vols. London: Methuen, 1903.

Howe, Mark deWolfe, ed. *Holmes–Laski Letters: The Correspondence of Mr. Justice Holmes and Harold J. Laski, 1916–1935*. 2 vols. Cambridge, MA: Harvard University Press, 1953.

_____. *Holmes–Pollock Letters: The Correspondence of Mr. Justice Holmes and Sir Frederick Pollock, 1874–1932*. 2 vols. Cambridge: Cambridge University Press, 1943.

Johnson, Donald. *The Challenge to American Freedom: World War I and the Rise of the American Civil Liberties Union*. Lexington: University of Kentucky Press, 1963.

Karsner, David. *Debs: His Authorized Life and Letters from Woodstock Prison to Atlanta*. New York: Boni and Liveright, 1919.

Kennan, George Frost. *Soviet–American Relations, 1917–1920*. 2 vols. Princeton, NJ: Princeton University Press, 1956.

Kennedy, Thomas C. *The Hound of Conscience: A History of the No Conscription Fellowship, 1914–1919*. Fayetteville: University of Arkansas Press, 1981.

Kettle, Michael. *The Road to Intervention, March–November 1918*. New York: Routledge, 1988.

Kielbowicz, Richard Burket. *A History of Mail Classification and Its Underlying Policies and Purposes*. Seattle: United States Postal Rate Commission, 1995.

King, Willard L. *Lincoln's Manager: David Davis*. Cambridge, MA: Harvard University Press, 1960.

Kirby, David G. *War, Peace, and Revolution: International Socialism at the Crossroads*. Aldershot, UK: Gower, 1986.

Klement, Frank Ludwig. *Dark Lanterns: Secret Political Societies, Conspiracies and Treason Trials in the Civil War*. Baton Rouge: Louisiana State University Press, 1984.

_____. *The Limits of Dissent: Clement L. Vallandingham and the Civil War*. Lexington: University Press of Kentucky, 1970.

Klaus, Samuel, ed. *The Milligan Case*. London: Routledge, 1929.

Kramnick, Isaac, and Barry Sheerman. *Harold Laski: A Life on the Left.* London: Allan Lane Penguin, 1993.

Lamson, Peggy. *Roger Baldwin, Founder of the American Civil Liberties Union: A Portrait.* Boston: Houghton, Mifflin, 1976.

Levy, David W. *Herbert Croly of the New Republic: The Life and Thought of an American Progressive.* Princeton, NJ: Princeton University Press, 1985.

Lief, Alfred, ed. *The Social and Economic Views of Mr. Justice Brandeis.* New York: Vanguard, 1930.

Link, Arthur S., ed. *Wilson: The Road to the White House.* Princeton, NJ: Princeton University Press, 1947.

_____. *The Papers of Woodrow Wilson.* 69 vols. Princeton, NJ: Princeton University Press, 1966–92.

Mandel, Bernard. *Samuel Gompers: A Biography.* Yellow Springs, OH: Antioch, 1963.

Marquand, David. *Ramsay MacDonald.* London: Jonathan Cape, 1977.

Margulies, Herbert F. *Senator Lenroot of Wisconsin: A Political Biography, 1900–1929.* Columbia: University of Missouri Press, 1977.

McGinty, Brian. *The Body of John Merryman: Abraham Lincoln and the Suspension of Habeas Corpus.* Cambridge, MA: Harvard University Press, 2011.

McPherson, James M. *Battle Cry of Freedom: The Civil War Era.* New York: Oxford University Press, 1988.

Miller, Sally M. *Victor Berger and the Promise of Constructive Socialism, 1910–1920.* Westport, CT: Greenwood, 1973.

Millman, Brock. *Managing Domestic Dissent in First World War Britain, 1914–1918.* London: Cass, 2000.

Moore, Howard W. *Ploughing My Own Furrow.* Syracuse, NY: Syracuse University Press, 1985.

Mitchell, Donald. *The Politics of Dissent: A Biography of E. D. Morel.* Bristol: Silverwood, 2014.

Morel, Edmund Dene. *Tsardom's Part in the War.* London: National Labour, 1917.

_____. *The Persecution of E. D. Morel.* Glasgow: Reformer's Bookstall, 1918.

Morris, A. J. A. *Reporting the First World War: Charles Repington, the Times and the Great War.* Cambridge: Cambridge University Press, 2015.

National Civil Liberties Bureau. *The Truth about the I.W.W.* New York: 1918.

Neely, Mark. *Fate of Liberty: Abraham Lincoln and Civil Liberties.* New York: Oxford University Press, 1991.

Nelles, Walter. *A Liberal in Wartime: The Education of Albert DeSilver.* New York: Norton, 1940.

Parrish, Michael. *Felix Frankfurter and His Times.* New York: Free Press, 1982.

Peterson, Horace Cornelius and Gilbert Courtland Fite, *Opponents of War, 1917–1918.* Madison: University of Wisconsin Press, 1957.

Peabody, James Bishop. *The Holmes–Einstein Letters, Correspondence of Mr. Justice Homes and Lewis Einstein, 1903–1935.* New York: Macmillan, 1964.

Prouty, Andrew Mason. *More Deadly Than War, Pacific Coast Logging, 1827–1981.* New York: Garland, 1985.

Randall, James Garfield. *Constitutional Problems Under Lincoln.* New York: Appleton, 1926.

Robins, Lucy Fox. *War Shadows.* New York: Central Labor Bodies Conference for the Release of Political Prisoners, 1922.

_____. *Tomorrow Is Beautiful.* New York: Macmillan, 1948.

Rowland, Peter. *Lloyd George.* London: Barrie and Jenkins, 1975.

Russell, Charles Edward. *Bare Hands and Stone Walls: Some Recollections of a Side-Line Reformer.* New York: Scribner, 1933.

Salvatore, Nick. *Eugene V. Debs: Citizen and Socialist.* Urbana: University of Illinois Press, 1982.

Schaffer, Ronald. *America in the Great War: The Rise of the War Welfare State.* New York: Oxford University Press, 1991.

Shannon, David A. *The Socialist Party: A History.* New York: Macmillan, 1955.

Shore, Elliott. *Talkin' Socialism: J. A. Wayland and the Role of the Press in American Radicalism, 1890–1912.* Lawrence, KS: University Press of Kansas, 1988.

Simpson, Alfred William Brian. *In the Highest Degree Odious: Detention Without Trial in Wartime Britain.* Oxford: Clarendon Press, 1992.

Smith, Donald L. *Zechariah Chafee, Jr.: Defender of Liberty and Law.* Cambridge, MA: Harvard University Press, 1986.

Snyder, Brad. *The House of Truth: A Washington Political Salon and the Foundations of American Liberalism.* New York: Oxford University Press, 2017.

Spiro, Jonathan Peter. *Defending the Master Race: Conservation, Eugenics, and the Legacy of Madison Grant.* Burlington: University of Vermont Press, 2009.

Stampp, Kenneth. *Indiana Politics During the Civil War.* Indianapolis: Indiana Historical Bureau, 1949.

Steel, Ronald. *Walter Lippmann and the American Century.* Boston: Atlantic Monthly, 1980.

Stoltzfus, Duane C. S. *Pacifists in Chains: The Hutterites During the Great War.* Baltimore: Johns Hopkins University Press, 2013.

Strum, Philippa. *Brandeis: Beyond Progressivism.* Lawrence: University Press of Kansas, 1993.

Sullivan, Mark. *Our Times, The United States, 1900–1925.* 6 vols. New York: Scribner, 1935.

Swanwick, Helena Maria Lucy. *Builders of Peace: Being the Ten Years' History of the Union of Democratic Control.* London: Swarthmore, 1924.

_____. *I Have Been Young, etc.* London: Victor Gollancz, 1935.

Swartz, Marvin. *The Union of Democratic Control in British Politics During the First World War.* Oxford: Clarendon, 1971.

Talbert, Roy, Jr. *Negative Intelligence: The Army and the American Left, 1917–1941.* Jackson: University Press of Mississippi, 1991.

Taylor, Alan John Percivale. *Beaverbrook.* London: Hamilton, 1972.

Thomas, James Henry. *My Story.* London: Hutchinson, 1937.

Thompson, John. A. *American Progressive Publicists and the First World War.* Cambridge: Cambridge University Press, 1987.

Thompson, Laurence. *The Enthusiasts: A Biography of John and Katherine Bruce Glasier.* London: Gollancz, 1971.

Trachtenberg, Alexander, ed. *The American Socialists and the War.* New York: Rand School, 1917.

Trefusse, Hans L. *Ben Butler: The South Called Him BEAST!* New York: Twayne, 1957.

Tupper, Edward. *Seamen's Torch.* Plymouth, UK: Mayflower, 1938.

Tyler, Robert L. *Rebels of the Woods: The I.W.W. in the Pacific Northwest.* Eugene: University of Oregon Books, 1967.

Ulam, Adam. *Expansion and Coexistence.* London: Secker and Warburg, 1968.

Urofsky, Melvin I., and David Levy, eds. *Letters of Louis D. Brandeis.* 5 vols. Albany: State University of New York Press, 1971–78.

Walling, William English, ed. *The Socialists and the War.* New York: Garland, 1972.

White, G. Edward. *Justice Oliver Wendell Holmes: Law and Inner Self.* New York: Oxford University Press, 1993.

Wilson, Douglas L., and Rodney O. Davis. *Herndon's Informants: Letters, Interviews and Statements about Abraham Lincoln.* Urbana: University of Illinois Press, 1998.

Winter, Ella, and Granville Hicks. *The Letters of Lincoln Steffens.* 2 vols. New York: Harcourt, Brace, 1938.

Wintour, Barry. *Britain and the Great War, 1914–1918: A Subject Bibliography of Some Neglected Aspects.* Englefield Green, UK: Greenengle, 2014.

Zeman, Z. A. B. *Germany and the Revolution in Russia, 1915–1918, Documents from the Archives of the German Foreign Ministry.* London: Oxford University Press, 1958.

Documents

Report of Proceedings of the Thirty-Ninth Annual Convention of the American Federation of Labor. Washington, D.C.: Law Reporter, 1919.

Report of Proceedings of the Fortieth Annual Convention of the American Federation of Labor. Washington, D.C.: Law Reporter Printing, 1920.

Report of Proceedings of the Forty-Second Annual Convention of the American Federation of Labor. Washington, D.C.: Law Reporter Printing, 1922.

Articles

Baldwin, Roger, and Alan Westin. "Recollections of a Life in Civil Liberties—I." *Civil Liberties Review* 1 (Spring 1975): 39–72.

_____. "Recollections of a Life in Civil Liberties—II." *Civil Liberties Review* 2 (Fall 1975): 10–40.

Chafee, Zechariah, Jr. "Freedom of Speech." *New Republic* 17 (November 16, 1918): 66–69.

_____. "Freedom of Speech in Wartime." *Harvard Law Review* 32 (June 1919): 932–73.

Debs, Eugene Victor. "Canton Speech." In Jean Y. Tussey, ed. *Eugene V. Debs Speaks.* New York: Pathfinder, 1970.

_____. "Indicted, Unashamed and Unafraid." *Eye-Opener*, March 16, 1918.

Dewey, John. "Conscript of Thought." *New Republic* 12 (1917).

_____. "In Explanation of Our Lapse." *New Republic* 13 (1917).

Eberle, Donald. "The Plain Mennonite Face of the World War One Conscientious Objector." *Journal of Amish and Plain Anabaptist Studies* 3: 175–201.

"Ending the Socialist Schism." Editorial, *New Republic*, 15 (May 11, 1918): 34–36.

Freund, Ernst. "The Debs Case and Freedom of Speech." *New Republic* 19 (May 3, 1919): 13–15.

Giffin, Frederick C. "Morris Hillquit and the War Issue in the New York Mayoralty Campaign of 1917." *International Social Science Review* 34 (1999): 115–28.

Haynes, John Earl. "Revolt of the 'Timber Beasts': IWW Lumber Strike in Minnesota." *Minnesota History* 42 (Spring 1971): 162–74.

Hunczak, Taras. "The Ukraine Under Hetman Pavlo Skoropadski." In Taras Hunczak, ed., *The Ukraine, 1917–1921: A Study in Revolution.* Cambridge, MA: Harvard University Press, 1977, 61–81.

Kennedy, Kathleen. "In the Shadows of Gompers: Lucy Robins and the Politics of Amnesty, 1918–1922." *Peace and Change* 25 (January 2000): 22–51.

Klement, Frank Ludwig. "The Indianapolis Treason Trials and Ex Parte Milligan." In Michael R. Belknap, ed., *American Political Trials*. Westport, CT: Greenwood, 1981, 101–27.

Lanier, Alexander Sidney. "To the President." *New Republic* 18 (April 19, 1919): 383–84.

Lovin, Hugh T. "Moses Alexander and the Idaho Lumber Strike of 1917: The Wartime Ordeal of a Progressive." *Pacific Northwest Quarterly* 66 (July 1975): 115–22.

Millman, Brock. "The Battle of Cory Hall, November 1916: Patriots Meet Dissenters in Western Cardiff." *Canadian Journal of History* 35 (Spring 2000): 57–84.

"Profiles: Mr. Chairman." *New Yorker* (March 11, 1933): 21–24.

Rader, Benjamin G. "The Montana Lumber Strike of 1917." *Pacific Historical Review* 36 (May 1967): 189–207.

Stoltzfus, Duane. "Armed with Prayer in an Alcatraz Dungeon." *Mennonite Quarterly Review* 85 (April 2011): 259–92.

Warren, Charles. "What Is Giving Aid and Comfort to the Enemy?" *Yale Law Journal* 27 (January 1918): 331–47.

_____. "Spies and the Power of Congress to Subject Certain Classes of Civilians to Trial by Military Tribunal." *American Law Review* 53 (March 1919): 195–228.

Wright, Chester M. "An Appeal for Peace." *The Western Comrade* 2 (April 1915): 23–24.

Newspapers

Canton Repository
New York Call
New York Times
New York Tribune
Nonpartisan Leader
Spokane Daily Chronicle
Spokane Spokesman-Review

Microfilm Archives

Debs, Eugene Victor. *The Papers of Eugene Debs, 1834–1945*. Microfilm. 21 Reels. Sanford, NC: Microfilming Corporation of America, 1982.

Harding, Warren. *The Papers of Warren Harding*. Microfilm. 263 Reels. Columbus: Ohio Historical Society, 1969.

Socialist Party of America Papers, 1897–1963. Microfilm. 142 Reels. Glen
　Rock, NJ: Microfilming Corporation of America, 1975.
Wilson, Thomas Woodrow. *Woodrow Wilson Papers*. Microfilm. 542 Reels.
　Washington, D.C.: Library of Congress, 1973.

Archives

National Archives, College Park, Maryland
　　Record Group 59, Department of State
　　Record Group 60, Department of Justice
　　Record Group 65, Bureau of Intelligence
　　Record Group 165, Military Intelligence Division, Army
　　Record Group 174, Department of Labor
　　Record Group 204, Pardon Attorney
Hoover Institution for Peace and War, Stanford University, Palo Alto,
　California
　　Hugh Gibson
　　John Lord O'Brian
Manuscripts and Special Collections, Yale University, New Haven,
Connecticut
　　Edward House
　　William Wiseman
University of Indiana, Bloomington, Indiana
　　Max Eastman
　　Upton Sinclair
University of Maryland, Hornbake Library, College Park, Maryland
　　Samuel Gompers
Harvard Law School Library, Harvard University, Cambridge,
Massachusetts
　　Zechariah Chafee
　　Learned Hand
　　Oliver Wendell Holmes, Jr.
Labadie Collection, Special Collections, University of Michigan, Ann
Arbor, Michigan
　　Agnes Inglis
　　Jo Labadie
Seeley Mudd Library, Princeton University, Princeton, New Jersey
　　American Civil Liberties Union
　　Roger Baldwin
University of Buffalo
　　John Lord O'Brian
Tamiment Library, Special Collections, New York University, New York
　　Eugene Victor Debs

Special Collections, New York Public Library, New York
    David Karsner
National Civic Federation
    Norman Thomas
    Lillian Wald
    Frank Walsh
Duke University, Durham, North Carolina
    Socialist Party of America
Swarthmore Peace Collections, Swarthmore College, Swarthmore,
Pennsylvania
    American Union Against Militarism
    People's Council of America
Manuscripts, Library of Congress, Washington, D.C.
    Louis Brandeis
    George Creel
    Norman Hapgood
    Charles Warren
    Woodrow Wilson
Wisconsin Historical Society, Madison, Wisconsin
    Victor Berger
    Adolph Germer
    Morris Hillquit
    Algie Martin Simons
Imperial War Museum, London
    Vernon Kell
National Archives of the United Kingdom, London
    Home Office HO
    Security Service KV
    War Office WO
    Cabinet CAB
Parliamentary Archives, London
    Herbert Samuel

Index